**The
Schools
and
American
Society**

THE SCHOOLS AND AMERICAN SOCIETY

SECOND EDITION

DANIEL SELAKOVICH

Oklahoma State University

Xerox College Publishing

Lexington, Massachusetts / Toronto

91684

Consulting Editors:

Lawrence A. Fink

Raymond Ducharme, Jr.

Smith College

Preface

This book is an attempt to explain American schools and their place in society. It was designed and written for use as a major textbook for courses in social foundations of education. It does not view the school from inside its walls, but is rather an exposition of the school as a major institution in American society, subject to the influences and pressures of the community it serves. This study of the school as a major social institution reveals that schools are particularly vulnerable to value controversies and troubles that plague the society in general.

The second edition of this book is substantially changed from the first. Many of these changes were made at the suggestion of colleagues and hundreds of students who used the book in the social foundations of education course. To these people I owe a great debt of gratitude. In addition, many changes were made because of interest in and concern about the schools which local, state, and national sources have shown during the six years since the first edition was published. The result is a substantially different book, one that should prove more useful to students and teachers. This book deals with three major questions: (1) how does society impose its values on the schools? (2) how are the schools organized to teach these values? and (3) can the schools change society? Although these are old questions, they continue to be relevant ones for those who study the school system in any society.

Every effort has been made in this edition to describe and provide some analysis of new problems facing the schools. Most notable among the forces at work are the efforts of minorities to make the schools more responsive to their interests; the impact of criticism from the "new left"; the free school movement; teacher accountability; private enterprise in education; the de-centralization movement; student unrest; and the search for new means of educational finance.

Part I deals with the general question of how society imposes its values on the schools. In this section the general subject of social values as they affect the schools is described and analyzed. This material has been substantially revised in this edition in view of the fact that the schools have been at the cutting edge of public value controversies and confrontation politics which have been so characteristic of the late sixties and early seventies. New definitions of the very meaning of democratic society and the role of the schools in that society have been developing in the years since the first edition of this book was published.

The content of the chapters in Part II describes and analyzes the manner in which our society imposes its values on the schools. No attempt is made to consider the whole range of social values; the discussion is limited largely to political values and to the manner in which these values affect schooling. A major assumption in the several chapters of Part II is that political values, as they apply to the schools, involve the use of power, its sources, its exercise, and its effects. Certain forces are selected which are important instruments in the imposition of values. These include the forces of tradition, the communi-ty, pressure groups, the law, and the system of educational finance.

Many changes were necessary in Part II of this edition. Although the schools continue, for the most part, to reflect traditional and often conserva-tive values, new forces are at work to push the schools in new directions. The militance of minorities and the massive outpouring of literature of criticism have threatened traditional conservatism in education. The chapters on school finance have been updated and revised, since the very basis of the system has been called into question in recent years.

Part III, which deals with the question of how the schools are organized to teach values, has been extensively revised in this edition. New forms of organization have evolved out of the ferment of the sixties and new concepts such as teacher accountability, differentiated staffing, and private contract-ing for learning have many implications for schooling in the seventies. New proposals and programs emanating from sources within the national govern-ment have become an annual part of the school picture.

Finally, the last part of this book asks: Can the schools change society? The answer to this question has been modified somewhat by events since the publication of the first edition. Certainly the schools have reflected some of the changes in society and have made others easier. The content selected to illustrate the role of the school as an agent of change includes certain more or less impersonal forces operating within the environment and demanding change. Although no one can predict the direction of this change or its ultimate impact on societal values, the potential for change exists within the schools. The increasing strength of teachers' organizations and the growing political consciousness of the teacher are sure to have some effect on the future of the schools. The great push for realization of idealized political values such as equality, freedom, and justice for minorities has already been felt and should continue to be a force for change. Technological development has also had a great effect on political values as they are expressed in such terms as "career education" and will certainly have some impact on future educational goals, programs, teachers, school organization, and students.

This second edition is neither more optimistic nor more pessimistic than the first about the future prospects of American education. Its job is to reflect the growing amount of interest in the strengths and weaknesses of American education and leave to the reader any value judgments about the present condition of the system.

D.S.

Contents

**The
Schools
and
American
Society**

PART ONE
Values and Education

The manner in which a society views its schools depends to some extent upon the values held by the people who make up the society. Sometimes, as in a totalitarian state, these values have an absolutist quality about them; that is, the "truth" is known and the schools function primarily to teach this "truth." In such a society, an explanation of the role of the schools is a simple task for there is never any question or debate on what the schools ought to do.

In a democratic society this is not the case. The schools can be described well enough in a given time and place, but the genuinely perplexing questions include the problem of what the "proper" role of the schools should be. Such questions are not easily settled in a democratic society; they often involve honest differences of opinion which stem from strongly held beliefs, preferences, and values that compete freely in the market place of opinion and policy-making.

Chapters 1 and 2 deal with the general nature of social values as they relate to education and as they function to give education and the schools some guidance in a free society. The nature of so-called democratic values is examined in an attempt to demonstrate a serious dilemma in any democratic society—the need for the society to reach basic agreement on values and operational goals in order to progress, while at the same time allowing for examination and criticism of existing values and goals.

PART ONE
Values and Education

1

Social Values and Education

"When *I* use a word," said Humpty Dumpty, "it means just what I choose it to mean—neither more nor less." Alice was worried: "The question is whether you *can* make words mean so many different things."

Humpty Dumpty replied with an air of confidence: "The question is which is to be master, that's all."

Perhaps many of us live in Wonderland when it comes to a definition of values. Nothing is more basic to a study of education than the subject of human values, nor is anything more difficult to define. Defining values is difficult in our society because values are always in the process of change. It becomes nearly impossible to list values and proceed with an orderly discussion and analysis. Someone will always quite properly inquire, "Whose values are these and why were they selected?" The validity of any group of values, as one attempts to utilize them to explain why people act as they do, depends upon the value orientation of those making the selection. Moreover, the substance of the content of values is highly controversial. It is difficult to discuss values objectively because it is difficult, if not impossible, for most of us to achieve a Cartesian aloofness from our environment. No matter how objective we may claim to be, a multiplicity of influences colors our vision. Consciously or unconsciously the total life experiences of the viewer have some influence on the manner in which he views human values. Even so, an academic definition and discussion of values and education is possible, and even necessary, if we are to arrive at an understanding of education and schooling in the United States.

Moreover, it is possible that at no time in our history has the subject of values had such relevance, even for our very survival as a nation. In recent years there has been ample justification that all is not well in the United States. The decade of the sixties has been characterized in part by violence and disorder. Responsible scholars, the news media, and politicians have referred so frequently to "growing racism," "polarization," and the "generation gap" in our society that these have become household terms. Urban riots, prolonged strikes by teachers and other public employees, and campus violence have become commonplace in the American social scene. For much of our society's youth it must seem that the generation just ahead of them, the over-thirty crowd, has at best been totally unaware of growing problems and conflicts in American society. At worst, they have seemed so much concerned with their individual efforts at material success that they have neglected their broader responsibility for building a better social order. Indeed, the more radical idealists of the student population on the high school and college level are quick to agree that the generation before them has made a mess of things. The lakes and streams and air have been polluted, seemingly without serious concern for future generations. There has been an apparent lack of concern about the responsibilities which go along with a high level of production and affluence. For many of the young, their elders' lack of concern about such serious problems borders on criminal neglect. Unfortunately, there is much evidence of this neglect. There continues to be a desperate need for better housing for millions of our citizens; large numbers of our youth have faced problems of unemployment and demeaning work; there is a continuing need for improved human relations, for more and better education, for improved transportation and communication, for more comprehensive health care—in short, for a more humane society, more concerned with people than with things.

The schools, of course, have a vital role to play if this society is ever to come to serious grips with its problems. Perhaps the best thing about them is that they are common knowledge: they are out in the open and people are willing to discuss them. For instance, fifteen years ago ecologists were considered quaint nuts at best and dangerous fanatics at worst. Obviously some progress has been made in this area. Prejudice and racism continue to plague us but there are signs that we are beginning to face them. Certainly equality, justice, and freedom mean much more in concrete terms to most people today than they did fifteen years ago. The most hopeful sign may be that the young are becoming involved in political and social issues. The schools and their teachers must play some role in this if for no other reason than that the students are demanding that they do. As students and teachers come to grips with these dilemmas, they will quickly discover that human values play a central role, not only in the resolution of problems, but in intelligent discussion of them. This is why a study of values and the process of valuing is relevant for teachers.

WHAT ARE VALUES?

Some have little difficulty with a definition of values. The totalitarian state has an official set which can be defined and outlined in detail and transmitted to the population with complete confidence in the inevitable justice of the cause. Even in a pluralistic society some have little difficulty with a definition. Such a situation is evident in John Patrick's play, *The Teahouse of the August Moon.* In this play, two U.S. Army officers, Colonel Purdy and Captain Fisby, are charged with the responsibility of building a schoolhouse in Okinawa. Captain Fisby, a professor of humanities in civilian life, has been a miserable failure as a military man. When he complains to his colonel that perhaps he was not meant to be a solider, Colonel Purdy explodes:

> Purdy: Captain—none of us was cut out to be a soldier. But we do the job. We adjust. We adapt. We roll with the punch and bring victory home in our teeth. Do you know what I was before the war?
> Fisby: (hesitates unhappily)—A football coach?
> Purdy: I was the Purdy Paper Box Company of Pottawatomie. What did I know about foreigners? But my job is to teach these natives the meaning of Democracy if I have to shoot every one of them.[1]

On almost any day one can read a similar statement in the editorial pages of some local newspaper, hear a politician extolling "American" values, or listen to a speaker at some local service club expressing the sentiments of Colonel Purdy. Moreover, many such well-meaning citizens really believe and often practice what they preach. The meaning of democracy is clear to many of our citizens. If asked, they can easily list the basic "American values," and are quick to criticize those who question them.

Teachers too may be tempted to impose their own values on their students, either unaware that they are doing so or convinced in an authoritarian way that what they believe is right. Filled with the heady stuff of "Christian virtues," the exploits of American heroes and the democratic creed, the advantages of the American political and economic system, and the great ideals of Western democracy, the teacher can hold forth in a classroom of children who may or may not share his understanding, much less his enthusiasm.

Even attempts to impose values upon which there is a national majority consensus create some rather difficult problems within our society, whether the attempts are made through the schools in the informal process of community living or by means of the law. Certainly secondary school

---

[1] Bernard S. Miller, "The Quest for Values in a Changing World," *Social Education* (Feb. 1965), vol. 29, pp. 69–73.

administrators and college deans have learned that it is not a simple matter to impose generally accepted adult community ideals of dress and behavior on high school and college students. School and university rules regarding dress, length of hair, and what constitutes "proper" coeducational conduct have been violently at issue between school administrators and students in the last decade. Nor have these issues been resolved. When the students gain concessions, the adult community is often shocked and repulsed. In some communities the school authorities have managed to have their way only by rigid and authoritarian enforcement. In recent years university students in various locations around the country have paid dearly for their various expressions of individuality, their often violent refusals to conform to the role assigned them by a majority of adults in the community.

On the national level, when the law attempts to implement basic values of our constitutional system in communities which are not prepared to accept them, the implementation can become difficult. During the last two decades, driven by the consensus of national moral conscience, Americans have attempted to improve political morality in some communities through the force of law. An example of the difficulty of this undertaking is provided by Bernard Miller, when he quotes from trial proceedings in Jackson, Mississippi. Jurors were being selected to determine whether Byron De La Beckwith, a fervid segregationist, murdered Medgar Evers, Mississippi field secretary for the NAACP.

> "Do you think," asked the prosecutor, "it is a crime for a white man to kill a nigger in Mississippi?" The prospective juror was silent. "What was his answer?" asked the judge. "Nothing, Judge," said the prosecutor. "He's thinking it over."[2]

The story illustrates as well as anything can the difficulty of providing the means for establishing a widely supported value such as basic human equality in communities where such a value is more an abstraction than a reality. It illustrates the difficulties encountered in a democratic society in utilizing the force of the law, sanctioned by a great majority consensus and implemented by representatives and agencies of the majority, when the law flies in the face of deeply held personal values. Where values are so deeply felt, the law, or other social agencies including the school, may not be able to do much to change them.

Perhaps all that the school can realistically accomplish is to examine values in the hope that such examination may have some effect on thought and, ultimately, on behavior. If we are to examine values intelligently, there should be an attempt to define them. Although it may not be possible to provide a good generalized definition of values, the late Clyde Kluckhohn

---

[2] Miller, pp. 69–70.

provided a working definition in the statement: "A value is a selective orientation toward experience, implying deep commitment or repudiation, which influences the ordering of choices between possible alternatives in action."[3] Kluckhohn took the position that values involve a "set of hierarchically ordered prescriptions and proscriptions." Without a hierarchy of values human behavior "would become a sequence of reactions to unconfigurated stimuli."

The idea of hierarchy in the value system of an individual or a society frequently appears in definitions of value. In the words of an economist, "value is the relative position of a good in a preference ordering, and the higher its position the greater its value." The preference ordering may be that of an individual or a group. "Preference is based on the perceived relative utility of different goods."[4] Obviously, any given value hierarchy depends on the individual and the society in which we view him. The utility of a good which is perceived by an individual is conditioned by his society and by his experience. So in some cases pure physical drives, such as hunger, may be lower in the hierarchy than eating forbidden food. Indeed, where physical need is in conflict with a strongly held value, the individual may face starvation, for example, rather than deny the cultural values. For that matter, the example need not be limited to deeply held values. Certain tentative and surface values within our own culture may be cited. Secretaries have been known to forgo breakfast and lunch in order to remain slim and dressed in the latest style. Who knows what great sacrifices are made by the American teenage boy in order that he may display his maturity (or lack of it) behind the wheel of a highly polished automobile? Or for that matter, what sacrifices are made by parents of teenagers who feel they must know intimately, at full volume, the latest LP release of the currently popular rock group?

In any definition of value we must be careful to distinguish between what Professor Kluckhohn described as "that which is desirable" and "conceptions of the desirable." It is in the first sense that the layman generally uses the term "value" in his conversation. When we define "that which is desirable" we are generally making evaluations of objects; that is, we may refer to democracy as the most desirable form of government, or we may say we believe that education is valuable. The "conceptions of the desirable," on the other hand, refer to the standards we set for what is valuable. These are the standards by which choices are made between competing values and by which evaluations are defended and justified to ourselves and to others.[5]

---

[3] Clyde Kluckhohn, "The Study of Values," *Values in America,* ed. Donald N. Barrett (Notre Dame, Ind.: Univ. of Notre Dame Press, 1961), p. 18.
[4] Alfred Kuhn, *The Study of Society* (Homewood, Ill.: Dorsey Press, 1963), p. 266.
[5] Robin M. Williams, Jr., "Values and Modern Education in the United States," *Values in America,* ed. Donald N. Barrett (Notre Dame, Ind.: Univ. of Notre Dame Press, 1961), p. 58.

The standards we set depend upon a number of things. Not the least important of these is the substance of the subject we are considering or the environment in which we are considering it. We have value orientations with regard to politics, religion, marriage, money, education, and so on; all are influenced greatly by environment.

In order to demonstrate the difficulty of the problem of tying down a specific set of values in a democratic society, the following typology of value orientations in American society has been suggested by Otto Dahlke and may prove useful:

I. The Religious Value Orientation
   A. Ultimate ends: God, Christ, Salvation, immortality; otherworldliness
   B. Character structure and life organization:
      1. The saintly or holy character; the Christlike character
      2. Virtues of humility, patience, purity, fidelity, faith, and service
      3. A life of prayer, penitence, and repentance; obedience to divine will and to divine love
   C. Person: each soul a unique and infinite value; worth of person and evaluation of person symbolized in the brotherhood and sisterhood ideal; redemption through love and grace
   D. Competition: devaluation of competition; man against man ultimately sacrilegious
   E. Cooperation: stress on mutual aid, sharing, communalism, service without ulterior motives
   F. Wealth and property: low valuation, a hindrance to the religious life; frugality and simplicity in living; stewardship concept
   G. Social change, intellectual inquiry, and creativity:
      1. Criticism of social institutions is regarded as contrary to divine will or divine law; may even be revolutionary
      2. Change and inquiry of little significance; the important values are not of this world
      3. Artistic creativity in service of the ultimate ends
   H. War: ambiguous, from pacificism to just-war principles, but ultimately the Kingdom of God is peace

II. The Nativist Value Orientation
   A. Ultimate ends: the national culture and/or the state, power, glory, honor, greatness as national attributes; sovereignty
   B. Character structure and life organization:
      1. The patriot-warrior
      2. Virtues: aggressiveness, discipline, toughness, hardness, ambition for fame, prestige in struggle
      3. Tradition-bound, mentally immobile, mentally conformist, ethnocentric

C. Person: instrumental or tool conception of person
D. Competition: life as a struggle for existence; survival of the fittest with the weak falling by the way, exterminated, or subservient to the winner
E. Cooperation: significant only as it contributes to the competitive struggle
F. Wealth and property: as an expression of and in service of the nation-state leads to public monumentalism and other display items of national power and glory
G. Social change, intellectual inquiry, and creativity:
  1. Conservative, status quo oriented; best ways are the old
  2. Fear of the new; inquiry suspect because questioning and skeptical; intellectualism debunked as mere talk, words
  3. Creativity to be channeled into the celebration of the grandeur and power of the nation and its heroes
H. War: proves the mettle of man and nation; the/or a main source of social progress

III. The Market Value Orientation
A. Ultimate ends: goods, wealth, profits, money, power, conspicuous consumption, prestige, fame
B. Character structure and life organization:
  1. The self-made man image or the successful manager or executive
  2. Virtues: exemplified in the hard-driving, shrewd, acquisitive, inventive, calculating, ambitious, aggressive individual, manipulative of persons and things
C. Person: instrumental and tool conception of person; "everybody has his price"
D. Competition: competition as the mainspring in life
E. Cooperation: same as nativist, and as cooperation contributes to the achievement of the main goals; pseudo-Gemeinschaft
F. Wealth and property: accumulation for the individual the summum bonum; a symbol of respectability, prestige; all things valuated quantitatively in monetary units
G. Social change, intellectual inquiry, and creativity:
  1. Inquiry into the manipulation of things (technology) and persons acceptable
  2. Inquiry into social institutions suspect: hence, conservatism
  3. Suspicion of intellectual and artist because they do not fit into the work categories
H. War: as an opportunity to move or advance rapidly to the ultimate ends

IV. The Common Man Value Orientation

A. Ultimate ends: collective action, mutualism, dignity of worker
B. Character structure and life organization:
1. The little man image—salt of the earth; the toiler, the worker-citizen
2. Virtues: hard work, self-sacrifice, cooperation, willingness to share; modest ambitions
C. Person: inherent worth and dignity of person; rejection of tool conception
D. Competition: collective action, working together, rather than individualistic competition
E. Cooperation: "Mutually stimulates cooperation—a much more fundamentally sound principle than profit at the expense of co-workers . . ."
F. Wealth and property: a comfortable level of living regarded as desirable; unlimited accumulation as unsocial
G. Social change, intellectual inquiry, and creativity:
1. Change as favoring the worker acceptable, but with the worker as the dominant factor in community living
2. Inquiry and creativity to be directed to the creation and support of a worker culture
H. War: devaluation of war and peacetime conscription or military service

V. The Humanist Value Orientation
A. Ultimate ends: knowledge, creativity, experimentation, man as the measure of things, the intelligent ordering of life as based upon knowledge
B. Character structure and life organization:
1. The scientist-citizen, the man of freed intelligence
2. Virtues: scientific habits of thought, suspended judgment, analyzing, criticizing, investigating or exploring, seeing both sides of a question, impartiality and objectivity, tolerance and sympathy
3. Mental balance, willingness to accept and evaluate change, sense of responsibility to self and others, sensitivity to others
C. Person: persons as ends, not tools; creative personalities
D. Competition: destructive of human nature and social living
E. Cooperation: living as an essentially cooperative venture, sharing and exploring with others
F. Wealth and property: as a means for personal and community development; no inherent worth in wealth and property; things needed as instruments for action and the aesthetic life
G. Social change, intellectual inquiry, and creativity:
1. Experimentalism as a fundamental way; no limits to inquiry; no blocks to creativity

2. Living as an exploration for and in support of intellectual, social, and aesthetic values
3. Ordering cultural living in terms of the findings of the sciences
H. War: a denial of man's human nature and of cultural living; war as cultural suicide[6]

This suggested typology of values is useful in that it represents, as vividly as anything can, the complexity of values and value systems. Even a quick glance at the typology suggests that it would be impossible to find a "pure" type in any society. In contemporary American society the pure nativist might be called a fascist while the pure common man might be labeled a communist. Such easy classifications would depend upon the value position from which the name-caller was taking his stand. Where values are not rigidly fixed within an official ideology of the state, and great variations and combinations are allowed, the possibilities for confusion and misunderstanding are tremendous.

The possibilities for misunderstanding are multiplied when differences erupt into violence, as they have in recent years on numerous occasions. The most common outbreaks of violence have been between established authority and students or Blacks. Dahlke's typology becomes an extremely useful tool for analysis of student protest and violence—so common in the late sixties. Although it is difficult to generalize with accuracy, there appeared to be a serious gap in value orientations between the more radical students and officials who tried to repress their activities. The more radical students were advocates of some of the elements of Dahlke's "religious" and "humanist" value orientation while those they confronted appeared to be more appropriately described by Dahlke's "market value" orientation. The more radical students were extremely critical of competition, appeared to see nothing sacred in wealth and property, favored experimentalism in life style over existing modes, and universally condemned war as a method of problem solving. Those who opposed them decried the students' lack of respect for wealth and property, were extremely suspicious of their contempt for existing institutions and customs, and failed to understand why so many rejected the obligation of military service. Many in the older generation were particularly shocked by some students' attitudes toward the virtue of work for personal gain. This kind of analysis could be extended indefinitely, but it should be obvious to the reader that Dahlke's typology has some practical applications.

Equally obvious should be the fact that the typology could be overextended in a pluralistic society, because it suggests that values spring from a variety of sources. Dahlke's listing attests to the influence of great religious leaders

_____

[6] H. Otto Dahlke, *Values in Culture and Classroom* (New York: Harper & Row, 1958), pp. 63–66.

and documents, historical tradition, the evolution of economic and political systems, and so on. The once-popular melting pot theory which described an American as a person who had somehow absorbed various features of foreign ethnic groups but maintained a special "American" identity is no longer generally accepted. The concept of cultural pluralism is more widely held today.[7] The melting pot theory was a comfortable one since it enabled us to view the United States as a nation of very few really basic differences even though we were populated by many diverse groups and individuals. The reality may be that there was never anything approaching a "pure" American. For generations our politicians have recognized the reality of foreign subcultures, particularly in their appeals to the ethnic minorities in large cities. In recent years this pluralism has taken on new meaning in the political, social, and economic realms. The Black power movement is a classical expression of the political pluralism that has long existed in our society. Moreover it has awakened similar efforts on the part of newer minority groups, such as the Chicanos, and has revived interest in the old ethnic alliances, especially among southern and eastern European descendants including the Poles and Italians, who were supposedly totally "American" in character. In the social realm the minorities, particularly Blacks, have rediscovered their social and cultural heritage and are pushing everywhere for recognition through such programs as Black studies, recognition of contributions by the American Indian, and fair treatment of other minorities in the school program. Blacks and Chicanos have recently discovered economic pressure as a means to achieve some of their demands for recognition and equal treatment. Black minorities have experienced some success with the economic boycott, or refusal to buy from retailers and producers who practice discrimination, while the Chicano has experienced some success in organizing grape vineyard workers in California and farm labor in other states.

Significantly for the teacher, America continues to be a split society in which a variety of minority cultures exist side by side, normally in harmony, but more recently with some problems of accommodation which occasionally flare into violence. This is significant within the context of values since it would be totally unrealistic for the teacher to view this as a society of fixed values in which every citizen was tirelessly striving toward the assimilation of a given value system. Obviously cultural pluralism is a fact of our existence. What may not be so obvious to the native-born white, middle-class teacher is the possibility that many American minority individuals cling to their identity *with a vengeance.* Clearly, pride in a Black heritage expressed in the phrase "Black is beautiful" is strongly felt by many Blacks. Moreover, in their view this difference, the identifying characteristics of their culture, is totally

---

[7] Charles F. Marden and Gladys Meyer, *Minorities in American Society*, 3rd ed. (New York: American Book, 1968), p. 68.

American and an article of faith. For many, it is the identification which makes them men, which makes them human. This is essentially no different from earlier expressions of cultural identity made by other groups. The progeny of eastern and southern European immigrants of two generations ago continue to delight in national conferences in native costume, with old country music, food, drinks, brotherhood, and mythology. It is probably safe to predict that the newly awakened minorities, particularly the Blacks, Chicanos, and American Indians, will continue to build on their special identity in the future, just as other minorities have in the past.

This discussion is not meant to imply, of course, that minority group identity or affiliation takes precedence over all other considerations. Minority affiliation cannot totally envelop an individual living in a pluralistic society. These allegiances have a way of waxing and waning depending upon the issue, the time, and the immediate environment. A Black citizen can no more "think Black" twenty-four hours a day than a Slav can "think Slavic." This is true because of the practical business of adjusting to one's immediate environment while performing the daily tasks of earning a livelihood in a society of many cultures. With few exceptions the masses of Blacks must deal with whites, the Italians must of economic necessity mix with Poles, and so it goes. It is this feature of our environment which tends to minimize the differences. It is this feature of our society which enables cultures to mix and individuals to begin to better understand each other. This economic necessity for association does not necessarily eliminate conflict. The confusion and conflict between subcultures and value systems remain serious problems. Perhaps this is most true in open societies and constitutes simultaneously their greatest weakness and greatest strength; their greatest weakness in the sense that there is a constant outcry from those who feel they know what our values "ought" to be, that ours is a rudderless society lost on the stormy seas of fortune and doomed to oblivion. All this because we have lost sight of the "true" values which made us the great nation that we are. Confusion and conflict in values constitute strength for the open society in that individuals are relatively free to develop and free to choose between the conflicting winds of opinion based on conflicting values. This free choice, if known, enables careful investigation of alternatives and greatly enhances the possibility of wise choices.

THE NATURE AND FUNCTION OF VALUES

The broad scope of the subject of values does not mean that their study has no utility, since a good case can be made for the functional nature of values. It must be admitted at the outset that even a very democratic society may strive to impose "democratic" values. By admitting that these may be difficult to define in any absolute sense any society may provide an opportunity for consensus on basic values and action based on this consensus. In the words of George Axtelle: "cooperative action demands common standards, common objectives, and a common frame of reference."[8] The alternative to this cooperation, according to Axtelle, is "War against all, each ready to perish in its own sense of rightness." Thus, a major function of values is to provide the means by which a measure of order, however tentative, can be achieved in any society.

One must be cautious in the degree of faith placed on the cementing or synthesizing aspects of values, however. A democratic society is such precisely because no particular set of values holds a permanent and absolute grip. Are we then confronted with a contradiction? Must a democratic society be a society without permanent values and hence without the direction provided by them? If so, what then provides guidance for the social system? Surely the major function of values is to provide the basic standards against which the people can judge a given act, the direction in which the political leadership is taking the society, and other things which determine the drift of society. A basic assumption here is that nihilism is incompatible with organized society. A society totally without values may be technically impossible. Values exist. They exist in any society at any given time. Their roots are deep and conceivably indestructible in their totality. Given any group of living, breathing human beings with a past, the nonexistence of values would be inconceivable.

Another absolute which can be stated about values is that they change, sometimes violently, as in the case of revolution, and sometimes by evolutionary process; but always there is change. Ortega y Gasset made this point when he observed:

> . . . a disassociation of past and present is the generic fact of our time . . . and the cause of the suspicion more or less vague, which gives rise to the confusion characteristic of our present day existence. We feel that we actual men have suddenly been left alone on the earth; that the dead did not die in appearance only but effectively; that they can no longer help us. Any remains of the traditional spirit have evaporated. Models, norms, standards are of no use to us. We have to solve our problems without any active collaboration of the past, in full actuality, be they problems of art, science, or politics. The European stands alone without any living ghosts by his side; like Peter Schlemihl he has lost his shadow. This is what always happens when midday comes.[9]

---

[8] George E. Axtelle, "How Do We Know What Values Are Best?" *Progressive Education* (April 1950), vol. 27, pp. 191–195.
[9] Ortega y Gasset, *Revolt of the Masses* (New York: W. W. Norton, 1932), p. 39.

Midday for Ortega was the passing of an old generation. He saw civilization as a series of ups and downs, each new generation losing its grip on a previous one at "midday." Somewhere in the process no new values had sprouted to replace the old ones which no longer seemed to fit. To some the result appeared to be a drift in society which lent itself to the idea that the civilization was on the brink of collapse. This does not mean that Ortega saw the total disappearance of values in a society all at the same time. Rather, the values of the older generation were eroded until few were left standing. In a word, where the institutions of the society allow it, values change.

This process of change is well illustrated in the school situation diagram by George Spindler[10] which follows:

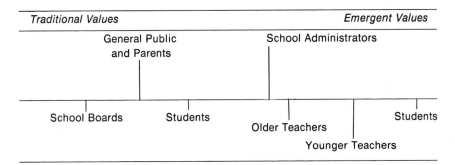

Spindler did not claim that it was possible to classify individuals or groups on his continuum as "pure" value types but he did suggest that "there is probably a modal tendency for the groups indicated to place on the . . . continuum line, in the way expressed in the diagram."

Spindler placed school boards on the traditional end, since he hypothesized that they were usually made up of persons representing the status quo power elements of the community. Admitting the difficulty of assigning a spot to the public on the continuum he hypothesized that the public "tends to be more conservative in its social philosophy" than professional educators are. This hypothesis was based on the assumption that parents represent the dominant values of the older generation. Students were placed at two points on the continuum on the assumption that some would be strongly influenced in a positive way by tradition-minded parents and some would be in a state of rebellion against old values.

School administrators and younger teachers were placed on the emergent end of the scale, since Spindler hypothesized that "professional education culture has a clear bias toward an emergent-oriented ethos." He based this

---

[10] George D. Spindler, *Education and Culture* (New York: Holt, Rinehart & Winston, 1963), p. 139.

hypothesis on the assumption that the literature of professional education, which was emergent-oriented, had some effect on values.

Although, as Professor Spindler admits, his continuum is hypothetical and perhaps contains some gross generalizations, it does illustrate the general concept of change, the changing environment from one generation to the next. Moreover, this changing environment is becoming increasingly more significant as it influences the traditional values held by any group in our society. This is true because changes have a geometrically accelerating quality about them in an advanced technological society. Certainly Margaret Mead's statement that "no one will live all his life in the world into which he was born, and no one will die in the world in which he worked in his maturity"[11] is a fact of our times. Nor is man-made environmental change necessarily induced by conscious efforts to effect change in values. Sweeping changes in environment which are man-made may occur without thought of consequences to existing values.

The discovery of the destructive power of the atom is a good case in point. Within nations, as well as within individuals, the power of the atom has caused some rethinking of values which has resulted in some changes in behavior of individuals and nations. The development of machine technology and the application of chemistry in agriculture has had a telling effect on a whole set of values based on the family farm concept of earlier generations in the United States. Who knows what alterations of belief and behavior may be forthcoming from the "fallout" from the current efforts to explore space? Perhaps the most pointed and immediate illustration of the impact of computer-assisted nuclear and space technology is the university campus. During the years following World War II, science and technology have drastically altered major activities undertaken in the large university. Once a place for teaching, quiet scholarship, and much individual research, many large university campuses have become research centers spending millions of dollars furnished by government and industry in the pursuit of pure and applied research. Indeed this new emphasis in the university has been one cause of serious student unrest in recent years. Huge sums for research have contributed to pulling experienced and talented professors out of the classroom and into the lab. The changes this has brought about in undergraduate and graduate teaching have caused serious concern among students on some campuses. An illustration might be appropriate to demonstrate what can happen. Suppose, for example, that a competent chemist is engaged in teaching undergraduates the fine points of his discipline. He enjoys his work and the students recognize him as a talented teacher. Then suppose that the chemist is offered promotion, salary, and other fringe

---

[11] Margaret Mead, "Thinking Ahead: Why Is Education Obsolete?" *Education Digest* (Feb. 1959), vol. 24, pp. 1–5.

benefit inducements to forsake the classroom for research. Funds are available for equipment, research assistants, secretaries, and most significantly, for graduate students to assume the professor's undergraduate teaching responsibilities. The resultant change in the students' environment can be immediate and dramatic and the derivative effects can range from mild grumbling to violence on the part of affected students.

Of course this kind of adjustment to the demands of science and technology can be rationalized by university administrators by bringing technology itself into play. Deans and other administrators can smooth the transition by putting the professor on video tape for one hour per week—a perfectly rational solution, making the most economical use of the professor's time since "he was only lecturing anyway." What may be most surprising about this illustration is that anyone bothers to object. Most technological innovations have been accepted in this society with scarcely a murmur of protest. Indeed, in most instances, such innovations have been enthusiastically accepted. The major point for consideration in this and similar illustrations is that few discoveries, inventions, and adaptations which grow out of technology are planned and determined efforts designed to change men's thinking with respect to traditionally held values or traditional ways of doing. Such effects are generally incidental or accidental.

A final characteristic of values to be noted is that the values an individual holds, or a group of individuals shares, are dependent upon the environment. Nor is it an easy matter to determine precisely if values must change in order for man to change his environment or if environmental change precedes changes in values. Examples can be provided which illustrate both phenomena. One could argue, as some economic historians do, that the medieval Church concept of a "just price," which was defined as the cost of producing an article, had to be modified before modern capitalism could develop fully. Once the concept of profit for the manufacturer and merchant was understood and accepted, a major obstacle to a capitalistic system of economic development was removed. Similarly, the medieval belief in the hopelessness of man's lot in this world, the belief that man could do little to improve his miserable condition, served for centuries as a major obstacle to material progress. In a word, values, beliefs, and attitudes had to change from hopelessness to a belief in the possibility of progress. Certainly, at least in Western society, part of this change began in the mind of man in a consciously revolutionary way fed by the rediscoveries of ancient philosophy, the Reformation, and the growth of national states. Part of the change was fed by natural features—population growth, the location of natural resources such as potential water power and minerals which supported the so-called industrial revolution in certain nations, and so on.

Nor is this a dead issue of the past. Values, beliefs, and attitudes, where strongly held, continue to act, in the contemporary world, as an effective obstacle to man's ability to modify his environment. Indeed, many of the so-called developing nations continue to face the obstacle of traditional values strongly held by large numbers of their population. Traditional tribal values in some of the nations of Africa and Asia continue to present a serious obstacle to progress even though a given nation may possess rich natural resources. It is interesting to note that values concerning the possibilities of material progress may change dramatically only by some outside influence. In a sense, the Crusades provided western Europe with its window to the world just as the technology of the television screen and the forced infiltration of foreign ideology is providing it for the underdeveloped nations and underprivileged peoples of the twentieth century.

Certainly the environment, both in a time and place sense, has some effect on values. A traditional or primitive society based on an agrarian or hunting economy has fewer alternatives from which to choose than a highly developed society. This is not to say that primitive life is simple while life in an industrial society is complex, for there can be great mystery and complexity in the most primitive of societies. Technology, however, does influence values and value systems. Technological development has forced man to make decisions which he does not have to face in a primitive society. In the industrial nations man is faced with a great variety of alternatives from which he must pick and choose, and these decisions may be so frequent and so demanding that values by which things are judged, the criteria which provide the bases for selection from several alternative courses of action, get a real workout. Indeed, the environment may be moving so rapidly that existing values, whatever they may be, are not adequate to serve man in industrial society. He may not have a system that is adequate to cover all the possible situations which rush upon him and which necessitate some decision on his part. Contrast this situation with that in a primitive society, in which things move more slowly and in which there are fewer questions and more answers. Custom and tradition thus can play a much stronger role and provide a more certain guide for behavior.

This aspect of values has a very great influence on the kind of education which exists in the society. Where alternatives are severely limited in a society which has limited material or economic development, education may tend to follow rather rigidly established patterns. On the other hand in a society which produces material goods and services in abundance and in which occupational choices are great, the manner in which education is conducted is never completely fixed. The highly developed society, regardless of its political system, must constantly face questions about the appropriateness and adequacy of its educational system. In both kinds of societies, regardless of time or place considered, perhaps a major problem is that of a serious lag between the realities of the present and the existing functions and organization of schooling. Regardless of time or place or the material condition of the society, values, real or fancied, play a significant role in the decisions which are made about schooling.

WHY STUDY VALUES?

The study of values then becomes important for many reasons in considering the role of education in the society. Perhaps we should not study values held by a given society at a given time in order to select some for personal guidance or to help us build a philosophy of education which would serve us as a guide through the maze of living in a modern society. A search for one's own set of values which can form the foundation for a philosophy of education may be an honorable undertaking, but in a society in which the ground is constantly changing such a search may prove futile. Even more futile perhaps might be an attempt to select some values to teach to our students. This task is beset with the same major pitfall, that is, the dynamic nature of the society which may leave us standing on the platform while the rest of the world revolves in some new orbit. This does not mean that the school makes no attempt to teach values or that individual teachers should be without them. It merely faces the reality of change. The school does attempt to teach values. One of its major functions is the transmission of culture, and values may be the most important aspect of any culture. It does mean that values are subject to critical inquiry, that they are subject to change, that they do change.

Perhaps the major reason for a study of values is to understand why things are the way they are, to explain why there is disagreement in our society over what the schools are supposed to do. A study of schooling in the context of values should help us to examine differences of opinion critically and to understand the basic position from which differences are argued, and it should give us some guidance in the resolution of the more serious differences. In the words of Spindler:

> In this perspective, many conflicts between parents and teachers, school boards and educators, parents and children, and between the various personages and groups within the school system (teachers against teachers, administrators against teachers and so on) can be understood as conflicts that grow out of sharp differences in values that mirror social and cultural transformation of tremendous scope—and for which none of the actors in the situation can be held personally accountable. . . . If these conflicts can be seen as emerging out of great sociocultural shifts—out of a veritable transformation of a way of life—they will lose some of their sting.[12]

---

[12] Spindler, p. 142.

Since we are concerned with values and education, we are generally interested in the standards Americans set for what is valuable with regard to the formal schooling aspect of education. The amount and kind and nature of schooling in any society depend upon the same basic authority which reflects a value system at least subject to description in a given time and a given place. In our society that authority is the political authority of the state. In a pluralistic society many influences play upon political decisions. Political decisions are influenced by tradition, by formal and informal power structures, by practical considerations of choice, as in the allocation of resources, and a myriad of other problems and considerations. In the chapters which follow an attempt has been made to describe and analyze some of those forces and to show how value systems or standards of value affect decisions on schooling.

REFERENCES

Axtelle, George E. "How Do We Know What Values Are Best?" *Progressive Education.* 27:191–195 (April 1950).

Barrett, Donald N. (ed.). *Values in America.* Notre Dame, Ind.: Univ. of Notre Dame Press, 1961.

Big Rock Candy Mountain. Partola, Calif.: Partola Institute, Inc., Winter 1970.

Buber, Martin. *The Knowledge of Man.* New York: Harper & Row, 1965.

Dahl, Robert A. *Polyarchy: Participation and Opposition.* New Haven, Conn.: Yale Univ. Press, 1971.

Dahlke, H. Otto. *Values in Culture and Classroom.* New York: Harper & Row, 1958.

Dodd, Stuart C. "On Classification of Human Values: A Step in Predicting Human Valuing." *American Sociological Review.* 16:645–653 (Oct. 1951).

Durkheim, Emile. *Education and Sociology.* New York: Free Press of Glencoe, 1956. Chapter 1.

Ericson, Erik H. *Childhood and Society.* New York: W. W. Norton, 1963.

Gasset, Ortega y. *Revolt of the Masses.* New York: W. W. Norton, 1932.

Hook, Sidney. *Education for Modern Man.* New York: Alfred A. Knopf, 1963. Chapter 4.

Kimball, Solon T., and James E. McClellan. *Education and the New America.* New York: Random House, 1963. Chapter 7.

Kluckhohn, Clyde. "The Study of Values." *Values in America,* Donald N. Barrett (ed.). Notre Dame, Ind.: Univ. of Notre Dame Press, 1961.

Kuhn, Alfred. *The Study of Society.* Homewood, Ill.: Dorsey Press, 1963.

Macmillan, C. J. B., and George F. Kneller. "Values and Education." *Review of Educational Research.* 34:34–37 (Feb. 1964).

Marden, Charles F., and Gladys Meyer. *Minorities in American Society.* 3rd ed. New York: American Book, 1968.

Mead, Margaret. "Thinking Ahead: Why is Education Obsolete?" *Education Digest.* 24:1–5 (Feb. 1959).

Miller, Bernard S. "The Quest for Values in a Changing World." *Social Education.* 29:69–73 (Feb. 1965).

Neal, Sister Marie Augusta, S.N.D. *Values and Interests in Social Change.* Englewood Cliffs, N.J.: Prentice-Hall, 1965.

Phi Delta Kappa Symposium Report. *Values in American Education.* Bloomington, Ind.: Phi Delta Kappa, 1964.

Rogers, Carl R. *Freedom to Learn.* Columbus, Ohio: Charles E. Merrill, 1969.

Roszak, Theodore. *The Making of a Counter Culture.* Garden City, N.Y.: Doubleday, 1969.

Spindler, George D. *Education and Culture.* New York: Holt, Rinehart & Winston, 1963.

Stoops, John. *Religious Values in Education.* Danville, Ill.: Interstate, 1967.

Williams, Robin M., Jr. "Values and Modern Education in the United States." *Values in America,* Donald N. Barrett (ed.). Notre Dame, Ind.: Univ. of Notre Dame Press, 1961.

2

Democratic Values
and the Schools

Democracy is all things to all men. As such, democracy has many meanings in many different contexts. In education such clichés as "education preserves democracy" or "the survival of our democracy depends upon the success of our educational system" are too often repeated without any definition of democracy. Frequently, our political system is labeled a democracy and its values are contrasted with the values of nondemocratic states. In the last twenty-five years the cry that we must preserve our democratic system against the threat of undemocratic communism has been a popular one. More recently student radicals have seriously questioned what has traditionally been called "American democracy" and some of the more extreme groups have been working to destroy the system so that it may be replaced with something they consider more democratic. The implications of these conflicting positions very often involve specific tasks for the schools. Such cries can cause some dismay in the minds of serious students of society. This is especially true when the advocates of democracy assume that everyone who hears their cry has a similar understanding of the term. The confusion is multiplied when it becomes evident that the communists claim democracy as their own invention and certain groups and individuals within the United States denounce it as an alien concept.

In the face of such confusion and apparent contradiction, few doubt that the generalized ideal of democracy is good and that the schools in America play a key role in its preservation and/or development. If school people must maintain and develop what is loosely called "democracy," they must know what it is. If it is desirable for the schools to promote the democratic ideal, it must be recognized that one of the most serious obstacles facing the schools is this difficulty in reaching an agreement on the definition of democracy and the basic values which underlie any definition.

Such an obstacle provides no excuse, however, for avoiding a discussion of democratic values. This chapter was written as an attempt to provide a definition of democracy which can be applied in education, and it outlines some of the major values associated with democracy. Any discussion of democratic values imposes an obligation to consider some of the major conflicts between idealized belief and practice in a society which professes to be democratic. Finally, in this chapter an attempt has been made also to deal with the role of the schools in the preservation and extension of the ideal.

A DEFINITION OF DEMOCRACY

Part of the confusion over the term "democracy" stems from the fact that those who use the term do not always make clear the context in which it is being used. As generally used in our society the term "democracy" has political, economic, and social implications. When used in the political sense, democracy generally refers to a particular kind of political system which incorporates such principles as that of majority rule with protection of the minority; equal access to the ballot box; freedom or liberty protected by custom, law, or constitutional guarantees; individual rights; and so on. *The American Political Dictionary* provides the following definition of democracy:

> The term is derived from the Greek words "demos" (the people) and "kratos" (authority). Democracy may be direct, as practiced in ancient Athens and in New England Town meetings, or indirect and representative. The Democratic Creed includes the following concepts: (1) individualism, which holds that the primary task of government is to enable each individual to achieve the highest potential of development; (2) liberty, which allows each individual the greatest amount of freedom consistent with order; (3) equality, which states that all men are created equal and have equal rights and opportunities; and (4) fraternity, which postulates that individuals will not misuse their freedom but will cooperate in creating a wholesome society. As a political system democracy starts with the assumption of popular sovereignty, vesting the ultimate political power in the people. It presupposes that man can control his destiny, that he can make moral judgments and practical decisions in his daily life. It implies a continuing search for truth in the sense of man's pursuit of improved ways of building social institutions and ordering human relations. Democracy requires a decision-making system based on majority rule with minority rights protected. Effective guarantees of freedom of speech, press, religion, assembly, petition

and equality before the law are indispensable to a democratic system of government. Politics, parties, and politicians are the catalytic agents which make democracy workable.[1]

One of the difficulties in any such definition of political democracy is the fact that genuine democracy does not lend itself to absolutes. Everything about the definition can be argued. It is this freedom to disagree upon the basic concepts within the definition which at once provides the key to the effectiveness of the system and at the same time constitutes the greatest threat to its very existence. In a discussion of the ideology of democracy, Carl Becker described the problem of this basic conflict in these words:

> Democracy, if it be consistent, must welcome the critical examination not only of its current institutions and policies but even of the fundamental assumptions on which it rests. Democracy is thus a stupendous gamble for the highest stakes. It offers long odds on the capacity of the human mind. It wagers all it has that the freest exercise of the human reason will never disprove the proposition that only by the freest exercise of the human reason can a tolerably just and rational society ever be established.[2]

Consistent democracy then, provides the seeds for its own destruction. The belief has been strong in the Western representative democracies, however, that the great majority of citizens are rational and humane and that the majority will somehow reach the decisions necessary to perpetuate democracy as a political system.

Nevertheless, within our society there is by no means unanimous agreement that the American political system should be defined as democracy. Some object to that designation on the grounds that democracy is a term which is too equalitarian in its implications and that ours is not, nor was it ever intended to be, a democratic political system, but rather a "republican" system. Indeed, this has become a serious debate in the United States in recent years. In the words of Max Lerner:

> This is not merely a closet controversy carried on by scholars: It crops up in editorials and newspaper columns and in heated Congressional debates. It seems to be the whimsical notion of the "republic" school of thought that "democracy" should be dropped from the American political vocabulary. They call it a word which (despite Jefferson and the Jacksonians, De Tocqueville, Bryan and Woodrow Wilson) didn't become popular in America until George Dimitrov used it at a Comin-

---

[1] Jack Plano and Milton Greenberg, *The American Political Dictionary* (New York: Holt, Rinehart & Winston, 1962), p. 5.
[2] Carl Becker, *New Liberties for Old* (New Haven, Conn.: Yale Univ. Press, 1942), pp. 126–127.

tern meeting, and which is today tainted beyond redress by the "People's Democracies" of eastern Europe.[3]

The position one takes on the political definition of democracy depends upon the values one holds with regard to the major concepts which have become accepted as part of the definition of democracy. Such concepts as equality and liberty have great ranges of possible meaning. Whatever the meaning, the debate over the definition has great educational implications which will be discussed later in this chapter.

The debate is not limited to the definition of political democracy. Many are not satisfied with only a political definition of democracy. Some citizens insist that the economic and social dimensions of our system are just as important as its political aspects. Perhaps the political definition of democracy gets much of the attention since twentieth-century America has experienced much political effort to define and implement the economic and social ideals which are embodied in the democratic idea.

In the battle with communist ideology which has been characteristic of our age, "economic democracy" has been a much-used phrase. Closely associated with political democracy, economic democracy is based on some of the same major concepts as political democracy. For many, however, economic and political democracy are not the same thing. Traditionally, major doctrines of economic democracy in the United States have included the belief in individualism; equality of economic opportunity; and freedom of choice for the consumer, producer, and worker. Time and conditions have wrought some changes in these traditional values, creating some serious debate over the meaning of economic democracy. Our recent history has been plagued with such questions as these: Does the worker gain or lose freedom if he must belong to a union in order to become employed? What is the proper balance between unrestrained individualism and the public interest? Should government regulate prices, quality, and quantity of production in the public interest? How is the public interest determined? There are many such questions on issues which are far from settled. Individuals and groups which take opposing views on such questions almost invariably support their argument within the context of the definition of democracy as they understand it. So the businessman may object to pressure from government to keep prices down on the grounds that such pressure is in the nature of interference with a well-established value of a democratic economy, that of individual freedom to operate in a free market. One farmer may object to controls on his production because the controls conflict with his particular interpretation of the value of economic individualism in a democracy, while another farmer may not see such a conflict. Certain groups may

---

[3] Max Lerner, *America as a Civilization* (New York: Simon and Schuster, 1957), p. 365.

peacefully resist laws which they believe to be unjust while others stand ready to reject the system and resort to the use of guns and bombs to make their point. The examples which could be given are endless, but each one illustrates the importance of values held and the manner in which these values affect the way any given individual views a particular act or practice.

The definition of social democracy offers similar problems, although social democracy would encompass both the political and economic dimensions of the term. However, as popularly used, social democracy may refer more to a style of life than a specific economic or political system. This style of life idealistically may involve such concepts as cooperation and general respect for the dignity and worth of man as a human being. Social democracy at least implies a genuine respect for human life in whatever circumstances it may be considered. The same kind of conflict arises within the concept of social democracy as that which comes out of the economic and political concepts. Some people may believe in the basic social equality of all men as a major tenet of social democracy while others may place great emphasis on individual differences. Each position may be defended within the framework of some generalized definition of democracy. For some, such a concept as the brotherhood of men may have rigid limitations, while for others it may be an absolute value within the definition of social democracy which cannot be qualified.

It is not difficult to see how problems can be created for those charged with "preserving the democratic way of life" in the schools. Without exception, the definition of democracy which finds acceptance among our citizens, young or old, depends upon the values they hold. Such problems and conflicts are too often ignored by educational writers when they merely refer to the schools as the major institution in our society which is responsible for the preservation and extension of democratic values. Once this rather useless generalization has been made, it seems incumbent upon those making it to define their terms. The heart of the democratic process may be the examination and analysis of the value position from which one views democracy. This is particularly vital in education, for most believe that the schools influence attitudes and beliefs and action based on these beliefs, whether this action be that of the worker-producer, the consumer, the voter, or whatever. This knowledge (correct or incorrect) encourages those with a particular axe to grind to attempt to convince the local school people that the school should teach a *particular* definition of democracy based on a *particular* value orientation. More will be said on this subject in Chapter 5.

To this point the attempt to define democracy clearly has not been completely successful. Perhaps there is no completely acceptable definition of democracy that can be general enough to be useful or specific enough to make sense. A way out of the dilemma may be to define democracy as a "way of life," as Ebenstein does in *Today's Isms.*[4] Although this still leaves much room for argument, the definition is general enough to include several dimensions of democracy (economic, social, political) and yet specific enough to have some real meaning. Ebenstein lists the following eight characteristics of the Western concept of democracy as a way of life:

1. Rational empiricism
2. Emphasis on the individual
3. Instrumental nature of the state
4. Voluntarism
5. The law behind the law
6. Emphasis on means
7. Discussion and consent in human relations
8. Basic equality of all human beings.

Rational empiricism is described by Ebenstein as perhaps "the most important element in the free way of life."[5] It is a condition in which people are willing to accept the certainty that there is no final truth; it is always changing and subject to constant checking and verification. Ebenstein sees three roots of individualism: the Jewish concept of one God, which leads to the conclusion that all men as children of God are brothers; the Christian doctrine of the indestructibility of the human soul, providing a spiritual equality among all men; and the Stoic view, to know oneself and to act in conformity with one's rational principles and purposes.

The instrumental theory of the state views the state as a mechanism to be used for ends higher than itself. Thus the state becomes a necessary evil. The major value underlying this is that of the Jewish-Christian belief, that there are higher laws than those which the state can provide and no earthly law can supersede God's law. In the words of Ebenstein, "the function of the state is to maintain peace and order, so that men can pursue their activities devoted to higher ends."[6] From the rational humanist viewpoint, the instrumentalist theory of the state affirms the ability of the individual to "use his reason" in discovering what is right and what is wrong, and rational reason is the ultimate test of political authority. In Ebenstein's view, the concept of the law behind the law is based upon similar principles; that is, "law is not the product of the state, but precedes it."[7] Certain basic rights such as life, liberty, and property are not a gift of the state to man, but these rights precede the state itself.

Voluntarism, in Ebenstein's view, means that there is a sort of primacy in

---

[4] William Ebenstein, *Today's Isms,* 4th ed. (Englewood Cliffs, N.J.: Prentice-Hall, 1964), pp. 133–141.
[5] Ebenstein, p. 133.
[6] Ebenstein, p. 137.
[7] Ebenstein, p. 138.

voluntary groups and associations. The state depends for its being upon existing institutions and groups such as political parties, schools, labor unions, and so on. Society is made up of such voluntary associations. The emphasis on means suggests that "democratic life is based on the realization that ends lead to no existence apart from means, but are continually shaped by them."[8]

Finally, discussion and consent are essential to the preservation of a democratic society, while equality of all human beings is a kind which professes that all men are equal in the sight of God. This is not to be confused with an egalitarian concept of equality. In the words of Ebenstein, "God's challenge to every human being is the same, although men's response to it varies enormously."

Harvey Wheeler, in *Democracy in a Revolutionary Era,* approaches the definition of democracy somewhat differently. He sees certain intrinsic characteristics in democracy which he calls its "inner logic." Wheeler identifies three basic elements in the "inner logic" of democracy. These are: scientific, organizational, and philosophic. The scientific logic, according to Wheeler, is based on the proposition that "despotism has no basis in genetics."[9] This proposition is related to the question of leadership and to the basic faith that man can govern himself, since there is a natural sort of equality which exists within the masses. Wheeler argues that such human characteristics as wisdom or common sense, virtue, intelligence, and courage are "more or less randomly distributed through the society."[10]

The organizational basis for democracy, according to Wheeler, can be stated in the following proposition: "The more complex a society becomes the more intricate are its functions and the more difficult is their coordination."[11] This proposition suggests that it would be difficult if not impossible for a complex technological society to continue to develop without a climate of free inquiry and investigation, which can exist to its fullest extent only in a democratic society. It is interesting to note the difficulties Soviet leadership has been experiencing in this context with its intellectuals.

According to Wheeler the philosophical basis for democracy is founded on the proposition that "politics is wedded to philosophy because of man's incomplete instinctual equipment. He must find compensations for this deficiency through the creation of values and purposes."[12] Wheeler bases this proposition on the assumption that the establishment of values is essential for human survival. In primitive societies these values can be

---

[8] Ebenstein, p. 139.
[9] Harvey Wheeler, *Democracy in a Revolutionary Era* (Santa Barbara, Calif.: The Center for the Study of Democratic Institutions, 1970), p. 72.
[10] Wheeler, p. 73.
[11] Wheeler, p. 73.
[12] Wheeler, p. 75.

relatively stable over long periods of time, but in a complex civilization where the society is dynamic, "the pace of change and innovation breaks out of the confines of customary and traditional values and it is necessary to create new norms and values in addition to preserving those of the past."[13] Moreover, Wheeler argues, since there is no way to prove that certain individuals are better equipped to formulate new norms and values, "there is no other valid source for them but the people as a whole."[14]

What this says to the teacher who is concerned about a definition of democracy and various challenges to the system from a variety of sources, is that every man is capable of developing his own definition of democracy. Such a definition, however, has certain limits which are rational and philosophic in nature. Therefore, it is necessary that rational men agree to some basic framework such as that suggested by Ebenstein or Wheeler, in order that existing values and norms can be evaluated from some point of departure which is at least within the context of what is generally understood to be democratic. The starting point can be a basic set of principles or certain general rules of procedure. In a democratic society the development of new goals and processes does not have to accept any philosophic framework as an absolute guide, but rational dialogue is greatly enhanced by the adoption of such a framework. Preferably the philosophic framework is one which contains elements encouraging the examination of the framework itself. This is why the works of Ebenstein and Wheeler are useful analytical tools for any teacher who wishes to grapple seriously with the definition of democracy.

CONFLICTS OVER DEMOCRATIC VALUES

From the foregoing discussion one might conclude that a definition of democracy is no simple matter, but that it may be even more difficult to arrive at a definition of the major values which make up any definition. This is true, since every value associated with democracy is subject to a great variety of meanings and interpretations—none of which would satisfy everybody. To some, the term "equality" is the keynote to the definition of democracy, while to others individual liberty or something loosely called "individualism" is the key. Even where there is agreement upon the inclusion of the concept of equality in the definition of democracy this term itself is subject to controversy. Is equality an egalitarian concept that cuts across political, social, and economic lines, or does it have clearly established limits? Obviously, there has always been much disagreement over this question in our society. With regard to the definition of individual liberty there is an equally serious

---

[13] Wheeler, p. 76.
[14] Wheeler, p. 77.

split. Some would agree with Mill that the essence of liberty is the "free development of individuality."[15] Others would agree with Leslie Lipson, who, in his excellent critique of Mill,[16] maintains that individuality considered in this way tends to ignore society and that what is good for the individual may not necessarily be a good act as defined by society. Lipson points out that "liberty consists in opportunities to act for socially beneficial ends." This definition would be immediately challenged in some quarters as holding the implication that it is not possible to determine in any given case what is good for society. The argument then revolves around means; that is, who is to determine what is good for society and how this good is to be determined.

Although freedom is often considered one of the basic values of democratic society, like liberty, it is difficult to get agreement on the definition of freedom. It is possible that there is no such thing as absolute freedom in an organized society, and freedom may be even less possible where there is no formal political control, as in theoretical anarchy. In an attempt to provide a definition of liberty, Lipson classifies three basic kinds of liberty (or freedom) as intellectual, economic, and political. By far the most absolute of these freedoms, as Lipson sees them, is intellectual freedom. In his words, "The case for intellectual freedom is simple and irrefutable: It is the necessary condition of human progress."[17] Nearly absolute intellectual freedom may be necessary for a measure of freedom in other realms of human activity. For only where there is a great measure of intellectual freedom (procedurally identified as freedom to think, to speak, to print, etc.) can encroachments upon the general principles be defined, discussed, analyzed, and acted upon. It is this very condition of freedom, however, which enables disagreement upon the definition and dimensions of freedom.

Set against such value concepts as equality, freedom, and liberty—which are implied in the definition of democracy—are such terms as self-respect. Self-respect is often used as a corollary to individualism and cooperation, which are deemed necessary as essential elements in organized society. As an ideal, few can argue with self-respect, but in operational terms it too is difficult to pin down. A major conflict in the ideal of self-respect is evident in the question: Whose self-respect? In operational terms self-respect is frequently measured against some other so-called democratic value, and the conflicts often come in the means for its attainment. In recent years there have been many pages of editorial comment devoted to the question of the means of preserving self-respect. To cite but one of many possible examples, the owner of a restaurant might choose to go out of business rather than

---

[15] John Stuart Mill, *On Liberty* (New York: Everyman's Library, E. P. Dutton, 1911), p. 161.
[16] Leslie Lipson, *The Democratic Civilization* (New York: Oxford Univ. Press, 1964), pp. 525–544.
[17] Lipson, p. 525.

serve Blacks. On both sides, the matter of self-respect is involved. The Black has a legal as well as a human claim to be treated equally in the matter of being served in a privately owned establishment which serves the public. The private owner may feel he is being unjustly treated by the law not only because his "rights" (property) are being violated as a procedural matter, but also because his ideals, his values, his self-respect are being violated. Obviously, there is no clear answer to this question outside of the law, the justice of which is measured against the generally accepted values of a democratic society. This, in turn, boils down in practice to what the majority permits, allows, or expects at any given time and place.

Nor is the concept of "majority" easily defined in a large pluralistic society. In matters which may count most in terms of personal freedom, such as dress, public behavior, and general style of life which is either acceptable or unacceptable to various American communities, the development of anything like a national majority view may always be in process. Thus the majority in one community may grudgingly accept the hippie life style, while majorities in other communities hound and harass and drive those who are markedly different from their ranks. Fortunately for the survival of democratic ideals, communities continue to be found within the larger society where differences can be openly expressed.

The value of cooperation is frequently given lip service by political as well as educational writers. Like the other terms which make up the structure of the definition of democracy it is beset with conflicts and confusion. Is there a basic contradiction between the competition of rugged individualism (a strongly held value by some of our citizens) and the idea of a society built upon cooperative effort? As in so many other terms used to explain the basic doctrines of democratic life and democratic systems, the meaning of cooperation depends upon the frame of reference of the one who is using it and the context in which it is being used.

These examples should give the reader some notion of the complexity of the problem of providing a clear definition of democracy. There is, first of all, a great amount of confusion in our society over the basic frame of reference from which one is viewing democratic values. If one happens to choose the classical liberal position of the nineteenth century from which to argue democratic values, his conclusions and the application of these conclusions to practical problems of the day are apt to be quite different from those who choose to view democracy from the point of view of twentieth-century liberal thought. A second major difficulty in defining basic democratic values is the confusion over means and ends. It is extremely difficult when considering a concept like democracy to separate means and ends. The ends may be idealized abstractions which stir little argument. The means in democracy involve procedural questions such as "Who decides?" and "How do they decide?" Such questions open endless avenues for honest disagreement. In very abstract terms it may be simple enough to list the basic values of democracy but these are meaningless until the society attempts through some act or procedure to achieve these ends. The argument over freedom comes when some procedural instrument of the society attempts to curb or expand it. The argument over individualism begins when the means of its expression are questioned.

Perhaps the greatest confusion of all in any consideration of democratic values is brought about by the most simple observation one can make about them; that is, they change. Values change because the environment which surrounds them changes. Rugged individualism may be a perfectly adaptable democratic value in a sparsely settled frontier but in the urban environment rugged individualism may be so anachronistic that its practitioners must languish in jail. The change which creates confusion, however, may offer the most hope for schooling, since it can be described, defined, and analyzed. Moreover, one can know with some accuracy the period in time upon which any given value is based.

Perhaps the problems involved in changing environment and changing definitions of values, and the confusion over means and ends, can best be illustrated by the changing interpretation of the term "freedom" over a period of nearly two centuries. In a contemporary context freedom may be an all-encompassing concept which includes political, social, and economic ideals or values. In a political sense, for some, freedom means as little government as possible. Individual freedom may be thought of more as freedom from governmental interference than anything else. For those who hold this position, the political ideals of classical liberalism have a great deal of appeal. The liberalism of the eighteenth and nineteenth centuries is expressed by Thomas Jefferson: "That government governs best which governs least." The proper functions of government for the nineteenth-century liberal involved education, defense, and a very limited number of services. In this system the individual had the highest value and he was to be left alone to develop according to his best interests and his own ability. It was, in short, the laissez-faire concept of government. The concept of nineteenth-century political liberalism extended into the economic and social realm. If political freedom meant an absence of governmental restraint, then economic freedom meant an even greater lack of restraint. Those who subscribe to these beliefs today tend to embrace many of the ideas expressed by Adam Smith in *The Wealth of Nations*, particularly the idea that free competition and the absence of governmental restraint in individual economic enterprise is the best way to achieve individual as well as common good. The viewpoint was buttressed by Charles Darwin's theory of the survival of the fittest. Deeply underlying nineteenth-century liberalism was the belief that man was basically good and his political and economic choices would be good ones if they were to be successful. The "freedom" defined by the classical liberals was by no means an absolute freedom, since man was ultimately controlled by the laws of God and the laws of nature. Although neither of these proved in practice to be very restrictive, there was the underlying belief that decisions and actions which were in violation of the laws of God or nature were bound to fail. Some of these ideas are prevalent in current conservative philosophy.

The conservative sees some of these ideas as the "good values" in our past which must be preserved or in some cases revived. The conservative of today would argue that the classical liberalism of the nineteenth century offers the individual the greatest amount of freedom consistent with an ordered society. Those who express this doctrine sometimes do so without being aware of its origin or implications, and they see modifications of the doctrine in the twentieth century as a real threat to freedom.

The modifications as they exist have been due in part at least to the search for security on the part of many Americans. Certain groups in our society, no doubt representing large numbers of our citizens and at times constituting a political majority, saw a real threat to individual freedom in the classical liberalism as it was being advocated and practiced in the closing years of the nineteenth century. To these groups, the freedom which was being enjoyed by individuals was a limited freedom, limited to a few individuals at the expense of the many. The critics of classical economic and political liberalism saw their own freedom being threatened by what they considered to be excesses of power being wielded by other individuals. The political and economic consequences of unrestrained individualism evident in monopolies and trusts became so unpopular by the end of the nineteenth century that laws were enacted to restrain the freedom of some so that the freedom of others could be protected.

During the administration of Theodore Roosevelt, and continuing under Taft and Wilson, the new definition of freedom directly involved the government. The New Freedom of Woodrow Wilson put a major responsibility for the protection of individual freedom in the hands of government. No longer was the best government that which governed least, but rather that which governed in what was loosely called "the public interest." Although the turning point in the definition of freedom had come with the beginning of the Populist movement of the last quarter of the nineteenth century, the advocates of this kind of freedom had to wait until the twentieth century to see the definition implemented in any broad sense.

There can be little doubt that the political majorities of the 1930's and 1940's were demanding certain modifications of classical liberal definitions of freedom. These modifications came in the form of the New Deal, which included such measures as the National Industrial Recovery Act (declared unconstitutional), the Agricultural Adjustment Acts, the Social Security Act, and the National Labor Relations Act. Collectively, these measures served to regulate large segments of our economic activity and materially altered the meaning of individual freedom as it was defined in the nineteenth century. Small and large business enterprises were affected. So were employees and employers, and the aged in our society. The 1930's saw a great acceleration of the trend toward government regulation in the public interest. A most remarkable thing about the sweeping measures of the 1930's was the fact that the trend has continued down to the present. Although there were serious objections from a minority who saw in these trends the assassination of old values, the majority continued to elect representatives who implemented change through law. In a very real sense a new definition of freedom has emerged for many, and the new definition rejects many of the classical concepts. This rejection has not been consciously revolutionary but rather a piecemeal rejection which has been essentially pragmatic in character. Problems in society have been faced in their current context, and solutions have been sought to specific problems without a great deal of regard for the old values.

The old values have served only to cause a certain amount of unrest, or at worst, internal conflicts within individuals who were able to see a real contradiction in the old definition of individual freedom as they understood it and something new which seemed to violate the old definition but appeared nonetheless to be good and necessary. To illustrate the point, part of the old liberal tradition may fairly be said to embrace the idea of individual initiative, thrift, and saving for a rainy day. The concept of social welfare for the needy and the aged found expression in the politics of the 1930's and appeared in the form of the Social Security Act, which seemed to meet a real need in spite of the fact that it violated some of the cherished values. When the choice was made it was clear that it was made at the expense of some of the old values. The particular definition of freedom that would allow the individual the freedom to provide for his own misfortune and his own old age is a definition that was effectively buried with the enactment of social security legislation. Today few seriously propose repeal of the act on the ground that it is an "un-American" definition of freedom. More typical are exhortations that the philosophy and provisions of the act be expanded.

What occurred with regard to social security has been true in very many other aspects of our national life; that is, many have accepted new definitions of freedom. In some ways, social security has limited the freedom of individual choice. However, it is doubtful that many young workers who are employed for the first time, and who have really had no voice whatever in the present status of the law, object seriously to having a portion of their income withheld by their employer for the social security tax. Similarly, although the agricultural program has seriously curbed the freedom of the farmer as his freedom was defined in the classical liberal tradition, few farmers appear anxious to free themselves completely from governmental programs and controls.

The new definition of freedom which has developed out of the environment of the twentieth century places the emphasis more on security and collective well-being than on the individual freedom as it was defined in the nineteenth century. That is not to say that the new definition has neglected the individual. It has viewed the individual differently. The individual, as an individual, continues to be a vital part of society. The fortune or misfortune of the single individual is still of great concern, but his well-being has become the concern of the society. The ends of political and economic activity are not in dispute between the two definitions of freedom; it is the means which are in dispute. In both cases, ends involve the highest possible development of the individual within the limits of his ability and diligence and the belief that this individual development will work for the benefit of the whole society. The nineteenth-century liberals believed that this could be best accomplished by limited government and a reasonably free economic atmosphere. The twentieth-century liberal approach has favored a positive role by government. That is, government somehow has the responsibility for seeing to it that the individual is given the opportunity to develop, and the political and economic regulatory activities of government are viewed as necessary and proper to this end.

There is a considerable amount of evidence that the twentieth-century liberal approach to individual freedom is being questioned in a different way in the last quarter of the century. The so-called "New Left" advocates "participatory democracy" and views the liberalism of the last three decades as oppressive. The very emphasis on collective well-being for which the liberal of the last generation worked so hard is being challenged. Collective well-being seemed to call in the past for some large national effort at providing for economic security, welfare, broadened educational opportunity, and so on. The result of this large national effort has been the growth of bureaucracies to cope with the sheer size and scope of unemployment, hunger, unequal schooling, and other problems. Recently certain groups and individuals have accused our bureaucratic system of being calloused to genuine human needs and problems and destructive of individual freedom. Unlike that of the nineteenth-century liberal, their definition of freedom is not steeped in tradition, nor have they formulated any utopian system to replace the existing one. Rather they would eliminate the "evil" bureaucracy which exists and replace it with a more humane society, the dimensions of which would be worked out in local communities through the democratic process.

In spite of the fact that the ends of all three points of view are similar, if not identical, the real conflict for individuals comes over a consideration of means. The extreme conservative would repeal much of the social legislation of the twentieth century and would return to the rugged individualism of the nineteenth. The liberal of the first half of the twentieth century would expand social legislation and hopefully reform the bureaucracy which administers it. The radical liberal who advocates the extremes of participatory democracy would tear down the existing political structure and replace it with a more humane system yet to be developed by honest and rational members of local communities. Perhaps a more serious problem for the schools is the fact that a great deal of this conflict is within individuals. Individuals may cling fervently to traditional values, yet they see current practices which violate the old values as good and useful and reasonable solutions to present problems. For example, the citizen who professes to believe strongly in the ideal of free competition may readily admit that free competition could lead to monopoly, which he considers bad. Or perhaps even more serious, he may believe that free competition is an absolute good, but declare that it no longer exists. Indeed, the citizen may see the specific and real violations of the ideal all around him. When pressed for an analysis of the reasons for the decline of the opportunities for free competition in our society he can find no really good reasons—he may keep coming back to the ideal, admitting that it doesn't exist, but refusing to accept or intelligently consider the conditions of the times. The result for some may be a kind of hopelessness or disillusionment with a system which has allowed one of their cherished values to become eroded. It is out of this disillusionment that the more radical liberal groups have grown and found converts. Obviously the conflict between old values and present reality provides many opportunities for the critics of American society.

The citizen who has embraced the idealistic concept of the "family farm" and the self-sufficient rural householder of whom Thomas Jefferson wrote may find serious abrogations of that ideal on the current scene. He sees the industrialization of agriculture and the numerous efforts on the part of government to regulate the industrial machine as violations of basic political and economic ideals. Similarly, the citizen who believes in the abstract concept of equality may find serious conflicts between what he holds as an ideal and what he really feels toward various racial, religious, and ethnic minority groups. For many there may be a serious conflict between the definition of terms under consideration here.

SCHOOLS AND THE DEMOCRATIC IDEAL

The problems facing schools and teachers, the major instruments for the preservation and extension of democratic doctrines, are immense ones. There are certain areas, however, in which school personnel may have primary responsibility. They are often charged with the direct responsibility of defining and practicing a belief in democracy as well as providing some leadership in the development of the democratic creed in the thought and emotions of the young. Although teachers may attempt to do this in various ways, because of the subjects they teach and the manner in which these subjects are taught, they have a difficult task. In spite of the difficulty of the task, however, it is evident that teachers have specific functions in at least teaching about democracy that go well beyond the process of simple indoctrination of a specific creed or single set of incontestable beliefs. Citizens must be schooled to perpetuate and improve the society. *How* this is done can go beyond simple indoctrination.

The school in our society is, after all, assigned the major responsibility for defining and explaining and analyzing democratic doctrines and practicing some of their broad general concepts. It is impossible to overestimate the idealized tenet that the surest means of protecting and expanding these democratic ideas which stand the test of analysis and open discussion is an enlightened citizenship. Generally, however, the means for the preservation of the ideal, the instrument for its implementation, is government. In the words of John Dewey, "The Key-note of democracy as a way of life may be expressed, it seems to me, as the necessity for the participation of every mature human being in formation of the values that regulate the living of men together: which is necessary from the standpoint of both the general social welfare and the full development of human beings as individuals."[18] It is clear that government can provide the opportunity for the exercise of this keynote of popular participation. It is equally clear that responsible participation requires not only a tradition of popular participation, rules to see that it can properly function, but also a citizenship that is disposed to function in this way. Although it must be admitted that popular participation and the use of the instrumentality of government to insure that participation is only a means, not an end. It is true, however, that the means must exist in order for the society to move in the direction of ends which are "democratic" in character. It is in this respect that schools play a vital role in the preservation and extension of the democratic ideal. Responsible participation requires training—a charge for the schools if there ever was one.

By the things which are taught and the manner in which they are taught teachers can at least imply a commitment to democratic values. Schooling can demonstrate what Dewey called a basic "faith in the capacities of human nature; faith in human intelligence and in the power of pooled and coopera- tive experience."[19] The manner in which teachers go about their business can also demonstrate a basic belief in equality, the kind which proclaims that all individuals are entitled to equal treatment under the law; this is not an easy task.

It has long been an article of faith that the schools have been a major in- stitution in American society to promote, extend, and defend the "democratic

---

[18] John Dewey, "Democracy and Educational Administration," *School and Society* (April 1937), vol. 45, pp. 457–462.
[19] Dewey, p. 458.

ideal." Even Washington and Jefferson, who had rather different views on some rather basic political issues, were in substantial agreement that democracy could best be achieved and maintained by an enlightened citizenry, and the surest means to that enlightenment was education. From the first days of our existence as a nation to the present, a strong case can be made that education and democracy were corollary developments and that the school had a significant role in the development of the democratic citizen and the nurture and growth of democratic values.

Whether the school has succeeded or failed in this charge has been an open debate for many years. The answer to success or failure depends largely on the evidence marshaled to support one's position. If one chooses to support the position that the schools have indeed been a major instrument in the development of the democratic ideal, all that is necessary is to point to the expansion of the system. There is no question that a much greater proportion of the population is in school today than was the case one hundred years or even a generation ago. There is no question that the schools have been responsive to the needs of society in terms of extending educational opportunity downward to state-supported nursery schools and kindergartens and upward to publicly supported community colleges, state colleges, and universities. There is no question that the schools have been responsive to the burgeoning variety of societal needs in terms of different kinds of training, which has resulted in a vast proliferation of programs at secondary and higher levels of education.

On the other hand, if one chooses to support the position that the schools have failed in their democratic role, evidence can be marshaled which demonstrates that in spite of polemics to the contrary, schooling remains substantially unequal. The poor and minorities continue to be neglected. Students continue to drop out because they are faced with economic hardships. College or university training continues to be out of the reach of many for a myriad of reasons. The schools are not yet fulfilling their promise of training enlightened democratic citizens.

Perhaps this is not the real issue in the waning years of the twentieth century. Perhaps the real issue is the definition of democratic values. An analysis of this problem seems to indicate that subtle changes in the definition of major democratic values have already occurred which have not been fully realized by those involved in education and which are having and will continue to have great impact on the schools in the years ahead. These changes can be stated in a rather direct proposition: *American society has reached a stage in its development where it must deliver on its promise of democracy. The great democratic values—equality, liberty, freedom, and justice—can no longer be considered abstract ideals but must be considered as working guidelines—platforms for action.*

Traditionally, democracy has been conceived as a body of law and practice that protects the individual in the free pursuit of his natural inclinations from the encroachments of various political agents and agencies of the society. This was the nineteenth-century liberal view explained and justified by the writings of such philosophers as Locke, Mill, Rousseau, Smith, and Jefferson. Traditionally most individuals in this society have viewed the substantive liberal values of the First, Fifth, and Fourteenth Amendments to the U.S. Constitution as inhibitions against actions by governmental agents or agencies. That is, in the words of the First Amendment, Congress "shall make no law respecting an establishment of religion, or prohibiting the free exercise thereof; or abridging the freedom of speech. . . "; in the Fifth Amendment, "No person shall be. . .deprived of life, liberty or property, without due process of law. . . "; and finally, in the Fourteenth, no state "shall make or enforce any law which shall abridge the privileges or immunities of citizens of the United States; nor. . . deprive any person of life, liberty or property, without due process. . . nor deny any person. . . the equal protection of the laws." The wording is negative and has traditionally been interpreted literally as such: in case after case which came before the Supreme Court the amendments have been interpreted as negative inhibitions against governmental actions.

More recently, however, there has been a clearly discernible trend to interpret these great democratic abstractions not as negative inhibitions, but as positive platforms for action. Thus, equality used to mean that a state legislature or the United States Congress could not pass a law which would support unequal treatment. More recently, minorities pushing for equal rights as citizens have said that it is the responsibility of government to legislate equality; that is, to utilize the force of law to make their particular definition of equality a reality. The fact that this pressure has been partially successful is a matter of record. In the 1940's and 1950's the courts were the battlefield in which minorities succeeded in gaining prohibition of discrimination on the basis of color in colleges and public schools. Later, and especially during the sixties, the major arena of activity has been in the legislative halls and in the administration of the law. Thus, in recent years, the force of law has been used positively to create integrated schools. Congress has moved through its power of appropriations to prohibit national funds from those school districts which have attempted to subvert the intent of the law, and to appropriate funds for the implementation of integration. Equality in educational opportunity, although a long way from realization in the United States, has been encouraged and implemented through special grants under the Elementary and Secondary Education Act to assist school districts enrolling an unusually large number of poor children.

There are examples of this positive role of the national government in areas other than education. Instead of the old negative stance of prohibiting housing discrimination on the basis of race and nationality, Congress has more recently used the force of law to create integrated housing. Although this has been accomplished in a number of ways, the most obvious one is providing low-rent integrated housing. Similarly, in its policies on employment, the government has moved from its position of merely prohibiting job discrimination to enactment of legislation requiring that minority individuals be hired where government contracts are involved.

There are many other examples, but these are significant changes in both philosophy and action. How could such significant change happen in such a relatively brief span of years? Certainly the pressure from various minorities, particularly the Blacks, can explain some of the change. But why have minorities been successful in goading the majority into the positive implementation of so-called democratic ideals which have waited so many years for positive action? The following hypothesis is offered as one possible explanation for the phenomenon: *The possibility of implementation of the basic tenets of democracy as a practical guide to action exists in the United States today because of certain realities of mass society. These realities can be generally classified as political, social, and economic.*

The major political reality is the reality of mass society or mass power. Thus, in a pluralistic democracy where the majority is made up of a loose coalition of conflicting and contending power groups, political leaders must deliver. In such a milieu, democratic abstractions such as "equality" must be more than easily mouthed clichés. Even "equality of opportunity" no longer suffices. The real and quite different meaning of equality becomes equal housing, equal pay for equal work, equal education, equal employment. For example, equal educational opportunity has traditionally been interpreted to mean that every child should have an opportunity to get the best education of which he is capable. The major justification for this position was that if he didn't, he had only himself to blame. Within the "democratic" context this meaning was justified in terms of such generalities as "individual differences." In its extreme there was the implication that some sort of genetic basis existed for substantially unequal treatment. Equal education, on the other hand, means equal education. Every child must have equal education and the law exists to see that he does. He must have equal facilities, substantially equally well qualified teachers, equal public investment in his training, and so on. Equality in education, as in other areas of pluralistic democracy, has a practical meaning. If politicians do not deliver they are harassed, badgered, and eventually driven from power. The most obvious manifestation of this phenomenon has occurred in recent years in mayoralty races in several of our largest cities.

The major social reality in mass society is one of numbers. Given the massive population concentrations that have resulted from urbanization, problems cannot go unsolved indefinitely. The days of manipulation and privilege based on uneasy coalitions may be nearing an end. The solution of social problems, guided by some concept of fairness, concern for humanity, and social justice, is unavoidable. Problems must be attacked and new programs initiated which attempt to resolve them because it is impossible to ignore a million people. Although it was possible in the past to indefinitely ignore the demands of urban minorities, conditions have changed so that this is no longer the case: those millions are organized, they have instant communication with each other and with the nation, and perhaps most significantly within the context of our own traditional democratic ideals, those clamoring for implementation of equality, justice, and freedom have a case. They are asking for proof that democracy can work. They are insisting that democracy deliver on its promises.

The major economic reality of mass society is the total interdependence of the system. No longer can our economic system be viewed as a system made up of millions of independent economic units acting in their own best interests. Every economic decision makes waves and ripples throughout the system. Giant industries cannot raise prices nor can labor gain increased benefits without setting off chain reactions affecting the whole system. In practice, the reality of economic interdependence means that we solve our problems and prosper or fail to solve them and die, possibly violently.

These, then, are the major realities which make the implementation of democratic ideals imperative. So what does all of this have to do with education? It has everything to do with education because the schools and their teachers can be the key to survival. If this society is to experience a genuine implementation of democratic values, teachers cannot preach and not practice them. Teachers are destined for a key role in the future of mass society, for masses can become intolerant, destructive, and vengeful. History is replete with illustrations. Obviously, the greatest opportunity for the young to learn to function effectively in mass society is in the schools. The major responsibility of teachers is to teach mass society to be a thinking mass, to utilize rational intelligence rather than white-hot emotion in the solution of problems. More than this, the teacher must himself become an active citizen willing to take the risks involved in speaking out against injustice and inequities—willing to work actively for the improvement of the human condition. A teacher who is not committed to the proposition that there is something that he can do to make this a better place, a teacher who contributes nothing to posterity, might as well be replaced by a computer.

There are many obstacles facing the schools in the exercise of this basic function, some of the most serious being the force of tradition, the attitude and actions of the community, the activities of self-interest pressure groups, the force of tradition-bound law, teachers who are narrow and restricted in their views and methods, and the limitation of resources. This is by no means a complete listing of problems but they are important ones, and they do illustrate the scope of the difficulty. Chapters 3 to 7 deal with several of these forces and problems as they influence the operation of the school in the United States. This is not meant to imply that they are antidemocratic in nature. Quite the contrary. In some instances they are basically democratic in themselves, and reflect democratic values. In other instances they are not so democratic. All, however, are affected by, and in turn affect, values and valuing in the society. They affect values in a way that has real impact on what the school is able to do. In total, they are forces which are oriented toward the democratic ideal but in a very real way tend to limit the freedom of operation of the local school. This is not to say that this is evil, but rather to recognize the fact that the schools, for all their potential as instruments for social change in the direction of achievement of democratic ends, are severely limited by the environment in which they find themselves. The next several chapters will describe and analyze the forces that influence the schools and will attempt to demonstrate how these forces are essentially conservative in nature. Conservative, in some cases in a deliberate way, in others, rather unconsciously so, but conservative in the sense that they make rapid and radical change difficult. Conservative in the sense that they tend to reflect the thinking and philosophy of an earlier generation at worst, and the status quo at best. The net result may be that the school will be cast in the role of a reflector of the society rather than a major agent or instrument for change.

REFERENCES

Becker, Carl. *New Liberties for Old.* New Haven, Conn.: Yale Univ. Press, 1942.

Becker, Ernest. *Beyond Alienation: A Philosophy of Education for the Crisis of Democracy.* New York: George Braziller, 1967.

Chambers, William N., and Robert Salisbury (eds.). *Democracy in The Mid-Twentieth Century.* St. Louis, Mo.: Washington Univ. Press, 1960.

De Chardin, Pierre Teilhard. *The Future of Man.* New York: Harper & Row, 1959.

Dewey, John. *Democracy and Education.* New York: Macmillan, 1916.

———. "Democracy and Educational Administration." *School and Society.* 45:457–462 (April 1937).

Ebenstein, William. *Today's Isms.* 4th ed. Englewood Cliffs, N.J.: Prentice-Hall, 1964.

Fuller, Buckminster. *No More Secondhand God.* Carbondale, Ill.: Southern Illinois Univ. Press, 1963.

Gabriel, R. H. *The Course of American Democratic Thought.* Rev. ed. New York: Ronald Press, 1956.

Kallen, Horace M. *The Education of Free Men.* New York: Farrar, Straus and Giroux, 1949.

Lerner, Max. *America as a Civilization.* New York: Simon and Schuster, 1957. Chapter 6.

Lipson, Leslie. *The Democratic Civilization.* New York: Oxford Univ. Press, 1964.

Mayer, Milton. *Man v. the State.* Santa Barbara, Calif.: The Center for the Study of Democratic Institutions, 1969.

Mill, John Stuart. *On Liberty.* New York: Everyman's Library, E. P. Dutton, 1911.

Padover, Saul K. *The Genius of America.* New York: McGraw-Hill, 1960.

Plano, Jack, and Milton Greenberg. *The American Political Dictionary.* New York: Holt, Rinehart & Winston, 1962.

Popper, Karl R. *The Open Society and its Enemies.* Princeton, N.J.: Princeton Univ. Press, 1971.

Revel, Jean Francis. *Without Marx or Jesus.* Garden City, N.Y.: Doubleday, 1971.

Riker, William H. *Democracy in the United States.* 2nd ed. New York: Macmillan, 1965.

Selakovich, Daniel. *Problems in Secondary Social Studies.* Englewood Cliffs, N.J.: Prentice-Hall, 1965. Chapter 5.

Smith, T. V. *The Democratic Way of Life.* Chicago: Univ. of Chicago Press, 1926.

Wheeler, Harvey. *Democracy in a Revolutionary Era.* Santa Barbara, Calif: The Center for the Study of Democratic Institutions, 1970.

PART TWO
How Does Society Impose Its Values on the Schools?

In spite of the foregoing discussion, which attempted to demonstrate the very real difficulty in defining the political, economic, and social values of American society, the schools do teach values. In some instances this may be a deliberate effort, in others the effort is incidental; that is, the schools reflect the community which surrounds them. The general purpose of the six chapters that follow is, first, to demonstrate how certain major forces which influence schools and schooling in the United States tend to have a conservative value orientation and, second, to explain in a limited way the means by which these forces operate in their relation to the schools.

3

The Force of Tradition

Tradition has been a particularly strong force in shaping the development of American educational values and the manner in which schooling has been viewed, and tradition itself, of course, is influenced by the environment in which a society finds itself. This has been quite evident in the United States, where no special set of political, social, or economic values has enjoyed anything approaching stability. The environment here has been too dynamic in a material sense or in human terms, and too pluralistic in economic, political, and social terms, to permit any prolonged rigidity of values. Whole groups in our society have had a way of modifying values and value systems in the face of the realities of the present. Certainly this has been true of immigrant groups, certain economic groups such as farmers and industrial workers, more widely representative groups such as political parties, and so on. Conversely, groups which have attempted to stand still in the face of environmental change have tended to become extinct or ineffective. History is replete with such examples of institutions, ideas, systems, and customs which were based on obsolescent values, for example, the Federalist and Whig parties, the plantation system, the "separate but equal" doctrine, and the extended family. Moreover, as indicated in Chapter 2, this is not solely a historical phenomenon. The present division and conflict within the two major political parties are largely the outcome of a search for, and conflict over, basic and permanent values.

Obviously the relationship between education and the force of tradition is much too broad a subject to discuss adequately in a few pages. What follows, therefore, is restricted to the relationship of education to one aspect of the historical evolution of the environment in the United States—the political aspect—and the major purpose here is to demonstrate how the political environment has influenced the development of schools in the United States.

Schooling in the United States has always been more or less dependent upon political values and the practical realities of politics. In this sense, the development of the schools has paralleled the development of the political system. As the base of political participation was extended and the system became more responsive to mass demands, schools followed close behind. Political change has been characteristic of the system. There has never been a time in American history when the formal political system was considered static. Political values, political organization, and political processes have always been in various stages of growth, decline, decay, or modification of one sort or another. Indeed, the great strength of our formal governmental structure may be its flexibility, its adaptability to new stresses and new conditions. So it has been with schooling. At times schooling, as well as the formal structure of education, has appeared to lag considerably behind political developments, but always there has been a close relationship between education and politics in the United States, and the relationship has remained a close one whether the political organization and process are considered as a system or as a means of expressing the values of the American people.

It is as difficult to speak of a tradition in American education as it is to speak of a tradition in American politics. In political development, as in education, the growth of the concept of states' rights might be cited as a genuine American tradition. With equal vigor one might defend the proposition that political institutions and goals, as well as educational institutions and goals, have a national rather than a state or local character. Thus, anyone who attempts to determine the "true" tradition of American development of politics or education is beset with all sorts of confusions. This is probably true in both the political and educational arenas because both have been greatly influenced by the needs of the times and the demands of a given environment.

It is perfectly natural that the American system of schooling has been influenced and directed by what is currently happening on the political scene. The school has been popularly conceived of as a working corollary of everybody's definition of democracy. For more than a century the idea of public education has been a popular one in the United States. As such, education has been accepted as a responsibility of a representative government. This responsibility has been exercised largely through the political arm of the state. For many years, public education has been a basic part of the political system and has operated within the framework of the American legal, constitutional, and political systems. The values of schooling in our society are public in nature and cannot be separated from the political values of the society as they are expressed by the political leaders of the times and reported by the public media. Whom the schools teach and what is taught are public concerns and always have been. This close relationship between the political environment, broadly conceived, and education has a long history.

The philosophy concerning the proper role of education in the society has passed through three rather distinct phases which were influenced by political values. The first was characterized by a tradition of limited education, influenced by a theocratic aristocracy; the second, by pressure for enlightened citizenship; and the third and present phase, by a movement toward grass-roots democracy and a compulsory, multipurpose, and comprehensive mass education.

THE TRADITION OF LIMITED EDUCATION

The Englishmen who colonized the Atlantic seaboard had a rather narrow view of the role of education in organized society. For more than one hundred and sixty years, in most of the English colonies, the school curriculum was decidedly religious in character and was provided at public expense only for the very poor. This limited view of schooling was natural to the English colonists for this was the system that was common in England during much of the seventeenth century, and the first settlers merely transplanted it and established it on American shores.

Jamestown was one of the first colonies to establish legal provisions for schooling. Occupied for the first few years with the problem of survival, the colonists directed their attention toward schooling for their children only after the Virginia colony had expanded and become a stable venture. The Apprenticeship Law in Virginia in 1642 provides a good example of the way the constituted legislative authority of Virginia viewed education:

> Whereas sundry laws and statutes by act of parliament established, have with great wisdom ordained, for the better educating of youth in honest and profitable trades and manufactures, as also to avoyd sloath and idlenesse wherewith such young children are easily corrupted, as also for reliefe of such parents whose poverty extends not to give them breeding. That the justices of the peace should at their discretion, bind out children to tradesmen or husbandmen to be brought up in some good and lawful calling. And whereas God Almighty, among many of his other blessings, hath vouchsafed increase of children to this collony, who are now multiplied to a considerable number, who if instructed in good and lawful trades may much improve the honor and reputation of the country, and noe lesse theire owne good and theire parents comfort. . . .[1]

This law provides an interesting insight into the view of the nature of formal schooling and the values held by the political leaders in Virginia. It is a simple statement of values. More significantly, it ordains that the major function of the schools is to teach these values.

---

[1] Edgar W. Knight and Clifton L. Hall, eds., *Readings in American Educational History* (New York: Appleton-Century-Crofts, 1951), p. 9.

Even though Virginia had been a royal colony since 1624, it managed to maintain a certain amount of local autonomy. For example, its House of Burgesses was a representative assembly which, among other things, assumed responsibility for legislation on apprentice training. The wording of the Apprenticeship Law suggests that the members of the House of Burgesses viewed this kind of education as a public responsibility. They were obviously concerned lest the talent of youth who could not afford to learn a skill would go undeveloped and they consequently would not be able to obtain gainful employment. Moreover, they expressed concern that either through poverty or neglect on the part of parents, society as a whole might suffer from the lack of trained or skilled citizens. The members actually viewed the training provided as a legitimate and proper function of the legislative authority acting in the name of the general public. Not only did this legislation directly involve the state in providing schooling for certain youth, but it furnished specific implementation. The legally designated officers of the colony were to select two children in each county to be sent to James City to learn specific skills under the direction of designated masters and mistresses. The expenses of the program were to be met by the colony, and two buildings were to be erected at public expense to house the program. Although the Apprenticeship Law applied only to children whose parents could not otherwise give their children an education, it did express a public commitment of sorts to education, although a narrowly defined and limited one. However, it was in keeping with a narrow and limited political state that was greatly influenced by the clergy and by a specific set of moral values. Massachusetts, New York, and other colonies had similar limited legislation on their books by 1700.

In spite of their concern for the education of the poor, the apprenticeship laws of Virginia and other states during the first hundred years of the colonial experience are more an example of the attitude of a paternalistic, and in some cases, a theocratic state, than of any real grass-roots movement which was dedicated to the principle of schools for children at public expense.

Educational efforts of the Massachusetts Bay theocracy provide a good example of the religious orientation of early school legislation in America. It would not be possible, by any stretch of the imagination, to call the Massachusetts Bay Colony a representative democracy in the 1640's. However, by 1642, the government of the Massachusetts Bay Colony had developed into a very limited representative government. The colony was ruled by a royal governor who was assisted by a council which he appointed. By 1634 the freemen of the colony were demanding greater representation in the General Court, the legislative body of the colony. In that year representation of the freemen was increased in the General Court, and by 1635 the General Court was divided into a legislature of two houses. The upper house consisted of the Governor's Council, and the lower house, the freemen's representatives. This does not mean, however, that the lower house represented a majority of the population. For all practical purposes the colony continued, long after 1635, to be dominated by the governor and his council and by the freemen who were part of the Puritan congregation. The only real concession made to the principle of political democracy was a recognition that those who paid the taxes (the freemen and property owners) should have some voice in deciding what the policy of taxation on property was to be and how the tax monies were to be spent.

Viewed in this light, the school laws could not be expected to do much more than express the religious values of the majority of property owners in the Massachusetts colony. School laws also represented the general feeling of these property owners concerning what constituted an appropriate public expenditure. In the eyes of the freemen and prominent Puritans of the colony, the School Law of 1647 expressed this aptly in its concern lest "ye ould deluder, Satan" would get control of the children of the colony through the clever device of keeping them ignorant of the words of the Scripture. Aware of this danger, the lawmakers directed every township with fifty families or more to appoint someone to teach the children to read and write. All towns of one hundred or more families were instructed by law to provide a Latin grammar school which would prepare students for the university. Moreover, the law imposed a penalty of five pounds in the event that this stipulation was not observed. The expense of this program was to be met by the parents or "the inhabitants in general." Without question, the 1647 law was specifically religious in its purposes and orientation. As such, it was probably an accurate reflection of the political climate in the Massachusetts Bay Colony in 1647.

The Massachusetts law became a model for some of the other colonies, Connecticut adopting it in its entirety[2] and Plymouth Colony enacting a similar statute in 1658. By 1673 the Plymouth General Court had provided that the expense of free schools be defrayed by the treasurer out of profits from the fishing industry.[3]

Pennsylvania is a good illustration of how existing political values influenced educational development. Pennsylvania was established in the form of a land grant to William Penn in 1681, and its constitution designated the freemen as the ruling group. However, the definition of freemen in Pennsylvania was more liberal than it was in any other colony at this point in history. Here a freeman was anyone who owned or rented one hundred acres and cultivated at least ten; or any freed servant who owned or rented fifty acres and cultivated twenty; or any artisan or other inhabitant of the colony who paid taxes.[4] The second assembly, which met in 1683, enacted the first

---

[2] Ellwood P. Cubberley, ed., *Readings in the History of Education* (Boston: Houghton Mifflin, 1920), p. 300.

[3] Cubberley, p. 302.

[4] Max Savelle, *The Foundations of American Civilization* (New York: Holt, Rinehart & Winston, 1942), pp. 259–260.

law on schooling in Pennsylvania. It provided that all parents be responsible for instruction of their children in reading and writing and that children be taught some useful skill or trade.[5] Those parents who failed to discharge this responsibility were to be fined five pounds. The declared purpose of the act was to enable children to read the Scriptures, and although the act was motivated by religious purposes and put the burden of schooling on the parents, it did recognize the importance of schools to the welfare of the colony. At this stage in its development, Pennsylvania was less able than the neighboring colonies to impose any sort of universal religious values on its citizens and to use the schools as an instrument for instilling them, since the population was not uniform in its religious beliefs and practices. Consequently, the law reflected a realistic recognition of the differences in religious practice and belief in the colony. In this context, the Pennsylvania law must be viewed as a general statement of the belief and policy of the most representative colonial assembly of the times on the importance of education as a necessary part of the development of the colony. Indeed, because of the very democratic nature (for the times) of the Pennsylvania Constitution, private schools organized by religious groups became an early and important feature of the educational system in the colony. Although considered a public responsibility, the needs of education in Pennsylvania were subordinated to what was believed to be a more important consideration, that is, the freedom of religious groups to develop according to their own lights.

The importance of these laws is not that they were great landmarks of progress but rather that they were reflections of the values of a society which tended to be narrow and restricted. Most of the early laws were narrow in purpose and limited in application, and all were realistic in that they attempted to legislate the possible.

EDUCATION FOR ENLIGHTENED CITIZENSHIP

By the time of the American Revolution the political environment in America had experienced some rather drastic changes which had their effect on thoughts concerning the schools. During more than a century of development in most colonies the base of political representation had been greatly extended. Partly as a result of this broadened representation, and partly as a result of the excesses of colonial governors in the name of the Crown, the colonial legislature on the eve of the American Revolution had become a real center of governmental power. By the time of the Revolution the colonial legislature had assumed power over the purse strings, there was generally

---

[5] Cubberley, p. 307.

free and open debate in the legislature, and the legislative assemblies were meeting at their own discretion. In total, the legislatures had become an independent agency of government and the real center of power over local or state matters in the colonial system. To be sure, the legislatures were a long way from being truly representative bodies, for the qualifications for voting in every colony retained property and other restrictive qualifications. Thus, the electorate was a decidedly limited one. However, the legislative institution in colonial America had gained most of its power at the expense of the executive, the colonial governor. Although this development had no direct and immediate effect upon legislation with regard to schooling, it was a development which laid the foundation for immediate post-independence provisions for schools which were significant. The pattern of legislative independence continued after the Revolution. With the rejection of political control from England and the removal of the royal governor and his council as a source of authority after the Revolution, the states made moves which were indicative of a new attitude toward education and which reflected changing political values.

Guidelines for political action had been spelled out by men like Jefferson, Franklin, and Washington during the revolutionary period and now these same spokesmen directed their attention from time to time to education and suggested guidelines in this area. As early as 1749 Franklin made several specific proposals for the education of the youth of Pennsylvania which went well beyond what was being done in that colony or any of the other English colonies at that time. Franklin's proposals began with the statement that education was important to the happiness of private families as well as to the Commonwealth, that education was a proper function of government and a most important function of education was to "supply the succeeding age with men qualified to serve the Publik with Honour to themselves, and to their country."[6] This is certainly a broader and much more enlightened view than that expressed in the Massachusetts law of 1647, which was concerned with the narrower aspects of religious education and education for the poor. Franklin saw education as a primary function of the state, by which it prepared men to serve, and he was thinking in the broad terms of enlightened and intelligent citizenship. So was Thomas Jefferson, who viewed education as the only means that could insure the survival of a democratic system. Jefferson expressed fear that even democratic government could be turned into tyranny and expressed the belief that the best way to prevent this "would be to illuminate, as far as practicable, the minds of the people at large, and more especially to give them knowledge of those facts which history exhibiteth, that, possessed thereby of the experience of other ages and

---

[6] Knight and Hall, p. 9.

countries, they may be enabled to know ambition under all its shapes, and prompt to exert their natural powers to defeat its purpose."[7] Jefferson believed that only the educated could be entrusted with the public confidence and with public power and that only a liberal education could "ensure that the servants of the people would guard the sacred deposit of the rights and liberties of their fellow citizens. . . ." Moreover, Jefferson believed that educational opportunity should be provided equally for all, and that the expense of education should be borne by the public. In a proposal before the Virginia legislature, in 1779, Jefferson suggested that the Commonwealth of Virginia be conveniently divided into school districts which should build and provide for schools in which the fundamentals would be taught at the expense of the state. Moreover, he felt that the best of the students from these schools should be sent to the university for further education at state expense. Jefferson's plan was not adopted, but there can be no question that it was the most comprehensive plan for public education introduced in America up to that time.

Like Franklin, Jefferson was thinking in the broad terms of education for intelligent citizenship. Education was envisioned as a means of serving the state by providing it with citizens who were educated. Indeed, Jefferson saw an educated citizenry as the only means whereby the democratic state could survive. The significance of Jefferson's 1779 proposal was that it laid the broad general philosophy of the idea of public education which was to become a pattern for educational development in the United States. The purpose of education, as Jefferson viewed it, should be openly and deliberately political, and education should be used as a means to promote democracy in the broadest sense of the term.

George Washington viewed education as an opportunity to instill and propagate a high sense of nationalism in a fledgling nation. In his message to Congress in which he advocated the establishment of a national university in 1796, Washington expressed the opinion that education could be used to help the youth of the new nation to assimilate the "principles, opinions, and manners of our countrymen" and he declared: "The more homogeneous our citizens can be made in these particulars, the greater will be our prospect of permanent union; and a primary object of such a national institution should be, the education of our youth in the science of government."[8] In this proposal Washington saw clearly what was to become a major role of American public education. No other institution in our society—political, economic, or social—has done more to weld together people of diverse

---

[7] Philip S. Foner, ed., *Basic Writings of Thomas Jefferson* (New York: John Wiley & Sons, 1944), p. 41.

[8] Jared Sparks, ed., *The Writings of George Washington* (Boston: F. Andrews, 1839), p. 42.

origins, languages, beliefs, and experiences than has the American public school system, in spite of the fact that Washington's idea of a national university has never been realized. Like Jefferson and Franklin before him, Washington viewed education as a major vehicle for helping the population develop a common system of political values.

After independence from England, some of the first state constitutions reflected the idea that education was a public enterprise with rather broad general purposes. Although several states did not mention education in their fundamental law,[9] seven of the original states, and Vermont, did. In these eight states the provisions for education appeared to vary a little in terms of philosophy. Some of these constitutions contained provisions for education with heavy moral, religious, and charitable overtones. These continued in the century-old tradition of severely limited education. Such was the provision of the Pennsylvania Constitution of 1776, which contained a general statement providing for education in every county in the state followed by a section which justified the provision in terms of the need to encourage virtue and prevent vice and immorality. Similar provisions may be found in the Vermont Constitution of 1777 and the New Hampshire Constitution of 1784. The New Hampshire Constitution placed greater emphasis on the importance of education as a means for preserving a free government and was more in line with the values of enlightened citizenship than with the old values of education to promote morality and virtue. The Massachusetts Constitution of 1780 turned its attention to education in providing for the establishment of a university, choosing not to disturb the pattern of the lower schools which had developed more as a matter of private, religious, and moral training than anything else. The North Carolina Constitution of 1776 and the Georgia Constitution of 1777 contained general provisions on education which said nothing about virtue, morality, or religion.

In summary, it might be said that the concept of education as a public function for the purpose of developing the values of enlightened political citizenship was beginning to appear in some of the constitutional provisions of the original states. This is understandable in view of the fact that the political environment of the times was the successful drive for independence, and although a complete feeling of nationalism had not yet had time to develop, there was a sense of dedication to new values developing in the political arena. The older concepts of education for narrow, religious, and moral training and education for the poor, as expressed in the Massachusetts School Law and other similar school laws of an earlier century, had been modified, expanded, and liberalized by the time of the American Revolution to include the idea of the importance of schooling as a citizenship function in

---

[9] These included New Hampshire, New Jersey, Delaware, Maryland, Virginia, South Carolina, New York, Connecticut, and Rhode Island.

the broad political sense. The relationship between the educational function of the state and its political aspects was made quite clear in some of the early state constitutional provisions on education.

This relationship was even more evident in constitutional provisions of new states which were admitted to the Union in the first generation of national independence and in the state laws during the first thirty or forty years of the system. The constitution of Ohio was a mixture of enlightenment and the tradition of education for moral and religious training. It clung to traditional values, yet expressed new ones. It provided in part:

> That all men have a natural and indefeasible right to worship Almighty God according to the dictates of their conscience; that no human authority can, in any case whatever, control or interfere with the rights of conscience; that no man shall be compelled to attend, erect, or support any place of worship, or to maintain any ministry, against his consent; and that no preference shall ever be given by law to any religious society or mode of worship; and no religious test shall be required as a qualification to any office of trust or profit. But religion, morality, and knowledge being essentially necessary to the good government and happiness of mankind, schools and the means of instruction shall forever be encouraged by legislative provision, not inconsistent with the rights of conscience.

The Indiana Constitution of 1816 reflected enlightenment and a sense of political values in its statement that knowledge and learning were essential to the preservation of a free government, and it did not mention the importance of religion, morality, and virtue; nor did it mention the need for education of the poor.

One must use caution, however, in making broad claims for education for enlightened citizenship. The political philosophy of the Federalists had a somewhat limiting effect on the development of ideals of the enlightened citizen. Based to some extent on the idea of a ruling elite and a severely limited electorate, Federalist political theorists could not conceive of a broadly based educational system designed to elevate the masses to intelligent citizenship. This was true in spite of the fact that certain Federalist leaders such as George Washington expressed the ideal in their speeches and writing. Even the most liberal-minded of the Federalists, however, were reluctant to go all the way in advocating the public school idea. This does not mean that Americans had to wait until the era of Jacksonian democracy for any really solid movement for public education at public expense for public purposes. The values associated with Jacksonian democracy did not spring fully mature on the election of Jackson. Nor did the public school idea spring fully mature upon the appointment of Horace Mann as state superintendent in Massachusetts. District organization for education was an established fact long before the Jacksonian period, and all of the states had assumed some of the responsibility for financial support of education. The common school movement of the 1820's, 1830's, and 1840's was well underway in 1820.

GRASS-ROOTS DEMOCRACY AND EDUCATION

The movement for public education for the masses was not so much an outgrowth of Jacksonian democracy as it was an evolutionary development which sprouted from the seeds of democratic political values during the early nineteenth century. The rise of political parties at the turn of the century had some influence, however indirect, on the public school movement. This political phenomenon is generally credited to the Jeffersonian Republicans and their attempts to organize support for candidates in the election of 1800. American politics has never been the same since. The political party as an outlet for the expression and coalition of a variety of special interests and pressures played a vital role in the development of the public school idea.

In addition to the rise of the political party as a method of political expression, the more liberal religious beliefs which stressed equality and religious freedom appeared as early as 1800. Thomas Paine's *Age of Reason,* which appeared in America after 1794, gained an audience which must have had some influence on educational thought in America. As the logic in *Age of Reason* loosened the stranglehold of the orthodox religious view which dated from the mid-seventeenth-century Calvinism in the colonies, it must have set men to thinking about the proper relationship between education and religion and education and the state. Spurred by this new liberalism in religious thought, the Unitarians, Congregationalists, Baptists, Methodists, and Presbyterians took the gospel to the frontiers and preached, in the earthy language of the masses, a religion based on mass participation. This kind of religion was a great contribution to the ideal of an equalitarian democracy.

In their writing, the Americans at the turn of the century were beginning to express interest in a broader definition of democracy and its functions and practices. Hugh Henry Brackenridge (1748–1816), in *Modern Chivalry,* was critical of the class system he saw in the new republic. He believed that the hope of the system was based on intelligence and education. Similarly, Charles Brockden Brown (1771–1810), in *Arthur Mervyn* (1800), portrayed a democratic hero who believed in the principles of human equality and justice. Newspapers expanded rapidly in America in the first generation of our existence. By 1810 there were 350 in circulation along with forty magazines. For the most part, these were political in nature and fed to the reading public a constant barrage of philosophy which laid the groundwork for a wider representative political state, one which took a more active interest in mass schooling.

In addition to these landmarks in the evolutionary development of a broadening concept of the meaning of a democratic state, Jefferson's attitude about class and protocol while he was president was sure to have had some effect on the development of education in America. Disdainful of what he believed to be Federalist pretensions, Jefferson was the sort of president who appeared to be sympathetic toward an equalitarian ideal in his manners, dress, and in the general way in which he conducted himself in the presidency. His encouragement of localism as an essential element in democracy and his conviction of the importance of an enlightened electorate must have had some influence in the development of public education as a public responsibility.

Growing out of these and other currents of a broadening concept of democracy, the public school movement of the 1820's and later takes on more meaning. It was in the enlightened political environment provided by the Republican leadership on the national, and in some cases, state level, that free school societies began to appear in such cities as Washington, Baltimore, Philadelphia, and New York. These societies collected money, trained and paid teachers, built schools, and generally promoted the idea of mass schooling. It was in this environment of enlightened political values that the legislature of Rhode Island was petitioned by the Mechanics and Manufacturers Association of Providence in 1799 to establish elementary schools at public expense. A General Free School Act was actually passed by the Rhode Island assembly in 1800 (repealed in 1803). However, by 1836 the city of Providence had 1,456 students enrolled in its public schools at a cost to the city of nearly $6,000 per year.[10]

By 1818 the city of Boston had established public primary schools for children from four to seven years of age.[11] By 1830, in Philadelphia and Lancaster, Pennsylvania, public schools, supported by public taxes, had been established by law, and those interested in a state system of public schools were petitioning the legislature of Pennsylvania for the establishment of a state-wide system of elementary education. Indeed, the movement for public education at public cost had achieved such notoriety by 1830 that certain criticisms of the idea found their way into the public press. The following criticism, which appeared in the *Philadelphia National Gazette* on July 10, 1830, is in some ways typical:

> . . . Education and general information—these must indeed constitute our only true National Bulwark. May the day soon come when in point of literary acquirements the poorest peasant shall stand on a level with his more wealthy neighbors.
> It is our strong inclination and our obvious interest that literary acquirements should be universal; but we should be guilty of impos-

---

[10] Cubberley, p. 550.
[11] Cubberley, p. 555.

ture, if we professed to believe in the possibility of that consummation. Literature cannot be acquired without leisure, and wealth gives leisure. Universal opulence, or even competency, is a chimera, as man and society are constituted. There will ever be distinctions of conditions of capacity, of knowledge and ignorance, in spite of all the fond conceits which may be indulged, or the wild projects which may be tried, to the contrary. The "peasant" must labor during those hours of the day, which his wealthy neighbor can give to the abstract culture of his mind; otherwise, the earth would not yield enough for the subsistence of all: the mechanic cannot abandon the operations of his trade, for general studies; if he should, most of the convenience of life and objects of exchange would be wanting; langour, decay, poverty, discontent would soon be visible among all classes. No government, no statesman, no philanthropist, can furnish what is incompatible with the very organization and being of civil society. Education, the most comprehensive, should be, and is, open to the whole community; but it must cost to every one, time and money; and those are means which every one cannot possess simultaneously.[12]

As a statement of values this editorial comment is interesting. In this brief selection there are several statements which express a mixture of values. There is the admission that general education is "good" but above this on the value hierarchy is the idea that "productive" work is of greater value to society generally, than schooling. This may have been a rather common position in a society which was more concerned with building the community (in a physical sense) than with "book learning."

By the 1830's, the opponents of the idea of free public education had every reason to be concerned, for there was a ground swell of feeling in favor of the establishment of elementary schools at state or public expense. Workingmen's associations, such as the one in Philadelphia, along with public spirited citizens who were leaders in the semiprivate free school movement, were advocating free public education. So were individual legislators speaking to their colleagues in several state legislatures. The governors of several states advocated free public education in their political speeches.

In the 1830's the forces of Jacksonian democracy were evident in the political arena, and they had their effect on education. Although not responsible for the sweeping political changes which opened the doors to a genuine feeling for public education, President Jackson is frequently given credit for the change itself. Nor did Jacksonian democracy instigate sympathy for public education, for the sympathy was already there. The Jacksonian period merely witnessed changes in the political values and practices which made the public school idea a more realistic one than it had been in the past. The political party convention as a method of nominating candidates for office

---

[12] Knight and Hall, p. 149.

was a genuine democratization of the nominating process. Started by the Anti-Masons in 1830, the convention system was picked up by the Democrats in 1832. The importance of the political convention, with its open and freewheeling style, the opportunity it provided for airing the concerns of the masses, such as the idea of greater educational opportunity, cannot be overemphasized. In addition to this political innovation was the replacement of the old method of the selection of electors by legislators to a popular vote for electors, merely another indication of the democratization of the system.

Perhaps the most significant political development to have an impact on the public school idea was the rapid development of the idea of universal manhood suffrage. The constitutions of some of the new states which entered the Union after 1803 contained provisions for universal manhood suffrage and often eliminated religious and property qualifications for voting. By 1830 most of the original states had modified their constitutions to the effect that universal manhood suffrage was part of the constitutional makeup of all the states of the Union. The impact of an expanded suffrage cannot be overemphasized. It gave the necessary policy-making power to the large groups of citizens who were most interested in providing for public schools at state expense—that is, those who could not afford private schooling for their children.

Moreover, political values were influenced by the growth of industry and the expansion of agriculture, both of which provided ample opportunity for investment and profit. The physical and economic development of the nation during the Jacksonian period was so rapid and so individualistic in nature that it almost seemed as if most were content to allow the state to provide for education because they were too busy to worry themselves with the problem. More realistically, perhaps, the growth of industry and towns during the period brought people together who were interested in providing a minimum of schooling for their children, a luxury which they could not afford themselves.

The provisions for education in the various states reflected the new political values. Jackson's own state, Tennessee, was one of the first to establish an ex-officio state board of commissioners to provide for a state-wide system of common schools in 1836. A year later Massachusetts created a state board of education charged with the general supervision of the schools in that state. Other states followed suit.

By 1852 the movement for free public schools had progressed to a point where state legislatures were becoming concerned with compulsory school laws. Massachusetts led the way with the first compulsory school law in the United States in 1852. Although this law provided for only twelve weeks of compulsory education, it was a beginning. Moreover, the law was comprehensive in nature. It included everyone who had any child under his control between the ages of eight and fourteen.[13] No less than twenty-six states had established compulsory education by statute before 1900.

MASS SCHOOLING AS A POLITICAL IDEAL

The last quarter of the nineteenth century and the first decade of the twentieth century witnessed some rather broad changes in education. The most notable trends which got under way in the last quarter of the nineteenth century and have continued to the present include: (1) the increasing number of students enrolled on all levels of education, particularly on the secondary and college levels; (2) a concern with accreditation according to some kind of national standard; (3) more emphasis on the child; and (4) certain innovative practices in school organization and teaching.

During the last quarter of the nineteenth century two major features of education were increasing enrollments on the elementary level with expanding state education budgets to meet the need, and a remarkable growth of the secondary school.

In 1871 there were approximately 7.5 million students enrolled in the first eight grades of public schools while only 80,227 students were attending high school. By 1890 the numbers had increased to a little more than 12.5 million in elementary school and a little over two hundred thousand in high school. By 1900 the elementary school attendance had increased to nearly fifteen million while secondary school attendance more than doubled to 519,251.[14]

By 1910, this number had swelled to nearly a million. The secondary school population increased much more rapidly during this twenty-year period than the population of the country. In 1890 there were approximately sixty-three million Americans, while in 1910 there were about ninety-two million. While the general population was increasing by one-third, the high school enrollments quadrupled. This trend has continued to the present. Moreover, the growth in school enrollments, as a proportion of the population, has increased geometrically on both the elementary and secondary levels. While the population of the United States during the sixty years from 1910 to 1970 multiplied by four times, the total school population in public and private elementary and secondary schools has multiplied sixty times, from one million in 1910 to nearly sixty million in 1970. Some reasons for this fantastic growth will be discussed below.

---

[13] Knight and Hall, p. 365.
[14] David B. Tyack, *Turning Points in American Educational History* (Waltham, Mass.: Blaisdell, 1967), p. 469.

The public school idea in the twentieth century has also come to include the community junior college, which in most communities relies to some extent on state support. The first junior college was established in Joliet, Illinois, in 1902, and this movement has spread throughout the nation. In most states the junior college provides an additional two years of education that is only slightly more expensive for the student than the free public high school. Another twentieth-century phenomenon has been the remarkable growth of the four-year college or university. College enrollment has increased from approximately one-quarter million in 1900 to more than seven million in 1970. This geometric increase in enrollment has been accompanied by a corresponding increase in public expenditures for higher education from both state and national sources.

With the growth of the public high school there was also a growing concern in academia with the matter of accreditation. By 1890, college professors had become concerned with secondary school preparation and the variety and quality of secondary school graduates who were seeking admission to college. The concern became widespread enough by 1891 that the National Educational Association was moved to appoint the Committee of Ten headed by Charles Eliot, then president of Harvard University, to examine the high school curriculum with a view toward establishing minimum requirements for admission to college. This effort was followed with the establishment of the Committee of Fifteen on Elementary Education (1893) and the Committee on College Entrance Requirements (1895). There can be little doubt that these committees greatly influenced curriculum in the secondary school. They set minimum standards in terms of course work and achievement for admission to college. By 1910 the requirements of specific courses, a fixed minimum number of courses, and minimum performance on achievement-type entrance examinations were familiar features of college entrance requirements. Although the influence of college and university entrance requirements on the secondary school curriculum has been seriously questioned in the years since 1910, these requirements remain a significant part of the educational scene up to the present.

Also characteristic of the last quarter of the nineteenth century was an increasing concern for the child as well as the subjects which were to be learned. Although Rousseau and Pestalozzi had concerned themselves with the child a century earlier, the movement languished in America until such leaders as John Dewey, G. Stanley Hall, Edward Shelton, and others began to advocate an understanding of the child and his needs as the central function of educational study. Some were scholars, such as Hall, who set about the study of children in a deliberate and organized way. Some, like John Dewey, were philosophers and theoreticians who were willing to test their ideas in experimental situations.

Practitioners in the public schools were quick to attempt some applications of the theories which grew from the writings of late nineteenth-century educational philosophers. Much of what is thought of by contemporary educators as innovative can be found in educational experiments near the turn of the century. A concern for individual differences, the needs of children, flexible grading and scheduling, grouping, and individually prescribed instruction, formed the basis for several large experiments in the early part of the century. The quarter system introduced by Gary, Indiana, Superintendent Will Wirt in 1908 was one such experiment. In general the Gary school system attempted to make the school a miniature model of society. The curriculum consisted of a balanced program of basic skills, shop and domestic science, health and physical education, and social development.[15] The program set a clear precedent for contemporary comprehensive school programs. Another widely heralded innovation in curriculum and school organization in the early part of the twentieth century was the so-called Winnetka plan. This plan divided the school day into two parts. The first part of the plan concentrated on the learning of basic subjects and basic skills. Mastery was the key in this part of the plan and students were guided in mastery of segments or units of content and on specific skills. There was individually prescribed instruction, such as one finds in the non-graded schools of today, which permitted students to proceed with mastery of basic subjects and skills at their own pace. The second part of the curriculum dealt with what has come to be called the "affective" area of learning, involving social interaction, values, and the development of communication skills. In the affective areas most of the emphasis was placed on exploration and investigation rather than on mastery of specific skills and information. The Dalton plan, introduced in Dalton, Massachusetts, in 1919, placed most of its emphasis on students' management of their own work. The school year was divided up into specific jobs or performance tasks assigned to students, who were then allowed to perform them at their own pace.

Although one can only speculate upon the forces in American society during the latter part of the nineteenth century and the early twentieth century which continue to influence educational theory and practice, certainly the growth of industry, the expansion of political democracy, and the contributions of philosophers and educational leaders have played significant roles.

The growth of industry in the United States in the period following the Civil War unleashed a multitude of forces which, directly and indirectly, had some impact on education. As industry grew so did the towns and cities. Some of the growth consisted of the attraction that steady jobs and more or less regular factory income had for the native rural population, but by far the

---

[15] Ellwood P. Cubberley, *Public Education in the United States,* rev. ed. (Boston: Houghton Mifflin, 1947), p. 530.

greatest boost in urban population in the years from 1870 to 1910 came from immigrants, largely from southern and eastern Europe. Education was affected not only by the numbers involved but by the character of the immigrants themselves. The cities, particularly those in the East, and the new industrial towns of the Ohio River Valley and the old Northwest, were inundated with immigrants. By the 1890's many thinking citizens in the urban areas affected were expressing concern about the children of immigrants. There was much concern on the part of the native Protestant white populations of the industrial cities about the "Americanization" of the children of immigrants. The schools, particularly the public ones, seemed to offer the best solution to this problem. Added to this concern, which was highly individualistic and personal, was the impersonal force of economics. As industry developed and the demands for labor grew, new immigrants were recruited and very young children were pressed into service. The willingness of industry to employ minors provided an added inducement to immigrant parents to produce more children. To complicate matters, the industrial system did not work perfectly in the laissez-faire days of the 1870's, 1880's, and 1890's. There were periodic breakdowns, such as the panics of 1873 and 1893, along with less famous periods of depression. The major result of significance to education during these periods was large-scale unemployment among the masses who were able to eke out only a bare subsistence even during prosperous times. Such personal catastrophies must have had some impact on the millions of individuals who hoped for something better for their children. This might be one reason for the dramatic growth of secondary school population in the years immediately following the panic of 1893. The very fact that there were so few jobs for the young during these years must have pushed them into the classrooms, just as has happened in the years since the 1890's.

Of course there were many other forces operating in the last two decades of the nineteenth century which were direct or indirect outgrowths of urban industrial development. The evils of child labor were recognized early in the industrial era and by the turn of the century there were determined efforts to see that it was eliminated. The early years of the twentieth century brought a wave of legislation on the state level prohibiting child labor. It was so successful that by the 1930's efforts to eliminate the evil by constitutional amendment were no longer needed. Obviously, once child labor had been successfully attacked, something had to be done with the children. In millions of individual cases, continuing in school must have provided a reasonable solution to the problem. Another significant force which grew out of the industrial revolution in the United States and which had direct and indirect influences on education was the growth of organized labor in the last quarter of the nineteenth century. As organized labor struggled first for recognition and later for better pay and shorter hours, the worker became more prosperous. In addition, organized labor worked diligently for more and better schools, and for the extension of compulsory education legislation; better training for more children became a realistic possibility for millions. Finally, the demands made by organized labor through the years has put economic pressure on industry to make its work force more productive. As workers became more expensive through their own organizational successes, industrialists had to devise ways and means to make labor more productive. The economic results are a matter of record. The results as far as the schools are concerned were less direct but no less significant. As the worker's share of income from industry increased, industry could make higher demands in terms of skills and special training. The need for increased schooling and different kinds of training became apparent. This phenomenon has persisted until the present. Moreover, the system has worked well in an economic sense. As the educational level of the population has risen, entrance requirements in the work world have risen along with wages and salaries. Obviously, the impact of the growth of industry on American education has been real and significant through the years.

The expansion of political democracy has also been a significant force in the expansion of educational theory and practice. During the rapid industrial growth of the last quarter of the nineteenth century, the Progressives and Populists and their muckraking intellectual partners made important contributions to the growth of education. Ida Tarbell, Lincoln Steffens, and Ray Stannard Baker described in popular journals corruption and graft in politics and excesses in industry at the turn of the century. In 1906 John Spargo provided the reading public with sensational exposés of child labor, while Upton Sinclair shocked his readers by exposing the deplorable conditions in the meat-packing industry. The outgrowth of these efforts was a general reform movement in business, industry, and politics. The muckrakers were generally on the side of labor in its attempts to organize, and they contributed to reform in local and state governments across the nation. This was the era of greater responsibility in government, the direct primary, the direct election of senators, and the women's suffrage movement, all of which conspired to make the system more representative and to expand mass participation in government. Out of this movement came a greater concern for the demands of the masses and, inevitably, larger budgets on the state and local level for such social programs as education. It was in this political framework too that experimentation with more comprehensive forms of education found a more favorable climate. Nor has the political scene been the same since. The more recent push for civil rights on the part of minorities and the expansion of the national government into local educational problems are natural descendants of the early political efforts of the Progressives and Populists.

Finally, the ideas of philosophers and the daring of educational reformers made some contributions to the growth and development of American education. Obviously from what has been said, the political, social, and economic climate was ready to accept some of the ideas of such early thinkers as Pestalozzi and Rousseau. In the 1890's the work of Johann Friedrich Herbart gave practical application to the theories of Pestalozzi. Colonel Francis Parker did much to popularize the work of both Pestalozzi and Herbart during the last two decades of the nineteenth century. John Dewey's theoretical and experimental work found a favorable climate in the early years of the twentieth century—favorable because the educational theories were in general harmony with the new politics. There was an emphasis on the individual as a unique human being with special problems, needs, and interests. There was the implication, at least, that man was more important than the products of industry and that it was the responsibility of democratic society to develop man to his full human potential through education. Education for a humane kind of citizenship was emphasized and traditional restrictive and limited education would not suffice in this task. Schooling came to be thought of not so much in terms of specific training in skills and content, but as a place where general enlightenment could occur. Indeed, progressive thought in education held that the schools could provide some remedies for society's ills and become a real working part of the society.

In spite of the tremendous growth of American education in the last hundred years, both in terms of numbers of students served and the broad extensions of the functions of the school, there remain to the present certain conservative forces in our society which continue to inhibit development. Mass schooling as a political ideal has yet to be realized. Religious values still influence education despite court decisions and other secular forces which have attempted to emphasize the wall of separation constitutionally standing between church and state. Anti-intellectualism is still not dead in American society. There continue to be significant numbers in our population who view education as a necessary evil at best, and at worst advocate the elimination of "socialistic" public education. Resistance to federal interference in education in whatever form continues to be popular with some individuals and groups. Most significantly, certain groups in our society continue to be shortchanged. Minorities, particularly the Blacks, Chicanos, and Indians, have not shared fully in the educational progress of the last hundred years. For the most part they continue to attend poor schools. Rural children, especially those in pockets of rural poverty, continue to attend schools which are actually little improved over the nineteenth-century models. Poor children everywhere find it difficult to extend their education much beyond that which their parents enjoyed a generation ago.

Yet progress has been made by the masses. In more than three centuries of development, education in the United States may be nearing the point where its role in the preparation of enlightened citizens is a realistic possibility.

With all the shortcomings of the system, it must be admitted that the means presently exist for the preparation of an enlightened and educated citizenry. The political development of the nation has enabled education to develop. There is virtually a total public commitment today to the ideal of free public education. It has become a fact of our existence. The burning questions of today are not so much questions concerning the propriety of state support of education but how much support is adequate and, perhaps more important, who should pay the bill, the national government or the state. In terms of philosophy, the next decade will undoubtedly continue to experience debate between forces which advocate open classrooms and free schools, and the existing educational bureaucracy with its emphasis on behavioral goals, accountability, measurement, and a product-oriented society.

The present attitude toward the universal nature of schooling, and the idealized as well as practical values of schooling which seem to have at last caught the imagination of a great number of Americans, have been influenced by many forces long developing in our society. The fact that the present attitude toward schooling is different from that of a century ago or even a generation ago cannot be denied. At the base of this change has been the changing nature of the society. The forces of industrialization, urbanization, and an increasing population have resulted in new movements and the growth of new values with regard to schooling.

The forces of industrialization, urbanization, and population were at the base of such movements as the organization of labor unions and other associations in our society which expressed interest in mass schooling. These forces also unleashed new ideas and new movements within the political arena. Such ideas as those advocated by the Populists in the political arena near the end of the last century had a telling effect on the development of new procedures on the state and national level which were in the direction of greater mass participation in government. Around the turn of the century the ideas expressed by Dewey and his followers greatly influenced thinking about the relationship between education and democratic values.

Following these movements was a rather sweeping democratization of the system (in terms of popular participation). The twentieth century has experienced extension of the ballot in women's suffrage, popular election of senators, and some liberalization of state voting laws. More recently the system has experienced new interpretation of the meaning of "equal protection of the laws" in the Fourteenth Amendment of the United States Constitution. The courts have decided to enter the political thicket of reapportionment, and there is a new concern for education as an important national responsibility. Collectively, these things reflect changing values in the society and are certain to have some effect on the way our citizens view the role of schools.

This brief history of the progress of public schooling in the United States has been presented to demonstrate that political values are a significant conditioner of educational policies and development. The schools have tended to mirror the society. The growth of free public schools was a slow and painful one and was successful only as the political values changed. The expansion of suffrage, the rise of political parties, the increasing power of organized labor, urbanization, and industrialization of the nation were perhaps more realistic forces in democratizing education than anything the schools or the leaders in the free school movement were able to do.

The assumption of this brief history is that the schools have not led the society down new paths. Genuine and effective change in education has been initiated and invoked through political pressure. The progressive ideas of men have found expression, not so much in the schools as on the political platform in our society. This should not be interpreted to mean that the schools have been such a reflection of tradition that they have had no influence on departures from tradition. Quite the contrary, they have been an instrument in social change as it has been articulated in the political forum. This is an argument that the schools have not been a primary force in social change, they have not been the instigator or innovator of such change, but they have served to facilitate it. They have facilitated the changes which have been implemented through the political process by gradually providing a public ready to accept innovation. In providing basic skills and gradually upgrading the educational level of the mass of the society, they have facilitated change. To claim the schools have done more would be difficult in a pluralistic society.

REFERENCES

Butts, Freeman. *A Cultural History of Education.* New York: McGraw-Hill, 1947.

Butts, Freeman, and Lawrence A. Cremin. *A History of Education in American Culture.* New York: Holt, Rinehart & Winston, 1953.

Cremin, Lawrence A. *American Education: The Colonial Experience 1607–1783.* New York: Harper & Row, 1970.

———. *The Transformation of the School.* New York: Alfred A. Knopf, 1961.

Cubberley, Ellwood P. (ed.). *Readings in the History of Education.* Boston: Houghton Mifflin, 1920.

———. *Public Education in the United States.* Boston: Houghton Mifflin, 1947.

Dunn, William K. *What Happened to Religious Education?* Baltimore, Md.: Johns Hopkins Press, 1958.

Foner, Philip S. (ed.). *Basic Writings of Thomas Jefferson.* New York: John Wiley & Sons, 1944.

Graham, Grace. *The Public School in the American Community.* New York: Harper & Row, 1964.

Illich, Ivan. "Education Without Schools: How It Can be Done." *New York Review of Books.* 15, XII:25–31 (7 Jan. 1971).

Knight, Edgar W. *Education in the United States.* 3rd ed. Boston: Ginn, 1941.

Knight, Edgar W., and Clifton L. Hall (eds.). *Readings in American Educational History.* New York: Appleton-Century-Crofts, 1951.

Lieberman, Myron. *The Future of Public Education.* Chicago: Univ. of Chicago Press, 1960.

Morris, Van Cleve. "The Philosophical Premises Underlying Public Education." *Progressive Education.* 34:69–74 (May 1957).

Reisner, Edward H. *The Evolution of the Common School.* New York: Macmillan, 1930.

Repo, Satu. *This Book is About Schools.* New York: Pantheon Books, 1970.

Savelle, Max. *The Foundations of American Civilization.* New York: Holt, Rinehart & Winston, 1942.

Sparks, Jared (ed.). *The Writings of George Washington.* Boston: F. Andrews, 1839.

Tyack, David B. *Turning Points in American Educational History.* Waltham, Mass.: Blaisdell, 1967.

4

The Force of the Community

In spite of the increasing influence of the national and state governments on matters of educational policy, the community remains a most important level of decision-making in the operation of the school. Although it is impossible to generalize about American communities, there seems to be a tendency for community influences on schooling to be on the traditional or conservative side. Leaders in positions of power, regardless of class or other affiliation, tend to be conservative on many issues. "Conservatism" might be defined as a situation in which the existing community power structure, whatever it may be, is interested in retaining power and believes that interest is best achieved by some considerable respect for the status quo.

This conservatism has imposed tremendous hardships on millions of inner-city children, whose parents continue to struggle to develop a sense of "community" on educational matters. Unfortunately, the inner city with its transient population and special problems does not lend itself to a traditional geographic concept of community. This does not mean that a sense of community does not exist. Perhaps it needs to be defined differently. Obviously, geographic boundaries are not the only definition possible for community. A community can be thought of as "shared institutions and values," a particular "distribution of power," a social system, or merely as "people," as Roland Warren suggests.[1] There is some evidence that new definitions of community have evolved in the last decade among citizens who live in the slums of larger cities. The efforts of inner-city residents to wrest some educational decision-making power from established groups has been a major educational struggle in recent years.

---

[1] Roland L. Warren, *The Community in America* (Chicago: Rand McNally, 1963).

This chapter is concerned with three broad general aspects of community life and values as they affect the schools: The first is the general nature of the class system as it has been identified by students of society, the things which each class values, and the effects that this system can have on schools. The second is the power structure in the community, that is, who makes the critical decisions which affect schooling in the community and what values influence such decisions? Finally, the chapter deals with the urban drive for decentralization.

SOCIAL CLASS AND EDUCATION

Some social comedian once remarked that everybody in America was equal; some were just more equal than others. Certainly as an abstraction the ideal of equality has been an important part of the spirit of America. Throughout our history, foreign observers such as De Tocqueville, Lord Bryce, and others have gone away impressed with our dedication to the principle of equality, while at the same time criticizing American society for not being as equalitarian in practice as we professed to be in theory. On the whole, however, most observers of American society readily admit that ours is perhaps the one in which equality is more easily achieved than any other.

As a matter of record, equality has been a realistic dream for many Americans. The old argument that any boy could become president had enough validity about it to make it plausible. Moreover, schooling had little to do with the historic dream of American equality. A man's chances of success in our system were based more on his ability to move up through his efforts in the economic and political arena, and it was not necessary for him to be well educated in order to achieve success.

Today the situation is reversed. It is generally conceded that the most certain route to upward social mobility is through formal schooling. The nature of the society requires it. The complexity brought about by industry and technology provides little opportunity for the unschooled. In nearly every phase of our national life, years of school, economic status, and social mobility are tied closely together. The old hope for education as it related to the general good of society was tied to a desire for enlightened citizenship. A major assumption of such enlightenment was that educated citizens were more intelligent guardians of the democratic ideal. The new hope continues to envision enlightened citizenship but an economic dimension has been added. The need today, which is widely recognized, is not only for enlightened citizens but for useful ones—useful in an economic sense.

The economics of education has lent reality to the consideration of education as an equalitarian force. This casts historical tradition in a new light. The definition of social status formerly tended to be based on economic considerations, and these have not always required a specific kind or quantity of schooling. Development along these lines has created a major problem when one considers the role of schooling as an equalitarian force; that is, the schools have traditionally reflected the existing social structure and have not been recognized as the instrument by which social change can be achieved. To consider the American school system historically as the great leveler, the great force for an equalitarian democracy, is perhaps to overstate the case. Certainly part of the tradition has been one in which the schools have reflected economic and social class lines in the society. The school as an equalitarian force is more a twentieth-century phenomenon, the full potential of which is just now gaining some genuine public attention.

This is particularly true in the inner city, where minorities have been demanding a greater voice in the education of their children. They have charged that the traditional middle-class school has failed them and their children, and in several cities minority groups have been actively working for control of their own schools. There is a great deal of legitimacy in the charge that schools operate for the benefit of the middle class.

As a social institution, the schools have tended to recognize social class in many ways. In practice they have tended to perpetuate the existing class structure. They have recognized class by organizing curricula best suited to dominant class needs and by the organization of the school districts. Until very recently they have even recognized and perpetuated a caste system by providing separate schools for Blacks. In addition, researchers have discovered certain class biases in teachers.

The problem with such unconscious or conscious recognition of class structure and its subsequent reflection in methodology, curriculum, school organization, and administration is that it is deeply established in tradition. That is, it is based on what used to be, on yesterday's society, on the needs and interests of an earlier generation. The needs and interests of the last quarter of the twentieth century have dramatically changed. The new interest in formal education as an equalitarian force has extensive political, economic, and social implications. A good example of this is the present belief in some quarters that the schools may be the best single weapon for combating poverty. The list of political figures who see formal education as an equalitarian force is growing. The problem remains, however, that the schools are not completely ready to play an equalitarian role.

However, it is in the new context of the realization that schools can be an effective force in a general improvement of the society that we must view the problems of education. School people can at least hope that a majority in our society is becoming committed to the use of the schools as a means for such improvement. This hope is fed by new approaches and new programs deliberately designed to provide greater equality of educational opportunity than has existed in the past. Is this a realistic hope or an idealistic dream? If the schools are to be used as a major instrument for the improvement of society, we must examine how this can be accomplished and the obstacles which stand in the way. This examination involves a look at what exists. The purpose of the examination will be to attempt to analyze the possibility of success of new programs and new approaches.

CLASS STRUCTURE AND VALUES

A most serious obstacle to equality in educational opportunity is the existence of class and caste in our society. There are many political and educational implications of class structure and values. The decision to move a whole class of people up the social and economic scale is a political decision which can be implemented by a Congress speaking in the name of the majority. The commitment of the public and its representatives to this goal, however, is only half the battle. There are many problems confronting those who would attempt to improve the lot of the poor in our society. Do the poor really want help? What kind of help? What role should the schools play? What directions should the efforts take and should the schools attempt to modify the values of the poor? And, if so, whose values should be taught? These are questions which we must continue to ask. So that we might ask them more intelligently, let us look briefly at the problem of class structure and values in our society as these relate to education.

Class Structure

The definition of class in American society is a difficult undertaking. Part of the difficulty lies in the existence of a belief in equalitarianism in the United States. Few want to admit that there is any rigidity to class structure and prefer to think of our society as fluid. In practice, however, there appear to be many distinctions within our society which constitute genuine barriers to economic and social mobility. Most students of class agree that the color of one's skin constitutes a serious barrier to practical equalitarianism in the United States, so much so, in fact, that the term "caste," which is a closed class with no movement in or out except by birth or death, might have applied until very recently to some Americans. In addition, questions of religion, nationality, wealth, family history, and other considerations affect social status within given communities. The contradiction between the ideological belief in equality and the practice of class distinctions is partly what motivated sociologists such as Warner,[2] Hollingshead,[3] Havighurst,[4] and others to attempt to define social class. This group of sociologists attempted to define social class in specific communities. Out of these studies and others like them a general definition of class structure in the United States

---

[2] W. Lloyd Warner, et al., Social Class In America (New York: Harper & Row, 1960).
[3] August B. Hollingshead, Elmstown's Youth (New York: John Wiley & Sons, 1949).
[4] Robert J. Havighurst, et al., Growing Up in River City (New York: John Wiley & Sons, 1962).

has evolved. Obviously, such general definitions pose serious problems. Consequently, no sociologist would claim that his specific study should be utilized as a general basis for the definition of class in the United States. Most community studies are limited in time and space to one community over a given period of years, and the only really valid conclusions about class which can be drawn from them are those about the specific communities studied. Even in the communities studied, generalizations are difficult since each author tends to establish his own criterion for class structure, so that the criteria for the determination of class vary. An absolute definition which will fit all places at all times cannot be applied.

However, there is a certain general agreement on the definition of class in our society. Social class has been defined in the following manner:

> A social class is any portion of a community marked off from the rest by social status. A system of structure of social class involves: first, a hierarchy of status groups; second, the recognition of the superior-inferior stratification; and finally, some degree of permanency of the structure.[5]

Most community studies have shown three major classes in the United States, with subdivisions within these classes. The largest group is the lower class, which is made up of about 60 per cent of the population. Above this class is the middle class, which makes up about 40 per cent of the population. Finally, there is a small upper class consisting of 2 or 3 per cent of the population.[6]

Leonard Reisman, in a discussion of "Hometown," pointed out that for those at the extreme ends of the social hierarchy there is a tendency to think of their community as consisting of only two groups: "people like themselves and everyone else." Reisman also cautioned against making broad generalizations about class structure since there are many variations from one community to the next and there are a great number of variables operating which affect class structure within a community, including the age of the town and its occupational structure. However, Reisman's description of class in "Hometown" is fairly useful for our purposes:

1. An upper-class whose title and privilege stem from its position as the class composed of the descendents of Hometown's past and tradition—the founders of Hometown and the men who gave the town and themselves whatever success can be claimed. This class is Hometown's version of nobility, and consequently, a high social wall has been built between this class and would-be aspirants to these ranks.
2. The lower-upper class includes those who have managed to achieve

<hr>

[5] Robert M. MacIver and Charles H. Page, *Society: An Introductory Analysis* (New York: Holt, Rinehart & Winston, 1949), p. 348.

[6] Robert J. Havighurst, "Social Class Influence on American Education," *Social Forces Influencing American Education.* The Sixtieth Yearbook of the National Society for the Study of Education (Chicago: Univ. of Chicago Press, 1961), p. 121.

many of the symbols of status, such as wealth, education, and the proper home. However, they are denied admission into the upper-most rank because they lack the prime requirements—a long, respectable, and traditionalized social standing. They are newcomers, or, if long residents, without the proper family background. Their gains are too recent. They are not yet socially aged to the proper mellowness that would properly condition them for upper-upper class membership. Although they try to emulate the upper-uppers, their mimicry is poorly executed, pathetically overdone, and manifestly gauche.

3. The middle class is also subdivided into two segments, principally on the basis of wealth. Less wealthy than those above them, the upper-middle class at least is a notch above others in the community. These are the upwardly mobile individuals who are ready to approach the next hurdle into the upper class itself. The lower segment of the middle class includes those individuals of solid respectability with a steady, sober life pattern. They are the average citizens of Hometown, its stable element, who never do anything outstanding or out of the ordinary. Respected in the community, they have little else to mark them.

4. The lower classes include those who by occupation, income, and education stand lowest in the hierarchy. They perform the skilled and semi-skilled work. They have modest incomes, and socially are the most invisible class of all. They are honest and steady citizens of Hometown, differing only from the class immediately above them by occupation and income. At the very bottom of the class hierarchy are the lower-lowers. They do the unskilled labor. They don't amount to much of anything, most people in Hometown believe, and they never will. If the upper-uppers are the contemporary versions of aristocracy, then the lower-lowers are the American version of the untouchables rejected by a caste system.[7]

The classification cited above is not made as an effort to demonstrate that there is a clear distinction between the classes in the society generally. Nor does Reisman claim that this is anything other than a description of "Hometown." There are enough exceptions to any such classification so that at best it is only a rough guide. Moreover, identifications of class structure are static; they describe a time and a place. Historically, ours has been a society which has been characterized by upward mobility. That is, the class lines which exist have been relatively fluid for individuals except for the extremes on both ends of the social hierarchy. The American dream of material success has been achieved often enough so that for many, if not most citizens, it still remains a realistic dream. The routes to upward mobility

---

[7] Leonard Reisman, *Class in American Society* (New York: Free Press of Glencoe, 1959), pp. 182–183.

are many. However, one can move up the social scale most readily by way of increased income and a "respectable" occupation. With increasing frequency, the route to increased income and a respectable occupation is through schooling.

This is not to say that lower-class individuals adopt the values of the middle class, once such individuals achieve middle-class economic status. However, some of the middle-class values are easy enough to adopt even though a renunciation of old values may be necessary. In any case, the relationship between class and values is educationally significant in that it helps explain some of the behavior of teachers, provides insight into the curriculum and organizational pattern of schools, and helps us to understand students better. Because social class values have such great educational implications, let us take a brief look at some of those associated with the major classes in the United States.

Social Class and Values

Since the great bulk of the population of the United States falls within the middle and lower classes, we shall limit our consideration of class values to these two general classes. In a discussion of the three general classes in the United States, Clyde and Florence Kluckhohn[8] attributed the following goals to the middle and lower classes:

Goals of the middle class:
1. Relating to the acquisition of property.
    a. Great stress is put on permanency of property and a piling up of capital goods. In part this is "family property" so long as the family remains a unit, but in part, it is made up of "individual" possessions.
    b. Thrift and hard work are emphasized: "Work for work's sake."
    c. Respect for both property and ownership is important.
2. Relating to "good" standing in the community; conformity with standards is important.
    a. Strict sex taboos are required.
    b. Cleanliness is stressed.
    c. Emotional control, especially adequate control of aggression, is stressed.
    d. The individual is expected to be a "good fellow" who is successful in a respectable and established job, but who is not outstandingly different.
    e. "Good" manners of a conventional type are important.

---

[8] Clyde and Florence R. Kluckhohn, "American Culture: Generalized Orientations and Class Patterns," *Conflicts of Power in Modern Culture,* eds. Lyman Bryson *et al.* (New York: Harper & Row, 1947), pp. 121–126.

f. Affiliation with the proper companies and organizations is expected.

g. A respect for law and order is inculcated.

h. "Good works" are stressed. However, "charity" is often taught in such a way that the child's sense of class distinction is strengthened.

3. Individual autonomy is emphasized.

4. A good education—specifically related to success—is a goal to strive for.

5. A "good" marriage is important; ideally there is no divorce.

6. Relating to family solidarity.

   a. The middle-class family is ideally an isolated conjugal unit made up of father, mother, and children. The relatives usually do not live with the family, and relatives who are considered "undesirable" are disregarded. The widowed are often under duress.

   b. There is segregation of the spheres of dominance of the father and mother. The father is the economic head of the family. The mother and children are usually ignorant of financial matters. The mother is the director of home activities, social life, and the main disciplinarian of the children, except in very serious matters, which are referred to the father. The mother ideally remains in the home and devotes much of her time to furthering the social contacts of her children and husband.

   c. The family is "child-centered" partly because children are the hope of improved family status.

7. Relating to recreation.

   a. Participation in various individualistic and organized sports is considered desirable.

   b. Travel is a frequent way of spending vacations.

   c. Various forms of commercial entertainment are an important form of recreation.

Goals of the lower class:

1. Relating to the acquisition of property (money and material possessions).

   a. Keeping the family fed, clothed, and housed is of vital importance.

   b. Immediate spending of material goods and money tends to be a subgoal in itself.

2. Relating to "good" standing in the neighborhood.

   a. The individual is expected to be a "good fellow" in the gang.

   b. Prowess in aggressive techniques brings prestige.

   c. Prowess in the sexual sphere is encouraged.

   d. Opportunism is a characteristic attitude toward law and order.

   e. Cleanliness is less stressed, partly because the mother often works as well as manages a household. This relative lack of cleanliness brings negative response from middle-class people.

3. Relating to education: Ideally there is a vague notion that education will help the individual to improve his status. Some stress is put on literacy but the person who is "too educated" is a misfit in the community.

4. Relating to family solidarity: (These are the general patterns; there are variations between ethnic groups especially in the first generation.)
   a. Family solidarity tends to be along the extended family line, usually the maternal. Members of extended family groups aid each other and all relatives are recognized. The emphasis on independence of the conjugal unit is not so great as in the middle class.
   b. Maternal dominance often exists in the economic sphere because, for one reason or another, the father is unable to support the family. The mother and children are aware of the financial situation. The mother frequently works as well as the father. Frequently the family consists of the mother and children.
   c. The home is not "child-centered," and the mother does not supervise the activities of the children closely.
5. Relating to recreation: Indulging in gambling and commercial entertainment is permitted at an early age.

Obviously this is a generalized classification to which there are many exceptions.[9] Even so, it is a useful classification for teachers. The classification is descriptive and in some instances can help explain the behavior of individuals. An immediate concern for teachers, of course, is the manner in which individuals within each class view schooling. Generally, all levels of the middle and upper classes recognize the "value" of schooling. In the case of the middle-class and lower-upper-class individuals, it is recognized primarily as a means for advancement on the social and economic scale. Lower-class individuals, on the other hand, may not see this value in schooling so clearly. Whether this is a studied attitude on the part of the lower-class member or merely a realistic recognition of his inability to make the necessary sacrifices for schooling is problematical. Whether economic factors create an attitude of apathy toward schooling or whether apathy creates economic problems for the lower-class members really matters little. The facts clearly indicate that the lower class does not get educated to the extent that the middle and upper classes do. In every study of the relationship between schooling and class, the lower classes contribute the largest numbers of school dropouts and contribute a relatively insignificant number to the total of college graduates.

---

[9] An interesting exception may be found in John Brooks, "Mr. White and Mr. Blue: Notes on the New Middle Class," *Harpers Magazine* (June 1966), vol. 232, pp. 88–91. Brooks describes in some detail the differences in values between white-collar and blue-collar neighbors who are in the same economic class. Other studies, such as the Komarovsky study in 1964, which discovered that lower-class citizens who have moved into the economic middle class still cling to lower-class values, do not necessarily destroy the meaning of Kluckhohn's general classification, but merely demonstrate its general nature, and that it is difficult to base class value orientations on classes defined solely on the basis of income.

The values or goals which are held by a given class at a given time are educationally significant. The values which are held by a social class as a whole generally affect attitudes of teachers and students who belong to this class. Research indicates that teaching draws heavily from the middle class.[10] As might be expected, many teachers hold middle-class values. In view of the economics of education, it is not difficult to understand why it has been the middle class that has supplied so many of the teachers in the United States. Teaching as a career generally requires a college degree. Since a degree is limited largely to the middle and upper classes in our society, it is natural that there are few teachers from the lower classes. Perhaps the most common reason cited in recent research is that a majority of all public school teachers are female and the vast majority of women teachers come from middle-class backgrounds. Studies of male teachers, especially on the high school level, however, indicate that a greater number of male teachers come from the lower class.[11] However, even where lower-class students do manage to acquire a degree and a teaching certificate, by the time they appear as teachers in classrooms they may have adopted some of the values of the middle class and for all practical purposes might be classified, in terms of such things as place and condition of residence, dress, and speech, as middle-class persons. One cannot safely conclude that all hold middle-class values, however. Any attempt to attach specific values to a certain class is theoretical. In fact, any class grouping is theoretical. Added to this problem, class values are not static; they are always in the process of change. New values are constantly emerging to replace old ones within every class stratification.

For example, teaching has traditionally tended to attract middle-class women. This illustrates the idea of changing or emerging values suggested above. Middle-class women may become teachers because teaching is "respectable." Although a "good" marriage may be considered more respectable for the daughters of middle-class parents, a second choice may be the comfort and security offered in the respectable occupation of teaching. In recent years there is some evidence that the middle-class value of the nonworking wife and mother has undergone some rather serious modification. Many middle-class wives and mothers are now working, in contradiction to an earlier view which was strongly opposed to it. The departure from the value has been subtle, since only certain kinds of work seem acceptable. Teaching appears to be high on the list of acceptable work for the middle-class working wives in today's society. Part of the explanation for this change

---

[10] W. W. Charters, Jr., "The Social Background of Teaching," *Handbook of Research on Teaching*, ed. N. L. Gage (Washington, D.C.: NEA, 1963), p. 721.
[11] Harmon Zeigler, *The Political World of the High School Teacher* (Eugene, Ore.: Center for the Advanced Study of Educational Administration, Univ. of Oregon, 1966), p. 24.

in attitude about working wives may involve values which are higher on the hierarchy of the middle-class list of values than the negative attitude toward working wives and mothers. Perhaps a whole cluster of values is involved which outweigh the old attitude toward work outside the home. For example, a well-established goal in the middle class is the ambition of its members to achieve a higher social and economic status. This involves a whole cluster of values, including the kind of neighborhood in which one can afford to live, the newness of furniture or the automobile, opportunities of various kinds for the children, the manner in which the family is able to dress and appear in public, and so on. Taken together, this cluster of values may be more important than the value: "Mother's place is in the home." There is strong evidence that the working wife (who holds a respectable job which promises a respectable career) is an emerging value for the middle class. In such cases the early efforts of the working middle-class wife may be almost solely economic. When this real or fancied need passes, justification or rationalization is almost always made in terms of social responsibility. Another example is the increasing interest of middle-class youth in teaching and service occupations. Many such youth appear to openly reject the middle-class values of their parents.

Perhaps the slowest to change is the general school environment which tends to reflect middle-class values. This applies to the school board, the curriculum, the care and maintenance of the school, and a myriad of other aspects of the school system.

One authority[12] on the subject theorized that school boards tended to be middle-class and conservative partly because they were past middle age. Other reasons which have been advanced in an attempt to demonstrate that school boards tend to be middle-class in origin and attitude include such factors as the educational and occupational level of school board members, the political and social values which they hold, and the fact that they are property owners and taxpayers.

Arguments that the public school curriculum tends to cater to middle-class interests usually revolve around the idea that the total public school curriculum is oriented toward what have been assumed to be middle-class values. The most notable of these include the observations that the curriculum is designed to prepare students for college, the program is designed in a way that encourages order and conformity, respect for law and order, "good manners," hard work, and so on. All of these are generally considered to be middle-class goals. At least one author disagrees with some of these conclusions, however. H. Otto Dahlke made the following observation in *Values in Culture and Classroom:*

---

[12] George D. Spindler, "Education in a Transforming American Culture," *Harvard Educational Review* (Summer 1955), vol. 25, pp. 145–156.

A current interpretation of the public school is that it merely reflects and upholds middle-class values. The norms apparently support this idea, but continuity of school and middle-class norms is incidental. Many of the norms and even value emphasis occur not because of middle-class influence but because the school is a group. Emphasis on work, punctuality, getting the job done, control of aggression, avoidance of conflict, and being relatively quiet are necessary conditions if any group is to persist.[13]

Even if one accepts the logic of Dahlke's statement, it is difficult to deny that the middle class has great influence on the curriculum and operation of many local schools. The parents who are really interested in the school and express such interest by joining the PTA, by attending various functions of the school, and in other ways working closely with the school tend to be parents who would be grouped somewhere within the middle class. These are the people who take great interest in school board elections, in proposed changes in the curriculum, and in the selection of textbooks, teachers, and the kind of school buildings which are provided for their children. The lower classes tend to be less articulate on school matters. This may be due partly to the fact that they are generally not well educated and many may feel that their knowledge about schools and schooling is severely limited. In addition, they may lack the time to concern themselves with school matters, or they may feel completely uncomfortable in the middle-class environment of the school. In addition, many do not or cannot vote in important school elections. For these and many other reasons the influence of the lower classes on the school program and the operation of the school may be small in some communities. In some urban communities this alienation of lower classes is such an acute problem that these groups have resorted to picketing and public protest to make their school demands known. In most places such groups have had only token success. Even so, such efforts, though mightily resisted, are beginning to be felt. This problem will be discussed below.

If the assumption can be made that the schools tend to be staffed by middle-class teachers, run by middle-class oriented administrators and school boards which favor middle-class value orientations and programs, what then is the significance of this situation? Perhaps it can be illustrated with a few examples.

Although it does not necessarily follow that teachers who spring from the middle class or are labeled as such will attempt to teach these values to their students, in cases where this is true, it raises some interesting problems. Even where school district boundary lines tend to follow economic and social class lines, there is a mixture of classes in virtually every public school. Thus,

---

[13] H. Otto Dahlke, *Values in Culture and Classroom* (New York: Harper & Row, 1958), p. 253.

if a teacher attempts to indoctrinate his students with middle-class values, he is sure to come face to face with some serious problems if he is alert enough to recognize them. To provide a specific example of what might happen in such a hypothetical, although possible situation, let us assume that an elementary school teacher is attempting to teach respect for property. It is conceivable that for some students from the lower-lower class there is no relationship between what the teacher is attempting to teach and his own real-life experience. Moreover, there may be genuine conflict between what the teacher is advocating and what the student has picked up in his home environment. Without some real effort on the part of the teacher to examine the values of each of his students on the subjects or topics he wishes to teach, he may never be aware of these kinds of problems. This should not be construed as an argument that the elementary teacher should not attempt to teach students to respect public property. Rather, it is merely an indication of how varying class values may make such teaching difficult.

As the lower-class student proceeds through school, the relationship between real life and what the school teaches as real life may become increasingly more remote. This could occur as the lower-class student matures and becomes increasingly observant of his real world and what is necessary for him to survive in it. The texts and other reading materials are of little help for such a student, since they tend to teach values which are somehow different from what he knows from experience. If the lower-class student is unfortunate enough to come into contact with an uninterrupted procession of teachers who are rigidly middle-class and care little or know little about differences in behavior which stem from class values, his chances for success in school become increasingly impaired.

It is even possible that a series of unfortunate circumstances might make advancement up the educational ladder a realistic impossibility for the lower-class student, who might be a member of a minority group, or migh have serious problems with the language, and of course he is not as well dressed or as "clean of mind and body" as his fellow students. His efforts to gain acceptance into the group in the only way he knows—by standards set by his own class, including the use of obscene language or disrespect for certain kinds of authority—can only lead to disaster if his fellow students happen to be predominantly middle-class with a teacher who holds middle-class values. From the middle-class teacher's viewpoint, the lower-class student may appear stupid, dirty, and generally impossible. No real effort is made to reach him. Year after year he is "written off" until the happy day that he finally reaches the legal age limit and can get out. For those who doubt the possibility that such situations exist, a day in the teacher's lounge of any school with a predominantly middle-class population should dispel any doubts.

A serious educational problem which exists throughout the nation and which is related to the question of class and class values is the problem of staffing schools which are situated in lower-class neighborhoods. Middle-class teachers are reluctant to serve in such neighborhoods. Since many of the "best" teachers with many years of experience refuse to teach in such schools in the larger cities around the country, administrators in these school districts have had to resort to placing young and inexperienced teachers in them, which is unfortunate; it is doubly so if the young teacher happens to be middle-class in background and orientation. All too frequently this situation spells disaster for the new teacher as well as the students. At present, the national government is attempting to help meet this problem by providing special inducements for teaching in areas with an extremely low socioeco-nomic environment. At best, this can only be a short-range solution to a difficult problem, for it tends to attack symptoms rather than basic causes for a serious social disease. Any permanent solution must wait for a multifront war on the causes of poverty, of class distinction, and a serious effort to utilize the schools as an instrument for social change. To be an effective instrument, schools will have to ignore traditional patterns of organization, school district lines will need drastic revision, and efforts will have to be made toward the practice of genuine equality in the schools, often in the face of great opposition by local majorities. Such change on the level of the community classroom would most certainly be felt in teacher education programs which would have to give *serious* consideration to such real problems as class values. That such change will be slow in coming should be readily apparent.

COMMUNITY POWER AND CLASS

Studies of status or class in American communities in the last fifteen years have tended to emphasize power in community decision-making rather than class structure. One of the earliest of such studies and one which has been widely quoted in the literature of community research is Floyd Hunter's study of Regional City, in which power is defined as "a word used to describe the acts of men going about the business of moving other men to act in relation to themselves or in relation to organic or inorganic things."[14]

In the study of communities a fine distinction needs to be made between power and class, for there may or may not be a relationship between the two.

---

[14] Floyd Hunter, *Community Power Structure* (Garden City, N.Y.: Anchor Books, Doubleday, 1963), p. 2.

This is a significant point, because some of the earlier studies on class seem to imply that there is a close relationship between power and class; that is, the powerful (usually upper) class makes most of the decisions in most communities. The later studies dispel this theory.[15] What appears to exist instead is a variety of control groups, some formal, some informal, some composed of upper-class members of the community, and some composed of middle- or even upper-lower-class persons. Thus, the source of influence on important decisions affecting schooling will vary from one community to the next. In some instances, a formal group such as the Republican party may decide major issues related to schooling, while in others a single individual may exercise inordinate power over such decisions. In any event, one would be almost totally in error to assume that decisions which affect schooling are based solely on social class considerations in American communities.

Nearly any alert teacher is aware that every community possesses some kind of power structure that has great influence on the decisions which affect the community school system. In some communities such power may be exercised through the formal groups such as the Chamber of Commerce, the Lions Club, the Democratic or Republican party organizations, or a local labor union. In others real power may be wielded by the duly elected officials of government. Many studies have revealed, however, that informal power structures may be quite common in American communities. Such structures may consist of one or two individuals or a small but powerful group who are not in public office, who may not be top leaders in formal community organizations, but who do exercise their control through various means (frequently by use of economic power) and make many of the important decisions in the community.

This kind of situation was described by Ralph Kimbrough in a study of community decision-making in 1964. Kimbrough described a fictitious community in which the teachers' association appointed a committee to work on a new salary schedule. The school depended heavily for support on three large textile mills. Pop Gregg was chairman of the board of the textile company and everyone knew he exercised great influence in local policy. The committee met for several hours and outlined a very comprehensive and difficult plan of attack on the salary problem which involved an "organized, grass-roots attempt to influence the thinking of status officials and formal interest organizations on the salary increase." A young teacher on the

---

[15] These include such studies as Delbert C. Miller, "Decision-Making Cliques in an American and an English City," *The American Journal of Sociology* (Nov. 1958), vol. 64, pp. 299–310; Robert A. Dahl, *Who Governs?* (New Haven, Conn.: Yale Univ. Press, 1961); George Belknap and Ralph Smuckler, "Political Power Relations in a Mid-West City," *Public Opinion Quarterly* (Spring 1956), vol. 20, pp. 73–81; and Gladys M. Kammerer, *et al., City Managers in Politics* (Gainesville, Fla.: Univ. of Florida Press, 1962).

committee was somewhat dubious about the results of such a comprehensive effort and in " . . . an exasperated tone exclaimed: Why do all of this? Why not let's go to Pop Gregg and ask him if we can have the money?"[16]

However difficult it may be to generalize about community power structures in the United States, we do know that they exist, and that in many cases they tend to be conservative on matters involving increased appropriations and new programs for schools. A hypothesis that might be supported in many communities is that the power-wielding group and/or individual in any given community tends to be on the traditional end of a traditional-emergent value continuum. The few studies of community power which exist tend to support this hypothesis.[17] One might expect this to be true for several reasons. In communities which are run by a single wealthy or powerful individual or a small group of such people who are large taxpayers, one might expect a certain amount of conservatism relative to tax increases. Moreover, such informal community leadership might be personally interested in the status quo since any great change might be viewed as a threat to their grip on the reins of power. In addition, if such individuals or power groups subscribed to the economic and political value orientation of classical nineteenth-century liberalism outlined in Chapter 2 of this book, one could clearly label them as conservatives. Such individuals might have a completely different view of the goals of schooling than most of the school people—or most of the community for that matter. They might view the school system as a place to "build character" in terms of nineteenth-century liberal values. They might see the school system as a vehicle for building individualism, self-reliance, and "Americanism" as they understand it.

This whole problem may or may not be related to the question of class or status as it has been defined in earlier sociological studies. For school people interested in studying community power and the manner in which that power affects school decisions, it would probably be much more fruitful to study the power structure in the community and then attempt to determine the value orientation of that specific power structure than to attempt to study class and values and generalize from that knowledge.

One note of caution is needed. Short of a comprehensive study of a particular community in a particular time and place, it can be very misleading to generalize from studies which exist at present. With regard to the hypothesis suggested above on the traditional or conservative nature of power-wielding groups or individuals, one might find some notable and significant exceptions. Groups and individuals which wield power are not all

---

[16] Ralph B. Kimbrough, *Political Power and Educational Decision-Making* (Chicago: Rand McNally, 1964), p. 25.

[17] Kimbrough, p. 25. (Kimbrough describes this problem in his own study and cites several supporting studies in Chapter 7.)

alike. There may be serious splits in value orientations within groups or individuals that make meaningful generalizations impossible. Pop Gregg could be a hard-boiled conservative in economic matters, but on the other hand he could be a real friend of progressive-minded school people. The salary committee might have been well advised to see Pop Gregg and forget their grass-roots campaign. On the other hand, the ruling clique in a community may hold power so precariously that they could be pressured to make concessions to emergent groups in order to avoid open conflict and risk a loss of power. By nature, no ruling clique can forever maintain absolute control of the decision-making process in any community. By definition, the emergent group will eventually become the power group, and the values of the emergent group, once it is in power, may be considered the conservative force in the community by the succeeding emergent group. Added to all of these variables, in any consideration of community power structure, is the fact that the power structure varies in different communities.

To mention just one problem which contributes to variety of power structure in American communities, we might consider the matter of geographic variety. At least one anthropologist has seriously considered this problem and has suggested that it might be easier to reach valid conclusions about power structure in New England towns and in communities in certain sections of the South than in other sections of the country.[18] This is true, because in certain New England towns, and in some areas of the South, there is a long tradition of a ruling elite and the absence, in many cases, of an emergent group which would challenge the existing power structure. In nearly every other section of the country, however, the emergent groups are not only there, but they are constantly shifting and changing personnel as well as value orientation. An outsider might move quickly into the ranks of the emergent group in a midwestern or west-coast city and within a reasonable period of time actually become a powerful voice in decision-making. This sort of fluidity and change tend to make community studies on power structure in certain geographic areas dated as soon as they are published.

COMMUNITY CONTROL—THE DRIVE FOR DECENTRALIZATION

The decade of the sixties witnessed a rather dramatic movement on the part of urban minorities as they attempted to acquire some power over their local schools. Leaders in the community control movement have advocated total control of their schools. They have demanded that large urban school districts be broken up and that smaller geographic boundaries be drawn for

---

[18] C. M. Arensberg, "American Communities," *American Anthropologist* (Dec. 1955), vol. 57, pp. 1145–1160.

the new districts. The advocates of community control have demanded that citizens in the new districts be given the power to elect their own school boards, have a real voice in the selection of teachers and administrative personnel, and gain complete autonomy in the use of funds for education. In recent years the demand for decentralization of the schools has gained national attention.

Much of the pressure for decentralization and community control of the schools has come from the large urban areas of the country. This is understandable in view of the educational problems which have long been developing in urban areas. As the problems of the inner city were neglected over the years and the more affluent residents of the inner city escaped to the suburbs in the last two decades, the minorities and the poor moved in to replace them. The population density increased, the number of children grew, and the character of the population changed. In the decades since the end of World War II the color of the inner-city population changed from predominantly white to predominantly Black. Many of the new residents were extremely poor, had been on the welfare rolls, or held marginal service jobs in what Galbraith referred to in *The New Industrial State* as "cockroach capitalism." The old ethnic groups of first- and second-generation Americans, largely from European stock with a tight sense of community, were pulled out by the attraction of the suburbs or frightened out by the new immigrants.

In the face of this changing population, the schools remained relatively unchanged. The decades of the 1930's, 1940's, and 1950's had seen great efforts at centralization of governmental functions in urban society, including the schools. Thus, school boards elected on a city-wide basis, with little or no representation from the inner-city population, were established and still exist in many cities. The result for the last two decades has been neglect of and indifference toward the educational problems of the inner city. Decaying school plants were allowed to deteriorate in spite of repeated complaints from local citizens. The responsibility for hiring teachers rested with the central city board which tended to ignore complaints that teachers hired for ghetto schools were not generally fit to teach there. They were outsiders who drove into the ghetto in the morning and left early in the afternoon and appeared to be little interested in the lives of their students. The same charge was made against principals and other supervisory personnel. They were outsiders who cared little for the community in which they worked. Advocates of a greater community voice in the education of their children also criticized a centrally formulated curriculum which, they claimed, was more relevant for middle-class whites in suburbia than for the kids who lived in the ghettos. Finally, and perhaps most significantly, the educational establishment in large cities was charged with financial discrimination against inner-city schools. Many residents of the ghettos felt that their children were being shortchanged in every conceivable manner by an educational establishment that managed to keep them on the outside looking in.

The inevitable result of this sort of neglect was serious and sometimes violent pressure for local control of the schools. Although the drive for decentralization has been a national urban phenomenon since the mid-sixties, its present status remains clouded in doubt and confusion. The most publicized struggle for decentralization occurred in New York City.[19] In some ways typical of the struggle in other cities, the New York City effort began in 1966, and continues to be a serious issue. In November of 1966, a group of parents from Black and Puerto Rican neighborhoods invaded the offices of the board of education and sat for three days demanding a greater voice in their local schools. Mayor Lindsay called in McGeorge Bundy of the Ford Foundation who was asked to arbitrate the differences between the board and its critics. The result was the establishment of three "demonstration" school districts which were to go into operation in the fall of 1967 with the assistance of a Ford Foundation grant. The three involved were Ocean Hill–Brownsville, Two Bridges, and the 201 Complex. From the outset, the organizational scheme was dubious. The central board authorized a planning council to organize and plan for the demonstration districts. After a few weeks of planning, the planning council became a governing board without ever gaining approval from the central board. The newly created board was conceived as broadly representative with limited power over the operations of the district.

Unfortunately for the advocates of decentralization, the plan was beset with difficulties from the beginning. The local board's difficulties with the United Federation of Teachers over the dismissal of nineteen teachers ultimately contributed to the prolonged strike at the beginning of the 1968–1969 school year. Throughout the experiment, the local board and its administrators had difficulty getting funds and supplies from the central office, teachers complained that their paychecks were a month or two behind schedule, and the powers and functions of the local board were never clearly outlined. Indeed, it would be difficult to declare the experiment a success by any measure.

Those who were most intimately involved in the New York City decentralization experiment tended to polarize into those in favor and those opposed. Both sides engaged in public debate over issues that were often petty and emotional, and more heat than light was undoubtedly generated by the

---

[19] A good summary of the New York City battle for local control may be found in Helen Shaffer, "Community Control of Public Schools," *Editorial Research Reports,* ed. William Dickinson (Washington, D.C.: Congressional Quarterly Inc., 1968), pp. 945–951. Also see: Marilyn Gittell, "Community Control of Education," *Academy of Political Science Proceedings* (April 1969), vol. 29, pp. 60–68.

experiment. Although there were many immediate problems related to the day-to-day operation of the experiment, the more basic obstacles to its success were long-standing problems which tinkering with school organization could not overcome. Even so, the efforts in New York were successful in that they brought change to the system. New York City now has thirty-one districts by order of the state legislature. Each district has its own governing board and administrative staff. The central board continues to control the secondary schools and fiscal matters.

What happened in New York City was repeated with varying results in other cities. Black citizens in the Roxbury district of Boston have repeatedly attempted to gain some local control over their schools with little to show for it. In Boston, the hope for local control rests more with the success of the Model Cities program and with outside money to fund the program than with any efforts on the part of local citizens or groups. The plans for decentralization in Philadelphia have been repeatedly delayed because of political and bureaucratic resistance and lack of funds.

However, decentralization has been moderately successful in other cities. Several cities began the 1970–1971 school year with various kinds of decentralized school systems.[20] The 1970 legislature in Michigan ordered the city of Detroit divided into regional school districts. The existing plan provides for eight regional districts, each with its own governing board. Seattle now has an inner-city district headed by a Black administrator and an elected board of community residents. St. Louis has established six districts within the city, giving limited autonomy to six superintendents and providing for the election of a parent congress in each district.

A study of the decentralization movement dramatically demonstrates the ability and realism of emerging Black leadership in America's major cities. The two key political issues which provide rallying points for Black leadership are poverty and education. The condition of poverty and the conditions of schools in poverty areas have been real issues which Black leaders have been able to exploit successfully. Moreover, there have been some genuine short-range successes in these areas. Black citizens have gained a measure of control over their local schools, but perhaps more significantly, Black leaders have been able to utilize the school issue and the various anti-poverty programs of the late sixties to develop an organized political power base where there had been none. The point made by many Black leaders, that true integration can have meaning for Blacks only when they enter into the process as equal partners, was something that Black people understood. The sham of integration solely on white man's terms was a condition that Blacks

---

[20] Kenneth G. Gehret, "Can People Power Save the System?" *The Christian Science Monitor,* 21 Aug. 1970, 2nd sect.

could not accept. The argument for decentralization and Black control of Black schools seemed a reasonable solution to the problem. This logic has not escaped Black politicians in urban and rural areas where Blacks constitute a majority or near-majority of the population in specific political jurisdictions. The reality of the power of the ballot box has resulted in the election of hundreds of Blacks to political office in recent years.

Most of this movement can be explained in terms of traditional American politics. Nearly every large minority group has traveled the route of political solidarity as a means for achieving its goals. The Blacks are thus practicing traditional American politics—in some areas—rather successfully.

Unfortunately, the politics of decentralization in education could create other problems. If the success of the decentralization movement is an outgrowth of a genuine demonstration of power by Blacks, it might be considered a positive movement. If, on the other hand, it is merely an abdication of responsibility by white leadership, it could prove tragic. It would be easy enough to conclude that state legislatures and central school boards in urban areas have been pressured into decentralization by the demands of inner-city minorities. Somehow this explanation seems too simple given the general conservative middle-class character of these institutions. It is just possible that state legislatures and central boards were willing to relinquish and diffuse power as a convenient method of dumping the serious school problems which they had been unable to solve into the laps of those who were complaining the loudest, the inner-city residents. In no case where a measure of decentralization has occurred is there any evidence that the state legislature involved has made any really serious effort to attack the basic problems of school finance. If the local district continues to be a major source of support then it would obviously be to the advantage of the predominantly white middle-class suburban majorities to grant total independence and control to inner-city districts, including the burden of raising a significant part of the operational costs. If the decentralization movement succeeds in gaining control without gaining a broader base of financial support from the community and state which surround it, public education in the inner city will be in for even more difficult times than it has already experienced. The result could be a new and more sophisticated form of segregation and apartheid than already exists. Unfortunately, this may be precisely the direction in which the urban school systems are headed, if one can assume that the character of the typical state legislature is not apt to change greatly in the near future. As it is presently constituted, it is extremely difficult for inner-city minorities to gain any real voice in the typical state legislature. Even with recent reforms in representation the minority groups are still on the outside looking in. The system makes it virtually impossible for minorities to gain the sort of legislative power necessary to radically alter state programs of school finance. Unless the state or national government is willing to bear nearly all of the cost of local schooling, there will continue to be gross inequities in the system. Given this situation, decentralization has little hope of improving inner-city schools; rather, there is the possibility that they will decline even further and fall even more behind the quality of suburban education. The process of decline may be greatly accelerated if state legislatures decide to go all the way; that is, to give complete control to the decentralized boards, including the matter of raising and administering local funds.

This is not to say that decentralization under existing circumstances is not a worthy goal. Obviously it seems more desirable for local taxpayers to have some voice in policy, curriculum, administration, and teaching in the school their children attend. But that voice without accompanying resources is a hollow one. Perhaps the real hope for the future lies more in a natural decentralization than a contrived one. The real hope may be that as the central city becomes virtually uninhabitable the population will leave it. Perhaps at some time in the future the miles of tenements that exist in our large cities will be torn down and the land converted to cow pastures or truck farms. There is no reason to think that the present condition, although persistent, is a permanent one. Already there are indications that large numbers of people are leaving the ghettos. Sadly, the exodus of the 1960's seems to have involved mainly whites, leaving the inner city of 1970 even more predominantly Black than it was a decade earlier. However, a trickle of Blacks have left and there is always hope that this could become a flood in the next two decades. Some of the forces which might encourage such movement are already in sight. The very difficulties of inner cities in recent years have contributed to the movement of industry and job opportunities. Paralleling this development has been the effort on the part of many states which have been slow to develop industrially to provide various inducements to industry to relocate in more bucolic surroundings. For more than a decade the national government has been making efforts to encourage this dispersal in a variety of ways, especially in granting government contracts to outlying and rural industries. Moreover, there is some hope that problems of human ecology—population density, pollution, and poverty—will gain greater national attention and the climate for a more active role by the national government will gradually improve. For some years new towns have developed and new plans are on the drawing board to provide a more humanistic definition of "community"—one where people can work and play and cooperate in community enterprises and, hopefully, build a better world for themselves. Thus the long-range solutions to the educational problems of the inner city may await some basic changes in the nature and character of the inner-city population.

SOME EDUCATIONAL IMPLICATIONS OF COMMUNITY POWER, SOCIAL CLASS, AND DECENTRALIZATION

Since the major decisions which are made in education are basically political, the political implications of community power, social class, and decentralization take on great significance. This is not an effort to list and discuss all of the possible political implications of the problem, but is intended as a discussion of a few examples of how the existence of community power, social class, and certain class values affect and are affected by political decisions and the political process. For purposes of illustration we shall deal with the two questions of who shall be educated and what should be taught.

The question of who shall be educated has been raised since the first time man began to think about education. It was raised by W. Lloyd Warner and others in the early 1940's[21] and much of what these authors had to say years ago still applies. They recognized that ours was not, in reality, an equalitarian society, and viewing ours as a society in which a status system existed, they felt the schools could do little to change the situation. They voiced the opinion that the schools had to operate within the existing social framework and that only as the social order changed could the schools hope to reflect this change. Moreover, they hoped for a change in the direction of a greater realization of the dream of an equalitarian society.

Some progress toward an equalitarian society has undoubtedly been made since 1940. There can be little question that the position of the middle class has been strengthened and that upward mobility within all but the very top stratum of the upper class has become more evident since 1940. Whether widening opportunities in education have been primarily responsible for this phenomenon is open to question, for other factors have also been operating in the society which are equalitarian in nature. The drive for equal educational opportunity for Blacks has been fought in the streets, in the courts, and in the legislative chambers. This drive has been strangely apart from, although part of, the educational scene; that is, this very significant movement for educational equality has succeeded in most of its goals in the past twenty-five years without really substantially altering the structure or offerings of the school system. In effect, in all too many instances, the Black has, through sheer political force, opened the doors of schools which may not really understand him or his problems. In this case, legal equalitarianism may be far removed from genuine social equalitarianism. What the Black may find inside the open door of opportunity may too often be the social system based on class which continues to frustrate his demands for equality. Even where

---

[21] W. Lloyd Warner, *et al., Who Shall Be Educated?* (New York: Harper & Row, 1944).

they are in a majority, as in the urban ghetto, Blacks continue to complain that they have no power over educational decisions.

In other ways, in spite of the obvious obstacle provided by power structure in some communities, there has been a kind of progress toward equalitarianism. Certainly the G. I. Bill enabled many to obtain college degrees who otherwise would have had no means to do so. This was the kind of program which could not have been blocked by community power structure even if the power structure had opposed it. Yet in this remarkable accomplishment no effort was made to politically justify the move within the framework of the equalitarian ideal. Rather, it was justified politically as a reward for services rendered or frequently as a recognition of the economic facts of life. Indeed, one might seriously argue that the political attraction for increasing appropriations, generally for higher education, with the ensuing increase in numbers of students pursuing this goal in the past twenty-five years, has been based more on economic realities than on any question involving the equalitarian ideal.

However it has been justified or argued, it cannot be denied that the movement of larger numbers of middle- and lower-class citizens into higher education has had the effect of increasing the upward mobility of those who have been fortunate enough to participate. In some communities a few of these fortunate individuals have managed to push themselves into the emergent power group. With the single exception of the G. I. Bill, however, it is very difficult to find general examples in the past twenty-five years of education's being primarily responsible for equalitarian gains. Perhaps any increasing equalitarianism which is evident in our society has been forced by considerations outside the schools and the schools themselves have merely reflected these forces.

The major force—economic, social, political, or whatever—in the past twenty-five years has been that of science and technology. Economically, this force has dramatically decreased opportunities for those who are not skilled or trained or educated. Socially, with respect to the class structure as well as the power structure, it has provided opportunities for upward mobility which were previously limited. At the same time, technology has created problems of hardened stratification in the lowest class, where son follows father not up the ladder of social class but deeper into the depths of the lower class. From a political as well as an educational viewpoint the force of science and technology must be dealt with—in terms of its social and economic consequences.

The remarkable thing about the force of technology as it involves education is that the existing system of schooling in the society has played a minor conscious role. Instead, school people have been characteristically struggling to find a role which will enable them to deal with the impersonal force of science and technology on its own terms. Far from being on the cutting edge of the force, blazing new trails, and opening new frontiers, school people are more often found trying desperately to discover what must be done in order to keep up.

However, the force of science and technology has provided an answer to the question of *who* should be educated. The answer is simple and direct and few disagree with it. That answer is everybody, and it is generally acknowledged that everybody must be educated, for there is no longer any place for those who are not. This realization, of course, plays havoc with the arguments over which class or which power group in the community places the greatest emphasis on schooling.

There remain, however, serious questions to be considered. All citizens might agree that everybody should be educated, but disagreement is still apparent in how much they should be educated, at whose expense, and the nature of their schooling. Throughout our history, the question of "how much" schooling has been left open. The conditions of the community have determined the answer in broad general terms and probably will continue to do so. Similarly, the question of financial support has been debated, but in the long run answered by conditions rather than by the logic or eloquence of the printed or spoken word. The threat of unemployment or military service has kept more students in the high school and college classroom than all of the rhetoric on record. The race for space has done more to raise the quantity and quality of schooling than all the learned journal articles and local struggles for adequacy combined. There are many other such examples. In the face of such realistic problems, the arguments over how much schooling and who pays tend to become more academic with each passing year.

A more serious question, however, is the problem of *what* should be taught. This, too, is perhaps influenced as greatly by the environment as by the views or the power of community decision-makers. As a political question, however, it is fraught with obstacles which are affected by the existence of power structures, demands of special interest groups, social class, and human values.

Every school system, large and small, is faced daily with the problems of the needs of the children and of the community. What these are, unfortunately, depends greatly on who is considering them. The answers are forthcoming from every possible direction. What should be taught in the schools is ultimately answered in the normal political process in the form of appropriations for approved programs designed to meet the needs of the children in a given community. Thus, the approved programs become the programs that teach those things which those in positions of power consider to be the values, the goals, and the needs of the community.

Although no real pattern of values can be discerned from the existing curricula in the elementary and secondary schools of the United States, certain generalizations can be drawn. The twentieth-century pattern of offerings in the public schools generally reflects the aspirations and values of the great middle class. Beyond the minimum-skill subjects, the public school continues to be traditional if not classical in its approach to schooling. Disciplines are taught as separate subjects which have been established for years. The social studies curriculum builds "good citizens" as this term is generally understood by the middle class. The language curriculum prepares more students more for language on a higher level than for anything else. Where the curriculum looks toward preparation for "real life," it is frequently looking toward the real life of the middle class. The mathematics and science curricula, even with the innovations of the National Science Foundation, continue, for the most part, to teach the "truths" which have long been established and are passed on to new generations by college professors of science and mathematics. The wide range of electives in the comprehensive high school, whether in class work or extra-class work, may be more dedicated to the principle of adjustment to real middle-class values than anything else.

Perhaps the best illustration of this point is the generally accepted community view of what constitutes the "best" school. All too often, the "best" of the local schools are judged largely by middle-class standards and aspirations. The "best" schools are always those which have good discipline, little public trouble, good football teams, new buildings, the largest number of Merit Scholars—and above all, a high percentage of graduates who succeed in college, most frequently in repetition of a course of study similar to that provided by the high school.

This does not mean that the local community does not find exceptions to this kind of "best" school. There is, in some communities, another kind of "good" school. A "good" school can be a trade school or a vocational school, or a comprehensive school which has such a curriculum. Apparently many citizens have become convinced that equalitarianism in education does not have to mean the same kind of education for everybody. The problem with the vocational school is that it has become so well accepted. Too often this becomes the easy solution for the education of the lower class and its offerings justified by the reasoning that "these people cannot possibly hope to go on to college anyway." The political implications of this kind of thinking are dangerous. Such a practice tends to solidify class lines. It threatens to create a whole new class of automatons who could become totally alienated from intelligent and enlightened participation in the process of governing the society.

Although the foregoing discussion of middle-class schooling might appear as carping criticism, it is not meant to be. Rather, it is merely a description of what appears to exist. Indeed, it does not seem possible that it could be otherwise. The school and its program, for good or evil, continue to be a reflection of the majority viewpoints in communities which they serve, and in a broader sense, the society. Dependent as it is on majority support, both moral and economic, the school can do little more.

In spite of these problems, the schools have served as an equalitarian force in our society. There are too many individual examples of this to deny it. The millions of second-generation Americans who are now working in the professional ranks of the society know the value of schooling as a major means of upward social and economic mobility. Too many millions of Americans have exceeded the fondest dreams of their parents via the school route to deny that schooling is an equalitarian force. It is a remarkable, if not an almost unbelievable, fact of our existence that in little more than a generation whole groups, minority groups, which only yesterday seemed poorly prepared to cope with a modern industrialized society and lived huddled together in ghetto areas of large cities, have been almost totally assimilated into a new culture. Millions of children from these groups are scattered across American communities living the "good life" of the suburbs and are demanding for their children a better chance than they had. In many millions of such cases, schooling made the difference. It enabled escape from a life of privation—from hunger, from illness, from the dirt and grime and poverty of the ghetto. No volume of criticism of middle-class values, of power elites, of ruling cliques, can change that fact. Our society has been fluid and flexible enough to enable it to accommodate large numbers of "strangers." Perhaps more significant, these strangers effected some subtle changes in the society. In the whole process there has been movement spurred by environmental change. This movement has been, and continues to be, reflected in the schools. Indeed, a vital part of the movement as well as the environment has been the increase in the quantity and quality of educated citizens who continue, quietly but effectively, to enable our society to move in desirable directions.

REFERENCES

Arensberg, C. M. "American Communities." *American Anthropologist.* 57: 1145–1160 (Dec. 1955).

Belknap, George, and Ralph Smuckler. "Political Power Relations in a Mid-West City." *Public Opinion Quarterly.* 20:73–81 (Spring 1956).

Bell, Robert R. *The Sociology of Education, A Sourcebook.* Homewood, Ill.; Dorsey Press, 1962.

Brookover, Wilbur B., and David Gottlieb. *A Sociology of Education.* New York: American Book, 1964.

Brooks, John. "Mr. White and Mr. Blue: Notes on the New Middle Class." *Harpers Magazine.* 232:88–91 (June 1966).

Charters, W. W., Jr. "The Social Background of Teaching." *Handbook of Research on Teaching,* N. L. Gage (ed.). Washington, D.C.: NEA, 1963. Chapter 14.

Collier, K. G. *The Social Purposes of Education.* London: Routledge Kegan Paul, 1959.

Dahl, Robert A. *Who Governs?* New Haven, Conn.: Yale Univ. Press, 1961.

Dahlke, H. Otto. *Values in Culture and Classroom.* New York: Harper & Row, 1958.

D'Antonio, William, and Howard J. Ehrlich (eds.). *Power and Democracy in America.* Notre Dame, Ind.: Univ. of Notre Dame Press, 1961.

Gehret, Kenneth G. "Can People Power Save the System?" *The Christian Science Monitor.* 21 Aug. 1970. 2nd section.

Gittell, Marilyn. "Community Control of Education." *Academy of Political Science Proceedings.* 29:60–68 (April 1969).

Halsey, A. H., Jean Floud, and C. Anderson (eds.). *Education, Economy and Society: A Reader in the Sociology of Education.* New York: Free Press of Glencoe, 1961.

Havighurst, Robert J. "Social Class Influence on American Education." *Social Forces Influencing American Education.* The Sixtieth Yearbook of the National Society for the Study of Education. Chicago: Univ. of Chicago Press, 1961.

Havighurst, Robert J., Paul H. Bowman, Gordon F. Liddle, Charles J. Mathews, and James V. Pierce. *Growing Up in River City.* New York: John Wiley & Sons, 1962.

Henry, Jules. *Culture Against Man.* New York: Vintage Books, 1963.

Hollingshead, August B. *Elmstown's Youth.* New York: John Wiley & Sons, 1949.

Hunter, Floyd. *Community Power Structure.* Garden City, N.Y.: Anchor Books, Doubleday, 1963.

Kahl, Joseph A. *The American Class Structure.* New York: Holt, Rinehart & Winston, 1957.

Kammerer, Gladys, Charles D. Farris, John M. DeGrove, and Alfred B. Clubok. *City Managers in Politics.* Gainesville, Fla.: Univ. of Florida Press, 1962.

Kimbrough, Ralph B. *Political Power and Educational Decision-Making.* Chicago: Rand McNally, 1964.

Kluckhohn, Clyde and Florence R. "American Culture: Generalized Orientations and Class Patterns." *Conflicts of Power in Modern Culture,* Lyman Bryson, Louis Finkelstein, and R. M. MacIver (eds.). New York: Harper & Row, 1947.

Levy, Gerald E. *Ghetto School: Class Warfare in an Elementary School.* New York: Pegasus, 1970.

Lipset, Seymour M., and Reinhard Bendix. *Social Mobility in Industrial Society.* Berkeley, Calif.: Univ. of California Press, 1959.

MacIver, Robert M., and Charles H. Page. *Society: An Introductory Analysis.* New York: Holt, Rinehart & Winston, 1949.

Maxtell, George. "Parents in the School: Community Control in Harlem." *This Magazine is About Schools.* 4, IV:72–109 (Fall 1970).

Mercer, Blaine E., and Edwin R. Carr (eds.). *Education and the Social Order.* New York: Holt, Rinehart & Winston, 1958.

Miller, Delbert C. "Decision-Making Cliques in an American and an English City." *The American Journal of Sociology.* 64:299–310 (Nov. 1958).

Nisbet, Robert A. *The Quest for Community.* New York: Oxford Univ. Press, 1953.

Reisman, David. *Constraint and Variety in American Education.* Garden City, N.Y.: Anchor Books, Doubleday, 1958.

Reisman, Leonard. *Class in American Society.* New York: Free Press of Glencoe, 1959.

Report of the Task Force on Children Out of School. "The Way We Go To School: The Exclusion of Children in Boston." Boston: Beacon Press, 1971.

Shaffer, Helen. "Community Control of Public Schools." *Editorial Research Reports,* William Dickinson (ed.). Washington, D.C.: Congressional Quarterly Inc., 1968.

Spindler, George D. "Education in a Transforming American Culture." *Harvard Educational Review.* 25:145–156 (Summer 1955).

Warner, W. Lloyd, Robert J. Havighurst, and Martin B. Loeb. *Who Shall Be Educated?* New York: Harper & Row, 1944.

Warner, W. Lloyd, Marchia Meeker, and Kenneth Eels. *Social Class in America.* New York: Harper & Row, 1960.

Warren, Roland L. *The Community in America.* Chicago: Rand McNally, 1963.

Woodring, Paul. *A Fourth of a Nation.* New York: McGraw-Hill, 1957.

Zeigler, Harmon. *The Political World of the High School Teacher.* Eugene, Ore.: Center for the Advanced Study of Educational Administration, Univ. of Oregon, 1966.

5

Pressure and the Schools

A group of militant Blacks has staged a sit-in in the city's board of education offices demanding redress on a list of specific grievances. A group of radical students has taken over the principal's office at Central High School demanding reinstatement of several students who were expelled from school. The local commander of the American Legion accuses the high school social studies faculty of promoting un-American ideas. Any of these statements could have been the substance of headlines in local newspapers almost anywhere in the United States in recent years.

Pressure in various forms from a multiplicity of sources has been a common feature of the community school scene in recent years. At times the aims of those responsible for pressure have been quite clear, at other times somewhat vague. One can be sure, however, that much of the pressure on schools grows out of a belief that the schools should operate in conformity with certain values strongly held by the pressuring group or individual. Such pressures, coming from one place or another, have been a regular and continuing feature of the American public school system, and they have always existed. This chapter will present a brief history of pressures on the schools, look at contemporary pressures, and attempt to determine why schools are susceptible to them. Finally, an attempt will be made to point out some of the implications for society which often grow out of the existence of pressures on the schools.

A BRIEF HISTORY OF PRESSURES ON THE SCHOOLS

Historically, pressures on education have been similar to a fever chart which fluctuates with the patient's condition. These fluctuations have followed the political destinies and fortunes of the nation. In times of peace and prosperity, when there appear to be no threatening domestic or foreign crises, pressures on education in the United States have been at a low ebb. During periods of domestic or international crisis, on the other hand, education in the United States has come in for more than its share of public interest.

The colonial experience was one in which schools were established to present the prevailing religious views in the community. There were certainly pressures during those times to see that the religious views were adequately represented by educational practitioners. One of the earliest and most notorious examples of pressure was the dismissal of the first president of Harvard College when he accepted the Baptist view of infant baptism.

During the American Revolutionary period, political as well as religious conformity was required of teachers. All states established some kind of test oath for civil officials, including teachers.[1] As early as 1776, Massachusetts had enacted a loyalty oath for teachers, and in 1777, New Jersey required schoolmasters to take oaths of allegiance. The New Jersey oath contained a kind of self-enforcing provision, which made it the citizen's responsibility to discover and bring suit against any teacher who might not have taken the oath. As an added inducement, the law provided that the fine for the offending teacher was to be six pounds and that the person bringing suit was to have one-half for his own.[2]

Sometimes during the early years of our history, objections were voiced to the whole idea of public education. In spite of a slowly growing recognition of the need for state educational systems, many might have agreed with the comments of the *Philadelphia National Gazette* editorial on July 10, 1830, which pointed out that education was wasted on most people. The "peasant," said the editor, "must labor during those hours of the day, which his wealthy neighbor can give to the . . . culture of his mind; otherwise, the earth would not yield enough subsistence for all."[3]

The battle lines were drawn during the 1830's between forces favoring public education and those opposed. A Philadelphia union, The Workingmen, did not agree with the position of the *Gazette.* The Workingmen lamented the fact that education was handled as charity in the Commonwealth of Pennsylvania. They expressed the opinion that "all who receive the limited knowledge imparted by the present system of public education are looked upon as paupers."[4] They also felt that public schools conformed

---

[1] Howard K. Beale, "Teacher As Rebel: His War for Freedom," *The Nation* (May 1953), vol. 176, p. 412.

[2] Edgar W. Knight and Clifton L. Hall, eds., *Readings in American Educational History* (New York: Appleton-Century-Crofts, 1951), p. 37.

[3] Knight and Hall, p. 149. (See Chapter 3 for a more complete quotation from this editorial.)

[4] Knight and Hall, p. 342.

with the spirit of free institutions which was part of our national character.

The late 1830's and early 1840's witnessed the beginning of a type of pressure on education that was to last well into the twentieth century. The cause was the conflict between the North and South which found expression in the classrooms of America. A great deal of sentiment against sending southern scholars to the North to be educated appeared in the South long before the Civil War. Moreover, there were certain restrictions placed on southern teachers. During a decade or so preceding the Civil War it was dangerous for teachers in the South to advocate freedom for the Negro, and there were many instances in which teachers were dismissed and sometimes driven from the community for taking a position in opposition to slavery.[5]

After the Civil War the issues which divided the country were still strongly felt. Militant patriotic groups became the watchdogs of materials used in the schools in both the North and the South. The Grand Army of the Republic and the United Daughters of the Confederacy attacked teachers and textbooks and tried in every way they could to influence the curriculum in a direction which would be favorable to their own interests. This battle continued until the turn of the century. By this time, publishers had succumbed and were turning out materials which were inoffensive to either side in the dispute. In 1899 General Lee, head of the United Confederate Veterans historical committee, could announce: "The style of historical authors has become less sectional and controversial and much more liberal and patriotic."[6]

The Spanish-American War created an expression of chauvinistic nationalism which was readily apparent in the press of the times and which had its influence on the public schools as well. There were local demands to instill patriotism and the values of American democracy into the school curriculum. These influences were so strongly felt in some areas of the country that some state legislatures were moved to enact legislation requiring the teaching of a nationalistic history and of the Constitution in the schoolrooms of the state.

World War I created a great concern for teacher loyalty in America. During the war, teachers themselves demanded dismissal of disloyal teachers. There were periodic outbursts of fear and hysteria, and this atmosphere found its way into the classrooms and legislative chambers as they considered school matters. The requirement of loyalty oaths for teachers became a universal practice in the states and hundreds of teachers were called to task for being pro-German, un-American, or otherwise "subversive." The hysteria created by the war caused public school teachers some serious moments of anxiety.

During the interwar years the schools experienced pressure from various groups and individuals. Some of these were social and political in nature;

---

[5] Beale, p. 413.
[6] Wallace E. Davies, *Patriotism on Parade* (Cambridge, Mass.: Harvard Univ. Press, 1955), p. 230.

some were economic. Along with dissatisfaction from every conceivable source and direction with the course of events in America during this period, there were numerous external threats used by groups and individuals to justify their criticisms and pressure on the public schools. The pressures of the period between 1920 and 1940 had a serious and unsettling effect on the teacher in the classroom. In a particularly penetrating analysis of academic freedom on the secondary school level, Howard Beale[7] saw some general forces during the 1920's and early 1930's which tended to limit freedom in the classroom. Beale pointed out that the war itself created some disillusionment with the old order of things. In Beale's opinion, the war bred hatred and prejudice which added to confusion in the society and created problems for the schools. Added to the war and its heritage, the rise of communism created a state of panic in some quarters that tended to class any criticism of the status quo as a real menace.

Political pressure on education in the 1920's frequently took the form of pressure on textbooks and teachers, pressure which found expression in legislative enactments on school matters. During the early 1920's many states passed laws which attempted to ban books which were "unpatriotic" or which tended to "degrade" national heroes. During the 1920's many states passed so-called "monkey" laws and pure history laws which attempted to restrict and dictate the content of courses in science and history.

During the 1930's pressures on education were most characteristically directed toward the idea of free public education, certain topics which were being taught in the schools, textbooks, and the loyalty of teachers. It was, in many ways, a continuation of the dreary pattern which had been established in the preceding decade. The advent of the Great Depression and the changing political and economic ideas in America of the 1930's created a multitude of problems for the schools. In the 1930's some Americans were not yet convinced that free public education was essential or even desirable. Although almost universally accepted at the elementary school level, free public education was not so accepted on the secondary school level. No doubt some of the stimulation for the arguments to curb the program in the secondary schools came from tax-conscious citizens at a time when tax resources were seriously depleted. Some critics of education in the 1930's were opposed to what they called the "fads and frills" in the secondary school and suggested in some of their writing that free public education was subversive of the essential values of the American tradition. Some of the arguments heard in the 1930's along these lines have a singularly contemporary ring. The *Memphis Commercial Appeal,* concerned with a legislative cut in normal school appropriations in Tennessee, made for the purpose of

---

[7] Howard K. Beale, *Are American Teachers Free?* (New York: Charles Scribner's Sons, 1936).

providing more funds for working with "subnormals" in elementary schools of that state, demanded:

> Will the state continue to save money to half educate those best capacitated to receive it and then try to waste money on expensive but futile methods by trying to educate those incapable of being educated? In other words, will we keep the frills and discard the essentials to a real education?[8]

The *New York Daily News* sounded its accord in a March 18, 1932, editorial which objected to such frills as child guidance, homemaking, music, sewing, speech, and kindergartens, adding that "it is a question, we think, whether our schools aren't turning out too many white collar workers for the nation to absorb." Other newspapers and individual critics of the 1930's tended to compare free education with the dole and insisted on an end to this drain on financial resources.

Pressure in the 1930's made itself felt in the classroom in the criticism of certain topics which were controversial in nature. The number of topics which seemed to be taboo were legion during the 1930's. Perhaps no better illustration could be found of this than a letter from a leading industrialist to a school superintendent who was assisting Bruce Raup in his study on pressures on education in the early 1930's. The letter was in response to a questionnaire which had been sent to the industrialist for the purpose of gathering material for the study. It is quoted in part here:

> I am returning herewith the questionnaire which I have filled out. After examining into this matter I have reached the conclusion that this questionnaire is nothing more than a clever piece of propaganda. I mean by this that it is not so much directly a piece of propaganda but that the questionnaire itself is suggestive of the kind of answers that are desired, and it is my belief that the replies will be answers that are desired, and it is my belief that the replies will be so handled as to permit the American Historical Association to single out the kind of material the backers or heads desire to send out.
>
> The Columbia University is a hot bed of communism and socialism. And I would not be at all surprised to find that Professor Raup is mixed up with the activities, as are a number of other professors. . . .
>
> While the questionnaire appears to be completely frank and open and entirely fair, there is a suggestion running through it. . . .
>
> I would not be surprised to find, after investigation, that Professor Raup, who is sending this questionnaire out, is one of a large and well

---

[8] Charles R. Foster, *Editorial Treatment of Education in the American Press* (Cambridge, Mass.: Harvard Univ. Press, 1938), p. 39.

organized group of Communistic or socialistic professors and teachers who are associated with our various colleges and universities. . . .

As a superintendent of schools, I would be interested in having you advise me just why such subjects—as Pacifism; Disarmament; Socialism; Communism; Soviet Russia; Differences in religious belief; Birth control, etc.—should be discussed in a high school or any public school? What is the idea or need of such discussion?[9]

Although this is the opinion of a single individual, it does illustrate highly opinioned interest in topics which were normally discussed in some courses in the public schools.

Certain patriotic groups were busy attacking textbooks during the 1930's. Generally, the complaints against textbooks were that they contained a pacifist influence, were favorable to internationalism, and that they debunked heroes. When the textbooks did not conform to the critics' values, they were declared subversive of American institutions and ideals and unfit for use in the public schools. Professor Harold Rugg neatly summed up the criticism of textbooks in the late 1930's when he wrote:

The books were denounced as "subversive . . . un-American." It was said they undermine patriotism . . . twit the Founding Fathers . . . have an alien ideology . . . plan to substitute a new social order for our American Government . . . would regiment private enterprise . . . debunk our great heroes of the past.[10]

Attempts to influence the textbooks were of little avail if the teacher using the text was suspect or not "100 per cent" American according to the definition of some critics of the 1930's, so there was a great deal of pressure on teachers during the period of the Great Depression. About half the states in the 1930's enacted loyalty oaths to protect children from "subversive" teachers. The Ives Law in New York, passed in 1934, was typical of loyalty oaths in many states during the period, the general terms of the law being that no one could teach in any school, college, or university until he or she took the oath of loyalty to the constitutions and laws of the state of New York and the United States.

The period since 1945 has experienced two great waves of pressure on the public schools. The first, which continues to the present, might be characterized as right-wing. The second, beginning in the late fifties and reaching some sort of peak in 1970, might be labeled an attack from the radical left. Such general classifications are, of course, oversimplifications. As indicated

---

[9] Bruce Raup, *Education and Organized Interests in America* (New York: G. P. Putnam's Sons, 1936), pp. 49–50.

[10] Harold Rugg, "Education and Social Hysteria," *Teachers College Record* (March 1941), vol. 42, p. 498.

in the preceding section, those who might be classified as politically conservative have long been interested in the public schools. The most radical elements within conservative political ideology are the groups that have gained the greatest amount of publicity and have dealt the schools the greatest amount of misery. Similarly, there are all kinds of liberals. Liberal school critics range from advocates of school reform to those who reject the possibility of reform and advocate total destruction of the system.

THE RADICAL RIGHT

In his work *Academic Freedom in Our Time,* a study of the late 1940's and early 1950's, Robert MacIver summarized some of the activities of the radical right:

> Minute Women are out to purge the libraries, American Legion Posts are at work to prevent unorthodox speakers from being heard, members of a post of Veterans of Foreign Wars hunt for subversives in their locality, textbook committees find subversives in unexpected places—perhaps the most notable discovery being that of a member of the Indiana Textbook Commission who revealed the Communist line in Robin Hood. This is something different from the older but still sufficiently vigorous censorship carried on in the name of morals and religion. It doesn't usually go as far as the book-burning affair that occurred in a town in Oklahoma, but it exhibits the same spirit. The favorite charge is that of being subversive —an accommodating label to stick on any doctrine that deviates to the left.[11]

Although MacIver was referring to the period from 1945 to 1954, the years since that period have shown few signs of abatement in this kind of pressure from the right. If anything, the various anticommunist crusades of the period since 1954, led by dynamic and sometimes emotional individuals, did not spare the schools in their attacks on the internal communist threat. Since the early 1950's new groups have been formed which have undertaken attacks on so-called "subversive" and "communist" teaching in the public schools, they have launched local and state-wide textbook examinations, harassed teachers out of their jobs, and generally stirred communities to some kind of action against schools. As recently as January 1965, the national president of the PTA, complaining that extremists were attempting to gain control of local PTA organizations, warned that "the extremists are not really after the PTA, they're after public education itself."[12]

---

[11] Robert M. MacIver, *Academic Freedom in Our Time* (New York: Columbia Univ. Press, 1955), p. 35.
[12] *Newsweek,* 1 Feb. 1965, p. 57.

Conclusive evidence on sources of radical right-wing attacks on education since 1945 have been obscure. There have been many opinions, however, on the sources of the attacks. The Select Committee on Lobbying of the Eighty-First Congress in 1950 looked into the educational activities of the National Economic Council, the Committee for Constitutional Government, and the Foundation for Economic Education, and found these groups to be the source of many attacks and much agitation on the problems of public education.

Dr. Hubert C. Armstrong, director of the Public Education Association of New York, pointed out that complaints against textbooks came from three major sources:

> First, the . . . super-patriots who for the most part are plain ordinary, uninformed, good-hearted American citizens. Second, a group composed of organized minorities, usually racial or religious, who find passages which they feel are prejudicial. Third, are the full-time complainers . . . who are zealous to make the literary world over in their own image.[13]

The number and variety of pressure groups in existence in the United States today is legion. No one could seriously propose to list them all. Ellsworth and Harris, in a study of the American right wing, suggested over a thousand in this classification alone.[14] In recent years there have been estimates of membership of the so-called American right wing which vary from one million to eight million operating on a budget which approached $25 million in some of the years of the early 1960's. The right-wing groups have no monopoly of interest in the public schools. Hundreds of groups, not specifically interested in the schools, become interested from time to time. These vary in political orientation from right-wing to left-wing and any position between the two extremes. Indeed, most organized pressure groups, of whatever political persuasion, have been known to exert occasional pressure on the schools.

Much of the pressure on education which has occurred since 1945 seems to have come from groups which might be called "patriotic" and groups which may be classified as extremely conservative in their economic and political value orientation, although the pressure has not been limited to these groups. In discussing the topic "propaganda and the curriculum," Gwynn[15] mentioned the efforts of various pressure groups to get their influence felt in the public schools. In this respect he listed religious

---

13 *New York Times,* 25 May 1952.
14 Ralph E. Ellsworth and Sarah M. Harris, *The American Right Wing: Report to the Fund for the Republic* (Washington, D.C.: Public Affairs Press, 1962).
15 Minor J. Gwynn, *Curriculum Principles and Social Trends* (New York: Macmillan, 1950), pp. 648–655.

pressure, patriotic pressure, pressure by civic organizations and governmental agencies, commercial advertisements, and propaganda by professional educational groups.

The literature of some of the pressure groups which have been most active in the last twenty-five years indicates a broad general pattern of techniques with regard to attempts on the schools. By far the most popular position has been that of the true conservative. In this role many individuals and pressure groups have identified their cause with "pure Americanism" and have attacked anything with which they disagree as subversive, socialistic, or worse. The "red scare" has been a favorite with groups attempting to influence education. In this connection, the so-called "progressive education" of an earlier era was branded as "communist-inspired," "Godless," and was accused of being a "red plot" in some of the literature of the extreme conservatives. Criticism of progressive education and the position of political conservatism have often been interwoven and inseparable. Progressive education has been attacked many times in the past twenty-five years on the grounds that it was new, or advocated change, or would be too expensive.

The right-wing attacks on education in the past twenty-five years have been many and varied. Most, however, played on the same theme. The communist threat was used by the majority of critics regardless of the nature of the criticism. It mattered little whether the attacks were against progressive education, high taxes, neglect of the fundamentals, the teaching of social studies, poor discipline in the classrooms—a way was usually found to tie in the criticism with the communist threat. This has been the major indirect technique of the past twenty-five years.

RIGHT-WING PHILOSOPHY AND TACTICS

The charge of subversion in education as it has been made by certain groups since 1945 has often been in the nature of a smoke screen. Since the groups with a particularly conservative or right-wing orientation have been so active in their attacks on education in the last twenty-five years, it might prove interesting to briefly analyze their position. The right-wing extremists have appeared to be opposed to many aspects of the school program, teachers, and sometimes education generally. They have taken a strong position in favor of states' rights, a policy of isolation for the United States, the teaching of fundamentals in the schools, a particular and somewhat narrow interpretation of the Constitution, and an emphasis on American heroes.

Defenders of states' rights to a man, these extremists have been very critical of what they refer to as the expanding power of the national government at the expense of the states. Such groups universally neglect to mention the expanding functions and responsibilities which have been assumed by state governments. Very often, the literature of the right wing has been opposed to increasing federal support of education and the increasing size of the national budget for what they believe to be welfare functions of the national government. Moreover, many extreme right-wing spokesmen have declared that the expansion of the functions of national government is a deliberate and planned attempt to remake the United States into a socialistic system or worse. In terms of their political and economic values, leaders of the American right wing have preached the doctrines of the eighteenth- and nineteenth-century economic and political philosophers. They idolize the economics of Adam Smith and agree with Thomas Jefferson that government should be very limited in its functions. These advocates of nineteenth-century values see any departure from these values as subversive of the American ideal.

Accompanying this particular economic and political philosophy, the right-wing extremists view America as the sole worldly possessor of the ideal modern "republic." Many right-wing extremists view America as a world leader but not in the role of leadership it has played during most of the twentieth century. Opposed to foreign aid and any hint of compromise with the socialistic nations of the world, some extremists have criticized foreign aid or any form of compromise in foreign policy as sinister plots designed by communists to destroy American ideals. Some right-wing groups have expressed the belief that America should push its ideals without compromise throughout the world as a protection against domination by socialism and communism.

Moreover, the right-wing spokesmen argue that these ideas should be taught in the schools; that efforts to teach any other view of American social, political, and economic development is somehow subversive; and that departure from the classical economic and political values of the nineteenth century is part of a sinister communist plot. Believing this, they feel that any means used to see that only true "American" values, as they view them, are taught in the schools are justifiable.

In line with their extreme conservatism the leaders of such groups argue that the schools need to concentrate on teaching "fundamentals" in the schools. Some of the stumping lecturers for the extremist point of view have been eager to point out that public school classrooms allowing discussion of significant and contemporary problems in which a great variety of points of view are aired, only tend to confuse students, and if such discussions are not openly led by teachers who are communist sympathizers, such teachers are at least dupes of the communists. This is true, they argue, because such teachers leave students without ideals and values which can be used to oppose communism in our society. The "fundamentals" for many extremists not only include the basic three r's, but the advocacy of a kind of fundamentalism for nearly every course taught in the public schools. These are the so-called fundamental values in the society (conveniently defined by extremists), the fundamental values in the United States Constitution, and so on.

The success of these groups has been rather remarkable, a most notable area being in school textbooks. It is a fact of our existence that in recent years the public schools have been cursed with a plethora of textbook examinations by legislative committees, state textbook committees, and other groups. The great bulk of these investigations has been initiated and encouraged by the right-wing extremist groups. In some instances, they have been successful; in others, they have not. However, the techniques utilized by the groups for investigation into texts have been generally similar. Normally, the charge is made that the textbook material is somehow subversive of American values or the author of the textbook is subject to suspicion. Committees which have the responsibility for selecting texts are pressured into hearing the evidence of such charges. Where such committees balk, the state legislature is implored to undertake state-wide textbook investigations in which the members of extremist groups are only too happy to serve as witnesses before the committees. During the course of these hearings the right-wing groups produce "evidence" of the subversive, communist, or socialistic character of the book.

Accompanying this technique, the right-wing critic may question the loyalty of the teacher. Teachers who do not agree with extremist values have been attacked in letters to the editor, in open investigations, by visiting delegations to the school board or superintendent of schools, and in various other ways. When board members or superintendents choose to support a teacher, they, too, are accused of subversive leanings. The whole battle, of course, is heavily publicized in whatever medium of public opinion is available in the community. Such publicity is not difficult to achieve, since schools are newsworthy and any attack on the schools, from whatever source, tends to get good coverage from the news media.

In addition to its attack on textbooks and teachers, the American right wing has found certain topics which are being taught in the schools a good point of attack. The United Nations has been a favorite in recent years. Teachers and school programs which have included the United Nations as part of their regular course of study have been blasted by the extremists for their stupidity or sometimes for their sympathy with the communists. The attack on this topic has generally followed the assumption that the United Nations is an organization which was originally the brain child of international communists and has been serving their purpose from the beginning. A favorite agency for attack is UNESCO. This has been pictured in recent years by certain extremists as an organization dedicated to the destruction of the American system. The most frequently cited evidence is the effort of UNESCO to rewrite the world's history in a way which tones down nationalism and de-emphasizes the history of wars. To some right-wing extremists, this is viewed as a scheme to debunk the history of America and attack the ideals and philosophy which made us the great nation that we are.

The American right wing has been successful in some of its efforts to enact its particular prejudices into law. In the past fifteen years there have been a number of state laws providing for the teaching of Americanism in the public school curriculum. Although these provisions are sometimes very general in nature and their implementation can come through the regular course work in the social studies, some have been very specific. In a few states, the teaching of Americanism is spelled out in some detail. Where it is, it may include such objectives as "teaching about the dangers of socialism" or "demonstrating the superiority of American capitalism" or "teaching the basic values of the American Republic." Where details are provided for the implementation of these goals, they are almost always provided in terms which harken back to the good old days of the nineteenth century before "big government" became a way of life in America.

Even though such a program may prove to be somewhat unrealistic for children in the 1970's, such units on Americanism have enjoyed widespread success in their application both on a state-wide basis and in local school systems. This success has been due to a number of factors. The post World War II successes of international communism, of course, have been a major reason for the success of a "patriotic" approach to education. Communist imperialism has been a genuine manufacturer of fear. For many years after World War II, America seemed to be losing the cold war and many were ready to accept any solution offered in order to change the tides of fortune. The schools, in many instances, fell victim to the fear of international communism, and, as no other institution or agent in our society, provided a convenient scapegoat and outlet for a frustrated public. The violent anticommunists discovered in the schools a vehicle through which they could promote their own particular values. The anticommunist extremist was offering explanations for our failure in the struggle against communism and he was doing more—he was offering solutions. The solutions were almost always phrased in terms of a return to the tried and true—the tested values of earlier generations. The fact that earlier generations were not faced with the sort of communist threat which faced the United States during the post World War II period was of little concern to the anticommunist crusader. He found in anticommunism the issue which made it possible to push his own program.

The confrontation with communists in Korea furnished the anticommunist critics of American education with new ammunition. The term "brainwashing" was coined and soon became a household word. The unfortunate cases of turncoats in Korea were used by most extreme anticommunists in their attacks on education as immutable evidence that the American public schools were failing in their task to instill American values into the minds of students. Indeed, some of the more extreme critics openly charged that the schools had been so thoroughly influenced by world socialism and world communism that they had deliberately taught the youth in such a way that they would be openly susceptible to communist brainwashing. This whole-sale indictment of the public schools was almost always followed by the plea to return to the teaching of good old American values. Nor did the critics need to be pressed for a comprehensive definition of what needed to be taught in the public schools in order to inoculate innocent children safely against the future possibility of brainwashing. Those who were bold enough to speak out against this kind of indoctrination of school children found themselves in the position of defending their Americanism as they were brought under suspicion by the critics. Needless to say, only the very brave or the very idealistic dared speak in opposition.

A new kind of fear appeared on the scene in 1957. As if the general although vague fear of communist domination were not enough, the success of the Soviets in their space efforts in 1957 induced a new wave of criticism of the public schools. Sputnik was made to order for critics of education. Just as the more violent and unreasonable charges against the schools were beginning to lose credibility and public support, Sputnik beeped its orbit around the earth. The extremists could then say, "We told you so!" Sputnik I was followed by a deep and searching evaluation of American education. Some of the examination was justified and some of the criticism was immediate and gratifying. Certain changes were made in methods in mathe-matics and science, curriculum studies in other areas were stimulated, examinations were made of teacher education programs, and the national government became seriously interested in many aspects of elementary and secondary education. However, actual changes have, for the most part, been minor rather than basic, for many of the critics displayed a remarkable ignorance of what the schools were really doing. On the other hand, the extremists released a new broadside at American education which has not subsided to this day. There can be little doubt that hysteria created by dramatic incidents on the world scene will continue for an indefinite time to play into the hands of those who would make over the public schools of America in their own image. This may very well be the greatest single threat facing the American public school for many years to come.

The threat is genuine for several reasons. In the first place, those who would make over American education possess the dedication of the true fanatic. For individuals and the groups representing them, there are no ground rules. The democratic process is derided and held as weak and inefficient. The contemporary literature of the American right wing is replete with denunciations of democracy, often labeling the term as an invention of the communists. Certain groups and authors of the right wing have openly charged that democracy was not used to describe the American system until after the Communist Revolution in 1917, and for them the connection is self-evident. Such an attitude toward democracy, of course, gives extremists a frightful advantage when dealing with those in the public schools who have great faith in the democratic process. The true fanatic is not so concerned with means as he is with ends. This has been a known fact among school people with regard to the Communist party for many years and the school people have been able to resist communist influence with considerable success. The fanaticism of the right-wing extremist is quite another matter. He is able to wrap himself in the American flag and the traditional values of American capitalism. To complicate matters for school people, this sort of extremist is more apt to be chairman of the board of a leading local corporation than the characteristic wide-eyed radical of an earlier era or the groups on the new left who cast their lot with the so-called "underprivileged masses."

In the second place, the threat from the right wing has been genuine because these people operate on the basis of a genuinely felt fear. Fear of communism has had some real justification in the post World War II world, for the successes of communism have been real. This fear has been used with great success by certain extreme groups in their attacks on education. Where examinations of textbooks have been made, it was not at all uncommon for teachers to be so afraid of being branded as communists or sympathizers that they would not appear at hearings to defend the books in question. Similarly, no legislator who valued his political life dared stand in opposition to a bill which would encourage the teaching of Americanism when introduced in the legislature. Administrators in the public schools have been very reluctant to risk a head-on confrontation with extremist groups for fear of the personal or professional problems such confrontation might cause. Finally, there have been some scattered examples of genuine personal fear of physical or psychological attack. There are many accounts in the past twenty-five years of professors, preachers, and public school teachers who have suffered threats to life and limb, serious beatings, unbelievably obscene phone calls at all hours of the night, and all manner of physical and psychological harassment from sincere fanatics who may honestly believe that they are fighting the evil of communism in their own backyards.

Finally, the threat from the right wing is genuine because the public has been reluctant to take the danger of its methods seriously. The general attitude has been that it is better to remain silent than get personally involved. Many people seem to feel that as long as it is another who is getting hurt, it should not concern them. Although the general public may not necessarily condone pressures on education by the right wing, their ignorance, or silence, or both, leads the attacker and those attacked to assume that the public stands in silent agreement with the substance of the charge and with the techniques of the attacker. Of course, this is due partly to the advantage the attackers have in organization. There may be no such thing as organized public opinion. The public is a disorganized mass which can be stirred to action by good leadership, perhaps only by the commission of the gravest sins and the most gross indecencies. In the case of the expressed goals of some of the extremist groups, this may be too late.

THE RADICAL LEFT

More recently, especially since 1960, a new source of pressure has appeared on the school scene. Much of the storm of controversy which surrounds the schools most recently has come from militant students and Blacks who appear alienated from the system. These attacks have been far less subtle than those from the radical right. Whereas the radical right critics found words relatively effective weapons, many groups on the radical left resorted to physical action which often included violence.

Early in the sixties liberal extremists, particularly minorities and some student groups, discovered the values of confrontation with what they liked to call the establishment. A favorite tactic of Black militants and militant students was to present school authorities with a list of "non-negotiable" demands, a tactic which was very often accompanied by some overt action such as a walkout or sit-in or the capture of the president's office or a building on campus.

Very often militant Blacks and student groups began their campaigns with a general concern such as the issues of war, poverty, or civil rights, and moved from there to specific attacks on universities or public schools.

Black militancy had a beginning of sorts as early as 1955 when a Black woman, Mrs. Rosa Parks, refused to relinquish her seat to a white man on a Montgomery, Alabama, bus. Willing to accept arrest for her civil disobedience, Mrs. Parks inspired a subsequent boycott of the transportation system in Montgomery, providing a successful pattern of active resistance on the part of Black leaders and Black citizens which has continued to the present. As Black students and others expanded their attack on segregation to include other public facilities, they were joined by other groups, most notably the Student Nonviolent Coordinating Committee. By the mid-sixties the Blacks had been joined in their attacks on segregation by student groups across the country.

Taking their cue from the success of nonviolent resistance in the form of freedom marches and sit-ins, student groups began to use the same tactics in order to make known their demands for general reform of society and specific reform of the university. In 1964 the American public was treated to its first large-scale campus demonstration by the Free Speech movement at

Berkeley, California. A year later a group of students was able to close the University of Chicago for a time.[16] The period from 1965 to 1970 was characterized by increasing militance on the part of students and Blacks and sometimes combinations of both. New groups sprouted, often charging the old with loss of faith and selling out to the establishment. Thus, the Students for a Democratic Society became progressively more active and radical in their position with each succeeding year after 1965, until their dissolution in 1970. Even so, the Weathermen were so much more radical that they looked upon the SDS as a tool of the establishment. Within the Black movement, the Black Panthers tended to view the earlier predominantly Black organizations, particularly the NAACP and the Southern Christian Leadership Conference, as "Uncle Tom" organizations.

By definition, the radical left leadership has been pushing for radical change—in the political system, in the economic system, in the social system, and, of course, in education. Unlike earlier left-wing radicals such as the communists and the Trotskyites, the new radicals have no utopia with which they plan to replace the existing system. The most radical would be content with total destruction of the existing system, perhaps on the theory that anything would be better. Although much, if not most, of such extreme radicalism is directed toward the conditions of society in general, some direct attention has been paid to the schools. Students on every level of schooling and in all parts of the country have utilized the tactics of left-wing radicals in efforts to influence the course of the war in Viet Nam, in the name of social justice, and, most frequently, in defiance of what they consider to be repressive schools, irrelevant curricula, and prejudiced teachers. The Third World Liberation Front at San Francisco State College is an excellent example. This group of radicals called specifically for a non-white faculty, an improved Black studies program, a more relevant curriculum, and a clear student voice in the administration of the college. On the high school level, the Montgomery County Student Alliance made a plea for what they called a "humane education" for students of Montgomery County, Maryland, and found a receptive audience in high schools across the country. In 1969, the Student Alliance accused their school system of dishonesty; of placing a premium on conformity; of destroying eagerness to learn; and of alienating large numbers of students through a repressive administrative system, an archaic testing and grading system, and a curriculum which was not in any way responsive to student needs.[17] Radical student organizations have become a familiar feature of the American secondary school. In some

---

[16] For an excellent description of student activism in the 1960's, see Jerome H. Skolnick, *The Politics of Protest* (New York: Ballantine Books, 1969).

[17] Montgomery County Student Alliance, "Wanted: A Humane Education" (Bethesda, Md.: Montgomery County School Alliance, 11 February 1969).

districts they are called student unions, and are independent local organizations. In other districts high school students have affiliated with existing groups including the Weathermen, the Panthers, and other groups.

At the current stage of development it would be difficult to find any common philosophy or set of goals to which all radical left groups would subscribe. It would be even more difficult to describe with any accuracy common goals for education or common tactics used to achieve their goals. However, there can be little doubt that individual radical students and groups have been influenced by some of the literature of educational criticism in recent years. For example, the Montgomery County Student Alliance makes references to Jonathan Kozol's *Death at an Early Age* and John Holt's *How Children Fail,* along with several others. Nor is it surprising that the radical critics of education have gained a large following, particularly among the victims of the system. Anyone from the rural slums or urban ghettos could not help but agree with much of what is said in Nathaniel Hickerson's *Education for Alienation.* The same might be said for a dozen other books, including Herbert Kohl's *The Lives of Children,* Leslie Hart's *The Classroom Disaster,* and Neil Postman and Charles Weingartner's *Teaching as a Subversive Activity.* While C. Wright Mills and Michael Harrington have provided direction and information for radical criticism of the society generally, these books and others like them have provided the same sort of support for radical pressure for reform in education.

Extremely idealistic in their philosophy, many left-wing extremists place personal values high above property values. Many tend to reject the argument that capitalism is absolutely "good" because it has been so productive. Some argue that Americans have paid too high a price for productivity in human terms and tend to reject material values in favor of what they like to term "human values." Although it is difficult to generalize about the goals and philosophy of the left wing since the term encompasses such a large number of disparate groups, most would agree with the Ten-Point Program of the Black Panthers. The major points of this program call for individual freedom, full employment, improved housing, better education, an end to war and military service, and an end to police brutality. Although in agreement with such specific goals, most groups in the new left tend to disdain specific programs and place their faith in what they call "participatory democracy," which relies heavily on the ability of citizens to build a new social order on the ruins of the old. Some of the groups and many of the individuals within the radical left movement reject the notion that it is possible to work within the existing system and insist that the existing political, social, and economic institutions must be destroyed before a new order can be built.

Regarding the schools, the radical left groups tend to be critical of what they call the "educational bureaucracy." Some charge that teachers and administrators are more interested in their jobs and in themselves than in the students they teach. Proposals for elimination of the bureaucracy range all the way from decentralizing large systems to the establishment of store-front and free schools as a substitute to public education. Generally critical of middle-class education, the more radical leftists see no in-house solution to the problem, and the most idealistic leftists would reconstruct the schools using the human needs of pupils as their major guideline.

The success of the radical left has been limited largely to the decentralization effort, the initiation of Black studies programs, and the establishment of a number of new free schools with no fixed curriculum or standards. Beyond this, the radical left movement has had some impact on the educational establishment in that teacher training institutions have added programs in human relations and courses on the culture of the disadvantaged and Black studies. The school systems, particularly in urban areas, have been goaded into human relations projects of various kinds; efforts have been made to attack problems of prejudiced teachers, especially through sensitivity training programs; and there is some evidence in the literature of education that the idealistic and humanistic contributions of Rousseau, Pestalozzi, and John Dewey are becoming more popular. In addition, textbooks and curriculum guides are being examined with a view toward eliminating racial bias. How far such reforms will go or how successful they may be is an open question.

Perhaps the major problem facing the schools and the society in general is the impatience of extremists. In radical reform movements it is always difficult to sort out those who are honestly interested in reform and those who are more interested in personal gain. Serious problems could arise if conservative majorities become convinced that the only solution to unrest and violence is counter-violence and suppression. If the reaction to left-wing extremists is bloody repression, there can be little hope for the schools or the society. If, on the other hand, the difficult work of reform is undertaken seriously and the most grievous ills are attacked, there is reason for hope. The great hope is that the most serious economic and social problems can be attacked in some rational manner and that solutions can be found which lie within the democratic framework. If the radical left has demonstrated anything clearly, it is that there is a close relationship between the general problems of society and the problems of the schools.

WHY EDUCATION IS SUSCEPTIBLE TO POLITICAL PRESSURE

In the past twenty-five years sudden and sometimes vicious attacks on public education in general, and local schools in particular, have been characteristic of the times. In recent years, citizens, teachers, and school administrators have been shocked and puzzled by violent criticism of the local school. There is scarcely a community in the land which has not witnessed some sort of "school trouble" in the past twenty-five years. It may take the form of dissatisfaction with the principal, the superintendent, some teacher in the system, the cost of education, the school program, the neglect of Black culture, the irrelevance of the curriculum, or any one of a hundred different aspects of the local school system. Sometimes community opinion is split down the middle by such local problems; sometimes the people of the community are able to meet the problem, whatever it is, in an intelligent and forthright manner. In either case, there is frequently a great deal of soul-searching on the part of the school people who may wonder why their school has suddenly found itself in the glare of publicity.

The classroom teacher or the school administrator should not be surprised, however, when his school system is suddenly and violently attacked by some individual or group in the community. The school in American society has always been particularly subject to various kinds of political pressure. Some of the reasons for this include: (1) the public nature of education in America; (2) the belief that the schools influence attitudes, beliefs, values, and subsequent citizen behavior; (3) the fact that the educational enterprise is decentralized and local in character; (4) the absence of any general agreement on the precise role of education in the society; and (5) the inability of school people to provide an adequate and clear statement of purpose.

There is a long tradition in the United States which makes education part of the political process. The schools have always been close to the public. From the first school law in the Massachusetts Bay Colony in 1642 down to the present there has been a genuine public interest in education. Paralleling this interest has been a particular development of schooling in the society along relatively simple and democratic lines. The simplicity of the development was conditioned by the demands of the environment; that is, the environment did not demand a complicated structure or professional establishment in public education; but it demanded that the masses be trained in a simple way in the three r's. There was very little that was mysterious or beyond the comprehension of the common (and often nearly illiterate) man. Control of the schools had been in the hands of the lay citizens, who had no particular reason to believe that the nature of schooling was in any way mysterious, complex, or beyond their comprehension. Public education was, for more than a century, a simple problem, solved by men with relatively simple tastes and demands, and in many cases conducted by those who were little better prepared than those they served. Although there were some innovations, for the most part these were limited largely to the extension of the public school upward and to methods of organization in schooling which would extend opportunity to larger numbers of students without materially increasing the cost of the process. Public education began to take on an air of complexity and mystery for the masses only in the twentieth century. As the process became more complex and less comprehensible to the average citizen, serious problems arose. As the practitioners in education attempted to experiment in a wholesale way with new ideas and processes in education, as they did in the so-called "progressive movement" of the 1920's and 1930's, and as this experiment took them away from more than a century of tradition, local opposition developed. In some instances this opposition was pronounced and successful in blocking change. It has been difficult for the schools to move rapidly in the face of tradition in spite of the fact that the environment which surrounds them has experienced some revolutionary changes. So long as the public, through its elected school boards, continues to influence educational policy, change is difficult.

With respect to change, the local school often finds itself in a unique position. People in local communities who may be ready to accept change in many other avenues of human activity may be reluctant to do so in their schools. Part of the reason for this may be that the public schools are so "public" in nature; that is, they are close to the public and the public is vitally interested in what they do. For example, the slightest criticism of the schools gets immediate public attention and generally some kind of following. Moreover, criticism of the schools is a simple undertaking. The organization for public education remains so simple that it is easy for individuals and groups to make their influence felt in school matters. In total, this adds up to a particular and peculiar susceptibility of the local school to public beliefs, attitudes, whims, or fancies, and makes school people especially conscious of, and sensitive to, community pressures.

It should be noted that the twentieth century has experienced some attempt on the part of the typical state legislature and the several state educational agencies to establish a standard curriculum pattern for all schools in the state. However, the total amount of change has been relatively small and the innovations few and generally undramatic in character. There may even be a tendency for state agencies to be much more conservative than the more progressive school systems in the state. Indeed, standard curriculum patterns may constitute a serious obstacle to innovation and experimentation. Where state agencies have suggested new courses or new curricula, they have been adopted only very slowly on the local level, and where the new courses have departed seriously from any traditional pattern they have been characteristically short-lived. The successful innovations, or the innovations which have been widely implemented, such as the modern math and science programs, do not question the established place of these courses in the curriculum, but concentrate largely on method of teaching. Notwithstanding, there has been some resistance on the local level against even these innovations. The fact that such resistance has been minor may indicate only that the changes have been minor. The voice of the local citizen in his own school still comes through loud and clear as an expression of traditionally held values in American society. Groups as well as individuals who have a special reason for attempting to influence local school programs and policies are well aware of this.

A second reason that schools have been subjected to pressure, particularly in recent years, is the long-standing belief that education can influence values and citizen behavior. In a rather thorough investigation of lobbying before the U.S. Congress, the House Committee on Lobbying of the Eighty-First Congress (1950) discovered, among other things, that some of the lobbyists were interested in influencing curriculum in the public schools. The committee discovered that leaders of some groups felt that the most certain method of establishing their point of view and getting it ultimately enacted into the statutes was to train children to their way of thinking. This was a long-range technique used by some pressure groups which was considered preferable to open efforts to influence individual legislators who might not be disposed to listen to their arguments. Evidence was presented to the House committee which indicated that leaders of some pressure groups were interested in the public schools because they felt if they could get their own values established in the public school curriculum, and if the job was seriously and efficiently undertaken, they would not have to worry about future legislators because they would have "educated" the future voters. These ideas were based on an almost classical assumption that the school has a great deal of influence on the building of beliefs and attitudes. There is, of course, evidence of this point of view in the literature of the American Communist party, and more recently a great deal of evidence may be found in the literature of the American right wing which advocates a similar "educational" point of view. There has also been a great deal of criticism of the schools, their teachers, and the system from the new left. This criticism often describes the schools as "prisons" where humanistic values are ignored and where students are forced to conform to a conservative ideology in direct opposition to the new left philosophy. Whether schools can and do, in fact, influence attitudes and beliefs is somewhat beside the point. The real point is that many leaders of pressure groups believe that they can, and they base their actions on this belief.

Unfortunately there is too much evidence that many groups have been successful in their efforts to get their point of view into the classroom. Many units have been introduced into the curriculum, most frequently in social studies, at the behest of a local, state, or national pressure group. In some instances the entire K–12 curriculum has been revised and influenced by such pressures. A typical pattern of such "curriculum development" is the introduction of units of varying length on "Americanism" or "democracy versus communism" on all levels. More recently, Black groups have experienced some success in introducing various kinds of Black studies programs into the schools. New courses and units have been added in many school districts as a direct result of local pressure on the part of individuals or groups outside the school; that is, by people who know little or nothing about curriculum-building, but have decided opinions on what "values" they want taught in the schools. Very often committees of teachers have been formed to work out the details of these units. Frequently the teachers selected share the values of the extremists, and are aided in their task of curriculum-building by great quantities of advice and printed materials from leaders of local pressure groups. One can only guess what parts of the existing program have to be sacrificed for the new units and courses. Of course, this is the central point.

Even if what happens in the classroom does little if anything to change the values of the children, materials and units forced on the teacher at the behest of some pressure groups take the teacher away from other important tasks. Indeed, the whole process is abortive in a way, since time thus spent in this kind of curriculum revision is valuable time wasted, time that might be better spent on deep and searching and intelligent analysis of the existing curriculum.

Although the success these groups have enjoyed may be due in large measure to the fact that the changes they recommend do not represent any really basic change, and they have been invoked by teachers who hold the same values, their success has also been due partly to the fact that the educational enterprise is decentralized and local in character except in the larger cities. Even there the trend is toward decentralization, as indicated in the preceding chapter. Decentralization of the educational system has many of the obvious advantages of democracy, but it is also an open invitation for pressure which has a good chance of success in the local community. In the past twenty-five years a sort of guerrilla warfare has existed in public education. Pressure groups with a particular axe to grind in terms of local and national politics have attacked schools in one community after another in an attempt to get enough local support to implement desired changes. A community thus may be rocking along rather smoothly in the operation of its schools, only to discover quite suddenly that an organized and often well-planned attack is underway on the local school, its program, or its teachers. Charges and countercharges are made. The enemy (school people) are attacked on many fronts and the school leadership may never be sure where the next shot will be fired or the direction from which it will come. School leaders are often ill prepared to defend their system against this kind of attack. Some school administrators have found the support and the resources within their community to resist such tactics successfully. Others have succumbed to the attack. To the attacking groups, success is important but not vital. Where they fail they merely regroup, try again on some other issue, or move to a new community. Local control and the decentralized nature of the system enhance the success of such attacks.

The school people and the friends of the schools have a difficult time resisting pressures because there is an absence of any general agreement on the precise role of education in the society. Although there have been many efforts throughout the twentieth century to determine the proper role of American education, its philosophy, and the values it should promote, none has been universally accepted. Most such statements are very general in nature and eclectic in philosophy. To provide one illustration of the difficulty in arriving at any kind of reasonable consensus on the values which should be taught, the idea of citizenship might be cited. Nearly every study of American public education places training for citizenship high on the list of priorities for major functions of American schools. Almost always the citizenship which is advocated is "good" citizenship. Herein lies the difficulty. What is good citizenship? It is difficult to get agreement in our society on this. Every group has its own list of qualities which its members believe should be included. Any statement which finds broad general acceptance with anything like a consensus is apt to be so broad that it is meaningless. Implementation, in any practical way, is impossible. Other illustrations could be given. Pressure for "education for democracy," or "developing appreciations of the American heritage," and so on, present the same problems as the illustration given.

This is not meant as criticism of any clearly defined value orientation for American education; as we pointed out in Chapter 1, only a totalitarian state can be absolutely certain it has the "right" goals. In a democratic society there is a delightful flexibility which permits differences, allows experimentation, and enables the possibility of change to meet needs which are not yet known. The danger remains, however, that such looseness of purpose makes the schools open to all sorts of pressure. It is interesting to note that in local situations where there are elaborate and definitive statements of policy or purposes, these are, as often as not, collecting cobwebs in some remote place in the central office. Indeed, in schools where detailed statements of policy are worked out democratically by the faculty and by the public or its representatives, they may be enforced only with the unbending will and power of a strong individual such as the local superintendent of schools. What begins as a democratically derived statement of policy may develop in practice into an authoritarian and rigidly administered code.

A final reason that pressures have a good chance of success in the local school district is the inability of school people to provide the necessary guidance in terms which can be understood by the public. Although related to the absence of general professional agreement on the role of education in society, this is more than mere lack of agreement. Even in areas in which there is agreement among the so-called professional educators, they may view the public as an ignorant mass which doesn't really understand them or their function in society. The field thus becomes befogged with what the critics may refer to as "educationese" or the peculiar and mystifying language of the professional educator. So in practice, a curriculum expert may be found explaining the mysteries of role theory, structure, taxonomy, and idiosyncratic material to a lay group from whom he expects unflagging support. The "cognitive and affective domains" may be so much gobbledygook to the untrained layman. The "ever-widening upward spiral of development" may look like a vicious circle to the uninitiated. This is a doubly unfortunate problem, since there is really not a great deal in the significant literature of education which cannot be described in clearly understandable language.

Added to this is the problem of disagreement among educators themselves on the proper approaches to the various areas in education. Obviously there is need for professional argument. It may be the cauldron out of which new ideas and significant research flow. But significant research in education often requires a classroom laboratory and students and parents who are willing to cooperate. Such experimentation needs to be clearly explained to anxious parents. Most important, perhaps, adoption of new ideas and procedures needs to await the results of legitimate experimental verification. Too often, unfortunately, eager teachers and principals rush forward with new ideas which are neither legitimate nor verifiable. When results are disappointing to a public which was possibly oversold at the outset, school public relations can become strained.

IMPLICATIONS OF PRESSURE

The history of pressure on education is a long one. At times the pressures have been particularly acute, and in the view of school people there have been times when pressures have proved confusing and frustrating. These pressures have come from a variety of sources, each with a particular purpose in mind. National and international crises have tended to stimulate certain kinds of pressures on American education. Moreover, there is no evidence on the current scene to indicate that political pressures from every conceivable source will not continue to plague American education and its practitioners. Educators must realize that political pressures of all sorts are something that they will have to live with for an indefinite time.

If anything, the pressures will increase in the future. The technology of mass communication has made political pressure a big business. With regard to pressures on education, the stakes are high. The hope of being able to influence millions of American school children at a time and in an environment in which they seem most susceptible to influence is a great temptation. Add to this a kind of fanaticism which is often associated with extremist views which find saintlike justification in any method, and there exists a genuine threat from certain pressures on the schools.

Pressure from the traditional pressure groups constitutes no genuinely serious problem. The old established groups in the society, such as the labor unions, the National Association of Manufacturers, the various farm groups, and others, have evinced an interest in education and have had considerable success in some instances. However, the political ends of these groups have been reasonably clear to anyone who would take the trouble to check into them. Moreover, the techniques of the established political pressure groups have been studied and publicized and there is general information available on how they operate and what their immediate goals are.[18] The techniques of these groups with regard to the schools have been reasonably open and free to examine. The most irrational extremists, however, present a different face. As often as not, they do not classify themselves as pressure groups and are organized in such a manner that they are not legally considered as such. Some of the more militant student groups totally reject any responsibility to the system and are not pressure groups in the traditional sense. Yet they are willing to use any technique to push their cause of the moment. Similarly, the extremists on the right will use any means to an end. Many extremist groups that have been active in their pressure on public education are not legally classified as pressure groups, but fall under other such designations as patriotic or religious "educational" groups. As such, they may escape the legal controls imposed on the regular political pressure groups and are free to operate in the same arena of dignity which cloaks genuine religious and educational groups. The implications for school people of this aspect of the more extremist groups are that the true motives of these groups may be difficult to discover and expose.

The major problem facing American education with regard to this kind of pressure, however, is that the advice of such groups is all too often taken seriously by an unsuspecting or apathetic public or fearful school officials. This is a serious problem because the advice of the extremist pressures on education, if taken seriously, will curb freedom of the schools to serve the society. The freedom of the teacher in the classroom to discuss important but controversial issues will be curbed. The use of materials of certain types will be severely restricted. The free exchange of ideas in the classroom will be affected. The organization of the curriculum could be greatly influenced by a small minority of Americans who have a particular objective in mind. In total, the effect could very well be the remaking of the schools in the image of the extremist.

Although this may sound alarmist in nature, any attempt to subvert the

---

[18] There are many studies on specific groups, but two comprehensive and general studies on traditional pressure groups are: David Truman, *The Governmental Process* (New York: Alfred A. Knopf, 1951) and V. O. Key, *Politics, Parties, and Pressure Groups* (New York: Thomas Y. Crowell, 1942).

public nature of public education needs to be viewed with alarm. School people and the public need to be made aware of the motives and techniques of this kind of pressure and every effort sould be made to beat down attempts to alter the basic democratic spirit of American public education. That democratic spirit is the essence of freedom—the freedom to examine any idea, however radical; the freedom to examine any alternative, no matter how shocking; the freedom to agree with public policy or to dissent intelligently; and the freedom to pursue intelligent inquiry, wherever it leads. This kind of freedom stands, by its very nature, in opposition to indoctrination from the right or the left, and it supports the human right to be different—it allows man to believe what he chooses to believe so long as he is willing to extend this right to his fellow man.

REFERENCES

Association for Supervision and Curriculum Development. *Forces Affecting American Education.* Washington, D.C.: NEA, 1953.

Beale, Howard K. *Are American Teachers Free?* New York: Charles Scribner's Sons, 1936.

———. "Teacher As Rebel: His War for Freedom." *The Nation.* 176:412–414 (May 1953).

Burton, W. H. (ed.). *Power, Politics and the Teacher.* New York: John Dewey Society, Fourteenth Yearbook, 1960.

Chase, Stuart. *Democracy Under Pressure.* New York: Twentieth Century Fund, 1945.

Counts, George S. *Education and American Civilization.* New York: Bureau of Publications, Teachers College, Columbia Univ., 1952.

Darling, E. *How We Fought for Our Schools.* New York: W. W. Norton, 1954.

Davies, Wallace E. *Patriotism on Parade.* Cambridge, Mass.: Harvard Univ. Press, 1955.

Ellsworth, Ralph E., and Sarah M. Harris. *The American Right Wing: Report to the Fund for the Republic.* Washington, D.C.: Public Affairs Press, 1962.

Ellul, Jacques. *Propaganda: The Formation of Men's Attitudes.* New York: Alfred A. Knopf, 1969.

Foster, Charles R. *Editorial Treatment of Education in the American Press.* Cambridge, Mass.: Harvard Univ. Press, 1938.

Friendenberg, Edgar. *Coming of Age in America: Growth and Acquiescence.* New York: Vintage Books, 1963.

Gross, Beatrice and Ronald (eds.). *Radical School Reform.* New York: Simon and Schuster, 1969.

Gross, Neal. *Who Runs Our Schools?* New York: John Wiley & Sons, 1958.

Gwynn, Minor J. *Curriculum Principles and Social Trends.* New York: Macmillan, 1950.

Hall, Gordon D. *The Hate Campaign Against the U.N.* Boston: Beacon Press, 1952.

Kaufman, Arnold S. *The Radical Liberal: New Man in American Politics.* New York: Atherton Press, 1968.

Key, V. O. *Politics, Parties, and Pressure Groups.* New York: Thomas Y. Crowell, 1942.

Knight, Edgar W., and Clifton L. Hall (eds.). *Readings in American Educational History.* New York: Appleton-Century-Crofts, 1951.

Lazarsfeld, Paul F., and Wagner Thielans. *The Academic Mind.* New York: Free Press of Glencoe, 1958.

Lens, Sidney. *Radicalism in America.* New York: Thomas Y. Crowell, 1969.

MacIver, Robert M. *Academic Freedom in Our Time.* New York: Columbia Univ. Press, 1955.

Melby, Ernest O. *American Education Under Fire.* New York: Anti-Defamation League of B'nai B'rith, 1951.

Montgomery County Student Alliance. "Wanted: A Humane Education." Bethesda, Md.: Montgomery County School Alliance, 11 Feb. 1969.

Postman, Neil. "Alternative Education in the Seventies." *The Last Supplement to the Whole Earth Catalog.* 40–42 (March 1971).

Postman, Neil, and Charles Weingartner. *The Soft Revolution: A Student Handbook for Turning Schools Around.* New York: Delta Books, 1971.

———. *Teaching as a Subversive Activity.* New York: Delacorte Press, 1969.

Raseberry, Salli, and Robert Greenway. *Raseberry Exercises: How to Start Your Own School.* Freestone, Calif.: Freestone, 1970.

Raup, Bruce. *Education and Organized Interests in America.* New York: G. P. Putnam's Sons, 1936.

Robb, Herbert E., and Raymond Sobel. *From Left to Right: Readings on the Socio-Political Spectrum.* I & II. New York: Benziger, 1969.

Rugg, Harold. "Education and Social Hysteria." *Teachers College Record.* 42:493–505 (March 1941).

Selakovich, Daniel. "The Techniques of Certain Pressure Groups Attempting to Influence the Teaching of American History and Government 1945–1960." Unpublished dissertation, Univ. of Colorado, 1962.

Skolnick, Jerome H. *The Politics of Protest.* New York: Ballantine Books, 1969.

Truman, David. *The Governmental Process.* New York: Alfred A. Knopf, 1951.

6

The Force of Law

In recent decades there has been a great deal of controversy over court interpretation of law which applies to the schools. As in no period in our history, the courts have been active in legal matters affecting the schools. Judging from the great number of cases involving educational matters which reach the courts, there is reason to believe that there are great differences of opinion over the meaning of law as it applies to education. Out of these differences have come many serious attacks on the courts, particularly the federal courts and the United States Supreme Court. In their more extreme form, these attacks have advocated the impeachment of the chief justice of the Supreme Court or the adoption of a constitutional amendment to the national Constitution which would establish a super-court with judges from the fifty states with the power to overrule the Supreme Court of the United States. The intensity of the argument and the near-success of the amendment's ratification indicate the great differences in values which are brought into the open by certain actions of the Court.

A good part of the antagonism which has been directed toward the Supreme Court in recent years has been an outgrowth of some of the recent decisions which have been made with regard to public education. Supreme Court decisions on school prayer and on segregation have kindled opposition to the Court from some quarters. In some sections of the nation, whites who oppose the integration principle laid down by the Court in *Brown v. Board of Education of Topeka* have devised ingenious schemes to avoid the directive of the Court. Since 1954 the Court has been fairly consistent in its interpretation of what constitutes an unconstitutionally segregated school system. Even so, if all the schools in the nation were desegregated, white and Black children would still be separated because private segregated schools nave been growing in number since 1954. Although this is a national phenomenon, the private school movement has made its largest gains in the South. In 1969 the Southern Regional Council estimated that three hundred thousand of the nine million white school children in the South were attending private schools. The opposition to the decisions of the Court on these matters may be best summed up by the sweeping generalization made by one of the honorable members of the United States Senate in reaction to the *Vitale* case, which declared school prayer provided by the New York Board of Regents a violation of the First Amendment to the Constitution. One senator who was gravely upset by the decision remarked on the floor of the Senate: "They have put the Negroes into the schools and now they have taken God out of them."

The public reaction to the school prayer cases and the major segregation case (*Brown v. Board of Education of Topeka*) was immediate and controversial. A large minority in our society was extremely vehement in its criticism of these two major definitions of the First and Fourteenth Amendments to the Constitution by the Supreme Court. Although the critics were not able to gain enough support to take action to curb the Court and hopefully overturn the decisions on these cases, they came close. The proposal to amend the United States Constitution in order to alter the structure of the court system was ratified by enough state legislatures to create alarm in some quarters. Not enough to constitute the necessary three-fourths majority, the critics of the Supreme Court were represented in large enough numbers to constitute a genuine threat to the continued existence of the system as it has developed for more than a century and a half.

To understand this outcry of opposition to Court decisions one must look behind the dissatisfaction expressed over a single decision or a series of decisions. Behind the criticism of the Court was a large ground swell of opposition to the decisions based on traditional values and attitudes which were not in keeping with the decisions.

The story of the relationship between the courts and the schools in the historical development of the United States can be very illuminating. This relationship provides an excellent case study in the way the courts have operated in our society to maintain the status quo or encourage change by interpretation of the law. The action of the courts goes right to the heart of the values, beliefs, and attitudes which constitute the meaning of our society in a given time and place.

In this respect education is not unlike other institutions in our society. There is a long and complicated history of the relationship of the courts to the working man, with what might be called a "modern" judicial view of organized labor dating back to the case of *Commonwealth v. Hunt* in 1842 and continuing down to the rather sweeping decision on labor in the *Jones and Laughlin Steel* case in 1937. Similarly, there is a long and often contradictory history of the interpretation of state and national laws by courts attempting to define and outline the constitutional limits of government regulation of business. Other segments of our society have grappled with questions of what "ought to be" in terms of public policy. The farmers in the last generation or so have seen the institution of the "family farm" and public policy on agriculture go through stages of development and control in which division of opinion on what "ought to be" found its resolution in the courts of the land. So it has been with education. As with other developments in our society, education has been unable to stand still. It has moved in certain directions, each new direction requiring some justification in terms of law and often demanding an interpretation of that law along lines of constitutional propriety. On the other hand, established practices and principles in education have been defended from time to time as having deep roots in tradition as well as in the law.

THE SCHOOLS AND THE LAW

Any consideration of the role of the courts in relation to the schools must begin with a consideration of the schools and the law, for it is the law which the courts are established to evaluate, to interpret, and to apply. The system as it exists in the United States cannot, as implied by some critics of the courts, enable the courts to interpret and apply that which does not exist. Every act, every court decision, must have some basis in law. The point of disagreement with the courts comes when there are conflicting views on the meaning and intent of the law. Few but the most extreme persons doubt that courts are acting within the framework of the law when they make decisions, controversial or not. Since the work of courts is thus based on law, let us look briefly at the most significant aspects of the laws which involve schools.

Ours is a society based on the law. It has been characteristic of education that each innovation, each extension of the system upward, has been accompanied by a legal provision or interpretation. Perhaps it would be more accurate to speak of a legal system rather than the law when referring to any institution in our society. Generally, this system of laws as it affects the schools involves some principles of common law; state and national constitutions; state and national legislative enactments; previous decisions of the courts; and a whole collection of rules, orders, and directives which we shall label administrative law.

Common law may be generally defined as judge-made law which conforms to the traditions and customs of the society. Normally, common law as used in the language of political science refers to that body of judge-made law which was brought to American shores by the colonists from England. Common law thus forms the basis for legal procedures in all of the American states except Louisiana, which, of course, has a French rather than English heritage. The common law tradition has very little relevance to present educational practices in the United States except where tradition, custom, and previous judicial decisions with regard to education and educational matters are concerned. In a historic sense, however, common law is significant in education in that the prevailing customs and traditions with regard to education were transplanted from England to America by the colonists. In the case of education, this common law tradition was the tradition that the state had some responsibility for providing schools for the poor, and schools were considered in the English common law heritage as charitable institutions. The emphasis was more on the welfare of the individual child rather than the well-being of the society. This tradition was well on its way out even before the end of the colonial period, although the idea has enjoyed a recent rebirth in the form of the so-called "child benefit" theory in the argument over the question of federal aid.

The state constitutions form another part of the United States legal system. At the present time, every state in the Union is guided by a constitution and each has a provision or provisions on education. Not only are the specific provisions on education important in state constitutions, but other general provisions in state constitutions may apply to educational policy and organization. Thus, in every state, the constitution places the responsibility for providing for a public school system on the legislature, and, in some instances, spells out in considerable detail the organization and administration of the public school system of the state. Beyond this, the various state constitutional provisions which parallel the national Bill of Rights contain provisions which have been applied to education by the courts of the state. Similarly, most state constitutions which outline the qualifications, duties, and responsibilities of the executive officers of state government have sections and clauses which either deal directly with the subject of education or have been applied to education by the courts of the state. The same is true of the provisions outlining the functions and powers of the legislature, and the jurisdiction and powers of the courts of the state.

Although the Constitution of the United States does not specifically mention education, it contains several provisions which have been applied to education. Some interpreters of the United States Constitution point to the fact that education was not mentioned in the Constitution as evidence to support the theory that the Founders did not consider public education as an appropriate or necessary function of the national government. Such theorists maintain that education is one of the "reserved" powers of the states which are mentioned in the language of the Tenth Amendment of the Constitution: "The powers not delegated to the United States by the Constitution, nor prohibited by it to the States, are reserved to the States respectively, or to the people." Carried to its most extreme conclusion, those who see education as one of the "reserved" powers would declare that any national law which dealt with the subject of education in any shape or form is a violation of the Tenth Amendment and therefore unconstitutional.

Obviously, this is not the manner in which the national Constitution has developed in the United States. The Constitution of the United States has proved to be a flexible instrument of government in the hands of the executive, legislative, and judicial branches. The Constitution has undergone a great variety of interpretations by the agencies which were created by it. These interpretations have affected the lives of our citizens in ways which could not possibly have been foreseen by the Founding Fathers. The relations between workers and management, farmers and railroads, the public and business—as well as the definitions of basic values in our society—have been affected by administrative, legislative, and especially judicial interpretation of the Constitution. The school, as a most vital institution in our society, has not escaped these interpretations of its role and function.

Several provisions in the national Constitution which made no mention of education have, from time to time, been instrumental in the development of legal policy with respect to the schools. The most notable of these have been the First Amendment provisions relative to freedom of speech, press, and religion, and the "due process" clauses of the Fifth and Fourteenth Amendments. Taken together, these may be classed as provisions which provide the substance of personal or human rights in our system. In practice, these provisions have come to mean that no state law, agency, or agent; no national law, agency, or agent, may deprive an individual of the substance of his freedom provided in these sections of the Constitution. Parts of the Fifth and Sixth Amendments to the Constitution have applied in a less direct way to education. The procedural rights to which a citizen is entitled under the provisions of the Fifth and Sixth Amendments have been applied from time to time to those persons who have been connected with education, either as teachers or administrators.

It is essential that the student of education gain some understanding of certain provisions of the Constitution as they have been applied to public and private education. Perhaps the most significant of these have been certain provisions of the Fourteenth Amendment. Although specific illustrations from cases will be utilized in the material following, it might prove useful here to outline the general method which has been utilized by the Supreme Court in applying the provisions of the Fourteenth Amendment to education. To gain a clear understanding of this, one must understand the way the process has operated.

As any student of American government knows, the first ten amendments were proposed in 1789 and adopted in 1791. That is, they were not part of the original document. As a whole, they may be described as limitations on the authority of the national government, prohibiting it from restricting certain basic liberties and privileges of individual citizens. These were basic because there was a long common law tradition of these rights which was in development for centuries before the Constitution was written. Specifically, most of the provisions of the first ten amendments to the Constitution were observed in English and colonial practice before the government of the United States was established. Indeed, some delegates to the Constitutional Convention objected to any attempt to list basic human and individual rights on the grounds that the very act of listing them might be construed as a limitation of such rights.

For many years these rights appeared to have little or nothing to do with education. This was particularly true since education was generally accepted as one of the "reserved" powers of the states, and the individual rights listed in the first ten amendments constituted a protection of the citizen against an arbitrary or capricious *national* government. State governments could violate these provisions and, in fact, the Supreme Court said as much in several cases. State legislatures, governors, courts, and other agencies could, with impunity, disregard or violate the provisions of the Bill of Rights of the national Constitution.

This situation underwent a subtle but significant change in 1868 with the ratification of the Fourteenth Amendment. Whereas the first ten amendments make specific reference to Congress, that is, "Congress shall make no law respecting an establishment of religion," the Fourteenth Amendment makes specific reference to states. "No State shall make or enforce any law which shall abridge the privileges or immunities of citizens of the United States; nor shall any State deprive any person of life, liberty, or property, without due process of law; nor deny to any person within its jurisdiction the equal protection of the laws." Although some groups and individuals in our society insist that the Fourteenth Amendment was intended to be limited in its application to Blacks and their rights, the Supreme Court's interpretation of the Fourteenth Amendment has been very broad in its application. For many years after its ratification, it was applied mainly to questions involving state regulations of private business rather than to the rights of Blacks. In practice, well into the twentieth century, where a state legislature regulated a business through the legislative process, the affected business sometimes appealed to the Supreme Court on the grounds that the state law violated the provision of the Fourteenth Amendment, which stated that no state shall deprive a person of property without due process, and found a sympathetic Court. However, as the years passed, the Fourteenth Amendment came to have a much broader meaning. In case after case, especially since 1937, the Supreme Court has elected to apply the wording of the Fourteenth Amendment to implement the provisions of some of the first ten amendments and to apply them to acts of the states.

For example, a citizen may challenge a state law which he believes violates one of the freedoms listed in the first ten amendments. The many cases brought by the Jehovah's Witnesses are illustrations of this point. Many of these cases involved the schools. In one case a salute to the United States flag was required by a ruling of the school board. A child refused to salute the flag. His parents had instructed him that the flag salute constituted "bowing before a graven image." The parents considered the enforcement of the rule a violation of their basic religious beliefs. Counsel for the Witnesses argued that the school was a legal and constitutional agent of the state and its officials were acting under the authority of the state and in the name of the state. The ruling of the school board which required the flag salute was challenged by the Witnesses on the grounds that it was a violation of the "establishment" clause of the First Amendment. Yet, this was a state case, involving the citizen of a state and a ruling of a school board which was an agency of the state. How could the First Amendment be involved in such a case? The Supreme Court ruled that the First Amendment was violated and that this was possible since the wording of the Fourteenth Amendment applied; that is, no state could abridge the privileges and immunities of citizens or deny equal protection of the laws. In this case the Court ruled that the state was depriving a citizen of freedom of religion. In a word, the Supreme Court of the United States utilized the wording of the Fourteenth Amendment to apply restrictions of the First Amendment to an agency of a state government.[1] In the words of Justice Jackson, who delivered the opinion of the Court: "The Fourteenth Amendment, as now applied to the state, protects the citizen against the state itself and all of its creatures—boards of education not excepted."

The reader is cautioned, however, about drawing any sweeping generalizations from a single case. Many other cases could be used to support the position that the wording of the Fourteenth Amendment has been used by the Supreme Court to "bring down" the provisions of the first ten amendments to apply to the states. However, many cases might also be utilized to illustrate that there have been times when the Supreme Court has refused to do this. About the only safe generalization which can be made with regard to this matter is that the Constitution is what the Supreme Court says it is in a given case. With regard to the broader interpretation of individual and human rights, however, there has been a tendency for the Court in the last thirty-five years to expand the meaning of the basic freedoms listed in the first ten amendments and apply them to states which have, in one way or another, provided some obstacle to citizens' enjoyment of these basic privileges.

State and national legislative enactments are the major body of law which affects education in the United States. One might accurately claim that the state and national laws provide the body and mind of education in the society by providing the broad general outline of educational policy, while the courts, particularly the Supreme Court, have provided the heart and soul of the system in a concern for the broader issues and values of the society which affect education and are affected by it.

State law implements any state constitutional provisions regarding educa-

---

[1] *West Virginia State Board of Education v. Barnette,* 319 U.S. 624 (1943).

tion which may exist. Beyond that, the state law sets the broad framework for education in the state. In its lawmaking activities, the state legislature is the policy-maker for education. More than any other agency, it decides what will be done, how much will be spent, and the direction education will take. As a policy-maker, the legislature tends to follow public consensus as nearly as it can be interpreted. The result, at least as far as many school people are concerned, is built-in resistance to change, repetition of old mistakes and old programs, and extension of the system only in painfully slow steps. Generally, little that is revolutionary can be expected from the law. It is, more often, a reflection of the society. The law does not provide the vanguard of leadership. In spite of this, innovations do sometimes come through the legislature. It is possible for the legislature to enact into law a sweeping and comprehensive program that departs radically from what has existed. Although such occurrences have been rare, they have taken place. This is possible because of the nature of the federal system. Just as the existence of fifty separate state systems provides an occasional innovation in other areas such as city administration, labor legislation, and so on, the system also provides opportunity for innovation and experimentation in education. So it becomes possible for one state to completely revamp its requirements for the preparation of teachers, as in California under the leadership of Max Rafferty, where the number of hours of education courses required for a certificate was drastically reduced. Other examples of sweeping change have occurred in New York, Michigan, and other states experiencing serious problems with city schools. In these states the legislatures allowed city school districts to reorganize, permitting large school districts to break up into a number of smaller districts with local or "neighborhood" control. State legislatures have also been innovative in recent years in allowing collective bargaining for public employees and teachers. Some of these innovations may be copied by other states, while others are ignored. The federal system allows states to become huge experimental laboratories for educational policy and practices. The fact still remains, however, that legislative policy which innovates in education is the exception rather than the rule.

Teachers who are concerned to the point of agony with the machinations of a legislature over programs which teachers and their friends see as absolutely worthwhile, frequently display a real ignorance of the legislative process as it affects education. Those who accuse the legislature of playing political football with educational policy are either ignorant of the legislative process or are themselves attempting to make political hay out of treatment afforded them by the legislature. Teachers are not the first group, nor will they be the last, to be frustrated in their fondest dreams by a legislature that fails to appreciate the quality of their cause. As long as the system exists in which the state legislature is a major policy-maker for education, some will see only agonizingly slow progress—if there is progress at all. However, criticism of the system needs to be tempered with a consideration of possible alternatives to what exists.

Like the state legislatures, the national legislature is also a reflection of the majority of society (or sometimes the collective reflection of local majorities with conflicting values). The great bulk of national legislation which deals with educational problems is of a traditional nature. That is, it supports traditional viewpoints and programs, and supplements on-going programs. In most of national legislation, Congress goes out of its way to attempt to make it clear that states are "sovereign" in this area and what Congress does should in no way affect the goals and policies of state systems. There is an important difference, however, between the national and state legislative policy-making systems. The difference lies in the much broader view of education which can be taken by Congress. The Congress of the United States is interested in the welfare of the whole nation and looks at problems of education on a national and even an international scale. This is not to say that congressmen do not have their local and parochial interests in education as in other matters. However, congressmen are compelled from time to time to think in broader terms. In its educational innovations Congress has most frequently related education to some broad domestic or international problem which faces the nation. The approach to agricultural education is a good case in point. So are the many specific programs such as the Job Corps, the Teacher Corps, and the Head Start program which have been enacted into law under the headings of national defense and the "war on poverty."

Another broad area of law which affects education and educational policy is previous court decisions. By their very nature, these tend to be conservative or traditional. The great bulk of school law, as interpreted by state courts, is concerned with relatively minor issues, dealing with specific problems which arise under the law. These involve such matters as teacher-pupil relations, the legal authority of school boards, and matters pertaining to local and state finance. In these cases, precedent figures prominently. Only rarely do courts strike out in new directions with sweeping new legal definitions which have serious and significant effects on the direction of educational policy. These few exceptional cases will be discussed in the following pages.

Finally, administrative law is an important aspect of the legal basis of the public schools. Administrative law refers to those countless orders, rules, explanations, and directives provided by executives or administrators on all levels of public education, which become necessary in order to implement public policy set by the legislative bodies. Such policy-making by administrators becomes necessary where the legislature deems it unwise, is pressed for time, feels incompetent, or for any other reason does not spell out in detail the programs which it authorizes.

Broad general legislative policy on education is administered by a myriad of officials in high and low places. In the implementation of legislative policy on education, the administrator frequently finds it necessary to issue directives, orders, and rules which spell out the general policy in some detail. This is actually a lawmaking process in itself. Perhaps it is on this level of lawmaking and implementation where the greatest amount of innovation occurs in education. At least the opportunity is there. Even though the administrator cannot create new programs, when he has large areas of discretion in implementation of policy and expenditure of funds, he can innovate. The great obstacle to innovation at this level is a bureaucratic tendency to follow established patterns. Innovations may be encouraged on the bureaucratic level in education where there is a close relationship between the administrators and academicians who may not be part of the official bureaucratic hierarchy, but who have a close clientele relationship with it. Thus, college professors are sometimes sought out for advice which may somehow filter into the system in the form of new plans. This assumes, of course, that administrators of state educational programs are in close touch with the researchers and imaginative teachers in the colleges and universities.

In summary, there is a great body of law, practice, and custom which underlies school policy at any given time in any given place in American society. Such a body of law emanating from so many different sources necessitates frequent interpretations by the courts.

THE MECHANICS OF INTERPRETATION

In the process of adjudication, the courts do not address themselves to matters which are in controversy except in cases where someone wants a court clarification of the law. Controversy determines the work of the court in a very real way. This is true of all courts in our system—local, state, and national—in most civil cases. With regard to education, the courts are frequently called upon to settle matters of controversy such as those which involve differences in views on the interpretation of the body of law underlying the educational system. It is true that the chief legal officer of the state, the attorney general, may be asked for an advisory opinion from the governor or the legislature when the administration of the law or the passage of some new law on the subject of education is being considered. In any state the attorney general may then review the proposed executive action or the proposed law, and give an opinion as to whether he feels that the proposed action or law is in conformance with the constitution of the state. The opinion of the attorney general is not binding in such cases, but it generally carries a great deal of weight. Compared to the courts, however, such interpretive functions on the part of the attorney general are limited. The great bulk of interpretation of the law as to its conformity with the constitution is done by the regular court system in most states.

There are many reasons for conflict in the application of the body of law which applies to education. One of the more important ones is brought about by poorly written laws. Another common reason for conflict is disagreement over the interpretation of the law by those who are responsible for administering it and those who are affected by it. The possibility of personal injury, either fancied or real, which might result from legislation, can be another reason for conflict.

Even with good help in the form of professional bill-writing services it is possible for laws on educational matters to be poorly written just as on any other subject under consideration by a state legislature. There are many reasons for this: legislators may lack experience in bill-writing, bills are often hastily considered, or the normal push and pull from interested groups and individuals can complicate an already difficult process, resulting in a poorly written bill or one containing serious errors. The possibility of conflict between state law and the state constitution is greatly increased in states where constitutions have numerous detailed provisions on education. As if these problems were not serious enough, there are few important bills on education finding their way into the statute books which do not represent some major compromises from contending forces. Every bill thus enacted into law has a ready-made opposition, ready to challenge it at the first opportunity.

Disagreement over the interpretation of the law once it is on the statute books is a major reason for court consideration of school law. Even the most carefully drawn legislation cannot anticipate every application. Moreover, it is quite common for the legislature to lay down broad general policy guidelines in its laws and leave the details of administration to the regular channels of administration. Where administrators are delegated discretionary powers by broad general grants of authority, they are frequently called upon to make decisions which are interpretive in nature. In a sense they must make value judgments. It is at this point in the process of administering the law that there arise many possibilities for disagreement. A great deal of the work of the court may arise from differences of opinion on the part of administrators and those they serve as to the proper interpretation of the law.

The implementation of the law by administrators charged with its implementation may be challenged by individuals or groups who are directly and adversely affected. For example, the legislative authority may set some broad general policy with regard to school district reorganization. The many details for implementation of the policy might be left to the state superintendent who may delegate this responsibility to county or district superintendents. Enthusiastic implementation of district reorganization on the local level might result in closing certain one-room schools. Those who oppose such a move on the local level might do so on legal grounds; that is, they might argue that local implementation of a law on reorganization is not in the spirit or letter of the law, and challenge the local action in the courts with a view toward getting a sympathetic interpretation of the law from the courts.

Sometimes citizens challenge school law or school officials operating under the law on the grounds that the law or its administration causes them personal injury of one sort or another. There are many cases in the history of any state court system which involve matters of school district liability where persons or property are involved and where citizens attempt to gain remuneration or other satisfaction from the school board which represents the district. In such cases, the courts find it necessary to examine the constitutional provisions and the laws governing school districts in order to fix legal responsibility. Similarly, many court cases have arisen over such questions as those involving the business affairs of a school district, the acquisition of land by school boards, the legality of bond issues and taxation, the constitutionality of loyalty oaths for school employees, and local rules on attendance of pupils.

The process of judicial review of the legal framework which surrounds education is no different from the process as it applies to other aspects of our society. A case originates in any number of ways, most commonly as a difference of opinion which cannot be settled out of court. A case in education may involve the interpretation of state law or national law; the state or national constitution; or an administrative rule, decision, or directive. To use a hypothetical illustration of the process, let us assume that a citizen (who becomes the plaintiff) decides that a state law which requires that the school day begin with a prayer is a violation of his rights under both the state and the national constitutions. He may first challenge the requirement in the state courts on the grounds that the law violates a provision in the state constitution. If a state constitutional matter is really at issue, the state supreme court may get the case on appeal from a lower court. If either party wishes to appeal this case (the appeal may be made by either party) to the Supreme Court of the United States, he may do so if the case involves a provision in the United States Constitution (which this one does). The Supreme Court will then decide if it wishes to hear the case. If it does, the Court can order the case upon a writ of certiorari. Then the case is placed on the docket of the Supreme Court, the arguments are heard, and the decision is made. Obviously, this is a simple explanation of a very complex process. A case could follow this process through the state and national courts, or it could follow any number of alternative courses. Generally, cases in which state law or the action of state officials is at stake are handled exclusively in state courts, while cases in which national law or the national Constitution are involved go directly into the national courts. Similarly, a state law which appears to violate some provision of the national Constitution may go directly to the national courts. The mechanics of the system are not nearly so important as the decisions of the courts on broad general education issues. Some of these broad educational issues have been decided by state courts, some by national courts; but there can be little question that the courts have played a significant role in the development of educational policy in the United States.

THE COURTS AS INTERPRETERS OF EDUCATIONAL POLICY

The State Courts

In the federal system the courts operate on two distinct levels—state and national. Generally speaking, the state courts are involved in the interpretation of state laws, while the national courts are concerned with the interpretation of laws enacted by Congress. However, in educational as in other matters, the Supreme Court has found it necessary to review acts of local and state educational agencies and officials as well as acts of state legislatures. Such review becomes necessary when it appears that there is a conflict between state action and the Constitution of the United States.

The great bulk of court action on educational matters is that which is taken by state courts, because the states are most active in the educational sphere. Moreover, state courts are called upon with frequency to decide a great variety of issues concerning education. In any recent year nearly any state supreme court might have on its docket cases which require interpretation of some state law on teachers, pupils, school property, school finance, school districts, and school officers, along with any number of other matters pertaining to the operation of the schools under state laws.

Sometimes cases that originate in state courts can deal with very basic issues. Recent examples are the cases brought by taxpayers who questioned the legality of the property tax as a means of school support. Although such cases were heard in a number of states by both state and national courts in 1971, the Alabama and California cases have received the greatest amount of publicity. In Alabama a three-judge United States district court, in the case of *Weissinger et al., and Vulcan Realty and Investment Company et al., v. Boswell,* ruled that Alabama's present property tax program was in violation of the equal protection clauses in both the Alabama and United States Constitutions. In California, the state supreme court in *Serrano v. Priest* ruled that the property tax denied children equal protection of the laws because it produced wide disparities among school districts in the amount of revenue available for education. The major principle involved in these and other property tax cases is that of equality. In most states, approximately half of the total cost of operating local schools comes from the property tax. Since property values, regardless of how they are assessed, vary greatly from one school district to another, there are sure to be inequities in the amount of money produced. There can be little doubt that property taxes as a means of school support will be challenged in a number of states in the next few years. Since it is a certainty that some of these cases will ultimately be appealed to the United States Supreme Court, one can only speculate on the long-term effects of state court action. For a more complete analysis of the property tax as a problem in school finance, the reader should see the following chapter.

Another example of state court consideration of school matters is the action of state courts in relation to teachers. Court interpretations of state laws designed to apply to teachers provide an excellent example of the many situations which may arise in a state and which require some kind of court action or interpretation. State laws on certification and qualification of teachers, contracts, loyalty oaths, tenure, union membership, and many others have been examined by state courts in recent years. Each year state courts hear many cases which involve the dismissal of teachers by a school board acting under the authority of state law. In some states if the teacher disagrees with the board's interpretation of the law, he may challenge that interpretation in the courts. To illustrate the nature of these kinds of uses, in a recent California case[2] a teacher who did not have his contract renewed by the board brought action in the courts. The board did not believe that the tenure laws of the state applied to this teacher and felt that they could legally refuse to reinstate him upon the expiration of his contract. The statute under which the board acted provided for tenure status, following a probationary period, for all employees in high school districts having an average daily attendance of 850 or more. In this particular case the court had to decide if the statute meant to include the seventh and eighth grade as part of a high school district. It decided that they were included, and that the teacher in question was under tenure. Although this case may seem insignificant and may apply to only one question and one teacher in a single school district, it does illustrate the kinds of questions which state courts are called upon to settle, and there are hundreds of such cases each year in these courts. No great principle is defined, no great precedent is established, but the decisions which are made on such matters are of vital concern to the individuals who bring suit.

Many actions have been brought by pupils and their parents against teachers on matters of discipline. This type of case may arise under a state law which prohibits corporal punishment. Let us suppose a teacher has a classroom of students who have tried his patience to the near-breaking point.

---

[2] *Meyer v. Board of Trustees,* 15 Cal. Rptr. 717.

As he attempts to restore order, he is insulted by a student and in a fit of rage he slaps the student. If the law provides for the dismissal of teachers who employ corporal punishment and the parents of the child wish to push the incident, they may demand the removal of the teacher. Let us assume further that the school board agrees with the parents and the teacher is dismissed. In this situation the teacher may have a court case. He may ask the courts to reverse the decision of the school board on the grounds that he has been dismissed illegally. Or, he may question whether the act he committed upon the student constituted corporal punishment as defined in the law. In this case, the court may be called upon to make the decision.

More recently, students have expressed concern over "student rights." The past decade has seen students challenging school rules on such matters as skirt and hair length. In some cases the courts have supported school officials, while in others the students have won their cases. For the most part, the battle over dress codes has been won by students; in many parts of the nation, in fact, school authorities have conceded that archaic dress codes are unenforceable. Students in many parts of the country have turned their attention to more basic issues. A most interesting recent case involved a particular form of protest against the war in Viet Nam. Some students in Des Moines, Iowa, decided to wear black armbands in protest of the war, violating a school rule prohibiting this form of protest. As school officials saw it, the wearing of armbands constituted disruptive conduct, and was grounds for dismissal. The students challenged the ruling in district court, where their lawyers argued that the rule was a violation of freedom of expression, a denial of the protection of the First Amendment to the United States Constitution. The court agreed with the students that the wearing of an armband for the purpose of expressing certain views "was closely akin to 'pure speech' which is entitled to comprehensive protection under the First Amendment . . . and that the school regulation . . . violated the students' rights of free speech under the First Amendment. . . ."[3]

As students have become more actively concerned with their rights as citizens, they have expanded their demands for protection of the exercise of these rights. In many school districts students continue to insist on freedom of expression in the burning issues of the day. Very often this involves the publication of journals of opinion without the censorship of school officials. Students are also demanding some voice in school policies which directly affect them. Most commonly this includes demands for some voice in curriculum, a greater choice of elective courses, a meaningful voice in the disciplinary rules under which they are expected to live, some consideration of student opinion in the selection and retention of teachers, criticism of

---

[3] *John F. Tinker v. Des Moines Independent Community School District, et al.,* 393 U.S. 503 (1968).

arbitrary systems of student evaluation, and "due process" for students who have somehow crossed the system. Most significantly, they are willing to face the risk of expulsion in order to bring such student rights to the attention of the community. Student groups seem willing to utilize whatever means are available to make their demands known, ranging from walkouts and picket lines to court battles. As students become more active in their concern over their rights as citizens, there is every reason to believe that the number of cases they bring to the courts will increase.

The courts are called upon to decide a tremendous volume of cases involving education and personnel in education. The reasons for this volume of work are many, the most important of which include the very quantity of law which surrounds education on the state level and the great number of people involved in and affected by the educational system. In spite of this volume of court work on educational matters and the large number of people involved, the typical school district is poorly prepared for legal action. A corporation located in a large city may retain a staff of several lawyers to handle the legal problems which develop in the normal course of its business. By contrast, the school district in the same city, which may operate on a much larger budget than the local corporation, and which operates under a large volume of state and national law which it is expected to interpret, implement, and observe, normally will retain a single lawyer on a part-time basis (provided the school can find the funds to do so or the lawyer who will be willing to serve in this capacity). Such a casual approach to school law creates many serious problems for school districts. With the proper legal assistance, local school boards and school officials might avoid some of the litigation, which can become burdensome.

Another problem which needs serious study is the relationship of the teacher and other school personnel to the law and the courts. Although some school districts have assumed liability for all of their employees so that they may bring some order out of the chaos of numerous suits against teachers, employees, and administrators, this is not yet general practice. For the most part, teachers still must rely on their professional organizations for legal assistance. In view of the great number of cases involving teachers in every state, this proves to be a poor solution at best. Good legal advice and assistance are not always available to the teacher. In practice, these problems become very serious when one considers the possibility that a single lawyer who is retained on a part-time basis by a school district, or by a professional organization acting in behalf of a teacher or group of teachers, may be pitted against a battery of lawyers for whom no expense has been spared in the attempt to enable them to win their case. Much remains to be done in the general area of school law in working out processes which will facilitate the interpretation and application of the law governing the educational enterprise on the state level.

The National Courts

The national courts have become increasingly involved with educational matters in recent years. Generally speaking, national courts have been involved in the broad general issues which have faced education in the past forty-five years. The Supreme Court of the United States has been called upon to interpret the acts of state educational agencies, officials, and state legislatures in the light of the conformity of these acts with the Constitution of the United States. Most of these cases have involved the Court's interpretation of the First and Fourteenth Amendments to the United States Constitution. In recent years the Supreme Court of the United States has acted in three broad general areas—education and religion, equal educational opportunity, and the loyalty of school personnel. No attempt will be made here to provide a full discussion of each, but examples will be provided to demonstrate how the Supreme Court becomes involved in issues which go right to the heart of the beliefs and values of American citizens.

Religion and schooling have been closely associated throughout history. Until very recently, few have questioned the place of certain kinds of religious practices in the public school classroom. From the first colonial experience there has been some dedication to the principle that the schools had a responsibility to at least acknowledge the existence of religious faith in the society, if not to attempt to promote it deliberately. The proper legal role of the schools with regard to religion was left to the states until well into the twentieth century, because the United States Constitution merely provided that "Congress shall make no law respecting an establishment of religion. . . ." Since the First Amendment was limited to a specific prohibition of the acts of Congress, the states were free under the Constitution to do anything they wished with regard to questions of religion. True, many states had provisions similar to the First Amendment in their constitutions, but throughout the nineteenth century and well into the twentieth there seemed to be little concern about the religious practices of schools. In fact, many religious denominations had established private schools, and state legal provisions on public schools frequently included references to the moral and religious purposes of public education. It is not uncommon to this day for school laws to contain statements of faith in God, or openly declare that "our society is based on Christian principles," or make other such references to religious faith.

This situation changed legally with the adoption of the Fourteenth Amendment in 1868. The wording of the Fourteenth Amendment which has application is the clause in the first section: "No State shall make or enforce any law which shall abridge the privileges or immunities of citizens of the United States; nor shall any State deprive any person of life, liberty, or property, without due process of law. . . ."

In many cases, especially in recent years, the Supreme Court of the United

States has interpreted the Fourteenth Amendment in a way that makes the provisions of the First Amendment applicable to the state and its agents and institutions; that is, where a state law, in the opinion of the Court, abridges citizens' rights contained in the First Amendment, the Court may nullify the law.

The reader should not get the idea, however, that the Supreme Court has, or can, settle the general questions of the proper relationship between the schools and religion by ruling in a number of specific cases. Quite the contrary. The only claim which can be made with reference to specific cases on religion and the schools which are decided by the Court is that the Court has ruled in that specific case and it may or may not have general applicability. Moreover, even in very similar cases involving identical points of law, the Court has reversed itself. Each case involves specific parties to a dispute, a particular constitutional issue, and a specific state law or ruling by an agent of the state. It would not be accurate to generalize from the cases which have come before the Court on the question of education and religion. One can only conclude that a specific case produced a specific decision.

Each case which comes before the Court that involves the question of religious freedom as defined by the First Amendment and applied by the Court through the Fourteenth Amendment is a difficult one. The legal definition of religious freedom is difficult because it always involves values which are deeply held by the contestants in the case. Moreover, the differences of opinion represented in any case reflect similar differences among large numbers in our society. This is true since there is such a great diversity of religious belief in the United States. The depth of feeling about religion and schools is illustrated by the fact that many religious denominations maintain their own elementary and secondary schools. There are, in fact, more than six million elementary and secondary school children enrolled in private schools in the United States. Many of these are schools maintained by church groups. The diversity of religious groups in the United States is illustrated by the following figures:[4] Buddhist, 60,000; Old Catholic, Polish National Catholic, etc., 497,527; Eastern Churches, 3,094,140; Jewish, 5,585,000; Roman Catholic, 44,874,371; and Protestant (226 bodies), 66,-854,200.

With such diversity in our population it is not difficult to understand why any position the Court takes relative to religion in the schools is sure to be a controversial one.

In recent years the Court has ruled in several broad general areas which involve education and religion.[5] The most controversial have been questions

---

[4] National Council of Churches of Christ in the U.S.A., *Yearbook of American Churches, 1965* (New York: Council Press, 1965).

[5] These areas are discussed and cases cited to illustrate them in Sam Duker, *The Public Schools and Religion* (New York: Harper & Row, 1966).

involving the use of tax money for what appears to some as a religious purpose or religious practice and activity in the public school classroom.

With regard to the question as to whether tax money can be used for religious purposes, the Court has generally said yes. In most of the cases which have been brought before the Court, the general principle of the "child benefit theory" has been followed. This general theory is based on the assumption that when a state or national law which provides financial assistance to private religious schools benefits the child rather than a specific religious denomination, the law does not violate the "establishment" clause of the First Amendment. Under this theory the Court has ruled that a state can provide textbooks[6] and transportation[7] for parochial school children without violating the First Amendment.

With regard to religious practices and activities in the public school classroom, the Court has taken the general position that these violate the First Amendment. Even when the practice does not appear religious but may "offend religious beliefs," the Court has ruled against them.[8] In an Illinois case, members of the Jewish, Roman Catholic, and Protestant faiths obtained permission from the board of education to allow students in grades four through nine to attend weekly classes in religious instruction. These classes were instructed by qualified persons of these faiths during the regular school day, and students were released from regular school activities to participate. Those who did not choose to participate were not released from regular school activities, but were requested to continue their regular school work. In this case the Court ruled that such activity on the part of the public schools was a violation of freedom of religion as defined in the First Amendment.[9] However, in a New York City case, where released time was provided by the school so that students could leave the school building and attend services of their choice, the Court ruled that this was not a violation of freedom of religion.[10] A key difference between the two cases was the fact that in the Illinois case, the facilities of the school were used and in the New York case they were not.

Another religious practice which has been rather common in American schools and has recently been considered by the Court is the practice of beginning the day with a prayer. A most controversial case was considered on this subject in New York.[11] In this case the New York State Board of Regents required that the following prayer be recited at the opening of each school day: "Almighty God, we acknowledge our dependence upon Thee,

[6] Cochran, et al., v. Louisiana State Board of Education, et al., 281 U.S. 370 (1930).
[7] Everson v. Board of Education, 330 U.S. 1 (1946).
[8] West Virginia State Board of Education v. Barnette, 319 U.S. 624 (1943).
[9] Illinois ex rel. McCullom v. Board of Education, 333 U.S. 203 (1948).
[10] Zorach v. Clauson, 343 U.S. 306 (1951).
[11] Engel v. Vitale, 383 U.S. 1261 (1962).

and we beg Thy blessings upon us, our parents, our teachers, and our Country."

A group of parents brought suit on the grounds that the requirement of such a prayer was a violation of the First Amendment. The Supreme Court agreed with them. The Court reasoned that the board was an agent of the state of New York acting in the name of the state and that this gave an official state stamp to a specific religious practice. In the opinion of the Court, this constituted a violation of the "establishment" clause of the First Amendment. The Court said in part:

> . . . We think that the constitutional prohibition against laws respecting an establishment of religion must at least mean that in this country it is not part of the business of government to compose official prayers for any group of the American people to recite as part of a religious program carried on by government.

In this case the Court also explained how it applied the First Amendment to the act of the state in these words:

> . . . The First Amendment was added to the Constitution to stand as a guarantee that neither the power nor the prestige of the Federal Government would be used to control, support or influence the kinds of prayer the American people can say, that the people's religions must not be subjected to the pressures of government for change each time a new political administration is elected to office. Under that Amendment's prohibition against governmental establishment of religion, as reinforced by the provisions of the Fourteenth Amendment, government in this country, be it state or federal, is without power to prescribe by law any particular form of prayer which is to be used as an official prayer in carrying on any program of governmentally sponsored religious activity.

Respecting the specific issue of the Regents' prayer, the Court said:

> Neither the fact that the prayer may be denominationally neutral, nor the fact that its observance on the part of the students is voluntary, can serve to free it from the limitations of the Establishment Clause . . . of the First Amendment. . . . A union of government and religion tends to destroy government and to degrade religion. . . .
>
> The Establishment Clause thus stands as an expression of principle on the part of the Founders of our Constitution that religion is too personal, too sacred, too holy, to permit its unhallowed perversion by a civil magistrate.

The Court held a similar view on Bible reading and prayer in *Schempp v. Abington* (1962), a Pennsylvania case; *Murray v. Curlett* (1963), a Maryland case; and in *Chamberlin v. Dade County Board of Public Instruction* (1963). In the *Chamberlin* case, the Court merely remanded the case to the Supreme

Court of Florida (which had upheld the school board and its program of religious activities) for review in light of the *Schempp* and *Murray* cases.

In 1968 the spectre of the old Scopes "monkey trial" reappeared after thirty years in the state of Arkansas. It involved a 1928 Arkansas law which prohibited the teaching of evolution in the schools. In 1965 Mrs. Susan Epperson, a science teacher, challenged the law as a violation of the First and Fourteenth Amendments to the United States Constitution. The case reached the Arkansas Supreme Court in 1967 and the anti-evolution law was upheld by that body on the grounds that it was a valid exercise of the state's power over the school curricula. In a unanimous decision, the United States Supreme Court agreed with Mrs. Epperson. The Court held that the Arkansas law was a violation of the First Amendment because it selected one segment from the "body of knowledge" which could not be taught merely because it seemed to conflict with a particular religious doctrine; that is, a particular and specific interpretation of the Book of Genesis. Justice Fortas, speaking for the Court, pointed out that "the First Amendment mandates governmental neutrality between religion and religion, and between religion and non-religion."[12]

The reader should not get the idea from this brief review of cases that the Supreme Court can provide any final definition of the First and Fourteenth Amendments which will have general application. In the first place, the Court has been known to change its view. For example, it changed its view on the flag salute issue in a very short period of time. Perhaps more important, even if one admits that the Court has been fairly consistent in its definition of the "establishment" clause, one must recognize that the Court cannot completely enforce its decision. The matter of religious practices in the schools is so deeply entrenched that complete elimination of religious exercises in the classroom seems a remote possibility. Millions of school children continue to start the school day with a prayer and in many communities this practice will not be challenged.

It has been challenged often enough, however, to demonstrate the controversial nature of religious practices in the public school. Perhaps controversy is most likely to occur in certain kinds of communities. Controversy which finds its way into the courts is most apt to occur in communities in which religious views are fervently defended and which are characterized by a great variety of religious groups. Frequently a community will have a strong numerical majority of one denomination with a large number of minority denominations. In such communities the majority group might be tempted to use the schools to promote its religious views. In such cases minority religious groups might understandably object, in a clear and sometimes emotional voice. In such circumstances in which peaceful resolution is impossible because of deeply held feelings, the national

---

[12] *Epperson v. Arkansas,* 393 U.S. 97 (1969).

government, represented by the Supreme Court as it interprets and defines the First Amendment, becomes the spokesman for the national conscience.

A similar situation has developed with regard to the question of equality. The Court has taken a rather clear position on the meaning of equality as it is expressed in these words of the Fourteenth Amendment:

... nor shall any State ... deny to any person within its jurisdiction the equal protection of the laws.

For many years the Court followed the principle set down in *Plessy v. Ferguson* (1896) in considering the definition of equality provided in the Fourteenth Amendment. In *Plessy v. Ferguson* the Court held that a Louisiana statute requiring railroads to provide "separate but equal" accommodations for whites and Blacks did not violate the "equal protection of the laws" clause of the Fourteenth Amendment. This ruling provided the justification for separate schools for Blacks for many years, not that Blacks and others who were interested in a more liberal definition of equality were satisfied with this definition—they were not—but they were unable to change the situation.

Step by step the Blacks worked toward a more liberal definition of equality under the Fourteenth Amendment. In *McCabe v. Atchison T.&S.F. Ry. Co.* (1914) the Court ruled that an Oklahoma law did not provide equal accommodations to Blacks and whites because it did not provide equal facilities on trains. In *Missouri ex. rel. Gains v. Canada* (1938) the Court ruled that the state of Missouri could not deny a Black admission to the law school of that state. Similarly, in *Sweatt v. Painter* (1950) the Court ruled that Texas did not provide equal facilities in its new law school for Blacks. In *McLaurin v. Oklahoma State Regents* (1950) the Court ruled that under equal protection of the laws, as stated in the Fourteenth Amendment, the Black student must be given the same treatment by the state as other students. There were other cases pointing in the same direction, but the great breakthrough came in 1954 in the case of *Brown v. Board of Education of Topeka.*

The *Brown* case was considered along with similar cases from South Carolina, Virginia, and Delaware. In each case Blacks were seeking the aid of the courts to obtain admission to the schools on a nonsegregated basis, and in each case the Blacks had been denied admission by laws which established segregated school systems. The Blacks claimed that such laws denied them equal protection of the law under the Fourteenth Amendment. In this series of cases the Court decided to look at the general effect of segregation on public education. Chief Justice Warren delivered the opinion in the *Brown* case, which said in part:

... In approaching this problem we cannot turn the clock back to 1868 when the Amendment was adopted or even to 1896 when *Plessy v. Ferguson* was written. We must consider public education in the light

of its full development and its present place in American life throughout the nation. Only in this way can it be determined if segregation in public schools deprives these plaintiffs of the equal protection of the laws.

Today education is perhaps the most important function of state and local governments. Compulsory school attendance laws and the great expenditures for education both demonstrate our recognition of the importance of education to our democratic society. It is required in the performance of our most basic public responsibilities, even service in the armed forces. It is the very foundation of good citizenship. Today it is a principal instrument in awakening the child to cultural values, in preparing him for later professional training, and in helping him to adjust normally to his environment. In these days, it is doubtful that any child may reasonably be expected to succeed in life if he is denied the opportunity of an education. Such an opportunity, where the state has undertaken to provide it, is a right which must be made available to all on equal terms.

. . . Does segregation of children in public schools solely on the basis of race, even though the physical facilities and other "tangible" factors may be equal, deprive the children of the minority group of equal educational opportunities? We believe that it does.[13]

In its reasoning, the Court quoted the following from the Kansas court which "nevertheless felt compelled to rule against" the Black plaintiffs:

Segregation of white and colored children in public schools has a detrimental effect upon the colored children. The impact is greater when it has the sanction of the law; for the policy of separating the races is usually interpreted as denoting the inferiority of the Negro group. A sense of inferiority affects the motivation of a child to learn. Segregation with the sanction of law, therefore, has a tendency to retard the educational and mental development of Negro children and to deprive them of some of the benefits they would receive in a racially integrated school system.

Then, in the words of Chief Justice Warren:

Whatever may have been the extent of psychological knowledge at the time of *Plessy v. Ferguson,* this finding is amply supported by modern authority. Any language in *Plessy v. Ferguson* contrary to this finding is rejected.

We conclude that in the field of public education the doctrine of "separate but equal" has no place. Separate educational facilities are inherently unequal. Therefore, we hold that the plaintiffs and others similarly situated for whom the actions have been brought are, by reason of the segregation complained of, deprived of the equal protection of the laws guaranteed by the Fourteenth Amendment.

---

[13] *Brown v. Board of Education of Topeka,* 347 U.S. 483 (1954).

The Court has ruled on a number of segregation cases since 1954. For the most part, they extend and support the basic position stated in the *Brown* case. In *Griffin v. County School Board* (1964) the Court interpreted the meaning of "all deliberate speed" urged in *Brown v. Board of Education of Topeka.* In the *Griffin* case, the Court said that "all deliberate speed has become a 'soft euphemism' for delay," and that "the time for mere 'deliberate speed' has run out and that phrase can no longer justify denying . . . school children their constitutional right to an education equal to that afforded by the public schools in other parts of Virginia."[14] In the *Gould* case (1968) the Court ruled against a freedom of choice plan in Arkansas as "inadequate to convert a racially segregated school system to a unitary, non-racial system. . . ."[15] In *Green v. County School Board of New Kent County* (1968) the Court ordered New Kent County school officials to present a plan for integration of its schools "that promises realistically to work, and promises realistically to work *now.*"[16] In a case involving the schools in Mississippi *(Alexander v. Holmes County Board of Education,* 1969) the Court ordered segregation ended immediately.

Nor have the courts limited themselves to extending and defining principles laid down in the *Brown* case. One of the most interesting and perhaps most significant school cases dealt with the inequalities within an integrated school system. For many years the Washington, D.C., school system had provided a two-track curriculum for students. One track consisted of traditional college preparatory subjects, while the other provided specific technical and vocational training. In practice, it developed that the vocational track was overwhelmingly populated with Black students. A group of Blacks protested that this was the worst sort of discrimination, since the vocational tracks provided only limited opportunity. In *Hobson v. Hansen*[17] District Judge J. Skelly Wright agreed. Judge Wright reasoned that the track system was undemocratic and discriminatory because "it is designed to prepare some children for white-collar, and other children for blue-collar, jobs." Judge Wright felt that the tests used to classify students were not reliable and the "danger of children completing their education wearing the wrong collar is far too great for this democracy to tolerate."

In April of 1971, the United States Supreme Court delivered a unanimous opinion on several cases involving the issue of segregated schools.[18] The

---

[14] *Griffin v. County School Board,* 377 U.S. 218 (1964).
[15] *Arthur Lee Raney, et al., v. The Board of Education of the Gould School District, et al.,* 391 U.S. 443 (1968).
[16] *Green v. County School Board of New Kent County,* 391 U.S. 430 (1968).
[17] *Julius W. Hobson v. Carl Hansen,* U.S. Federal Court 269, Federal Supplement 401 (1967).
[18] *Swan v. Mecklenburg Board of Education, et al., Law Week* (20 April 1971), vol. 39, no. 40.

major issue involved the bussing of students in order to achieve racial balance. The cases affected students in Charlotte, North Carolina; Athens, Georgia; and Mobile, Alabama. In Charlotte, the issue was whether or not a state law prohibiting bussing to achieve racial balance was constitutional. The Athens, Georgia, situation involved a school board plan to achieve racial balance by bussing students. In Mobile, the issue was the right of a school district to retain some all-Black schools.

In general, the Supreme Court ruled that the school districts involved must do everything possible to achieve racial balance. The Court supported bussing as a means for desegregation and gave its stamp of approval to desegregation plans which gerrymandered or paired school districts to achieve a racial mix. Although the decision is in keeping with the position of the Court since the *Brown* decision, it is difficult to predict what general effects it will have on segregated schools in the future. The decision was not a broad declaration of principle, but rather an application of constitutional principles to specific cases in selected southern school districts. The decision did nothing to resolve the issue of de facto segregation in the North or South. The immediate effects will be to give support to desegregation plans ordered by federal judges in specific school districts. The long-range effects will depend greatly on the enthusiasm of federal judges for integration within their jurisdiction and upon the action of the Justice Department in enforcing the law. In final analysis, the movement toward integrated education may hinge upon leadership provided by the president of the United States.

The Supreme Court of the United States has also been involved in educational matters when asked to rule on the constitutionality of state loyalty oaths. In the case of *Wieman v. Updegraff* (1952) the Court held an Oklahoma loyalty oath invalid. The Oklahoma law barred from public employment all state employees who could not swear that they had not been members of any subversive organization for the preceding five years. The Court ruled that the oath was a denial of due process since it made simple membership in listed organizations conclusive evidence of disloyalty. The Court reached a different decision in *Adler v. Board of Education.*[19] In this case, the Feinberg law of New York State was at issue. This law provided for the removal of all school employees who advocated the overthrow of the government by unlawful means, or who belonged to organizations that advocated overthrow of the government. Under the law, the Board of Regents was directed to list the organizations which advocated overthrow of the government by force and violence. Adler and others attempted to have the statute declared unconstitutional on the grounds that it constituted an

---

[19] *Adler v. Board of Education,* 342 U.S. 485 (1952).

abridgment of speech and assembly. Justice Minton delivered the opinion of the Court, saying in part:

... It is clear that such persons (the plaintiff) have the right under our law to assemble, speak, think, and believe as they will. ... It is equally clear that they have no right to work for the State in the school system on their own terms. ... If they do not choose to work on such terms, they are at liberty to retain their beliefs and associations and go elsewhere. Has the State thus deprived them of any right of free speech or assembly? We think not.

... A teacher works in a sensitive area in a schoolroom. There he shapes the attitude of young minds towards the society in which they live. In this, the State has a vital concern. It must preserve the integrity of the schools. That the school authorities have the right and duty to screen the officials, teachers, and employees as to their fitness to maintain the integrity of the schools as a part of ordered society, cannot be doubted.

In his dissent Justice Black said in part:

... This is another of those rapidly multiplying legislative enactments which make it dangerous—this time for school teachers—to think or say anything except what a transient majority happen to approve at the moment. Basically, these laws rest on the belief that government should supervise and limit the flow of ideas into the minds of men. The tendency of such governmental policy is to mold people into a common intellectual pattern. Quite a different governmental policy rests on the belief that government should leave the mind and spirit of man absolutely free. Such a governmental policy encourages varied intellectual outlooks in the belief that the best views will prevail. This policy of freedom is in my judgment embodied in the First Amendment and made applicable to the states by the Fourteenth. Because of this policy public officials cannot be constitutionally vested with powers to select the ideas people can think about, censor the public views they can express, or choose the persons or groups people can associate with.

In his dissent Justice Douglas said in part:

... The very threat of such a procedure is certain to raise havoc with academic freedom. Youthful indiscretions, mistaken causes, misguided enthusiasms—all long forgotten—become the ghosts of a harrowing present. Any organization committed to a liberal cause, any group organized to revolt against an hysterical trend, any committee launched to sponsor an unpopular program becomes suspect. ...

The law inevitably turns the school system into a spying project. Regular loyalty reports on the teachers must be made out. The principals become detectives; the students, the parents, the community become informers. Ears are cocked for tell-tale signs of disloyalty. The prejudices of the community come into play in searching out the disloyal. This is not the usual type of supervision which checks a teacher's competency; it is a system which searches for hidden meanings in a teacher's utterances.

What was the significance of the reference of the art teacher to socialism? Why was the history teacher so openly hostile to France, Spain? Who heard overtones of revolution in the English teacher's discussion of *The Grapes of Wrath*? . . . What happens under this law is typical of what happens in a police state. Teachers are under constant surveillance; their pasts are combed for signs of disloyalty; their utterances are watched for clues to dangerous thoughts. A pall is cast over the classroom.

. . . This, I think, is what happens when a censor looks over a teacher's shoulder. This system of spying and surveillance with its accompanying reports and trials cannot go hand in hand with academic freedom. It produces standardized thought, not the pursuit of truth. Yet it was the pursuit of truth which the First Amendment was designed to protect. . . .

In the *Elfbrandt* case (1967)[20] the Court struck down a loyalty oath in Arizona. In this case Mr. and Mrs. Elfbrandt, who were teachers in Arizona, refused to sign the Arizona loyalty oath because they felt it was a denial of their constitutional rights. The Court supported the Elfbrandts on the grounds that the particular wording of the Arizona oath implied guilt by association and thus infringed on freedoms protected in the Constitution.

In a purely local issue, the Court upheld the position of a teacher in the *Pickering* case in 1968. Marvin Pickering was a public school teacher in Illinois who wrote a letter to the local editor criticizing the manner in which the board of education and superintendent had handled proposals to raise revenue for the schools. Mr. Pickering was dismissed from his position and the dismissal was upheld by the Supreme Court of Illinois. The Supreme Court of the United States reversed the Illinois court's decision on the grounds that the dismissal violated Pickering's constitutional right to free speech. The Court found nothing in Mr. Pickering's letter to indicate libel or malice and reasoned that "a public school teacher's substantially correct comments on matters of public concern, although critical of school officials, may not, consistently with the constitutional guarantee of free speech, furnish grounds for dismissal. . . ."[21]

The above quotations illustrate some of the types of cases that affect school people, and questions of value which the Supreme Court of the United States has been called upon to settle. The divided opinion of the Court merely reflects a similar division in the society.

---

[20] *Elfbrandt v. Russell,* 384 U.S. 11 (1967).

[21] *Marvin L. Pickering v. Board of Education of Township High School District 205, Will County, Illinois,* 391 U.S. 563 (1968).

SOME CONCLUDING COMMENTS

The law which directs the operation of the educational enterprise in the United States is detailed, complex, and dynamic. The great bulk of the law which governs the daily operation of the schools in our society is state law enacted and placed on the statute books by the state legislature. Much of this law spells out in rather lengthy detail the things which school districts and school personnel can or cannot do. Even so, there remain large areas of discretion for school personnel and school officials.

The nature of the law on education reflects the nature of the society at the time the law was enacted. Generally speaking, the law does not innovate, but reflects the values of the community which it represents. Such values tend to be based on traditional ways of doing things.

When a conflict arises over the interpretation of the law as it applies to a specific problem in education and the conflict cannot be settled by other means, the courts must decide the meaning of the law in our system of government. State courts generally decide matters of state law, but there are times when the law which is in contention involves some basic principle of the national Constitution. Cases involving equality of opportunity, equal protection of the laws, the separation of church and state, and the loyalty of teachers have found their way into the Supreme Court of the United States in recent years. The questions involved in these cases and in others of a similar nature have been constitutional questions involving the First and Fourteenth Amendments. Even a brief study of the decisions of the Supreme Court on the pressing issues of society illustrates that the Court, historically at least, has been in general conformance with the prevailing beliefs of the national community. It might be argued that the Courts do not *make* policy, but rather reflect the thinking of the majority on any given case at any given time in our history.

The two major cases involving equal protection of the laws under the Fourteenth Amendment are a good case in point. The *Plessy v. Ferguson* case of 1896 provided one interpretation of the "equal protection" clause of the Fourteenth Amendment which apparently satisfied most Americans for several decades. As the environment and public feelings changed, values changed on the question of separate but equal facilities for Blacks. The Court reflected this change in the decision in *Brown v. Board of Education of Topeka* in 1954.

This was not a decision grasped out of thin air. There were many indications that it was on the way as the Court gradually changed its rulings on cases in higher education in the decade preceding the *Brown* case. These cases, too, were reflections of popular belief rather than moral or ethical value directives provided by the Court for a public which was unwilling to change. It would be extremely difficult for the system to operate otherwise.

Even though the Supreme Court spelled out in some detail how the decision in the *Brown* case should be implemented by the states, the application of the decision would have proved very difficult if a good part of the public had been unwilling to go along with it. This is apparent in the slow progress which has been made by some states. In truth, several states continue with a kind of de facto segregation in the face of the Court directive to integrate with "all deliberate speed." In 1971, seventeen years after the decision, the U. S. Office of Education estimated that more than one-quarter of the school districts in seventeen southern and border states continued to operate as segregated systems. No state which had segregated schools before the decision has totally integrated its schools. In fact, a majority of states which provided segregated schools before the *Brown* case have accomplished only token integrations. More than one thousand school districts in the South and in border states were segregated in 1970, while hundreds of de facto segregated districts in northern urban areas continued to operate schools which were 90 per cent or more Black or white. The implementation of judicial decisions, whether state or national, still requires cooperation of inferior courts, the legal administrative establishment of the national government and of the states, and the general approval of the public.

Court decisions, like the law, are not static. What is a majority opinion of the Court in one decade may become the minority opinion or dissenting opinion in the next. Moreover, it is difficult on some issues to determine the period of time during which a decision of the Court will stand. Court decisions tend to change with public feelings. Although the First Amendment freedoms appear to be absolute guarantees of freedom to citizens, they have been subjected to conflicting interpretations within the Court itself. During periods of fear of infiltration by communists and the real or imagined threat to the system's existence posed by the ideology of communism, many states sought to protect their children and their citizens from communist influence in the schools. There can be little doubt that loyalty oaths passed for this purpose during certain of the more trying periods of our recent past were eminently popular. The Court reflected the popular feeling in the *Adler* case cited above. However, there was a strong dissent from two justices, which, during calmer times and under different circumstances, might some day become the majority opinion of the public as well as of the Court.

All of the agencies and personnel involved in the educational enterprise operate in our society with an eye to public feeling, values, and tradition. The legislative policy tends to reflect current values. Constitutional provisions and legislative policy are viewed by the courts within the framework of an existing value orientation. The interpretation and implementation of policy by the legal agents and agencies of the state are made within this same framework. If one is looking toward these institutions and agencies to provide bold and imaginative leadership in education, he may have a long wait.

The situation is not hopeless, however, for change has been the rule rather than the exception in our society. Values reflected in customs or in the law have changed in the society. The pluralistic forces of the society have influenced change. In spite of the fact that the law is not a great innovator, neither is it a serious obstacle to change. One need only compare the educational system provided by law today with that provided by law of a generation ago to recognize change as an undeniable fact of life in education. New programs have been added—by law. Certification changes have been made—by law. The system has been expanded upward—by law. There are many such examples. Though there may be no sure guidelines which direct this change, few doubt that most of it has been in the direction of progress.

REFERENCES

Benson, Charles S. *The Cheerful Prospect: A Statement on the Future of Public Education.* Boston: Houghton Mifflin, 1965.

Butts, R. Freeman. *The American Tradition in Religion and Education.* Boston: Beacon Press, 1950.

Callahan, Raymond E. *An Introduction to Education in American Society.* New York: Alfred A. Knopf, 1956. Chapter 10.

Coons, John E., William Clune, and Stephen Sugarman. *Private Wealth and Public Education.* Cambridge, Mass: Belknap Press, 1970.

Cushman, Robert E. *Leading Constitutional Decisions.* 11th ed. New York: Appleton-Century-Crofts, 1958.

Duker, Sam. *The Public Schools and Religion.* New York: Harper & Row, 1966.

Edwards, Newton. *The Courts and the Public Schools.* Chicago: Univ. of Chicago Press, 1939.

Garber, Lee O. *Handbook of School Law.* New London, Conn.: Croft, 1954.

———. *Yearbook of School Law.* Danville, Ill.: Interstate (pub. ann.).

Levin, H. M. (ed.). *The Community School Controversy.* Washington, D.C.: The Brookings Institute, 1969.

McCord, John (ed.). *With All Deliberate Speed: Civil Rights Theory and Reality.* Urbana, Ill.: Univ. of Illinois Press, 1969.

National Council of Churches of Christ in the U.S.A. *Yearbook of American Churches, 1965.* New York: Council Press, 1965.

National Education Association. *School Law Series Research Report, The Pupil's Day in Court: Review of 1963.* Washington, D. C.: Research Division, 1963.

Nolte, Chester M., and John Philip Linn. *School Law for Teachers.* Danville, Ill.: Interstate, 1963.

Nunbaum, Michael. *Student Legal Rights: What They Are and How to Protect Them.* New York: Perennial Library, 1970.

Southern Education Reporting Service. *Statistical Summary of School Segregation–Desegregation in Southern and Border States.* Nashville, Tenn.: Dec. 1965.

Spurlock, Clark. *Education and the Supreme Court.* Urbana, Ill.: Univ. of Illinois Press, 1955.

7

Political Values and School Finance

The values held by Americans play an important role in school finance in the United States. In a very real sense, the things our citizens value determine how public resources are used, how much is spent on education, and the kinds of sources which will be tapped for support of the schools.

There has never been a time in our history when it was not necessary for the voters and their representatives to make hard choices on how public resources should be employed, and in spite of our present affluence this holds true today. Affluence does not solve the problem of the great range of alternative uses for public funds. Currently in the United States there are many possible uses for public funds, each of which promises to be insatiable. We must choose among space programs; defense needs; welfare needs; the needs of cities, roads, schools; and so on. There is no single activity in which government—local, state, or national—is engaged which could not profitably employ greatly increased appropriations. Where to allocate funds necessitates great and difficult choices which, in a democracy, are frequently based on what the majority seems to value most at a particular time.

The problem is further complicated by the fact that questions concerning the amount that ought to be spent on the schools are always considered on local, state, and national levels of government within some value framework or orientation. School people often claim that whatever amount they get is inadequate, while others in the society may see current expenditures for schools as more than necessary to provide adequate schooling.

Similarly, the question of values enters the problem of the kinds of sources which provide support for the schools of our society. A person who views schooling beyond a certain level as a privilege to be enjoyed by a limited number of our citizens is sure to have an entirely different view about where the money should come from than one who believes that schooling should be provided for all on an equal basis. Some might feel that the income tax provides a most equitable source for schooling, while others see a sales or property tax as the source which ought to be used for support of the schools. Again, whatever position is taken, it is generally defended from the value orientation of the person making the defense.

Whatever values are held in our society regarding adequate public spending for education, one can be reasonably sure that their general nature seems to be on the conservative side. This is generally true in any given community or state at any given time, since those who control spending tend to be conservative about it, in spite of frequent and sometimes emotional political oratory which deplores "reckless" or irresponsible spending of public money. The school board, which requests and appropriates funds for schools, may be conservative on economic questions by the very nature of its composition. Politicians who are seeking a place in the state legislature or in the governor's office rarely seek a reputation as "big spenders." More often such political candidates promise economy in government on the theory that this is the kind of government a majority of voters will value. The voters, in turn, often appear uninformed, or misinformed by political candidates, on the real money needs of the schools.

It is possible that the problem of school finance is less understood by the layman and the classroom teacher than is any other aspect of the educational system. This lack of understanding has serious consequences for the taxpayer, the school people, and the society. In practice, the lack of understanding results in the success of certain financial programs which may be of limited value to society and the failure of others which might adequately support a first-rate educational system.

There is a great deal of current evidence that school people and citizens generally do not understand either the process of educational finance or the financial needs of education. In many parts of the nation the general attitude prevails that so long as the schools are able to open their doors in September, so long as there are enough classrooms and seats to accommodate students and enough teachers to staff each classroom, there is no financial crisis in education. The evidence is there in the form of local school bond issues that fail to pass, revenue bills which fail to get out of legislative committees or are vetoed by governors, proposals for increased taxation which go down to defeat at the polls, and so on.

The layman approaches the problem of money for education with an attitude of ignorance, apathy, and ambivalence. The ignorance is often evident in the fact that he is rarely aware of the real needs of his local school system; the apathy stems from the fact that schooling seems to proceed in spite of all the wailing of the school people; and the ambivalence grows out of a concern for good schools on the one hand and an aversion to increased taxes on the other.

The school people, including teachers and administrators, have some of the same problems. There is reason to believe that large numbers of teachers (possibly a majority in many communities) are basically ignorant of the facts of political life. There has been a long-standing myth among teachers that there is little they can do or should do about school money matters. They have long considered problems of school finance a province reserved for the voter, taxpayer, or legislature. In the past, this belief has been supported in some instances by teachers' professional organizations. Historically, the organized profession of teaching has worked under the real or imagined assumption that the concern of a teachers' organization should not be with the realities of the politics of school finance, but with the qualifications of teachers or the standards of the profession. In the past, through their major professional organization, teachers have argued that excellence should come first and demands for adequate finance second. The history of the NEA (until quite recently) has been particularly altruistic in respect to matters of school finance. Many older teachers continue to argue that they are teaching not for money but for the psychic rewards of teaching. Although such missionary asceticism is difficult to find fault with, it must be admitted that it has not been realistic. Moreover, this philosophy has not only proved a financial handicap for teachers, but it has had a conditioning effect on the society which has slowed progress in the adequate financing of education.

Where teachers have labored for years under the assumption that if they do a good job and are professional in their attitude, the community will somehow reward them, there exists a reluctance on their part to become effectively involved in the politics of school finance. Moreover, when they do, they have so effectively sold the public on their nonpolitical role that their pressure in the political arena is often resented as unbecoming by politician and public alike.

Even where teachers do become militantly involved in local or state efforts for adequate finance through the political process, their efforts often look foolishly naive and, as often as not, end in disaster. This occurs because teachers have notoriously failed to apprise themselves of a basic minimum knowledge of the politics of school finance. One example should suffice to demonstrate the point. In a recent teachers' meeting in one of the western states, the state president of the Classroom Teachers Association informed his members that a measure, being referred to the people and providing for a large increase in state appropriations for education, "was sure to pass." The speaker was convinced beyond question that this was true since there were many groups behind the measure. When asked which groups were behind it, he named the state Chamber of Commerce, "the real estate people," the bankers, and the PTA. When asked about the support of the farmers and laborers, he said he wasn't sure about that. This occurred in a state where the combined potential vote of farmers and union members constituted more than 75 per cent of the electorate. One scarcely need comment on this situation.

Teachers have been notorious in their failure to study the economic and political situation in the states. Demands have been pushed on the legislature, the voters of the state, and the local voters, which have not been carefully prepared or properly studied. Support has not been cultivated and programs have not been prepared with proper consideration of political forces and pressures. In a word, teachers and the organizations which have represented them have displayed some genuine ignorance of the real world of politics.

Unfortunately, there is little literature in professional education on the problem of the politics of school finance. Moreover, those capable of writing on the subject have ignored it. Jesse Burkhead made an interesting comment on this point in a text on public school finance:

> The fact that there have been so few attempts to illuminate the politics of education is in itself worthy of comment. Part of the puzzle is that the profession of political science itself, with a few notable exceptions, has ignored the subject. Academics with an interest in the sociology of knowledge could well address themselves to the question of why it is that the two areas in our political culture which take the biggest slices of public money, defense at the national level and education at the state and local level, have received so little attention from professional political scientists. Political scientists seem to be attracted to subjects for research and analysis in inverse relation to their fiscal importance.[1]

The purpose of the next two chapters will be to outline some of the ways in which political values are associated with the effort to provide adequate educational finance.

EDUCATIONAL EXPENDITURE AS A POLITICAL PROBLEM

By its very nature, educational expenditure is a political problem in our system. The great bulk of support for education comes from the state and local levels, and the financial decisions are made by politically elected officeholders. This is also true on the national level.

Political values as expressed by successful politicians have always figured prominently in matters of school finance, but in the early days when schooling was simple, when it was controlled and administered locally, there was no serious problem. In any community citizens could band together and "raise" a schoolhouse with a minimum cash outlay. They could also hire a teacher, in many cases during much of the nineteenth century, without a cash outlay, or at least with a very small one. It was not at all uncommon for

---

[1] Jesse Burkhead, *Public School Finance* (Syracuse, N.Y.: Syracuse Univ. Press, 1964), p. 93.

teachers to be paid in surplus crops or to be boarded by families who would take their turn keeping them. This was a simple system for a largely unschooled population.

Contrast this with the problem of school finance today. During the 1969–1970 school year, according to various estimates by the United States Office of Education, the total expenditure for all public and private education, including higher education, was approximately $66.8 billion. Moreover, this figure had grown more than five billion dollars over the previous year. The increased costs have been reflected in per-pupil expenditures on the elementary and secondary levels. In 1953, the average per-pupil expenditure was $296 per year; in 1960 it had grown to $375; and by 1970, average per-pupil expenditures were estimated at $766.[2] This represents an increase of 104.3 per cent for the ten-year period.

Increased costs have been due more to a rapid increase in population and subsequent school enrollments than to any other single factor. During the ten-year period between 1953 and 1963, public and private school enrollment increased from 34.5 million to 51.4 million. In the fall of 1970, there were 59.1 million students enrolled in public and private schools, including colleges. Projections by the U.S. Office of Education predict an enrollment of 62.0 million in 1975. In order to meet this increased enrollment, the two most costly items—teachers and classroom space—have increased dramatically. The total instructional staff for all educational needs in the United States in 1953 was approximately 1.5 million. By 1963 this staff had increased to 2.3 million. The figure for 1971–1972 was estimated at 3.9 million full- and part-time professional workers.[3]

The great bulk of the billions spent on education in the United States can be placed in two general categories. The first is what we shall term capital outlay. Anyone who has traveled around the nation in recent years sees evidence of this type of educational expenditure all around him. New schools seem to sprout everywhere and even so they do not quite manage to keep pace with the need for physical space. The great bulk of capital outlay goes into new school buildings for all levels of education. The second category is current operating costs. This includes all of those items which are needed to staff and operate the school buildings. Where do the billions required for these two expenditures come from? Generally the money is raised by two methods: (1) legislative appropriation and/or permissive legislation which allows for funds to be raised locally, or (2) the sale of bonds.

No matter how the money is raised it is a political problem, since revenue for education requires a vote of the people or the representatives of the

---

[2] National Education Association, *Financial Status of the Public Schools, 1970* (Washington, D.C.: Committee on Educational Finance, 1970), p. 37.
[3] NEA, p. 18.

people. The methods of raising revenue will be discussed in some detail in a later section of this chapter. However it is raised, the money for education has become the most expensive and generally the most difficult problem facing state and local governments. The problem is enormously complicated in most states by a historical tradition which has provided serious obstacles to the development of an adequate financial system for the public schools. Most states are governed in their revenue-raising ability by archaic constitutional provisions dealing with the kind and amount of taxes which can be levied, provisions which closely prescribe acquisition of funds for capital improvements, and others which make a comprehensive program of school finance a difficult problem. Generally speaking, the school people and their friends have been content to push for temporary relief, for financial programs for education that are little more than stop gap moves which will enable them somehow to survive from one legislative session or one academic year to the next.

Any intelligent, adequate, and long-range program of school finance has been difficult to come by in most states because of the politics of the situation. Most states are in dire need of thorough reform in tax structures, procedures for raising revenue, and the machinery for administering state funds. Until now, the states have been very slow in providing the kind of overall reform that would be necessary for efficient fiscal operations. This has been true in most states because there is no great pressure group primarily interested in the kinds of governmental reform necessary to improve the state's ability to adequately finance its functions. The special interests and pressures which are effective before the legislature are more apt to be opposed to any general change in the tax structure, fiscal procedures, etc., in the state for fear that any change of the state financial structure might affect them adversely. No pressure group on the state level really speaks for the people. The result is the patchwork, "make-do" temporary expedients in tax programs which come out of the legislature each year or each biennium.

This problem is complicated by the fact that much of what the schools accomplish or fail to accomplish is not directly measurable. The problem of accountability for the success or failure of learning has always plagued the schools. In recent years, however, pressure for accountability in education has become acute. Leadership in the National Education Association has long claimed that one of the responsibilities of the profession is a self-policing function in order to maintain high standards of professionalism. Traditionally this seemed to mean that teachers should merely be competent and ethical in fulfilling their duties. For the most part, this continues to be the preferred definition of accountability for the leaders of teachers' organizations. Private entrepreneurs, however, mean something different when they speak of accountability; they mean the direct responsibility of the teacher to see that the student learns. Indeed, "learning accountability" has become so respectable that the U.S. Office of Education is now promoting it. The Bureau of Elementary and Secondary Education has assumed the duty of holding schools responsible for the learning successes and failures of their students. In this task, the U.S. Office of Education established a program in 1969 for the purpose of training "independent educational accomplishment auditors" whose job would consist of evaluating learning accomplishments of students involved in projects supported by the office.[4] Directly related to the learning accountability concept are the efforts of private organizations to contract with school districts for specific learning tasks. An example of such a program is Dorsett Educational Systems, which promised in a contractual arrangement with the Texarkana schools to raise, by a specified amount in a specified time, the math and reading levels of selected students in that system. Dorsett would be paid only for those students who succeeded. This particular contract has been under a cloud of suspicion because it was alleged that Dorsett people were directly preparing the students for the final test that the parties agreed upon as the means of progress evaluation. Even so, the U.S. Office of Education saw fit to grant more than a quarter of a million dollars for the project's continuation into a second year. Moreover, in the 1970–1971 academic year the U.S. Office of Education invested $5.6 million in performance contracts to six private companies and eighteen school districts. In addition, Philadelphia; Flint, Michigan; Ossining, New York; Gary, Indiana; and Camden, New Jersey were negotiating on their own for performance contracts in 1970.[5]

Obviously such private enterprise activities constitute some threat to teachers and their organizations. Perhaps the real problem which plagues school people however is the assumption upon which "learning accountability" rests: that there is indeed a specific quantitative measurement that will gauge learning. Professional educators have never really been completely sure that learning can be accurately measured. Obviously no test has been devised that can measure learning which takes place in the affective areas of human motivation, feelings, beliefs, values, and so on. Many educators feel that these are the most important areas. Given the resources and time, most teachers would agree that all normal children can be taught the three r's to whatever level of competence the community desires, but that this is not the most significant end of education. The end of education for many elementary teachers has always been—and continues to be—to develop human beings, to teach man to think for himself so that he may use the content and skills he has for some intelligent purpose. If specific and temporary accumulation of knowledge and skills is all there is to

---

[4] *Education U.S.A., The Weekly Newsletter on Education Affairs,* 10 Nov. 1969.
[5] *Education U.S.A.,* 3 Aug. 1970.

schooling, existing schools might well be replaced by a single teaching machine and a television receiver in each home. In the face of the real problems of war, race, and poverty which plague this society, one can't help but wonder if specified levels of accomplishment in math and reading are really what society should be demanding from its schools.

In view of the many long-standing claims that the major function of schools in a democratic society is to produce enlightened citizens, it is strange that teachers have expressed little opposition to the currently popular definition of "accountability." At any rate, teachers seem reluctant to attempt to prove to funding agencies that they are getting their money's worth in specific terms.

Unfortunately for the teachers and children, other pressure groups are not so reluctant to oppose increased educational appropriations. Existing pressure groups become most active when the legislature is considering revenue for adequate finance of state functions. These pressure groups are more often than not guided by self-interest rather than any idealized values. Adequate finance usually means taxes and most of the prominent pressure groups are in favor of new taxes only if they are levied on someone else. Under such circumstances, it is difficult to obtain agreement. Labor groups oppose sales taxes but favor corporation taxes. Corporation lobbyists, in turn, may work hard for a sales tax and oppose other taxes. Farmers want exemptions from general tax programs; politicians win elections on "no tax" campaigns; businessmen want tax programs which will encourage industrial development; and so it goes—no one speaks with any dedication for the general public, or for the children.

If teachers were politically alert, they could speak for the public. Teachers' groups could lobby for general reform in a continuous and, perhaps, effective way. As a group, teachers have the numbers and the resources to become a major and continuous reform agent in every state of the Union. Instead, they have been directing their efforts at intensive and too often futile attempts to gain just enough funds from the legislature to operate some kind of minimum school program for the next year or the next biennium. A year or two later they fight the same battle over again. It becomes an endless and too often fruitless battle.

There can be no question that every state in the Union staggers under serious financial problems, as there are always many more demands than there are available funds. There are many reasons for this, but one of the most serious is that states are handicapped by the patterns of historical development; that is, great numbers of people, legislators included, are still thinking in terms of an earlier day. The old myths persist in the face of new needs. A brief history of the development of educational finance might give the reader a better perspective within which to view current popular dollars-and-cents valuing of schooling.

A BRIEF HISTORY OF EDUCATIONAL FINANCE

The use of public money for the support of education has been a long uphill struggle in America. As a nation, we have not always been committed to a program of tax-supported education. Moreover, the move into tax-supported free public education has not been a carefully planned process. It has been, rather, a hit-or-miss process which has grown out of the environment of need. Under such circumstances the program has been characterized by little long-range planning and has managed, at best, only to keep pace with the need.

The tradition of school support in the United States is more one of localism than of state or national support. The Massachusetts school law of 1647 and the similar one in Connecticut in 1650 did not provide state support, but left the matter of securing funds entirely up to local agencies. The pattern was changed somewhat in Connecticut in 1795 when the state provided money received from the sale of its western lands to be distributed for educational purposes. A New York law in 1795 provided that funds were to be taken from the state revenues and given to municipalities for school use. However, this act was not renewed when it expired in 1800.

Localism continued to be the major pattern for school finance throughout most of the nineteenth century, although there were a few notable efforts to broaden the base of support for free public education during this period. During the years between 1835 and the Civil War, there was a great deal of propaganda and agitation for state support of public education. The battle for free public education was waged in the legislative halls of the various states by interested individuals and groups who brought pressure on the legislature to provide funds for public education.

Although those connected with the public schools in the present decade may at times become discouraged about the attitude of the public toward financial support of public education, the problems today are mild compared with those of an earlier century. The advocates of state aid for education were forced to undertake a major educational campaign to overcome deeply felt opposition to it. Referring to the attitude of the public toward school finance during much of the nineteenth century, Henry Morrison said:

> Less than half a century ago, citizens could be found in abundance who would "sacrifice the last dollar, sir, before, they would submit to the injustice of being taxed for the benefit of other people's children." Much more recently, individuals would proclaim their willingness to "rot in jail before sending my boy to school, if I don't want to."[6]

Much of nineteenth-century America was characterized by the existence of

---

[6] Henry C. Morrison, *School Revenue* (Chicago : Univ. of Chicago Press, 1930), p. 84.

a frontier and the predominance of agriculture as a way of life. An attitude in opposition to publicly financed mass schooling was realistic not only from the point of view of tradition but from an economic standpoint. Why should a man's son idle away his time in the schoolroom when he could be profitably employed on the farm?

Progress for tax-supported education was slow because of this kind of opposition. The first act which even approached a comprehensive system of public support of education came in 1745 in New York State in the form of an act for the "Encouragement of Schools." This act provided the sum of twenty thousand pounds per year to be appropriated for the purpose of "encouraging and maintaining schools in the several cities and towns" of New York State. In 1802 the Massachusetts legislature took a slightly different approach. Rather than appropriate money out of state funds, the legislature merely provided for the education of the poor at the expense of society. However, the money was to be raised locally within the township.

New York State once more took the lead in 1812 when it established the office of State Superintendent of Common Schools. The act specified in detail the duties and responsibilities of the superintendent, and was particularly detailed with regard to the so-called permanent school fund. This fund was created out of appropriations by the state legislature and from funds which were derived from the sale of public lands in New York State. According to the provisions of the act, the interest from this school fund was to be distributed on the basis of population during February of each year. Although population was used as a basis, the law required towns to raise a sum equal to that which was to be distributed by the state.

In the 1820's Vermont, Maine, New Hampshire, and Connecticut enacted school laws which provided supervision, the use of state funds, or both, in the support of the common schools. By the 1830's many states were moving in the direction of state support for public education. The laws which created a state superintendent of schools in Tennessee in 1836 and a state board of education in Massachusetts a year later were typical of the period. In Tennessee the state superintendent was given limited authority over the common school funds in the state. However, he was carefully limited in his powers and in the use of the funds. Under the Tennessee law, the local authorities who were legal custodians of school funds retained a large measure of responsibility for the collection and distribution of school money. In Massachusetts the board was empowered to handle money bequeathed to the state for educational purposes but was not given any real authority over the common school fund. The duties of the state school board were more regulatory in nature than they were financial. In Pennsylvania the first so-called free school law dates from 1834; in New Jersey a law in 1838 made the first effort to establish a system of state support.

The states which came into the Union under the provision of the Land

Ordinances of 1785 and 1787 provide a slightly different example of educational financial development. Ohio set the pattern when it was admitted in 1803. When Ohio was being considered for admission, the question arose in Congress as to whether the state ought to have the right to tax the public lands of the United States which were included within her proposed boundaries. The legislature of Ohio resolved this problem with Congress by agreeing not to tax the land owned by the United States. In return, Congress was to provide the new state of Ohio with the sixteenth section of each township to be used for purposes of education. This pattern was followed by all the states admitted to the Union after Ohio, with the exception of Texas, West Virginia, and Maine.[7]

The effect of this policy was to force states to consider some kind of system for the sale or administration of its school lands, and there followed, throughout the years preceding the Civil War, many state laws which provided for the establishment of a common school fund. Very often such laws provided for the establishment of some kind of state level organization for the administration and supervision of the fund. It was not until 1825, however, that Ohio passed a law which established a state system of education. In Indiana the foundation of a state-wide school system was laid in the constitution of 1851, and it was not until 1870 that Illinois had a state-wide system, established in its constitution.

By the time of the Civil War most of the northern states had the beginnings of a system of state-supported free elementary schools. The South continued to rely on local control and finance for the most part, in some cases until well into the twentieth century.

Thus, for more than a century after the Constitutional Convention of 1787, the pattern for the development of free public education was a mixture of education for the poor provided at the expense of taxpayers in the district or township, and state funds from the sale of public lands which were used to supplement local funds. Various patterns of organizational control developed for disbursement and administration of state funds. Really comprehensive patterns of state-supported education have been a twentieth-century phenomenon. In spite of the slow development of state support for education, however, one cannot overemphasize the importance of the efforts of individual states to provide for state financing of public education during the nineteenth century. This is particularly true when there is so much evidence of localism and such a long tradition of individual or private responsibility for schooling. Although there were many forces working against the traditional patterns, it was an uphill battle. When one considers the long period during which education was controlled by religious groups, the antagonism to-

---

[7] Ellwood P. Cubberley, *Public Education in the United States,* rev. ed. (Boston: Houghton Mifflin, 1947), p. 92.

ward taxation for education—in some cases even for the poor—and the general attitude that education was an unnecessary luxury, it is quite remarkable that so much was accomplished during the nineteenth century.

Many explanations for the development of free public education in the United States have been offered. However, three major forces which worked for the development of tax-supported state systems of education stand out sharply. These include the forces of political coincidence or accident, leadership provided by a number of idealists, and the growth of industry. Although each of these forces is interrelated, in themselves each one contributed significantly to the enactment of legislative and constitutional measures which established state-supported and state-directed educational systems.

The two major political coincidences worth noting are the admission of Ohio under the Land Ordinance of 1787 and the extension of suffrage in the new states which were admitted after 1803. It is doubtful whether the citizens of Ohio, for example, were very much dedicated to the ideal of a state system of public education when they were admitted to the Union in 1803, because at that time they were in the frontier stage of their development. By 1803 only a few states had dabbled in the establishment of such a system. Localism in education was the rule rather than the exception. This would have been particularly true in Ohio, where, because of its totally rural environment, only a few were seriously concerned with public education. However, the national provision that a section of land be set aside within each township to provide for education was legal fact with which the legislature had to deal. The existence of this public land in Ohio, and other states which were admitted later under the same terms, had a direct and fortuitous influence on the development of state support and supervision of education.

The other political coincidence of great significance for public education was the extension of the suffrage. This was a coincidence in the sense that it occurred at a time when certain other forces were working in conjunction with it to push forward for state support for public schools. These forces included the rise of the workingman, industrialization, the growing cities, and a rapidly expanding population. By the time of the election of Andrew Jackson in 1828, the suffrage had been widely extended in the United States. Although there were many reasons for this extension, it was widely reflected in the more liberal provision on suffrage which characterized the constitutions of the new states admitted after 1800. While the original thirteen states had erected many barriers to suffrage, the states admitted after 1800 tended to place fewer restrictions on universal manhood suffrage. Following this example, the original states extended the ballot within their own borders. For the most part this movement was led by politicians who were eager to extend voting rights. The extension of the suffrage to the propertyless masses is nowhere better illustrated than in Pennsylvania, where there were only forty-seven thousand votes cast in the election of 1824; four years later the number of votes cast in that election reached nearly one hundred fifty thousand.

The significance of the extension of suffrage during the period from 1820 to 1850 is very great with respect to state-supported public education. The masses who had gained the ballot were not at all reluctant to favor tax support for schools. Moreover, they were not completely unsympathetic toward some state political control over education.

In this environment, limited success was possible from some of the most ardent and articulate supporters of public education. The advocates of state support could write proposals and see them enacted into law or written into the constitution. As secretary of the state board of education in Massachusetts, Horace Mann was able to make some progress toward public support and control of education in that state. A politician as well as an educator, Mann had presided in the Massachusetts Senate when the bill which created the state board of education was passed. He became secretary of the board in 1837 and remained in that position for twelve years. Mann used the device of the Annual Report to the State Board of Education to make his views on education known. Not one to shun controversy, he took on any individual or group who appeared to be in opposition to the idea of public education. The most notable of these controversies was the public debate he carried on with the leaders of various religious groups in Massachusetts who were opposed to free public education. Perhaps the greatest indication of Mann's success in his struggle for state-supported and state-controlled schools was the fact that state appropriations for education more than doubled during his tenure as secretary to the board of education.

Henry Barnard played a similar role in Connecticut and Rhode Island. He was state commissioner of education in Connecticut for four years from 1838 to 1842 and held the same position in Rhode Island from 1843 to 1849. Barnard was very active in Connecticut in assembling statistics on school attendance, organizing libraries, making speeches, helping organize union schools, and many other projects. Perhaps his greatest contribution was that of propagandist for the public school movement in Connecticut. He was so effective in arousing and channeling public interest in education there that he succeeded in offending some political leaders. Governor Cleveland decided he could do without the services of Barnard, as they were sometimes conducted with such zeal that it was embarrassing to the governor. Barnard then moved to Rhode Island. When the political climate became more favorable, he returned to Connecticut, where he served as ex-officio secretary of the Connecticut state board of education. During the 1850's Barnard was successful in pushing for new school laws which increased state appropriations and state control over the school system.

Although Mann and Barnard are the two most outstanding examples of men who were at the vanguard of the movement for state support and state control of education, nearly every state in the Union has had one or more of the same type. The more prominent of these included Calvin Stowe and Sam Galloway in Ohio; Caleb Mills in Indiana; Ninian Edwards in Illinois; Isaac E. Crary and John Pierce in Michigan; Robert J. Brekenridge in Kentucky; and Calvin H. Wiley in North Carolina.[8]

Although the influence of these great educational leaders is impossible to measure, it can be overemphasized. Leaders alone do not make a movement. The generation before the Civil War did experience a real grass-roots movement in the direction of state support and state control of education, which has continued down to the present. As great as they were, such leaders as Mann and Barnard probably could not have been successful without the proper environment. Where such leaders did achieve success was where the people who could made their feelings known through the ballot box were ready to accept the kind of leadership they had to offer. The sentiment for state support and state control of education existed; men like Barnard and Mann capitalized on this sentiment and provided the practical suggestions for its implementation which could be enacted into law.

Perhaps the greatest force pushing the various states into the area of financial support and control of public education was that of industry. Industry was developing rapidly in the United States during the generation from 1830 to the Civil War. The effects of early industrialization in the United States is a familiar story. It encouraged immigration, which increased from approximately 100,000 per year in 1840 to nearly 410,000 in 1854; it encouraged the development of cities and the growth of a large group of propertyless workers. Most significantly for education, this growth of the working class enabled the workers to gain political control in some of the areas in which suffrage had been extended to include them. Workingmen's parties were organized in the more heavily populated sections of the country, and these experienced some success in politics. Not only did the early workingmen's associations work for political candidates of their liking, but they were very effective in New York, Pennsylvania, Massachusetts, and other states in pushing demands for free schools. Typical of the workingmen's expression in favor of free education was the following resolution by the Workingmen of New York City in 1829:

That the most grievous species of inequality is that produced by inequality in education, and that a national system of education and guardianship which shall furnish to all children of the land equal food, clothing, and instruction at the public expense is the only effectual remedy for this and for almost every species of injustice. Resolved, that

---

[8] For a comprehensive discussion of the battle for state-supported schools and the leaders in the movement, see Chapter 7 in Cubberley.

all other modes of reforms are, compared to this particular, inefficient or trifling.[9]

It was largely as a result of the pressure of the workingmen's associations that the first aid and state control programs for free education were established in the industrial states of the Northeast. These states, in turn, set the pattern for the development of state aid and state control in other states. It is interesting to note that complete local financing and control of education was slowest in coming to the rural states of the South. To this day, the localism which persists in education is more apt to be found in the rural agricultural states than it is in the industrial states of the nation.

Industrialization created other problems as well which worked in a more or less impersonal way to force the states into a more active educational role. Early industrialization encouraged child labor, which had become a serious problem by 1870. Many politically oriented groups, on both the national and state levels, were denouncing it. There followed a series of child labor laws enacted by state legislatures. This movement was so successful by the late 1920's that a proposed child labor amendment to the Constitution was not ratified by the states largely on the grounds that the states already had so many such statutes on their books that a national Constitution provision was no longer necessary. Accompanying the child labor provisions in state statutes and constitutions were provisions in several states for compulsory school attendance.

The nature of the industrial system as it developed during the late nineteenth and early twentieth centuries was such that it was plagued by recurrent depressions characterized by panics and mass unemployment. This feature of the system also had its effect on pressure for the upward extension of years of schooling.

The twentieth-century effort of the states in support and control of education has been a story of geometric expansion. During the period from 1900 to 1915, state aid to local school districts increased by one and one-half times. Local support doubled during the same years. During the next fifteen-year period from 1915 to 1930, state aid increased another two and one-half times, while local support of schools increased in an even greater amount. Increasing state aid and state control of public education has been an outstanding feature of this century. Whereas only ten states provided more than 50 per cent of the financial support for education in 1890, by 1960 eighteen states provided more than 50 per cent.[10] Because of increasing contributions by the national government since 1965, only fourteen states provided more than 50 per cent of the financial support for education in

---

[9] Harry J. Carman and Harold C. Syrett, *A History of the American People* (New York: Alfred A. Knopf, 1956), p. 459.

[10] Paul R. Mort, *et al., Public School Finance* (New York: McGraw-Hill, 1960), p. 197.

1970.[11] Perhaps more significant than numbers is the fact that the twentieth century has experienced much greater financial centralization in state educational systems. Without exception, the local school district in every state is dependent upon the state legislature. Even where a major part of the school money is raised locally, permission to do this is granted by the state legislature if such provision is not spelled out in the constitution. Moreover, there is a great deal of control from the state level concerning proper or legal school expenditures.

The most serious and continuing problem in public education in the twentieth century has been the search for money. Total expenditures for public elementary and secondary schools have increased tremendously during this period. The next two sections of this chapter will deal with the questions of how this money is spent and where it comes from.

HOW THE MONEY IS SPENT

School money is spent for three very broad general purposes; current expenditures, capital outlay, and debt services. The great bulk of the expenditures is spent under the first category. For the 1969–1970 school year, for example, from a total expenditure of approximately $39.5 billion for public elementary and secondary schools, about $32.3 billion was budgeted for current expenditures while approximately $7.2 billion was allocated to capital outlay.[12] Of course, averages can be misleading; some school districts have spent virtually nothing on capital outlay while others have spent great amounts. Obviously the school district which has experienced tremendous problems of population growth has been forced to spend a great deal more than rural districts where the school population has remained relatively stable.

The Nature of Current Expenditures

Current expenditures may be generally defined as the money spent by the school district in the day-to-day operation of the school. Obviously, such expenditures include a wide variety of purposes and activities. By far the most costly of all operations for the public schools is instruction, of which the most expensive item is teachers' salaries. Most school districts spend more than 60 per cent of their total available money on this alone. Of course, it is very difficult to generalize about it in any school budget as some districts may

---

[11] National Education Association, *Estimates of School Statistics, 1969–1970* (Washington, D.C.: Research Division, 1969), (R-15), p. 35.
[12] NEA, *Financial Status*, p. 36.

spend less than 60 per cent on teachers' salaries, while others may spend most of their current operating expenses on salaries.

Aside from teachers' salaries, there is a multitude of operating expenses which makes demands on the money available to school districts. Some of the most important of these include: maintenance, transportation costs, fixed charges, fringe benefits for teachers, and administration and auxiliary services. Any attempt to classify such expenditures in a general system is fraught with the possibility of error, since each state has its own system of budgeting for schools. Even districts within a single state may have a different system. However, in most districts, both rural and urban, transportation of students and maintenance costs represent a significant outlay of current operating expenditures. Moreover, in most school districts it is extremely difficult to effect economies of any great significance in either of these areas. Fixed costs might include such items as premiums for insurance and charges for utilities; in some school districts there may be fixed costs on workmen's compensation and unemployment insurance for certain employees. Some school districts budget the costs of retirement and insurance benefits for faculty and school administrators under salary, while others might list these costs under the heading of current operating expenditures. Most school districts operate what we shall term auxiliary enterprises, which would typically include such things as bookstores, athletic or band programs, and cafeterias. In some school districts these functions are self-supporting; in others they are not.

An item which is conspicuously small in educational expenditures is research and development. While it is not uncommon for private industry to expend as much as 20 per cent or more per year for research and development, it is not uncommon for local school districts to spend less than 1 per cent for this purpose. Moreover, much of what is spent on research and development comes from the national government and is a fairly recent phenomenon in education. For example, during the five-year period from 1960 to 1965, the total estimated expenditures for educational research in the United States grew from about $33 million in 1960 to approximately $98 million in 1965.[13] As might be expected, the local share of the 1965 total was about 3 per cent, or approximately $3 million; the state's share amounted to $11 million; while the national government contributed more than $69 million. The remainder was made up by foundation aid to research. The bulk of the national funds for research in education has gone to nine university research and development centers and fifteen regional educational laboratories which were initiated in 1965. In fiscal 1970 these centers and laboratories were allocated $70 million by Congress. The total national outlay for

---

[13] *Digest of Educational Statistics* (Washington, D.C.: U.S. Dept. of Health, Education, and Welfare, 1970), p. 127.

research and development in pre-school, elementary, and secondary education for fiscal 1971 was estimated by the Bureau of the Budget at $244 million.[14]

Although the dollar amount seems large, when considered in terms of a total educational expenditure of nearly $40 billion, it becomes an almost insignificant part of the total budget. Moreover, the fact that the national government provides the overwhelming share of funds for research and development is significant in itself, in that states and local school districts are not providing the stimulus for their own research on problems they consider important on the local level. When local districts are interested in research funds, they must present proposals which satisfy guidelines and goals laid down by funding agencies. Thus local researchers often find themselves guided more by national goals and priorities than by local interests and needs. In practice this is often translated by those interested in educational research and development on the local level into the question of what the national government is interested in funding, rather than what local problem needs to be researched. Nor is this picture likely to change unless local school boards see the need for funding research and development on the local level. Of course research and development is important to schools, as it is to industry, if reasoned changes are to be made in local schools and if the system is to be generally improved.

Perhaps the most effective way for the prospective teacher to learn about how the money in education is spent is to study the budget in a specific school system. Teachers and citizens have been somewhat apathetic toward school budgets in the past, a puzzling phenomenon in light of the great public interest which is normally expressed in state budgets and frequently in municipal budgets, and on questions involving taxation. Citizens have traditionally been quite interested in how money is spent by the state legislature and city council, but they have only infrequently expressed concern about how the local school board disposes of its funds. For many citizens, the whole business of school budgeting remains a mystery. This is even more puzzling in light of the fact that in many states the bulk of public money is spent on schools. Teachers and laymen should become much more aware of, and much more interested in both the nature and process of school budgeting. Most teachers and laymen would have no idea what proportion of the school budget was spent on salaries for instructional staff and what proportion was spent on auxiliary enterprises in their local school district. This is not meant to be an argument for petty teacher and lay criticisms of the local board and school administrator; it is rather an argument for intelligence in matters of public finance.

---

[14] *Special Analyses, Budget of the United States, Fiscal Year 1971* (Washington, D.C.: U. S. Government Document), p. 121.

School boards and administrators which serve them should encourage the curiosity of teachers and laymen and, where clear and thorough explanations of the school's budget are not made regularly, they should be demanded by teachers and laymen. This would be to the advantage of the board and the administrators, since teachers and laymen tend to grumble somewhat about the high cost of certain programs such as school cafeterias, the band, and athletic programs, without the slightest understanding of the problems of school finance. Indeed, an often heard complaint from teachers could be stated in these terms: "We might get a raise in salary if it weren't for the fact that our district spends so much money on football and band." Although such statements may be based on fact, they seldom are. More often the critic is assuming something to be true but has no real evidence. Moreover, if he attempted to get such evidence from those who have it, he would probably be cast under serious suspicion. This is an unfortunate situation which exists in all too many school districts. School budgets are a matter of public record and the more public they can be made the better. The teacher, and particularly the taxpayer-voter, need to be informed frequently and in some detail on how the local school spends its money. In all too many districts, the only realistic way to learn the economic facts of life about the operation of the local school is to serve a term on the school board—a privilege that is limited to only a few, since only a few have the interest, the time, and the public stature to run for the position in most communities.

The Nature of Capital Outlay

Funds for capital outlay include such things as money for buildings, land, and equipment. Since the end of World War II, the total expenditure for such items has increased greatly. During the 1952–1953 school year, total capital outlay for public elementary and secondary schools amounted to a little more than two billion dollars.[15] Seventeen years later it had increased to approximately $4.7 billion,[16] or a little less than 12 per cent of the total educational expenditure. The increase in capital outlay has been due to many factors: most important, of course, has been the increase of school enrollment. Added to this, the status of school facilities was not very good at the end of World War II. Little had been spent to keep up with the normal demands of population during the depression and World War II; even the normal processes of repair, renovation, and replacement were neglected. Added to this, the tremendous burst in school population beginning in the late 1940's and continuing to the present created a real problem in school finance. As if the sheer physical problem of numbers were not enough, financial pressures

---

[15] National Education Association, *Estimates of School Statistics, 1965–1966* (Washington, D.C.: Research Division, 1965), (R-17), p. 5.
[16] NEA, *Estimates of School Statistics, 1969–1970*, p. 21.

increased due to inflationary trends which tended to hit capital outlay needs in a way which complicated an already difficult problem. The price of land needed for new buildings has doubled on the average of once every ten years almost everywhere in the nation, and the cost of labor and materials has matched the increase in land prices. The total volume of money for capital outlay has had to double in each decade since 1945 in order merely to keep pace with normal growth needs. Expenditures for capital outlay were the most dramatically noticeable aspect of American education in the twenty-five years since 1945. Many medium-sized towns had poured effort, money, and pride into a single local high school during the school-building boom of the 1920's. These had become great and sometimes nostalgic landmarks in the small cities and towns across the country. Often they were the most magnificent buildings for miles around—a living testimonial to the dedication of the townspeople to education. The building of a school was undertaken with great care and pride and dedicated by the town fathers to serve the town for many generations to come. Since 1945 the picture has changed abruptly. For most students of college age today, the old building has become an eyesore if it has not already been replaced. Beginning with the elementary schools, every community of more than one hundred thousand population experienced a frenzy of school-building in the late 1940's. The process was repeated a few years later with junior high schools, and a few years later with senior high schools. Towns which had had only one high school for years suddenly found themselves with four or five, each of which housed more students than the original town high school. The present generation of college students more or less takes for granted the fact that the larger cities in their state may have two or three major school buildings in various stages of construction at all times. Providing the money for buildings adequate to house the rapidly growing school population since the end of World War II may be the greatest success story in the history of education. Still it has not been enough—funds for capital outlay have barely kept pace with the needs, and in many areas adequate or acceptable classroom space is still a long way from reality.

The great expenditure involved in the building program of the last twenty-five years has increased the cost of debt services. Debt service is defined in the following manner by one student of school finance:

> When a school district borrows money, the borrowed money is usually spent for capital outlay purposes and these expenditures are classified as capital outlay expenditures. The expenditures necessary to repay the borrowed money are debt service expenditures and include both principal and interest on the loan plus any costs which are incurred in employing a bank or some other financial agency to handle the details involved in retiring the loan.[17]

[17] John E. Corbally, *School Finance* (Boston: Allyn & Bacon, 1962), p. 47.

Most school districts have to go into debt to pay for the new schools, since few school districts have on hand the money to build new ones. This debt has become a very costly item in some school districts. One quarter of the nation's schools are spending a little over twenty dollars on school buildings for every one hundred dollars of net current expenditures. During the 1959–1960 school year, total expenditures for interest on debt amounted to a little less than half a billion dollars. By 1970, this amount had increased to a little over a billion dollars.[18] Unfortunately, those school districts hardest hit by the need to borrow in order to house increasing school populations have been the urban districts. Most urban districts have thus been caught in the double squeeze of increasing costs for current operating expenses and increasing interest burdens on money borrowed to provide the needed facilities.

WHERE THE MONEY COMES FROM

In a very general way, the public schools get their money from three major sources. These are intergovernmental revenue, borrowing, and taxation. Intergovernmental revenue includes the money provided for the local school district by the county or the municipality, the state, and the national government. Funds raised locally, within the school district or on the county and municipal level, remain the major source of revenue for our public schools. However, state and national support for local schools is becoming increasingly important. The following chart illustrates the major sources of revenue for public education during the five decades ending with 1970.

It is interesting to note that the proportion of state and local support for public education has not changed greatly in the last decade. Federal support,

Governmental Support for Public Education[19]
(Selected Years)

School Year Ending	Federal	(Per Cent of Total) State	Local
1920	0.3	16.6	83.2
1930	0.4	16.9	82.7
1940	1.8	30.3	67.9
1950	2.8	39.9	57.4
1960	4.4	39.1	56.5
1970 (estimated)[20]	6.7	40.8	52.5

[18] NEA, *Estimates of School Statistics, 1969–1970,* p. 27.
[19] Burkhead, p. 179.
[20] NEA, *Financial Status,* p. 49.

however, had increased significantly by 1960, and by 1970 it was an even more important part of the public school finance picture. The 6.7 per cent total represented more than two billion dollars of federal funds for use by local districts in the support of elementary and secondary education. The general elementary and secondary federal aid bill, HR 2362, which became law in the spring of 1965, provided for a total of $1.3 billion for education. Each succeeding year has witnessed increasing appropriations by Congress. In 1970 the total amounted to more than $2.3 billion.[21] Much of this has gone to school districts serving low-income families. Grants have been made on the basis of the number of children in families within the poverty classification. Such grants have amounted to as much as one-half the average state-wide per pupil expenditure for each child. In some states and localities this money has dramatically affected the percentage of support from various sources. In some school districts revenue from the bill has provided as much as one-third of the total for the school district. For the nation as a whole it has substantially increased the percentage of total aid provided by the national government to elementary and secondary schools.

A second major source of revenue for public schools is borrowing. Very few school districts can provide the needed facilities for education without going into debt. This situation has developed in a way which is very familiar to most families in the post World War II era. Few families are able to pay cash for the homes in which they live. It has been customary in the past twenty-five years or more for families to borrow the money with which to build a house and to spread the repayment cost over a period of years. The growing school districts have had to face the same problem. If anything, the school district has had even more serious problems with long-term financing than individuals and families have. In the first place it is extremely difficult for the school district to set aside money for future building needs. Although in some states the laws may provide for a reserve or sinking fund which is to be set aside to provide for major buildings as they are needed, this has become more the exception than the rule. With the pressures of population, increasing costs, and escalating needs, few school districts have been able to provide for future building needs. Consequently, school districts have found it necessary to borrow in order to build and equip the necessary classrooms.

The most common method used by districts for borrowing to provide necessary plants and equipment is through the sale of bonds. A bond may be defined as "a legal instrument or contract in which a corporate body promises to pay within a certain time the amount borrowed with interest at some fixed rate payable at certain stated intervals."[22]

Traditionally school districts have experienced very little difficulty in

---

[21] NEA, *Financial Status,* p. 49.
[22] Arvid J. Burke, *Financing Public Schools in the United States* (New York: Harper & Row, 1957), p. 195.

acquiring money for capital outlay needs through the sale of bonds. Every state constitution or statutes provides the means by which bonds may be sold. Generally, the first step is to write a proposal in language required by the constitution or the statutes. Generally speaking, the language of the bond issue submitted to the voters must be clear as to the amount which is being requested and the purposes for which it is to be used, along with the method of repayment. In most states, bond issues may be approved by a majority of those voting in the election. Very often this provision proves to be the key to the success of the bond issue, since there has been traditionally very little interest in bond issues and the turnout at the polls has often been very light. Many bond issues have passed with the approval of only a small proportion of those voters who are actually qualified to vote in the election.

The success of bond elections is rather clearly spelled out in the February 1965 report of the Department of Health, Education, and Welfare, which stated that voters approved a total of $735 million in bonds during the 1964 presidential election. Put another way, the voters approved a total of $58 billion in municipal bonds during the years from 1926 to 1963. Although not all of this was spent for the building of schools, a large part of it was. For the seven-year period from 1957 to 1964, school bonds averaged a 72 per cent approval record.[23]

Interest rates on bonds seem to make very little difference to the voter, and they vary considerably from one state to the next and from one school district to the next. The interest on bonds depends on a number of factors. The most important are the credit rating of the school district and the availability of money. If the credit rating is poor, as estimated by Dun and Bradstreet or some other major accounting firm, and there are good safe places to invest money for a good return, the interest rates on bonds may be high. If there is plenty of money looking for a good secure investment (free from U.S. income taxes) and the school district has a good risk rating, the interest rate may be low. Under these conditions, which vary widely with time and place, generalizations about interest rates can be misleading. However, averages can be useful when the student wishes to compare the interest paid in his own community with the national average, or to determine the direction of cost of indebtedness at some future date. From 1960 to 1965 interest rates varied from 3.19 to 3.54 for school and college bond issues. Higher rates offered in 1966–1967 in other relatively safe investments made bond money for lower interest rates hard to find, and exerted pressure to increase interest on school bonds. By 1970, average rates had reached 7.12 per cent.[24] During this same year, the lowest rate was 5.33. Since 1970 school bond interest rates have fluctuated, but the general trend has been downward.

---

[23] U. S. Dept. of Health, Education, and Welfare, *American Education* (Washington, D.C.: U. S. Office of Education, 1965), p. 20.
[24] NEA, *Financial Status,* p. 46.

Although bonds have been traditionally well accepted by voters as a means for financing long-term building needs for school districts, by no means do they provide a limitless pool of resources for the school district. Indeed, all the states of the Union have placed limitations on indebtedness that school districts may incur. These limitations vary widely among the states, from 2 per cent in Indiana to 50 per cent of assessed valuation in Minnesota.[25]

Besides this very real limitation on bonded indebtedness which exists in all states, there is some indication that voters are becoming a little more reluctant to pass every bond issue that is referred to them. Although the 72 per cent approval record cited above may seem impressive, one cannot help but wonder why more than one in four bond proposals went down to defeat during the seven-year period from 1957 to 1964.

The record has been even more dismal since 1964. Unfortunately for school people and for the children involved, there is evidence that taxpayers are becoming increasingly reluctant to increase their contribution to education on the local level. Bond issues and school levies, which in earlier years faced little opposition from the voter, are being voted down with increasing regularity in local school districts across the nation. Taxpayer resistance to increased taxes has reduced bond issues' chances of success to approximately 50 per cent. By the end of the sixties, many school districts were forced to close for lack of operating funds. In 1967 the school system in Versailles, Ohio, had to close its doors for several weeks in mid-year because it was out of funds. The 1968–1969 school year was a difficult one for many local school districts in Ohio. Several school districts were forced to suspend classes from several days to several weeks due to lack of funds. This happened in Youngstown, the Nelsonville–York City district, and Otesgo. In 1969 voters in Oregon rejected seventeen budget proposals for the operation of schools, while approving only twelve. These were operating budgets, because the law in Oregon requires that any school budget increase of over 6 per cent be submitted for voter approval. In September of 1970, five school districts in the St. Louis metropolitan area were forced to delay the opening of school following voter rejection of new taxes. The Los Angeles school system has been plagued by money problems for several years, and has recently found it necessary to cut budgets. The 1969–1970 school year cut was a significant $41 million in Los Angeles. Cleveland, Ohio, and Scarsdale, New York, were in serious financial straits at the beginning of the 1970 school year, along with hundreds of other school districts across the nation.[26]

Although the problems varied with the locality, there were many similar characteristics. A major factor in all cases seemed to be taxpayer resistance

---

[25] Mort, et al., p. 435.
[26] News stories on the financial problems of local school districts may be found in U.S. News and World Report, 9 Dec. 1968; 20 Oct. 1969; 19 May 1969; and 14 Sept. 1970. An analysis of the problems in Ohio may be found in The Nation; 30 Dec. 1968.

to an increasing burden of local property taxes coupled with the reluctance of state legislatures to provide significant increases in school appropriations. In some districts in the larger cities or in one-industry towns such as Youngstown, Ohio, school officials were faced with movement of more affluent citizens to the suburbs and a deterioration of real estate values in the central city. In others there was voter concern about efficient management of schools coupled with conservative leadership on matters of taxation. Everywhere the results are similar—closed schools, significant budget cuts, and school districts on the verge of bankruptcy. In the face of these problems, it is easy enough for school people to become discouraged. Unfortunately, these are not new problems for the schools.

There could be many reasons for reluctance on the part of voters to approve all bond requests. Although it is not our purpose to determine why the voter casts his ballot the way he does, we might speculate on some reasons for the failure of school bond proposals to gain support. A most serious problem is the fact that bonds have been referred to the people with increasing frequency during the past fifteen years or more in most of the communities which are heavily populated and require large sums for capital outlay. To the voter this means more taxes and more debt, both of which he has become increasingly reluctant to accept. In some communities the burden of debt has become a matter of serious public concern and the voter is becoming increasingly weary of new debt. This concern seems to be growing in spite of reassurances that public debt is not a serious problem from a purely economic point of view in a growing and expanding community economy. More and more frequently, voters are not so much concerned with what appear to be the needs of the schools as they are with the question: "What will it do to my taxes?" This attitude is understandable in a society in which every new year brings increasing burdens. Although the tax load has not become as heavy in the United States as in other nations, many taxpayers *believe* that taxes are a serious burden. This belief, in community after community, is enough to defeat bond issues. Added to this problem is the increasing publication of proposals providing alternatives to the existing system of public education. One of the most publicized alternatives is the creation of a voucher system in which taxpayers are given vouchers which they can utilize in any manner they wish for the education of their children. Most such plans suggest that vouchers could be used in public or private schools or perhaps in new schools which might grow out of consumer demand. This "free enterprise" alternative to the present system of tax-supported public education can have great appeal to heavily taxed citizens who see no real way to make the public school directly accountable for the learning of their children. For whatever reason, school people can no longer be absolutely sure of public support on bond issues. Citizens soon discover that the schools somehow manage to carry on after the failure of a bond issue, even though school officials may have warned that programs would be drastically curtailed if the bond issue failed. The school administrator of the future will have to undertake much more active public relations programs and educational programs on the needs of the school if he expects voter approval for needed expansion. More voters are going to have to be sold on the need for indebtedness in terms of how it will directly enhance learning if this system is to be used in the future as a major means of financing building and other capital improvement needs. With increased need for capital improvement, and voters reluctant to provide for indebtedness on the local level, new means must be found to finance public school improvements and building needs. Most bonds are paid out of the property tax and, of course, there is a limit to this source of revenue. Perhaps the financing of school building and improvement programs will shift to a new base at some future date. In some states the legislature has already assumed a part of this responsibility by guaranteeing the bonds which are sold by local districts. In the past, and continuing in the present, the national government has assisted with school building programs in many ways. These range from the Public Works idea of depression days to the present-day special grants for school buildings in so-called federally impacted areas, school equipment and materials under the anti-poverty program, federal money for transportation of pupils, and aid for vocational education training centers. There is every indication that the resources of the national government will be brought increasingly into the picture of assistance to local districts in their search for long-term capital. Effort will have to be made by school people in the future to educate the public in the need to seek new methods of support for school building programs. This could develop into a serious problem of political and economic education.

A third and major source of revenue for education comes from public taxation. This discussion of taxation is not intended as a thorough analysis of taxation for education. If the reader is interested in this general problem, he should refer to the many existing good works in school and public finance. The purpose of this section will be to outline the major sources of school revenue and to discuss briefly the major advantages and disadvantages of each. The most important taxes for education include the general property tax, the state sales tax, and the state income tax. Although there are numerous other kinds of taxes and fees collected by state and local governments, these miscellaneous ones do not contribute greatly to educational support.

The property tax is not only the oldest tax in the United States, but it remains the major source of local support for education. The theory of the property tax (or ad valorem tax, as it is frequently called) is based on ability to pay and the direct benefit idea. Real and personal property has long been considered an accurate measure of wealth in the United States. Throughout our history (including the colonial experience) those who have owned property were given certain privileges and certain responsibility. As was pointed out above, voting rights were restricted to property owners in state and national elections in many localities for more than half a century after 1776. These property owners consented to tax themselves for purposes of general government on the theory that the property owners benefited directly from the services which government could provide. These services included such things as police protection, the building of roads and streets, and other such direct services which theoretically improved the value of property. Later in the nineteenth century, education was one of the benefits of organized society which became the financial responsibility of government. It was natural to turn to the property tax as a means for financing the schools. This occurred despite the outcry in some quarters against using property tax money to educate other people's children.

Another aspect of the property tax which became dear to the hearts of many independent Americans was the fact that it could be locally collected for local purposes and it served to provide the local people with a great amount of local self-determination or local autonomy. So long as the local community could pay the total cost of whatever activities they desired, they did not need to fear interference from the state or national levels of government. Hence, the idea of the property tax as a means of support for all functions of local government, including education, became and still remains a strong part of the idea of federalism with its emphasis on state and local independence and state and local control of the "simple" functions of government.

The system of property tax as it has developed in the United States is a rather simple one. First, a taxing jurisdiction is outlined, usually in the state constitution. The original base for property tax may have been the county or township but, as new needs developed, special taxing districts were created by constitutional amendment or by the legislatures of the various states. Examples of geographic organization for taxing for specific purposes might include such things as sewer and street districts, fire districts, and of course, school districts. Assessors are appointed or elected whose duty it is to evaluate each privately owned parcel of property within the legally consti-tuted taxing district and to place these assessed values on the tax rolls. The next step is for the people, or their elected representatives on the school board, the county commissioners, the city council, or some other elected group, to determine the amount of taxes which will be paid. Normally this figure is set as a mill levy or a certain number of dollars of tax to be paid by the property owner on each one thousand dollars of assessed valuation. For example, let us assume that the county is the local taxing unit. All property is then assessed in the county on the basis of some formula. Let us assume that the formula in our hypothetical county is 50 per cent of current market value of the property. Each taxing unit (such as school district, fire district, police district, etc.) then determines its budget for the fiscal year. The total cost of local government is determined and that share which must come from property tax is determined. Let us further assume that the mill levy is set at sixty, or each taxpayer is paying sixty dollars per year in property taxes for every one thousand dollars of assessed valuation of his property. Let us further assume that the schools need more money than this will provide. The school's budget or finance officer has determined that school needs will require an additional five mills of property taxation. The voters (in some states, only the property owners) are then called upon to decide whether an additional five mills can be levied. Although a greatly oversimplified example, this is generally the way it works. The reader should check his own locality to determine how the assessment and collection of the property tax is determined. Teachers should become vitally concerned with this problem since the local property tax remains a major source of school support.

There have been many arguments, pro and con, on the property tax as a means of school support. It does have certain advantages. It is a stable tax which returns a fairly reliable yield. If the ownership of property can be used as a measure of wealth, it is based to some extent on ability to pay. It is a fairly easy tax to collect. However, there are many disadvantages to the property tax. It is very inflexible. There are serious limits to the property tax as a major source of income in a growing and expanding economy. Rates and assessments are traditionally difficult to change, and the source of revenue from the property tax grows slowly. In bad times, it becomes a very undependable source of income and the burden of high taxes on property have given rise to bankruptcies, foreclosures, and forced sales in the past. Property tax is a relatively expensive tax to collect, since it requires paid assessors and extensive records. Moreover, it is becoming increasingly evident that property ownership may not be the best measure of ability to pay. The fluctuations in property values have created certain serious problems in proper assessment. Property taxes, particularly personal property taxes, are easy enough to evade by dishonest taxpayers who merely neglect to report all of their personal holdings. Finally, there are notorious examples of unequal assessments on property from one state to the next and frequently from one neighborhood to the next within the same taxing district. The result is that a low tax rate in a district with much valuable property can raise many times more revenue than a high tax rate in a poor district. It is this basic inequity that has led citizens in several states to successfully challenge the constitutionality of the property tax as a means of school support. As a result of these challenges many state legislatures have been moved to reconsider their tax structure. It is possible that the property tax has outlived its usefulness as a major means of educational support in the United States.

In recent years the support of education has become more a concern of state governments. Perhaps a major reason for this has been the inadequacy of the property tax as a means of support. The major income producers on the state level are the sales tax and the income tax. The sales tax was born during the Great Depression and has expanded, until today more than two-thirds of the states have it in some form. The amount of tax varies from 1 per cent on all retail sales to as high as 6 per cent. In some states, sales taxes remain selective; that is, they are levied only on certain products such as tobacco and liquor, or goods sold at the wholesale level. In others they are selective in a different way. Some states have passed general sales taxes but have long lists of exemptions, which include such things as groceries, farm machinery, seed, and fertilizer. The sales tax has proved to be a lucrative source of income, not only for schools but for other governmental purposes as well. It is a very flexible tax inasmuch as income that it provides can be increased dramatically by merely raising the rate. In addition, sales taxes appear to be painless to the taxpayer since they are collected on a pay-as-you-spend basis, and the taxpayer is not called upon to make any lump-sum payments. Another great advantage of the sales tax is that it is fairly easy to collect and it hits all elements of the population in a similar way. The great argument against the sales tax, which is often made by organized labor and people on meager retirement or welfare payments, is that it is a "regressive tax"; that is, it takes a larger proportionate chunk of the income of the poor than it takes from the rich. Opponents of the sales tax argue that those with small incomes spend a majority of their income on the necessities of life and are taxed on their total income while the wealthy are taxed only on a small portion of their income.

Income taxes, which are collected in about two-thirds of the states, are not subject to this objection. In most states the rate of income tax has remained below 10 per cent of gross income. The income tax, unlike the sales tax, is based on ability to pay; that is, it is a graduated tax—the more one makes the more one pays. Like the sales tax, the income tax has proved to be a lucrative source of income, is easy to collect, and is relatively inexpensive to collect. It, too, is a flexible tax. Some object to the income tax on the grounds that it discourages initiative or penalizes the successful.

Other taxes which provide funds for education in some states include corporation taxes (usually levied at a flat rate on profits), city payroll taxes (similar to income taxes), death and gift taxes, and excise taxes on specific goods.

Most states have a long way to go toward the establishment of an adequate and equitable tax structure. Teachers should concern themselves with tax reform within their own states. Without tax reforms, education will continue to struggle along inadequately financed in most states. A comprehensive tax program for state government should be based on the following minimum considerations:

1. Ability to pay. Generally, the tax structure of a state should seek the money where it is and should tax those who are most able to pay for the needs of the state. However, punitive rates should be avoided in order to insure a healthy and growing state economy.
2. Benefits derived from taxes. Citizens should be encouraged to pay some taxes regardless of the source or the amount of their income on the theory that everyone benefits from governmental expenditures. This is particularly true of education.
3. Ease of collection. The tax structure in the state should be so designed as to minimize evasion and make collection of the taxes as simple as possible.
4. Cost of collection. Taxes which are extremely expensive to collect should be used sparingly.
5. Adequacy of yield or revenue. A total tax program for the state should provide enough resources to adequately meet the demands of citizens for governmental functions.
6. Flexibility and stability. A total state tax program should be flexible enough to provide for a stable income from year to year.

SCHOOL FINANCE AND VALUES

Many of the problems of school finance can be discussed under the headings of adequacy, equality, ignorance, and apathy. Although it may be a truism that every man in our society is interested in education, this does not mean that there is any general agreement on how it should be provided. Widespread public belief and commitment to the ideal of public education is not enough. There is, indeed, a great divergence of opinion in our society on how the money should be raised, for example. This debate is waged constantly in the political arena.

From the point of view of the teacher, the greatest single problem in education may be that of adequacy. By adequacy we mean sufficient plant facilities and teachers to do a proper job of educating. Adequacy for most teachers means more funds for next year than for last—in most cases, considerably more funds. For teachers, this increasing need not only involves the accelerating size of the public school operation in terms of numbers, but also mounting financial commitment from the public. Many teachers know that increased funds would enable them to do things they know to be in the best interests of a quality education, and to experiment with ideas which they have reason to believe will improve the process. They naturally expect the public to share their values. Moreover, they are easily frustrated when they know what they should be doing and are prevented from doing it solely because of limited funds.

The public is not so easily sold on this definition of adequacy. For the public which pays the bills, adequacy frequently means what the school is presently doing. This kind of attitude is encouraged by popular myths about education; by the expansion of education into new programs and specialties which are little understood by the public; by certain built-in problems such as constitutional or legal obstacles; by political disagreement on methods of support; and by competition from various agencies and institutions for the available funds.

The classroom teacher who has struggled with inadequate facilities, overloaded classrooms, and a myriad of other problems related to a poorly financed school system has difficulty understanding why parents are satisfied with this condition year after year. But part of the fault lies with the school people themselves, who are all too ready to demand increased support while carefully reassuring parents that they are doing an outstanding job with what they have. School seems to go on in spite of failures of bond issues, of new tax measures, or of other means to raise school revenue. The public is not as well informed as it might be on the real educational meaning of increased budgets. It isn't that improvements cannot be eloquently argued, but teachers seem reluctant, for some unknown reason, to argue them. So the myths persist. Moreover, they are frequently reinforced by the school people themselves. Such slogans as "we have the best school system in the state" or "our modern school plant" or "this year our seniors earned ten Merit Scholarships," which are quoted with great regularity by school superintendents before civic and business clubs, do little to convince the community of the needs of education. Parents may generalize such statements with the comment: "The schools sure are better than when I was a youngster." Perhaps if the real meaning of these slogans were examined, they would read somewhat differently. "We have the best school system in the state" might more realistically become: "Ours is a rotten system, but it's better than most." The other side of the reference to "our modern school plant," if truthfully made, might turn out to be: "our modern school plant, which was inadequate before it was finished." The propaganda on the Merit Scholars might more honestly be stated: "We have ten Merit Scholars which constitutes less than 0.01 per cent of our school population; what will happen to the rest? We have no real program for them." So long as these myths are encouraged by the school people, strong public support for greatly increased school budgets is going to be hard to achieve.

Even if the myths did not exist, there would remain the serious problems of constitutional and legal obstacles to adequate school finance. Archaic constitutional provisions setting such items as debt and tax limits provide serious obstacles to adequate finance. Constitutional and legal requirements on the assessment of property also constitute a serious problem in many school districts. Tax reform is another extremely difficult political problem. For every suggested reform, there is a vested interest with a built-in opposition. And so it goes; the legal and constitutional obstacles are many and serious.

The expansion of functions of education and of government generally has created new demands on the available money in local and state governments. With such expanding needs, there is never any real agreement on how the money should be raised. Certain groups will quite naturally oppose sales taxes while others will fight an increase in property taxes. The other major revenue source, the income tax, has been passed by state legislatures only with prolonged and well-organized opposition.

A most serious problem confronting adequate school financing in many areas is the inequality of economic ability which exists in such a large nation. Equality of educational opportunity has always been a problem involving political values. Although there seems to be general agreement that every child should have equal access to an education, the reality must await a broader base of financial support. With such a large proportion of money for the support of education provided on the local level, given the wide local variations in taxable resources, lack of equal educational opportunities constitutes a serious problem in our society. The only solution to this problem in our system has to be a political one. With the tradition of local autonomy in educational finance and local pride in one's school, this has been a difficult political problem. As state support becomes a more important part of the total school budget, this problem is somewhat relieved, but equal educational opportunity, when judged in terms of the economics of education, is a long way from being realized. Any measure can be used to illustrate this. One may examine differences in per pupil expenditure, in per capita wealth, in teachers' salaries, in classroom space available per pupil, and find tremendous inequality from one district to another in the United States. To practice what we preach about educational equality would involve great redistribution of tax wealth, a problem involving political values if there ever was one.

Finally, ignorance and apathy create serious economic problems for education. We have already discussed a peculiar kind of ignorance on the part of school people who, in some instances, prefer a good image to the painful truth. This suggests that public ignorance on the needs of educational finance may be perfectly innocent, because citizens cannot know, unless someone takes the trouble to inform them, of the specific needs. There is reason to believe that the public is committed to the best education that money can buy in spite of the outcry against bond issues and general tax increase. The poor in the society can easily be convinced that education provides the means for advancement. The middle classes and the wealthy need not be convinced of the values of education. Why, then, the reluctance to support it? One might speculate that a major reason may be poor leadership. Politicians who do not merit the public's respect cannot easily convince citizens that increased taxes will benefit the taxpayer's children. Poorly qualified teachers do little to inspire the kind of confidence which expresses itself in the public belief that increased appropriations will really matter. School administrators who play every side of the political game and who are fearful of making a stand for good education and explaining what this means to the public cannot be expected to provide the necessary leadership.

There is no serious doubt that our society can afford better schools. There is no question that money spent on education is a good investment for the individual and for the society. Nor is there any question that our citizens are committed to good education for their children. The major question in any consideration of the politics of school finance is this: Who will provide the necessary leadership? The teacher is left to draw his own conclusions on this problem.

REFERENCES

Bailey, Stephen K., Richard T. Frost, Paul E. Marsh, and Robert C. Wood. *Schoolmen and Politics.* Syracuse, N.Y.: Syracuse Univ. Press, 1962.

Benson, Charles S. *The Economics of Public Education.* Boston: Houghton Mifflin, 1961.

————. *Perspectives on the Economics of Education.* Boston: Houghton Mifflin, 1963.

Burke, Arvid J. *Financing Public Schools in the United States.* Rev. ed. New York: Harper & Row, 1957.

Burkhead, Jesse. *Public School Finance.* Syracuse, N.Y.: Syracuse Univ. Press, 1964.

————. *State and Local Taxes for Public Education.* Syracuse, N.Y.: Syracuse Univ. Press, 1963.

Carman, Harry J., and Harold C. Syrett. *A History of the American People.* New York: Alfred A. Knopf, 1956.

Committee for Economic Development. *Paying for Better Public Schools.* Washington, D.C.: Committee for Economic Development, 1959.

Corbally, John E., Jr. *School Finance.* Boston: Allyn & Bacon, 1962.

Crow, Lester D. and Alice. *Introduction to Education.* New York: American Book, 1960. Chapter 5.

Cubberley, Ellwood P. *Public Education in the United States.* Rev. ed. Boston: Houghton Mifflin, 1947.

Hartford, Ellis Ford. *Education in These United States.* New York: Macmillan, 1964. Chapter 6.

Illich, Ivan. *Celebration of Awareness: A Call for Institutional Revolution.* Garden City, N.Y.: Doubleday, 1970.

Kneller, George F. (ed.). *Foundations in Education.* New York: John Wiley & Sons, 1963. Chapter 9.

Kotler, Milton. *Neighborhood Governments: The Local Foundation of Political Life.* New York: Bobbs-Merrill, 1969.

Miner, Jerry. *Social and Economic Factors in Spending for Public Education.* Syracuse, N.Y.: Syracuse Univ. Press, 1963.

Morrison, Henry C. *School Revenue.* Chicago: Univ. of Chicago Press, 1930.

Mort, Paul R., Walter C. Reusser, and John W. Polley. *Public School Finance.* New York: McGraw-Hill, 1960.

National Education Association. *Does Better Education Cost More?* Washington, D.C.: Committee on Tax Education and School Finance, March 1959.

————. *Financial Status of the Public Schools, 1970.* Washington, D.C.: Committee on Educational Finance, 1970.

————. *Financing the Changing School Program.* Washington, D.C.: Committee on Educational Finance, April 1962.

————. *New Directions in Financing Public Schools.* Washington, D.C.: Committee on Educational Finance, April 1960.

————. *Research Report, 1963-R12, Estimates of School Statistics, 1963–1964.* Washington, D.C.: Research Division, Dec. 1963.

————. *Research Report, 1965-R17, Estimates of School Statistics, 1965–1966.* Washington, D.C.: Research Division, 1965.

————. *Research Report, 1969-R15, Estimates of School Statistics, 1969–1970.* Washington, D.C.: Research Division, Dec. 1969.

Peterson, LeRoy J., and Jean M. Flanagan. *Financing the Public Schools.* Washington, D.C.: Research Division, NEA, June 1962.

School Management. Annual Budget and Reference Issue. Jan. 1965.

Sly, John F. *Financing Education in the Public Schools.* Princeton, N.J.: Tax Institute, Nov. 1956.

U. S. Dept. of Health, Education, and Welfare. *American Education.* Washington, D.C.: U.S. Office of Education, Feb. 1965.

8

Values and Educational Investment

Political idealists, reformers, professional sociologists, educators, and others have long argued that education is the most certain means by which a society can provide its citizens with opportunity for upward mobility. Moreover, idealists have long believed that an educated citizen is essential to the maintenance of a democratic system of government.

The ideal of universal education at public expense has always been in process in our society, but it has never been completely realized. This is true and may always be true, since the definition of a necessary minimum universal education for enlightened citizenship has proved to be very susceptible to change. A minimum general and universal education for citizens meant one thing in the time of Jefferson. It means something quite different in the mid-twentieth century. This is because certain elements in the environment will not stand still. During the nineteenth century and even into the twentieth, the rudiments of schooling, the three r's, passed for an education that was adequate for providing citizens who could function effectively in most communities in the United States.

More than one hundred years of rapid industrial and technological development have dramatically changed this picture. By the end of the first quarter of the twentieth century, it was becoming increasingly apparent that the three r's were not enough, and by 1930, a major educational goal of the masses in our society was a high school diploma. The upward extension of formal schooling from elementary to secondary school for the masses had been nearly a century in its development. In contrast, during the generation since 1930, a college degree has become a popular educational goal—if not an economic necessity.

Considered in the past a luxury to be enjoyed only by those who had the time and money to dabble in it, higher education has come to be viewed by the masses as a necessity, is advocated by political figures, and has become a popular goal in the United States. Moreover, educational needs are no longer considered an idealistic abstraction, but have come to be considered in practical economic terms. Many who would rarely express concern about the advantages of education for enlightened citizenship become eager to acquire it for personal reasons—so they can become employable. It is becoming more and more apparent that those who are denied the maximum education or training of which they are capable feel they are being cheated of the good things in life.

The recent emphasis on schooling in the so-called war on poverty is prima facie evidence of a kind of national faith in the possibilities of education. There is a good deal of political idealism as well as realism in anti-poverty crusades. Both idealism and realism are involved in the concern stressed many times in recent years by those who felt that poverty is a breeding ground for ignorance. The argument states that citizens who do not share in the material abundance of the society also do not share in the privileges of citizenship in the society. The literature of the behavioral sciences is currently full of charges and implications that the poor in the affluent society are not only deprived but alienated.

The educational implications of the attack on poverty are tremendous. Political as well as educational leaders are generally coming to accept the theory that the major cure for poverty is adequate educational opportunity. This theory is based on the assumption that in the advanced technological society, skills which are necessary for economic independence can only be acquired in formal training. A second major assumption of schooling as a cure for poverty is that the schools provide the most certain means for breaking the cycle of poverty, the most certain means for raising the level of living for the large group of impoverished in the United States

This is not a new ideal in our society. For many years, most Americans have at least given lip service to the ideals of equality of opportunity in education and free education for the masses. In spite of the existence of these ideals in principle, however, it has been historically true that schooling beyond the elementary level has had a price tag for the individual as well as for the society. In the past, the society has provided some investment in schooling while leaving some of the financial responsibility to the individual. During most of the present century this individual responsibility has come in the form of direct and indirect costs for schooling beyond the elementary level. In much of this century, direct costs have included such items as tuition, fees, and living costs beyond the secondary school level, or in private or public training schools of various kinds beyond the elementary level. The major indirect cost to the individual has been the loss of income which results when schooling beyond the elementary level is chosen in preference to paid employment. To this day, this remains a choice that is really not a choice in many families in which income from teenage youth is essential to survival. Many studies of dropouts in secondary schools contain cases of students who have dropped out of high school because the income they could earn in employment was essential to meet the pressing needs of the family. However, leaving high school to help support the family has become more difficult in recent years, simply because the jobs are not there. As each year passes, the number of job opportunities for unskilled and uneducated youth diminishes. Partly for this reason the society is coming to assume more of the financial obligation for the education of its citizens. There are many pilot programs and experiments across the country today in which students of secondary school and college age are paid to stay in school. As the need for such programs grows they will probably continue to be supported by national funds.

The assumption by the society of the major, if not the total, financial obligation for schooling even beyond the secondary school raises some problems with which this chapter will be concerned. If society is to assume the total financial responsibility for schooling, the majority must be convinced that it is in the interests of the society for this to be done. In this connection, there follows a discussion of the nature of human capital and the relationship of educational investment to economic well-being.

THE NATURE OF HUMAN CAPITAL

Human capital may be defined as the capital, in the form of learned knowledge, skills, or abilities, possessed by individuals at a given time in a given society. For practical purposes this is translated in terms of time, money, and effort invested in schooling by the individual or by the society. In such a definition one can make an individual or societal application. Many students concern themselves more with their own store of educational capital, and think of education in terms of years of study or degrees obtained or in some other materialistic sense rather than in the idealistic terms of the store of knowledge that they have acquired. Even those who think in idealistic terms often attach a specific money value to their years of schooling. This practical money motive behind higher education for the individual is commonplace among college students, most of whom, if asked why they are attending college, can give some very practical reasons. Not infrequently they answer: "To prepare myself for employment" or "It is impossible to get a good job without a college education." Moreover, most of them expect a college degree to provide them with some economic advantages over those who do not have the benefit of such training. Although many students may dabble in general education, by the time they have invested two or three years of time and money in college, they begin to search earnestly for some major which will prepare them specifically for employment.

Anyone who has advised undergraduate students in a college of education is painfully aware of those who dabble around during the first two years of college and then suddenly decide they want to become teachers. When asked why by the advisor, they reply that they would like a teaching certificate so that they will have something to fall back on in case they can't find some other kind of job. Although this may be disturbing to the old-school advisor who believes himself to be dedicated to teaching, and who from time to time attempts to tell himself that he would continue teaching even if his salary were cut, to "have something to fall back on" such as a teaching certificate is not an unrealistic goal for the undergraduate student. Even good undergraduate students, when explaining their choice to their peers who are preparing for other occupations, tend to justify teaching as a career in terms of vacation time, hours of work, and other fringe benefits, not in terms of dedication to service, the needs of the society, or other such idealistic terms. It is difficult to be critical of this attitude, since ours is a society which emphasizes income, as much as the type of work, as a symbol of economic and social success. It might be interesting to determine the extent to which undergraduates pursuing a premedical course of study are doing so primarily because of the income possibilities of the medical profession. Quite pointedly, many college students place a dollar value on their educational investment.

Schooling is not only a personal investment but a societal investment as well. Society places a specific dollar value on that portion of schooling which is provided by the society. This dollar value in schooling has been the subject of some rather searching economic analysis in recent years. As the society becomes more highly industrialized and a higher level of skills is needed in order for individuals to function profitably in the society, both the quantity and quality of schooling have become important elements in the definition and analysis of human capital. As John Kenneth Galbraith pointed out in *The Affluent Society,* inventions during the early years of the industrial revolution were often the result of brilliant flashes of insight, not the product of a long period of formal education. Galbraith declared that inventions such as the flying shuttle, the spinning frame, and the steam engine represented great improvements in the capital which was put to industrial use, but for the most part these innovations were not related to previous education and preparation. In the words of Galbraith this situation has changed:

> However, with the development of a great and complex industrial plant, and even more with the development of a great and sophisticated body of basic science and of experience in its application, all this has changed. In addition to the entrepreneurs . . . who were more or less automatically forthcoming, modern economic activity now requires a great number of trained and qualified people. Investment in human beings is, prima facie, as important as investment in material capital. . . .

What is more important, the improvement in capital—technological advance—is now almost wholly dependent on investment in education, training, and scientific opportunity for individuals. . . . Benjamin Franklin is the sacred archetype of the American genius and nothing may be done to disturb his position. But in the unromantic fact, innovation has become a highly organized enterprise. The extent of the result is predictably related to the quality and quantity of the resources being applied to it. These resources are men and women. Their quality depends on the extent of the investment in their education, training, and opportunity. They are the source of technological change. . . .[1]

The most obvious examples of public acceptance of the idea that society should invest in human capital in the form of schooling are the various current attempts on the part of the government to train dropouts, to provide training for the unemployed, or to retrain those whose jobs have become obsolete. The most frequently used and perhaps accepted argument for spending tax money for this kind of educational program is that "education is cheaper than welfare." There is the supposition that once the cure of schooling is applied to the unemployed, the welfare burden will be lessened. Certain caution must be exercised, however. The job is not going to be an easy one even though a majority of Americans may be committed to the principle that economic progress is determined in part by our investment in education or in human capital. Those in whom we are attempting to invest may be the most serious obstacle to success. One of the most current problems with training programs where tax money is provided for those who are unemployed or underemployed in seasonal or marginal work is to convince these people that they should proceed with training. In several large cities, directors of such programs have experienced some difficulty convincing young men who are temporarily employed for two dollars or more per hour that they should attend school to be trained for better jobs. Two dollars per hour, even though temporary, looked better to some of these youths than the $1.25 they would have received for attending classes. It has been difficult to persuade them that the sacrifice of current income is not a loss, but an investment in their own stock of human capital. Ironically, others have been perfectly satisfied with their unemployed status. Such an attitude is naturally puzzling to many who have never questioned middle-class values and attitudes toward work and school.

Educators must somehow convince children at an early age that schooling is an investment for the society and for the individual. A considerably more difficult task will be to convince some that employment is better than unemployment. Great efforts need to be made, especially among the poor in our society, to convince people that schooling and subsequent employment

---

[1] John Kenneth Galbraith, *The Affluent Society* (Boston: Houghton Mifflin, 1958), pp. 271–272.

are the best means to material security. This can be undertaken successfully only by elementary school teachers who understand thoroughly the economics of education and the value systems of those poor who may resist schooling and gainful employment. For many millions of American elementary school children, basic value orientations will have to change before they will ever accept the notion that it may be an advantage to forgo present earnings in order to gain greater earnings in the future. Nor is this apt to be accomplished with mere preachments on the value of education. Efforts must be made to enable individuals to find some intrinsic rewards in school work. The sections which follow will give the prospective teacher some general information directed toward the proposition that education is an investment which pays in both a personal and a societal sense. It is not designed as a capsule which can be fed to the reluctant scholar, but should provide an overview of a general economic education problem for the teacher.

EDUCATIONAL INVESTMENT AND ECONOMIC WELL-BEING

The relationship between the amount of national effort in the form of time, money, and facilities and national economic well-being has national as well as international implications. In addition, there are also personal aspects of educational investment and economic well-being within any society.

On the national level, the relationship between the level of education and the economic well-being of the nation is direct. Evidence exists which shows that countries having highly trained and/or highly educated citizens tend to fare better economically than those that do not. No nation in the modern world is able to maintain a high level of living for the masses without a corresponding high level of education for the masses. The National Committee for the Support of the Public Schools turned its attention to the question of the relationship between natural resources, education, and income in 1963. John K. Norton prepared a chart which provides some interesting data for analysis and speculation. Column five has been added to Norton's original chart.

The Norton chart points up rather dramatically a relationship between educational development and per capita income. In countries such as Brazil, Colombia, and Mexico, where the known natural resources are high and the level of educational development is low, the per capita income stands near the bottom of the list. Educational development takes on great importance in relation to economic development when one considers the nations of Denmark and Switzerland, both of which rank high among the nations of the world in per capita income in spite of the fact that they are low in natural resources. The chart also illustrates very well the importance of the development of human capital or human resources in countries where natural resources are very limited. The generalizations which are suggested by the

Nation	Natural Resources	Educational Development	Per Capita Income (Average 1952–1954)	Per Capita Income (1968)
1	2	3	4 (dollars)	5 (dollars)
Brazil	High	Low	230	240
Colombia	High	Low	250	280
Denmark	Low	High	750	1,830
Mexico	High	Low	220	470
New Zealand	High	High	1,000	1,930
Switzerland	Low	High	1,010	2,250
United States	High	High	1,870	3,520

chart have applications to other nations and other areas of the world as well. It is generally true that the natural resources in many South American and African countries are very great, while the educational level is extremely low. It is also true that these areas of the world are characterized by very low per capita income; in fact, the great majority of the people live on the edge of starvation. The figures for 1968 tend to support the argument. With the exception of Mexico, the big gains in per capita income during the 1954–1968 period were made by nations with a high educational base.

The rate of growth of a nation is sometimes used by economists as a rough guide to determine the economic health of a nation, and this rate is generally stated in terms of the increase in gross national product from one year to the next. Generally speaking, there is a high positive correlation between the rate of economic growth and the educational level of the country. The countries which have shown the most rapid industrial growth in the period since World War II are those nations which have invested heavily in education. For example, growth in postwar Germany and Japan has been great, and correspondingly the percentage of gross national product which has been placed in education in these countries has been greater than in most, approaching an average of nearly 5 per cent during the post World War II years, compared to an average of 3.5 per cent in the United States and about 4 per cent in the United Kingdom.[3] Conversely, those nations which have invested a small percentage of national income in education have grown much less rapidly.

However, data such as this must be viewed with caution. One cannot

[2] John K. Norton, *Changing Demands on Education and Their Fiscal Implications,* National Committee for the Support of the Public Schools (Washington, D.C.: Public Affairs Press, 1963), p. 39.

[3] A. H. Halsey, *et al.,* eds., *Education, Economy and Society* (New York: Free Press of Glencoe, 1961), p. 39.

conclude from comparisons of investment in education, educational level, and growth that there is a direct and causal relationship between the amount of gross national product invested in education and high rate of growth or a high level of per capita income, for there are many things involved, including such items as the political system, economic systems, and other economic factors; climate, the types of resources available, and their uses; and the customs and traditions of the people.

A major question which must be raised in any consideration of the relationship between educational investment and economic well-being is whether a large number of schooled people (presuming a high level of investment) is the direct cause for economic well-being. One cannot make worldwide generalizations which apply to all places at all times. The role played by education in the industrial development of a nation and its subsequent ability to produce goods and income for its people are difficult to determine. In the United States as in the nations of western Europe, which experienced the effects of the industrial revolution even earlier than the United States, it is doubtful that formal education had a great deal to do with the initial stimulation of industrial development. The mass of human resources which fed the industrialization of the United States from the 1840's well into the twentieth century was not an educated mass. The very nature of schooling was antithetical to the needs of a nation struggling to establish an industrial system, for the schools of the United States continued to teach a classical curriculum. Such a curriculum was hardly designed to produce the kind of talent needed in our early industrial development. The problem was similar in England and other western European countries that took the lead in industrialization. The major elements which fed rapid industrial growth in the West during much of the nineteenth century were the availability of land, unskilled labor, capital, and other such basic factors of production. The only areas in which early industrialization depended on schooling were innovation and invention, and this was only to a limited extent. Moreover, the most notable inventions were not contributed by what we would call schooled men, but by practical men.

The technological revolution of the twentieth century has changed this. It is not our purpose here to examine the reasons for the tremendously increased sophistication of industrial society. Rather, we shall deal with the implications for schooling of broad and complex technological change. Every college student knows what the implications of the technological revolution are for his own educational plans. It has forced him to become more specifically trained if he is to find a useful place in the system. In a word, the process of industrialization has matured in many nations to the point that even the relatively meaningless tasks require a great amount of skill and a great amount of technical knowledge, which can only be gained in formal training. Invention and innovation have become big business. Millions of dollars are being poured into research that is conducted in impressive buildings housing large groups of men highly trained in the physical, biological, and social sciences. The day of the barnyard inventor working independently on some revolutionary machine is gone forever.

Moreover, this has great implications for education, not only in the highly developed industrial nations, but in those which are struggling to become industrialized. The developing nations of Asia, Africa, and Latin America cannot adopt the pattern of development followed in the countries which experienced the first industrial revolution. The pattern cannot be repeated because the environment has changed. Brazil cannot develop a steel industry just as it was done in the United States because the earliest mills in the United States would seem primitive today and their product could not compete in the market place. Thus, a country that wants industry must build a highly sophisticated technological plant from the start. Such a beginning requires a very high level of skills which can be obtained only through the process of formal education. The people needed to build and operate a modern industrial plant must be highly skilled and trained persons. Initially, the developing countries can import these people from the more developed nations, but in order to sustain economic growth and encourage industrial expansion, they need their own domestic supply of such human resources. On the other side of production, any nation needs educated masses who will demand the products of a sophisticated industrial plant. The leaders in developing nations generally recognize this need for schooling, and in most such nations the improvement of the school system has been the first priority for governments which desire to lead their people into the twentieth century. Although schooling may be a long and expensive process, in this age it is viewed as the shortest possible route to national economic well-being. This is a huge and tragic problem in many of the nations which desire rapid industrial development because it is in these nations that human capital in the form of trained citizens is spread pitifully thin. Illiteracy continues to be highest in the least developed nations. With few exceptions, illiteracy rates range from 30 to 70 per cent of the population in much of the Arab world, Asia, Africa, and Latin America. Even such schooling that does exist in much of the developing world is a classical system which relies heavily on foreign teachers and a curriculum which is not indigenous to the country. It is still not uncommon, for example, to find only the children of the upper classes enrolled in secondary schools in African nations, studying classical English or French literature.[4]

---

[4] For a good analysis of the relationship between education and economic growth in other nations, the reader should see Frederick Harbison and Charles Myers, *Education, Manpower and Economic Growth: Strategies of Human Resource Development* (New York: McGraw-Hill, 1964) and Don Adams and Robert M. Bjork, *Education in Developing Areas* (New York: David McKay, 1969).

There are compelling reasons why education has become the first item of business for many of the developing nations. Adams and Bjork list five reasons that they feel demonstrate that "education . . . is among the most important elements that explain the maintenance of societies in a developed form."[5] These include: (1) a monetary system, (2) written rather than oral communication, (3) a system of written law, (4) an absolute dependence on technology, and (5) the need for demographic balance. A monetary system suggests abstract and complex systems of accounting and "information gathering and storing, complex contractual arrangements, general comprehension of numerical relationships, and so on."[6] Obviously this cannot be accomplished without a rather comprehensive scheme of education. Adams and Bjork point out that it would be virtually impossible for the illiterate to survive in a developed society which depends on "written want ads, employment records, written applications . . . factory rules, employment regulations . . . and myriads of written notices. . . ."[7] The same would be true, of course, for the law. Not only must a society be literate in order to have written laws, but a certain level of literacy is needed to develop minimum loyalties which make the system operable. As societies develop, they tend to become urbanized, which increases dependence on technology. With urbanization and industrial development, the economic system becomes a system of complex interdependencies characterized by increasing specialization of work and an increasingly complex division of labor. Education becomes imperative in this situation. Finally, Adams and Bjork contend that "education is among the forces bringing fertility rates down in developed societies, and tends to reinforce the population's orientation toward the future."[8]

Still, one cannot overemphasize formal training at the expense of other factors. Even where it is apparent that little progress can be made toward increased industrial production in the developed countries without it, and that a beginning cannot be made in the developing countries without it, there are other important problems which need to be overcome if schooling is to provide the solution to economic problems in the developing countries. In some instances it may be a political problem. In many parts of the world, it will be difficult to achieve industrial progress without a stable political system that facilitates such development. This is as true of external political factors as it is of internal ones. Nations cannot develop unless they are free from outside restrictions, both political and economic. Nor can nations in the twentieth century develop within the framework of economic systems which do not lend themselves to rapid industrial development. In this case, forms

---

[5] Adams and Bjork, p. 21.
[6] Adams and Bjork, p. 21.
[7] Adams and Bjork, p. 21.
[8] Adams and Bjork, p. 22.

are not nearly so important as other obstacles. It matters little whether the economy is a planned one or a private enterprise economy—either can experience rapid industrial growth. What matters is the efficiency of economic operation which is conditioned in part by the level of education of the people, by traditions and customs, and other variables. A nation of people that has a traditional attitude antagonistic toward the type of discipline required of industrial labor faces a tremendous problem of education before it can join the industrial nations. This is only one of many problems which could be listed.

Middle-class parents have been known to lecture their children on the specific money value of schooling. At least among the middle-class parents in the United States, there is a strong feeling that schooling is the most certain road to economic success. Moreover, there is some evidence that this feeling among the middle classes has some support in the research.

There have been a large number of studies in recent years which have been concerned with the relationship between schooling and personal income. Although not overwhelming, the great bulk of the evidence collected points to the conclusion that there is a direct positive relationship between educational level and income. Moreover, this seems to be true regardless of the country—whether developed or developing.

For years many Americans have held the notion that schooling was a good investment. However, in the United States, there seems to be some evidence that social class has a very important influence on educational aspirations.[9] Generally, those of the lower classes express less interest in college than those of the middle and upper classes in our society. Sociologists have long speculated on the divergences in value systems among the classes in our society. Certainly part of the reason that the lower classes do not attach as much importance to education as the upper and middle classes do is because their values differ. However, one must not overlook the role that economics plays in these attitudes. Surely there are lower-class parents who believe strongly in a high level of education for their children, but who see only a remote possibility of its attainment. Thus they may deliberately discourage their children from thinking about a college education because they are certain that they will not be able to afford it. The attitude thus nourished may have nothing whatever to do with the way parents value education, but may be an attempt on their part to protect their children from cruel disappointment. In such instances, perhaps, the educator should help the promising child who is a possible dropout to find the means for an education rather than try to convince the child of the economic value of schooling. There is, of course, overwhelming evidence that the poor do not go to college. The Report of the National Advisory Commission on Civil Disorders called attention to the fact that in some urban ghettos fewer than 1

---

[9] Burton R. Clark, *Educating the Expert Society* (San Francisco: Chandler, 1962), p. 65.

per cent of the youth goes to college. For the nation as a whole, approximately 8 per cent of the so-called "disadvantaged" enter college.[10] In view of the tremendous economic importance of some training beyond the secondary school, the fact that only 50 per cent of all high school graduates enter college is significant. Although it would be difficult to prove precisely what percentage of America's non-college youth is in that category for purely economic reasons, it would be safe to assume that large numbers are too poor to attend.

Obviously, we are a long way from realization of the cliché that "anyone who really wants to go to college can go." Even after several years of effort by the national government, which provided various kinds of financial assistance to college-age youth, the proportion of non-whites who manage to finish four years of college presents a dismal picture. In 1957, 41.6 per cent of all persons in the United States had completed four years of high school. This had increased to 51.1 per cent in 1967. Non-white persons made a greater gain during the same ten-year period, from 18.4 per cent in 1957 to 31.5 per cent in 1967,[11] but the difference is still significant in terms of millions of students who face the dismal prospect of unemployment and dead-end jobs. Nor does this tell the whole story, since even those who are marginally poor, both white and non-white, who do somehow manage to get into college, very often find it necessary to attend the less well financed community colleges and low tuition state colleges, where programs are restricted and opportunities are fewer than at the large, prestigious, and expensive universities. For the twenty million in serious poverty, the hope of college training is remote. For the twenty or thirty million who are just above the poverty line—the working poor—the opportunities are severely limited. Thus, opportunities for training beyond the secondary school level remain severely restricted for nearly half of our youth. The only serious hope for improving this situation cannot come from the poor. Help must come in the form of greater public investment in higher education.

This is why we must concern ourselves with facts and figures on the value of school to the individual in a society which already accepts the generalized notion that schooling does materially improve one's ability to earn a livelihood. Perhaps the statistics should be used more to convince ourselves as members of a society that from the point of view of cold, hard economics the training of the individual contributes greatly to the economic well-being of the society.

In spite of the difficulties of controlling all the forces which contribute to earning power of individuals in any society, data provided by the census continues to make a compelling case for the economic returns on education.

---

[10] Report of the National Advisory Commission on Civil Disorders (New York: E. P. Dutton, 1968), p. 452.

[11] U.S. Bureau of the Census, *Pocket Data Book, U.S.A. 1969* (Washington, D.C.: U.S. Printing Office, 1969), p. 155.

The following chart, adapted from census data, illustrates as well as anything can the economic value of schooling to the individual.

Estimated Lifetime Income and Years of Schooling Completed[12]

Years of Schooling	Estimated Lifetime Earnings (In Dollars)
Less than 8 years	174,000
8 years	228,000
9 to 11 years	270,000
12 years (high school diploma)	320,000
1 to 3 years of college	381,000
4 years or more of college	520,000

Clearly, the investment in education pays dividends. Even when one considers the earnings by-passed by the individual who spends time in the upper years of high school and the years of college and adds this to the direct costs of school borne by the individual and society, it is still a good investment. One study of the problem[13] indicated that the return on investment in education was about the same as that on tangible capital during the period from 1940 to 1950. This study indicated that the return on investment in tangible capital in manufacturing was about 7 per cent after taxes. For all corporate earnings (during a growing and prosperous decade) the return was from 10 to 13 per cent and for unincorporated business from 5 to 8 per cent before taxes. With allowances for tax costs in education and individual investment, this study indicated a return on educational investment before taxes at about 9 per cent for urban white males.

Analysis of the relationship between income and education was given a boost as early as 1940 when the Census Bureau began collecting data which related family income to educational level. Theodore Schultz reported some of his findings on the economic value of education in the 1961 *Yearbook of the National Society for the Study of Education.* Some of his findings were rather startling. For example, for the year 1958, Professor Schultz discovered that college graduates could expect to earn $151,000 more during their working lifetime than those with only a high school diploma. He computed the cost of college at that time at $13,780 and concluded that the ratio of returns to costs was approximately 11 per cent.[14] Edward F. Denison of the

---

[12] Adapted from U.S. Bureau of Census, *Pocket Data Book, U.S.A. 1969.*

[13] Gary S. Becker, "Underinvestment in College Education?" *American Economic Review* (May 1960), vol. 50, no. 1, pp. 346–354.

[14] Theodore W. Schultz, "Education and Economic Growth," *Social Forces Influencing American Education, 1961* (Chicago: National Society for the Study of Education, 1961), p. 81.

Brookings Institution is also noted for his complex studies on the economic returns of education. In a study of the period from 1929 to 1957, Denison claimed that the contribution of education to national growth during this span of time was 23 per cent.[15]

In the mid-sixties, James Morgan and Ismail Sirageldin attempted to determine if there was a relationship between the amount a state spends per year on primary and secondary education and the later earnings of people who went through the school systems. In this task, the researchers looked at average per pupil expenditures for selected years in all the states and compared educational expenditure with income data. Their study attempted to control significant variables such as age, sex, race, rural or urban residence, and movement from one state to another. They found a pattern of positive relationships between a person's earnings and the expenditures on education. Generally, the individuals who reported the lowest hourly earnings were from states which had the lowest expenditure per pupil. Indeed, Morgan and Sirageldin claimed their study implied that "$1.00 more per year per pupil spent on education in a state means 24¢ an hour more earned by those who went to school there, other things equal."[16] Calculating an hourly rate in terms of lifetime returns on educational investment, the researchers found a return of more than 15 per cent. In applying their research to colleges, Morgan and Sirageldin found that those who graduated from what they called the "most selective" colleges had average annual earnings of nearly three times that of those who had no college, and nearly double that of those who graduated from what they termed "non-selective" colleges.[17] It should be pointed out that Morgan and Sirageldin were extremely cautious in drawing hard conclusions from their data. They admitted that the correlations between expenditures and earnings could be affected by the general economic condition of families, the state, and other significant variables. However, the pattern is fairly consistent. The causes and cures are another matter; it is difficult to determine whether the state's educational investment is low because the state is poor or vice versa. Such studies do demonstrate, however, that in general those who have the greatest number of years of schooling tend to fare best economically. It is also true that those communities employing large numbers of college graduates tend to rank high on per capita income charts.

Another interesting avenue of exploration has been the investigation of the productive value of education. Put simply, economists have been interested in whether or not education adds to the productivity of the worker. Obviously, if this could be demonstrated in specific terms, those who support education

---

[15] Edward F. Denison, *The Sources of Economic Growth in the United States and the Alternatives Before Us* (New York: Committee for Economic Development, 1962).

[16] James Morgan and Ismail Sirageldin, "A Note on the Quality Dimension in Education," *Journal of Political Economy* (Sept.-Oct. 1968), vol. 76, no. 5, p. 1074.

[17] Morgan and Sirageldin, p. 1076.

might be more easily convinced that they are getting their money's worth. There is some evidence that education does add to worker productivity. This has been particularly true in agriculture, which has experienced a tremendous input of research money, which in turn has been able to demand and utilize more training. Researchers studying the productive value of education have hypothesized that education may permit the worker to do more with the resources at hand. Moreover, in view of the complex nature of the economic system, more training and more sophisticated training become imperative. In the words of F. Welch, " . . . increased education may enhance a worker's ability to acquire and decode information about costs and productive characteristics of other inputs. As such, a change in education results in a change in other inputs, including, perhaps, the use of some new factors that otherwise would not be used."[18] What this says, in effect, is that education is indispensable to rapid technological development. Other studies[19] have placed the return on educational investment between 8 and 20 per cent. Although such studies have widely varying results, they all agree that education is a good investment with a high yield for the individual. Such studies are, of course, subject to criticism. For example, it is very difficult to control variables. One can prove nearly any rate of return he wishes, providing he selects the time and place and his subjects carefully. The popular hypothesis that schooling enhances earning power is always supported, however.

It really matters little whether economists will ever be able to determine accurately the exact return on educational investment (except that it may give them employment and provide endless research possibilities for struggling Ph.D. candidates). The argument is largely academic anyway. The major point to be considered in any study of the specific economic value of schooling is at once economic, political, and socio-psychological. With each passing year there are fewer opportunities for employment of the unskilled, the untrained, and the uneducated. For many years, unskilled labor needs have constituted less than 10 per cent of the demand. In recent years, this figure has fallen below 5 per cent. Because of this economic fact, it becomes increasingly apparent that the alternatives to more and better schooling for the individual in our society are becoming progressively limited.

These economic aspects of schooling have serious political and socio-psychological implications—political in the sense that large numbers of

---

[18] F. Welch, "Education in Production," *Journal of Political Economy* (Jan.-Feb. 1970), vol. 78, no. 1, p. 42.
[19] The student should see Mary Jean Bowman, "Human Capital: Concepts and Measures," *The Economics of Higher Education,* ed. Selma J. Mushkin (Washington, D.C.: U.S. Dept. of Health, Education, and Welfare, 1962); Lee W. Hansen, "Total and Private Rates of Return to Investment in Schooling," *Journal of Political Economy* (April 1963), vol. 71, pp. 128–140; and Michael Gisser, *Schooling and the Agricultural Labor Force,* Ph.D. dissertation, Univ. of Chicago, 1962.

unemployed in the ranks of the youth of our nation are embarrassing to either major political party in power. The political consequences of unemployment are recognized by both major political parties and the promise of full employment has become a standard campaign plank for Democrats and Republicans. This is true because there is genuine political recognition of the deleterious social and psychological effects of unemployment. For those able and willing to work, but who lack the necessary skills, welfare and unemployment benefits are a poor solution.

The day is gone, however, when employment can be promised to those who are not educationally qualified to fill a productive role in the society. Thus, it becomes necessary for political leaders to turn to the schools for help. This development raises questions about political policy relative to education which need to be faced seriously by political leaders.

The need for trained or skilled citizens could be met by: (1) maintaining the present educational system with its obvious inefficiency resulting from a wide range of individual choice, (2) greater planning with specific training established along the lines of needs of the economic system, or (3) any number of variations in between. There is a growing volume of literature suggesting more direct approaches to the problem of schooling for specific needs of the economy. In some ways, the various programs of the national government appear to be directed toward this type of approach. This is particularly true of the planning which is being done for the education of the dropout, and there are certain features in the war on poverty which tend in the direction of planned educational programs to meet specific needs of the economic system. The concern of officials in the U. S. Office of Education for "career education" seems to be the fad of the seventies. The trend in planning could be in the direction of providing a separate track system of vocational schools for large numbers of lower-class children in our society. Such planning on a large scale, involving millions of school children, would substantially modify the existing system of public education. It is doubtful, however, that the American public will give its full support to a double track system that has as its major objective specific labor demands. The greater probability is that the system will continue to provide the kind of training which it has in the past, but that the national government will increasingly enter the picture in attempting to provide educational opportunity for those in our society who have not, for one reason or another, been able to prepare themselves for gainful employment in a highly developed technological society. What this boils down to for practical purposes is the old argument over the advantages and disadvantages of carefully planned educational programs designed to train people for specific jobs, versus the general education point of view. Until now, the public has committed itself to the policy of allowing the individual to decide on the kind and amount of specialized training for specific occupations. The many exceptions to this policy which exist in the form of specific vocational programs in the larger urban secondary schools (in some instances, approaching a two-track system—one for college prep courses, one for training in vocational skills) have been subject to continuing and sometimes heated debate in the literature of education. What is most surprising about the current educational activities of the national government is the very sparsity of debate over the direction the programs are taking. The general feeling seems to be one of hopelessness—that something must be done for the impoverished in our society—it doesn't matter what. Yet, the political implications of educational programs and plans to meet immediate and pressing needs of the unemployed and underemployed with specific training programs are tremendous. In view of political implications, the small amount of public debate is puzzling.

There is a hidden danger lurking in the economics of educational planning. Planning can constitute a threat to freedom. In the case of the schools, the freedom threatened could be the freedom of choice for students and their parents. This threat exists because of the logical and irresistible economic appeal in comprehensive national educational planning. Such planning could be justified in terms of national economic well-being. Obviously, the unemployed and the underemployed represent a real economic waste. As a society we are, and properly should be, concerned about national growth. As a general rule, the rate of national growth is enhanced by full employment, a condition which can be achieved (given an otherwise healthy economy) only if training can provide the human resources to match the needs of the system. Total efficiency in this matching process would require total planning—a solution which would not be worth its price.

Finally, there are socio-psychological considerations involved in the problem of educational investment which have societal as well as individual implications. As we pointed out earlier, those who are unemployed or underemployed in an otherwise affluent society can become alienated from the mainstream of the social and economic system. The inability of large segments of our society to share in the benefits of the economic system is a condition which not only has serious social effects, but psychological effects as well. The educationally deprived in our society present serious problems of adjustment. Being unemployed does things to one's attitude and character that are, perhaps, beyond measurement. For these reasons society has accepted some of the financial responsibility for schooling beyond the elementary and secondary school.

As commendable as this effort may be, it remains true that everyone does not benefit from general public contributions to higher education. This is a double tragedy for the poor, because through their taxes, they are helping to subsidize college costs for the children of their more affluent neighbors. The result is injustice compounded; those who are thus educationally deprived become progressively more economically deprived with each passing year, partially because of the very relationship between level of educational attainment and income described in this chapter. In view of the importance of education in helping to break the cycle of poverty for families in this condition, what may be most needed is a general democratization of the system of higher education. Schooling beyond a certain point is least available for those who most need it—in economic as well as in other terms. The sort of reform needed to open the doors of higher education would vastly increase the costs, a condition which would necessitate the rallying of a majority of our citizens to invest more in education. Ironically, those who currently benefit most—the more affluent members of the society—are often the most outspoken critics of increasing tax funds for higher education. This kind of opposition must be overcome, not only because of the demonstrated economic return on educational investment, but as an article of faith in the justice of democracy itself.

No democratic society can continue to profess its democratic character while more than half of its young citizens are effectively denied minimum requirements for entering the competitive arena of the economic system. For the sake of the survival of what we like to call democratic education, the next two decades should witness great pressure for genuine equality of educational opportunity in higher education.

REFERENCES

Adams, Don, and Robert M. Bjork. *Education in Developing Areas.* New York: David McKay, 1969.

Becker, Gary S. "Underinvestment in College Education?" *American Economic Review.* 50, I:346–354 (May 1960).

Benson, Charles S. *The Economics of Public Education.* Boston: Houghton Mifflin, 1961.

Bowman, Mary Jean. "Human Capital: Concepts and Measures." *The Economics of Higher Education,* Selma J. Mushkin (ed.). Washington, D.C.: U.S. Dept. of Health, Education, and Welfare, 1962.

Burkhead, Jesse. *Public School Finance, Economics and Politics.* Syracuse, N.Y.: Syracuse Univ. Press, 1964.

Clark, Burton R. *Educating the Expert Society.* San Francisco: Chandler, 1962.

Denison, Edward F. *The Sources of Economic Growth in the United States and the Alternatives Before Us.* New York: Committee for Economic Development, 1962.

Eckland, Bruce K. "Social Class and College Graduation: Some Misconceptions Corrected." *American Journal of Sociology.* 70:36–51 (July 1964).

Galbraith, John K. *The Affluent Society.* Boston: Houghton Mifflin, 1958.

Gisser, Michael. *Schooling and the Agricultural Labor Force.* Ph. D. dissertation, Univ. of Chicago, 1962.

Groves, Harold M. *Education and Economic Growth.* Washington, D.C.: The Committee on Educational Finance, 1961.

Halsey, A. H., Jean Floud, and C. Arnold Anderson (eds.). *Education, Economy and Society.* New York: Free Press of Glencoe, 1961.

Hansen, Lee W. "Total and Private Rates of Return to Investment in Schooling." *Journal of Political Economy.* 71:128–140 (April 1963).

Harbison, Frederick, and Charles Myers. *Education, Manpower and Economic Growth: Strategies of Human Resource Development.* New York: McGraw-Hill, 1964.

Miller, Herman P. "Annual and Lifetime Income in Relation to Education." *American Economics Review.* 50, XI:962–985 (Dec. 1960).

Morgan, James, and Ismail Sirageldin. "A Note on the Quality Dimension in Education." *Journal of Political Economy.* 76, V:1069–1077 (Sept.-Oct. 1968).

Norton, John K. *Changing Demands on Education and Their Fiscal Implications.* National Committee for the Support of the Public Schools. Washington, D.C.: Public Affairs Press, 1963.

Report of the National Advisory Commission on Civil Disorders. New York: E. P. Dutton, 1968.

Schultz, Theodore W. *The Economic Value of Education.* New York: Columbia Univ. Press, 1963.

———. "Education and Economic Growth." *Social Forces Influencing American Education, 1961.* Chicago: National Society for the Study of Education, 1961.

Sexton, Patricia. *Education and Income.* New York: Viking Press, 1961.

U. S. Bureau of the Census. *Pocket Data Book, U.S.A. 1969.* Washington, D.C.: U.S. Government Printing Office, 1969.

Welch, F. "Education in Production." *Journal of Political Economy.* 78, I:35–59 (Jan.-Feb. 1970).

PART THREE
How the Schools Are Organized to Teach Values

Chapters 9 and 10 deal with the organization and functions, on the local and state level, of the school system in the United States, and the manner in which the national government has become involved in public education. Specifically, these chapters deal with the organization and composition of school boards and school districts, and the various agents and agencies on the state and national level which are concerned with educational matters.

In some instances the relationship between the organization and functions of the educational enterprise and values is self-evident, and in others it is not. In any case, the general question of values underlies the way schools are organized and the kinds of things schools are able to do. A few illustrations are provided to point up the relationship between organization and functions of the educational enterprise and social values. However, the major content of the following section is descriptive in nature, allowing the reader to draw his own conclusions.

9

Education As a State and Local Political Function

As a state and local function, education has been, and continues to be, a governmental function. As such, it is greatly dependent upon local political values, upon what is politically possible in the community. Education as a major function of state and local government is part of the political process and organization of the state. Very often the organization and often the basic functions of education are carefully outlined in the state constitution. Such constitutional provisions may be very general in nature or very detailed. Where the details of organization and function are not spelled out in the state constitution, they are spelled out in the laws which govern the school system.

Thus, one cannot consider education outside the general political structure of state government. At the top of the administrative hierarchy, most state constitutions provide for a chief school officer variously titled as the state superintendent of schools or commissioner of education. Where constitutional provisions establish the chief school officer of the state, there are frequently detailed paragraphs which determine his qualifications for office, the length of his term, and the manner in which he is to be selected.

Similarly, many state constitutions have provisions relating to a state school board or make some provision for a policy-making agency at the state level in education. If the constitutional provision is not there, certainly the statutes provide for the organization. The state constitutions provide the details of school district organization in some cases, and again, where not provided in the constitution, provision is made in state law. Moreover, the educational functions of the county and the local board governing the local school district are spelled out in detail either in the constitution or in state law. In any case the school system, its organization, and functions, is an inseparable part of the political organization of the state.

In spite of this close relationship between the schools and governmental structure, the American school and its functions have developed as a somewhat unique entity in our system. Although it is an integral part of governmental organization and process as established by law and by the constitutions of the several states, the school has some characteristics which historically have set it apart from the political scene. School people generally have been reluctant to consider themselves part of the regular political structure of state government. This has included teachers and administrators on all levels of education within any given state. Although this separate identity may have been more mythical than real, there might have been some basis for the existence of the myth. Two rather obvious examples of the separate character of the educational enterprise have been: (1) the relationship between the citizen and the schools, and (2) the lack of relationship between certain governmental processes and the schools.

It is possible that until very recently when the citizen thought of schools he did not think of them in the same terms he thought of his county, city, or state government. Education, in popular thought, has not been traditionally considered an integral part of the state and local political organization and process, but as a separate entity. In the past, schools and school questions have been frequently and sometimes deliberately dissociated from politics and political questions. Not only has education been deliberately nonpartisan (which is not always possible), but there seemed to be a popular belief in the complete independence of education from political organization and processes. School board elections thus have been traditionally nonpartisan, and have often proceeded as if the local school board—its election, its policies, and its membership—had no real-life relationship to what was happening in the political environment surrounding it.

In some communities there has long been a real gap in popular thought between the general government processes and policies and the public school. The power and control aspects of education and other governmental functions have been viewed differently. One illustration of this different framework has been the difference between reform movements in the organization of local and state government and the reform of school organization. Typical governmental reforms such as the merit system, and reorganization of the administrative structure of state and local government, such as the limitation of functions, functional reorganization, or the introduction of a city-manager-type government, have completely by-passed the schools. This does not mean that reorganization has not occurred in education. The initiative for such reorganization and reform has come not so much out of the political cauldron, however, as it has from those directly involved in education.

The result has been a difference in the manner in which formal and informal power groups as well as individuals have related themselves to schools and to government. There are many illustrations in general local or state government of the initiative for change or reform coming from power groups or individuals in the community when change or reform concerns general local or state government. On the other hand, when the schools are considered, a great deal of the innovation in organization and administration has come from within the profession of education.

There is much evidence that apathy toward the schools is undergoing some rather radical change. Recent movements for reform, particularly among minorities and youth, have frequently been directed toward the schools. There is much evidence that teachers are becoming more militant and openly political. As we pointed out in preceding chapters, the increasing costs of education have tended to make school finance a particularly sharp political issue in hundreds of communities in recent years. Beyond this, the increasing financial presence and influence of the national government in education has made education an open political issue on the national level. Even though this increasing politicization of the schools has been shocking and painful for some school people, hopefully it will work toward improvement of the schools. At least the increasing political role of the schools has shaken some people out of their apathy, more people are aware that schooling plays a central role in the real world of politics, and more people are becoming aware of the problems which exist in the educational system. Thus, citizens in increasing numbers are beginning to recognize that schools cannot be considered outside the total political and governmental structure.

Even so, the long tradition of localism in education continues to resist change. This tradition is, perhaps, most responsible for the belief that the schools are somehow outside the general political arena. A desire for continued local control of schools has supported the belief. Local power groups and individuals within the community have been able to hang on to a great amount of control of the local school system. In some communities there can be little doubt that a single individual or a few influential persons are instrumental in naming candidates for school board elections, constitute the power behind the local superintendent of schools, and in a general way, "run the schools" as they believe they should be.

For example, teachers soon learn that in some communities, "violating the standards of community behavior" may have a very limited definition. What is sometimes meant by community standards boils down to: "Don't cross old man Jones, he really runs this town." Naturally, where such a situation exists, it is in the interest of the controlling individual or group to maintain the status quo. This becomes even more vital as the leading power sources in the community see power in other areas slipping out of their grip due to increasing state or national activity. The phenomenon of decreasing local control is, of course, becoming more pronounced in education as well as in other areas in which political power is exercised.

However, localism in education has persisted well into the age of technology and urbanization in spite of many instances of rather obvious need for a more comprehensive view of the state's educational function. In practice, the localism expresses itself in many ways. School district reorganization, where it has been attempted, has been accomplished only after the most bitter struggle on the part of local communities to retain a major voice in the nature and extent of the reorganization. The matter of federal aid to education has often been opposed on the local level partly because of a serious belief that "federal money means federal control," a prospect which strikes fear into the hearts of some local school patrons. This tradition of localism has been a long time in building. Perhaps a look at the existing organization for education will help the reader to better understand the problem.

THE LOCAL BOARD AS A POLITICAL INSTITUTION

Historically, the local school board was a natural development growing out of the needs of the community. Although the present reality is that the education of the youth of the United States is a cooperative affair shared by the local, state, and national levels of government, it has not always been that way. The original drive for public schools came from leaders of the local community, the towns and villages of colonial America. Until the 1840's the function of schooling was considered by most citizens as primarily local, and it had developed as such. Early in our experience, local committees were appointed to see to the operation of the school and they had almost absolute power in this area. They could set the qualifications for the teacher or teachers, examine them with regard to their competence, determine the curriculum which could be followed, establish rules for the teacher as well as the student, and determine the location and provide the facilities for the local school. These local committees eventually came to be elected by the taxpayers in the community, and the local school board thus came into existence. The earliest boards inherited the broad powers of the local school committees. In many communities this pattern existed well into the twentieth century. The system of absolute local control was possible if not desirable in a nation which was primarily rural. The size of the nation coupled with the difficulty of transportation and the scattered and rural nature of the population encouraged the continuance of almost absolute control over the community schools by the local community as represented by its board of education.

As a political institution, the local school board grew as a democratic agency directly controlled by and responsive to local needs and desires. On the negative side, the local board was not completely democratic in that in most instances only property owners or taxpayers had a voice in the election of its members.

Moreover, it has always been possible for influential individuals and powerful groups in communities to exert varying amounts of control over local school board members. For example, if a school board member happened to be an employee of the town's largest taxpayer, it would be unrealistic to expect him to be a completely independent agent acting in the best interests of the masses on all issues. The drive for decentralization, described in Chapter 4, underlines the frustration experienced by many local citizens who feel they have little influence on the decisions made by school boards. In the large cities, those who have pushed for decentralization have done so partly because they believed they were not being represented in the existing system. While the decentralization battle is being won in the larger cities, in the smaller cities, towns, and rural areas of the nation minorities continue to be underrepresented on school boards at best, and at worst not represented at all. This becomes a particularly acute problem in areas where Chicano, Indian, or Black minorities are very small, since it has been possible for boards representing middle-class whites to proceed as if the minorities had no quarrel with the schools; indeed, to act as if the minorities did not exist. Generally, such a system can work great hardships on the children of minority groups. The board can neglect reading problems of such children, it can support track systems which provide inferior training, it can support prejudiced teachers at the expense of children, or it can neglect hunger by failing to provide a free lunch program. In short, where minorities are totally unrepresented on school boards, it can mean that schooling beyond a certain level becomes all but impossible for their children. This is why representation on the school board is so politically significant. For many minority group individuals, the schools are the front lines of political activism.

THE NATURE OF THE LOCAL BOARD

In the face of a tradition of local control, the revolutionary changes in many communities during the last thirty-five years have created serious problems for school organization. A major problem is the school board itself.

Before discussing some of the problems which are related to school boards, let us take a brief look at their organization. Although they vary from one community to the next, it is not uncommon to find boards which consist of from three to seven members generally elected for overlapping terms for periods of from two to six years. Most are elected on a nonpartisan ballot. A recent (1964) NEA study of a sample of 305 boards of education in school systems with enrollments of over twelve thousand students found that 82.2 per cent of the boards were elective on a nonpartisan basis. The median size board in this study was found to consist of seven members. This study also found that more than three-fourths of the local school boards were elected and one-fifth appointed by various groups and officials, generally the city council or mayor.[1]

The tradition of enabling only property owners to vote in board elections persists in some states even though the United States Supreme Court found a New York law limiting the school election ballot to those who owned or leased taxable real property a violation of the Constitution.[2] Presumably, any citizen who is denied participation by state law in a school election can now challenge its legality. Certainly the Court's decision is more in line with the realities of the present than existing limited suffrage provisions of many states. The election of school board members by the limited suffrage of the taxpayer may have been more realistic in the past than it is in the present. In the first place, the property qualification for voting in school board elections was reasonable in communities that were fairly stable and whose boundaries could be rather clearly drawn from a geographic point of view. In the past, communities were much more isolated and often more homogeneous than at present. Rapid industrialization, the urbanization of the nation, and the problems attending the advent of the technological society have greatly disturbed this homogeneous quality. Indeed, these forces have disrupted many old communities to the point where the sense of community no longer exists. Where community lines could be clearly defined and there were the neighborliness and personal acquaintance implied in such a definition, the suffrage qualifications were not so vital an issue. On the other hand, where community lines are not clear and there is little communication between citizens and voters on the local educational issues, the local school board and the local focus of power in education may be dated. Secondly, in the kind of mobile population which characterizes present society, the old property qualifications for voting in school elections have become archaic. This is dramatically true where rental property is more the way of life and where property owners and taxpayers may actually constitute a minority of the population. In addition to these problems, where the old idea of property owner control of local education may have been based on the valid premise that those who pay should control, support has been shifted to a broader base, and although local funds are still significant, they are gradually diminishing in importance. Indeed, many local schools are greatly dependent on state and national assistance. Where the state legislature provides a significant share of the cost of maintaining the local school, a major justification for limited suffrage based on local taxpaying has been removed.

---

[1] National Education Association, Research Division, and American Association of School Administrators, Educational Research Service, *Local School Boards: Size and Selection* (Washington, D.C.: Educational Research Service, Feb. 1964), Circular No. 2, 1964.

[2] *Kramer v. Union Free School District*, 395 U.S. 621 (1968).

These are significant problems because of the effect thay can have on the type of school board which is elected and the subsequent program of the local school. Merely the provision that school board members must reside within the school district which they represent, and that they be property taxpayers within that district, is no assurance that they are representatives of the majority of the people living within the district. It is possible that they are not representative at all. A few studies have been made of the nature and composition of the "typical" board. Such studies are so few and the samples so small that they are of little value in attempting to determine the nature of the "typical" school board, if indeed, such exists. For lack of better evidence, one can only speculate on the nature of school board membership. A few facts about school board members are known, however. The vast majority of them are elected. We also know that nearly all of the school board members of more than forty thousand independent school districts in the country serve without pay. In the most comprehensive study of its kind, Neal Gross[3] discovered that school board members in Massachusetts tended to be over forty-five years of age, Protestant in religion, and generally conservative with regard to the sort of things they would like to see taught in the public schools.

Some speculation is possible as to why school board members might adhere to conservative values. In many locations there may be a lack of available funds to experiment with new programs or new ideas in education. Even where funds are available, individual school board members may see no good reason why the local schools should be any different than they were thirty years ago when they came through the system and it provided them with an education which was "plenty good enough" to enable them to succeed. Perhaps the most realistic of all reasons for the conservative nature of many school board members is that they are conservative in matters of taxation. It costs money to experiment, to try new ideas, to implement what are known to be good practices in education. It costs money to hire the best available teachers and provide them with excellent facilities for teaching. Many of the school boards of our land are unwilling to impose the local taxes necessary to provide the kind of education that may be needed in the community, but they may be quite willing to accept innovation if it is financed by state or national funds.

Of course, there are many exceptions to the kind of conservatism described here. Some school districts have the resources, the people who are interested in excellence in education, and school boards which provide leadership for excellence. There can be little question that the local school board can provide any kind of leadership it wishes. Although in many states the legislatures have carefully defined the membership qualifications of

---

[3] Neal Gross, *Who Runs Our Schools?* (New York: John Wiley & Sons, 1958).

school boards, usually in terms of minimum educational requirements, residence, terms, the manner in which they shall be elected, and the general area of powers which are to be exercised by the board, the local school board is a powerful agency in the determination of school policy.

GENERAL POWERS OF LOCAL SCHOOL BOARDS

It is difficult to generalize about the powers of school boards since there are so many boards which represent such a wide variety of communities and conditions across the country. There are school boards in some rural communities in districts where there may be only a few teachers and perhaps no administrative personnel. In these cases the members of the board may actually administer the school. On the other extreme, there are boards in school districts with hundreds of teachers and with a complex administrative hierarchy; these boards may meet frequently and limit themselves to only the highest level of policy-making.

Regardless of the size of the district, however, the board is generally charged with responsibilities which include policy-making, administration, and advisement. In its policy-making role, the school board is generally acting as a miniature legislative body. Acting within the prescription of state law, the local board is frequently charged with the responsibility of providing for local funds which frequently involves determining the rate of school taxes. In addition, it has some responsibility for determining how the available money will be spent, and in this respect it has a very real influence on the nature of the local program. In terms of policy the local board also makes decisions about the location of new school buildings; the allocation of money for additions, repairs, and remodeling; and so on. Typical administrative duties of the school board include hiring the superintendent or other top school officials, making reports to higher agencies of government concerning the operation of the local schools, and accounting for state expenditures of school funds provided by the state. The local board also has at least the implicit if not the legal responsibility for the general supervision of the local school system and its employees. In its advisement function the school board acts as the representative of its public in advising school personnel on matters of general public interest. In certain cases it may be difficult to determine where advisement leaves off and policy-making begins. For example, there may be a great feeling in the community that a certain type of reading instruction be provided at the elementary level. The board may advise administrators to this effect but such advice may really constitute a directive rather than mere advisement. In most instances the superintendent who ignores the advice of his board is not interested in a long tenure in the community.

THE TEACHER AND THE BOARD

During most of its historical existence, the typical school board has been a democratic institution of sorts; a policy-making body elected to channel and implement the desires of a majority of the qualified voters in a community on educational matters. For the most part, the American school board has lived up to this high purpose. It has fallen short of the ideal where its members are not really representative of the population or where it ignores the counsel of the classroom teacher in its formulation of school policy. The problem of involvement of the professional classroom teacher in the formulation of school policy is at once one of the brightest spots and one of the most discouraging aspects of the role and function of the local school board. It is discouraging when local school board members treat teachers as "hired help." In such cases there may be no lines of communication between the classroom teacher and the local board. Fortunately, a policy of neglect of the classroom teacher and the minimization of his influence on educational policy may be an aspect of the school scene which is fast passing out of existence. Teachers are rapidly gaining influence in policy matters on the local level. This is true partly because education is becoming a highly complex and technological business that has moved beyond the competence of many lay board members, thus necessitating consultation with the classroom teacher, if not open and continuing communication and cooperation. Secondly, classroom teachers are demanding a greater role in the formulation of policy, and the organizations which represent them are backing them up in these demands.

The most common vehicle by which teachers are gaining some influence over their own welfare is the process of collective negotiations. Teachers everywhere in the country are pressing for some sort of legal arrangement which will enable them to negotiate as equals with their school boards. The first such agreement was reached between the New York City Board of Education and its teachers in 1961. Since that time, twelve states have enacted laws which specifically permit teachers' groups to engage in collective negotiations with their boards, and thirteen others allow other public employees to negotiate collectively. Several of the remaining twenty-five states are considering such legislation. For teachers, collective negotiations present a rather marked contrast to what has existed in most school districts. In the past, teachers would submit their demands to the school board, very often through the superintendent of schools. This was followed by an unencumbered, unilateral decision by the board. Generally, if teachers were not satisfied with the decision of the board, there was little they could do except seek employment elsewhere as individuals. Under negotiation contracts, the teachers make their proposal, the board makes its counter-proposal and the elected representatives of the teachers and the board then attempt to negotiate the differences. There is every reason to believe that the system of collective negotiations will spread, not so much because it is a better system (which it may well be), but because teachers will continue to insist on a greater voice in matters which vitally affect them.

THE SCHOOL DISTRICT

The creation of special districts for the execution of governmental functions is much older than the American system of government. As the original English colonial settlements near the Atlantic coast became more populous and the population moved inland, new towns were established at some distance from the original settlements. These towns needed some means of defense, some way to provide and maintain roads, and the people were interested in providing schools for the children. In order to furnish a convenient means for organizing and administering these functions as well as for financing their operation, the special district came into existence. Among the first to provide such special school districts were Connecticut in 1766 and Massachusetts in 1789.[4] These early school districts were independent of the other functions of government and were given authority, for example, to elect school board members who had autonomous powers to levy taxes and to select teachers.

This has been the pattern up to the present. Although the device of special districts is a common feature of local government, and they have been used for purposes of financing and administering such functions as fire and police protection, sanitation, street development, and conservation, by far the most numerous of the local independent districts are the school districts. Moreover, the system of district organization for the performance of the educational function is nearly universal in the United States. Only four states—Maryland, North Carolina, Rhode Island, and Virginia—do not have the school district.[5]

During the 1969–1970 school year, there were approximately 18,904 school districts in the United States. These varied widely in size and organization throughout the country. Generally, there are two types—independent and dependent. The independent districts are completely autonomous from the other local governmental agencies, although all of them presently have some relationship to the state government. In addition, many are involved in some way with the national government. The independent district system allows a great deal of policy-making power within the district boundaries. Local

---

[4] Ellwood P. Cubberley, *Public Education in the United States,* rev. ed. (Boston: Houghton Mifflin, 1934), p. 73.
[5] John C. Bollens, *Special District Governments in the United States* (Berkeley, Calif.: Univ. of California Press, 1957), p. 180.

independent school districts often have the legal power to levy local taxes, procure teachers and other personnel, purchase supplies, deal with curriculum matters, and a number of other functions. In twenty-nine of the fifty states, all of the school districts are independent governmental units.

The dependent school district is often in a subordinate position to some agency of local government. Such a district may rely upon the city council, which might exercise some budgetary authority over the district, or it may depend upon the county superintendent or some intermediate agent on supervision, records, or some other function or responsibility. Another example of dependency might be a school district which exists within the boundaries of an independent school district; that is, an independent school district may have within its boundaries districts designated as elementary school districts which are subordinate to a larger district for tax purposes or supervision of the schools within the district. Dependent districts exist exclusively in four states and in the District of Columbia. A little less than half the states have a mixture of both dependent and independent school districts.[6]

In addition to the variety of types of school districts, there exists a wide variety in size in the United States. There remain many one-teacher rural school districts in the United States. There is also a great variety in the geographic area of school districts. Some school districts in the more sparsely populated areas cover as much area as some of the smaller states. The Elko County, Nevada, school district, for example, has an area of more than seventeen thousand square miles, which is a greater area than the entire states of Rhode Island, Connecticut, and Massachusetts combined. The Elko County district has an enrollment of a few thousand pupils, while the combined enrollment of students in Connecticut, Massachusetts, and Rhode Island approaches one and three-fourths million pupils.[7]

Along with this wide diversity in area and number of pupils, there is also a wide variation in financial or taxable resources from one school district to the next. Indeed, even within the same county the differences in taxable wealth may be rather marked. In some areas of the West, for example, a school district which follows a river bottom containing most of the valuable farm land, the railroad, and such industrial development as exists in the county, may be a rich one in terms of taxable resources, while a district within the same county which lies out in semiarid or near-desert land, with sparse population and no taxable industry, may be extremely poor by comparison. Imagine the great differences in taxable wealth which may exist within the boundaries of a large state or from the poorest to the wealthiest school

[6] U.S. Bureau of the Census, *Census of Government, 1962* (Washington, D.C.: U.S. Government Printing Office, 1963), Gov't. Org., vol. 1, p. 4.
[7] American Association of School Administrators, *School District Organization* (Washington, D.C.: NEA, 1958), p. 82.

district in the nation. In some states with many small districts, it is not uncommon for the most prosperous district within a county to have twenty to fifty times as much wealth per pupil as the poorest.[8]

Such wide differences in wealth between school districts in the United States means that from one locality to the next there are great differences in ability to support education. The result is that some schools have a great quantity and variety of programs, materials, buildings, and teachers, while others consist of one or a few teachers holding forth in dilapidated buildings with small numbers of students in several grades and almost nonexistent materials for teaching. This is a particularly acute problem in some urban districts where inner-city schools have a low tax valuation base and a high-density school population compared to surrounding suburbs. These local differences are even more significant when one considers the fact that in most sections of the country, with the exception of the southeastern states, more than 50 per cent of public school revenue is derived from local sources. For the nation as a whole, local sources account for more than 52 per cent of the total.[9] The question of the constitutionality of these great discrepancies in taxable wealth is presently being brought in several states and could be the most significant school issue of the next decade.

Although there may be a wide variety in the size and resources of school districts in the United States, there is some similarity in the purposes of school district organization. The number and size of school districts in the country are what they are largely because of the purposes which they have had to serve. Originally, they were designed merely as convenient and frequently arbitrary geographic areas which would serve as a tax base for the support of the single function of education. The district was also a convenient administrative unit designed in many cases in the days when children walked to school. Walking distance and population concentrations thus generally dictated the size of the district, and in a very real way, its functions. As transportation improved and population grew and shifted, needs changed and so did district lines; but they have generally not kept pace with shifting population, improved transportation, and increasing financial needs.

District organization for schools illustrates as well as anything can the nature of the attempt to consider schools apart from general government and the political process. Many school districts are not only independent, but one might accurately say that many of them are stubbornly independent. Of course, the needs of schooling have changed, in some instances dramatically, over the years. The number of children to be served has greatly increased, the money needed for schooling has increased geometrically, and the school function has become a conprehensive and complicated one in

[8] National Education Association, *Estimates of School Statistics, 1963–1964* (Washington, D.C.: Research Division, 1963), (R-12), p. 7.
[9] National Education Association, *Estimates of School Statistics, 1969–1970* (Washington, D.C.: Research Division, 1969), (R-15), p. 34.

many of the school districts of the nation. These factors and others have created a greater need for state support and control of education. The result has been extensive modification of districts without really disturbing the basic idea of district organization. The major change which has taken place in the district system in the twentieth century has been the consolidation of districts. The extent of this change is pointed out by the Research Division of the National Education Association:

> The number of basic administrative units reported in 1931–1932 was 127,422. Primarily as a result of reorganization laws, which have facilitated the consolidation and annexation of school districts, the number of such units has declined steadily. The 1969–1970 total of 18,904 represents an 85.2 per cent decrease from the 1931–1932 figure, a 53.4 per cent decrease in the ten-year period since 1959–1960, and a 6.7 per cent decrease in the past year.[10]

Of course, other functions of government on the state and local level have been reorganized in this century, in some cases even more extensively than the reorganization movement in school districts. City government, for example, has experienced some genuine innovations which have been designed to make administration more professional and efficient. The most obvious example is the widespread adoption of the city-manager type of government. By contrast, the internal administration of the school district has changed little. The school board remains the policy-making body in the local school district. Administration of the district by a superintendent appointed by the board remains the major administrative feature of the district. Perhaps reorganization of the administrative structure of the school district has not been as necessary as it has been in city government. This may be true since the school district and its administrative hierarchy have always been a single-function agency of government, whereas local governmental functions are numerous. The problem of ineffective or inefficient administrative organization may not be so difficult in a single-function unit as it is in the multiple-function governmental unit. The single greatest problem with school administration has been the adequacy, administrative efficiency, and economic soundness of the school district itself—a problem relating to size and to the relationship of the school district to other governmental agencies and authorities. In this respect the imperative needs for reorganization of the educational function have provided the need for enlarging the size of school districts, and an increasing concern with centralization of the educational function, primarily on the level of state government. Both of these needs have presented serious problems. District reorganization has been resisted mightily in most local areas, and the centralization of school finance and control into the hands of state government has been seriously opposed.

---

[10] NEA, *Estimates of School Statistics, 1969–1970*, p. 4.

Some of the reasons for this are obvious. An immediate resistance exists because local patrons who are faced with reorganization have had no part in its initiation. Generally, movements for reorganization of school districts have not come from local groups, but have been initiated in the state legislature or by individuals or school officials interested in more effective organization for schools. This has not only been a proper development, but it has been a legal one. In the legal sense the local school districts, like other local districts, are creatures of the state legislature and can be changed or abolished by the legislature. If left to the local community, the matter of school district reorganization and consolidation might proceed slowly if at all. The tradition of localism in the United States is perhaps nowhere more strongly expressed than it is in the matter of schooling, and it is so old and so firmly entrenched that it is difficult to overcome. Local patrons and taxpayers like to have control close to home for reasons ranging from psychological to economic. Almost invariably, however, arguments on the local level against reorganization revolve around questions of what constitutes a "good" school and the issue of the cost of education. There is frequently a good amount of nostalgia involved on the part of local patrons who want the local school organization to remain as they remember it. Any admission that the schools had not been organized to do an adequate job of schooling would be an admission that the kind of schooling the patrons had received was somehow inferior. This is an admission that is difficult for many to face. Of course, there are many other obstacles to reorganization. Parents worry about the local school being removed from the scene because it has become a landmark, also about the possibility of their children traveling greater distances to and from school, increasing the social distance between the teacher and the parents, elimination of what may be locally considered to be a good school, mixing of students into a more heterogeneous population, and so on.

In addition to these kinds of worries, in nearly every case in which reorganization battles have been waged on the local level, there is the concern over how much more it will cost the local taxpayer. It is difficult to prove that reorganization is a cost-saving device, and local taxpayers are not easily convinced that an expansion of the size of the school district will have any effect other than to raise their taxes. For these reasons and others, communities have been seriously split over issues surrounding the reorganization of their school districts.

It is doubtful that the consolidation of school districts would have proceeded with such a rapid pace in the last thirty-five years if it had not been for the fact that the reorganization has been directed from the legislature rather than from the local districts. All of the states have passed legislation relating to school district reorganization. Such laws vary from mandatory legislation, which demands that school districts reorganize in a specific manner, to permissive legislation, which leaves the question up to the local people. In some states where the initiative or referendum exists, these methods have been used to accomplish either mandatory or permissive reorganization. Where mandatory legislation has been passed, it generally provides that districts must have a certain minimum number of enrolled students, or that the minimum size district be large enough to support a school system which includes grades 1–12, or that the minimum size should have some minimum financial base in terms of per pupil evaluation or some other formula. Similarly, there have been many permissive laws which include provisions that enable a majority of the voters in two or more reorganized districts to decide the issue. In some cases a majority of voters in each of the districts decides the issue. Whether mandatory or permissive, it is a matter of record that reorganization has proceeded rapidly.

There are many arguments pro and con for school district reorganization. With notable exceptions, school administrators and teachers have been strong in their support of it. The following criteria have been generally accepted by school people as practical for adequate local school districts, and have been frequently used as the major platform for reorganization:

School districts (or administrative units) should not be smaller than the areas of the natural sociological community; if possible, coincide with the local governmental unit; contain enough children to make possible a well-balanced but economical elementary and secondary school program;

have a pupil population large enough to permit provision of many essential types of educational services on an economical basis (supervision of instruction, attendance, transportation, guidance, health services, lunch program, vocational education, and special teachers in fields of art, music, etc.);

be large enough to locate high school attendance units within the natural community and permit elementary school attendance units at places which serve the children most effectively;

be large enough to afford the necessary administrative and supervisory staff at a cost deemed reasonable in terms of the total cost of the educational program;

contain sufficient assessed valuation and taxing capacity to provide the revenue required, when supplemented by state and federal funds, to finance an adequate educational program;

be large enough to attract and use to good advantage a high type of educational leadership (salary attractive to capable school leaders; program large enough to challenge best efforts of leadership).[11]

---

[11] Ellis Ford Hartford, *Education in These United States* (New York: Macmillan, 1964), pp. 159–160.

These criteria are open to debate, but they have been generally accepted by forces which have been working for reorganization. The success of the movement indicates they have a kind of face validity about them—at least the arguments have been capable of convincing voters across the land that reorganization is necessary. Obviously all of the arguments are not emphasized in every battle for reorganization. The criteria have been flexible enough so that in one community the major issue may be the cost of small districts, in another, inequality of educational opportunity may be emphasized, while in others the importance of a comprehensive educational program may be stressed.

Even the most dedicated advocate of school reorganization, however, must pause from time to time to reflect upon some of the negative aspects of reorganization. All of the good arguments for consolidation of school districts notwithstanding, perhaps the real moving force behind reorganization has been the condition of the society. Certainly the mobility of the society has been a factor. The closely knit rural community has been rapidly breaking down, and it is this factor as much as anything which has encouraged the reorganization forces. In addition, the obvious need in many localities to serve larger numbers of students at a lower per student cost has been a serious consideration. The large school district (in terms of numbers of students) does have the overpowering appeal of the economics of mass education. Finally, the comprehensive nature of schooling has found its way into the popular imagination. Perhaps reorganization has been more an outgrowth of the needs of the society than any real push on the part of those who are interested in school consolidation. Parents and taxpayers realize as never before the need for a comprehensive educational program in order to meet the academic and vocational needs of their children. These forces may have really very little to do with the educational soundness or intrinsic worth of consolidated school districts. No responsible advocate of consolidation attempts to make a blanket indictment of small districts or the schooling provided in the old one-room schoolhouse. Few people, including those in education, can help but be a little saddened that the impersonal forces of economics and technology have written the one-room school out of our life, for good teaching and real learning were possible there. In his weaker moments, the most ardent advocate of consolidation must admit that many of the ideas he advocates for creating a good learning environment were as likely to be achieved in the one-room schoolhouse as in the modern educational factory he advocates.

Perhaps the central issue in any consideration of the school district in the United States, its history, and its present status, is whether it is an appropriate unit for the implementation of the school function. Few question this in states where the district system is the basis of school organization. Yet, in some ways the school district itself persists on the myth that schools and other governmental functions do not mix and the school district provides enough independence from the governmental and political processes to make it a safe way to administer the school function. The myth continues to advocate a school system run on a day-to-day basis by those who know it best; that is, the professional educator, the superintendent, or the school people. Although there may be the formality of dedication to the principle that in the district and school board system the "people" really run the school, the realist knows that this is not actually the case, for the people have long since informally delegated this responsibility to the school people, the professional educators. In reality, the school function is closely and inexorably involved in politics and the general functions of government. As we pointed out above, reorganization must come from politicians who make up the state legislature, or less frequently the courts may implement some provision in the constitution which enables school district reorganization. In any case, the process of school district reorganization is basically a political process ultimately dependent upon the accumulation of votes in one form or another. Nor is it ever possible to separate the school from the immediate political environment. Change in educational policy or structure, right down to the district level, has always been a matter of politics. Local taxation rates are set by political officials, and state support to local districts is set by those in politics, not those in education. The school curriculum is determined politically for the most part. In general what the school does, how it is organized, how it is staffed, how it is housed—all of these are so closely related to the political environment and the elected political hierarchy that the separation of schools and politics is a genuine myth, despite contrary polemics of many schoolmen.

COUNTY GOVERNMENT AND EDUCATION

The American system of counties follows the English pattern. The system of local government in England at the time of the colonization of America was organized around the "shire," which became a county when transplanted to American soil. The county as a local unit of government was first used in Virginia, but soon spread throughout the South. New England also used counties, but by far the most important unit of local government in New England was the town, the county being more of a legal and geographic description than a basis for the organization of local government. The county system of government moved westward along with the people, and today the county unit exists in forty-seven of the fifty states. Only Alaska, Rhode Island, and Connecticut are without the county as part of the subdivision of state government. The county unit is the major form of local government in all sections of the country with the exception of New England, Louisiana, and the three states mentioned above.

The number and size of counties in the United States vary greatly from state to state. Delaware has only three, while Texas has 254. The largest county in the United States is San Bernardino in California, with 20,131 square miles, while the most populous county in the country is Cook County, Illinois, with nearly five million people. Loving County, Texas, has a population of only 227.[12] In addition, there are great differences in wealth, in geography, and so on. Therefore, in view of this it is difficult to generalize about counties in the United States.

One aspect of county government which is fairly general, however, is the fact that the county is normally a rather decentralized unit of government. Although nominally the general supervision of county government is in the hands of an elected board, very often a board of commissioners selected from district geographic division of the county, this does not mean that there is any very highly centralized locus of authority in county government. Indeed, quite the opposite is true in most counties. Dispersion of authority and responsibility within county government exists because there is very little in the way of policy-making authority in the county, and therefore very little need for a policy-making body. In most counties in the United States, these duties and responsibilities are spelled out in some detail by the state constitution or by the state law. Not only do such provisions spell out the detail of functions of county officers, but they often provide detailed qualifications for office.

In most counties where such an office exists, the county superintendent of schools acts as the agent of state government on the county level. Where this office exists, the qualifications for office usually include the provision that the county superintendent have a college degree and that he present some teaching and/or administrative experience in the public schools. In some states the office of county superintendent of schools is an elective one. In others, the superintendent may be appointed by an elected county board of education.

Some states have eliminated the office of county superintendent. In some cases the office has been eliminated by amendment to the constitution or by statute, while in others the need for the office no longer exists and the office goes by default; that is, no one runs for the post. It would be a simple matter to declare that the office of county school superintendent is no longer needed in the United States and that it should be eliminated. However, such general and simple solutions are not always acceptable. Although it is true that the forces of increasing urbanization and consolidation of school districts into larger systems have drastically cut into the need for the office in some localities, there are some instances in which the county superintendent of schools remains necessary and useful.

---

[12] John H. Ferguson and Dean E. McHenry, *The American System of Government,* 7th ed. (New York: McGraw-Hill, 1963), p. 669.

Where the county superintendent is active, he performs many administrative functions. As the representative of the state on the local level, he may have budgeting and accounting responsibilities. In this connection he may be responsible for keeping centralized records on daily attendance and he may have the primary responsibility for the distribution of state funds within his county. An active county superintendent can also perform an important function. This could include planning for meetings of county teachers to discuss any number of local problems or matters in which the state is concerned. In some counties the superintendent also serves as a key person in supervision. Representatives from his office make visits to classrooms and work directly with teachers and principals in the improvement of teaching. An active county superintendent may also be responsible for seeing to the legal qualifications for teachers in his county. Where the process is formalized in state law, the county superintendent may have to certify that each teacher has the appropriate teaching certificate for his position. In his supervisory capacity the county superintendent may be responsible for a centralized materials center which can be used by all teachers in the county. In some outlying regions of the country, such a materials center in the offices of the county superintendent provides resources that might not be available otherwise. In some counties the superintendent may actually procure teachers for the classrooms. The county superintendent may also serve as the chief coordinator of school activities in his county.

These are only a few of the many duties which may fall upon the county superintendent of schools. In many counties in the United States he still performs most or all of the functions that any superintendent of schools in a large district performs. In view of the many duties and responsibilities he can have, it would be inaccurate to say that the office is no longer necessary.

However, it is true that in many counties the office is no longer vitally important. In districts in some states, the office of county superintendent of schools still persists in spite of the fact that the state may have organized for educational purposes into county-wide school districts with a school board elected on a county-wide basis with an appointed superintendent of schools. In such a case, it is possible that all of the functions of the county superintendent could be performed by the regularly appointed superintendent of schools. In any event, each case must be considered as an individual one and recommendations for the elimination of the office of county superintendent of schools should proceed only after a careful examination of his role.

In rural areas of the country, where the county superintendent does have real and useful responsibilities, it cannot be denied that much could be done to improve the office, which has been severely criticized because of its political nature. However, this criticism may not be too serious since the school function generally is political in many ways. There are very few superintendents, county or otherwise, who are not influenced by the political environment of the community. No appointed superintendent can fly in the face of political forces in the community and expect a long tenure. Indeed, in some school districts the post of superintendent of schools is openly political. Political forces figure in school administration no matter how professional or separate from politics school administrators claim to be. Any schoolman who is doing anything is sure to be faced with a certain amount of hostility in the community, and in effect, such a superintendent is up for approval in every school board election. Hundreds of school board elections occur across the country every year in districts where the appointed superintendent of schools lays his career on the line. The idea that the elected county superintendent is a political creature, and the appointed district superintendent is nonpolitical and thus professional, may be one of the greatest myths in American education. There is a substantial difference in the two positions where the county superintendent of schools has to stand for direct election, in some cases every two years or perhaps every four years. This can be a waste of time and money, but even this problem has been worked out satisfactorily in many counties where county superintendents may outlast their appointed counterparts in city and rural districts by many years. Most of the serious criticisms of the county superintendent could be met in counties where the school patrons feel he has a real job to do. Most of the weaknesses of the office could be met in such cases by legislative means. Where the county superintendent is useful, his term of office could be lengthened, the qualifications for office could be raised if necessary, and his duties and responsibilities could be spelled out more carefully. Not infrequently such recommendations for improvement of the office of county superintendent have come from, of all places—the county superintendent himself. Students of the school scene in the United States must realize that the office of county superintendent of schools in some states and in some localities is apt to be around for some time to come. Emphasis perhaps should be more on attempts to study the office and its functions with a view toward improvement rather than a wholesale advocacy of its elimination.

THE ROLE OF THE STATE

In the past twenty-five years the state governments have been playing an increasingly important role in education. The state has moved in the direction of greater control of the certification of teachers and the development of the curriculum on all levels, and it has increased its support as well as its influence in local school matters. This has been true for a number of reasons. Perhaps most significant is the fact that a growing and shifting population has created educational demands which local communities have not been able to meet. The financial demands of an increasing school-age population have been severely felt in some localities. In the face of these demands, the state legislature has been called upon time and again to provide funds for the support of education. Indeed, the problems of what constitutes an adequate educational program and how much money is required for such a program have become the most important political problems in many states of the Union.

THE GOVERNOR

What the governor does with regard to education depends greatly on the system of organization for performance of the educational function in the state. In most states the governor is a powerful figure in the educational hierarchy. This is true regardless of the kind of organization which may exist in a state to perform the educational function. In some states great pains have been taken to keep education out of politics on the state level, but even the most casual observer must realize the impossibility of this goal in these times. Even if it were possible to separate education and politics at the state level, it might not be desirable to do so. No magic device has yet been invented which would make state policy on education a nonpartisan affair even if such a device were desirable. In most states the politics of the two-party system operate on the state level and the candidates for governor very often embody the public image of the party. Even in so-called one-party states, the primary allows the voter some choice of candidates and programs. In his role as a popular leader in the ranks of his party, the governor plays a vital part in the educational development of the state. Considering the great amount of funds in any state which must go to support the educational system, political candidates for governor cannot possibly ignore educational needs in their bids for election.

Of course, in the state's political process the governor is a key to the educational program. In every state the governor has at least the opportunity to present to the legislature a proposed program in education. This is frequently done by the governor in an early address to the legislature in which he outlines the needs of the state for the following year or biennium. A governor's recommendations on education may come from a variety of sources. He may dream them up on his own or he may lend an ear to the classroom teachers' organization in his state, the president of the state school board association, some lobbyist, or any number of interested individuals.

In some states the process of educational needs follows a rather formalized and time-worn structure in which demands are channeled from the grass roots through established agencies of government all the way to the governor's office. In such cases the governor may adopt a program for education worked out through established channels which allow for all sorts of conflicting ideas and feelings about the educational program of the state. In the final analysis, however, the governor is free to recommend anything he wishes to the legislature regarding his state's educational needs. Moreover, he frequently does just this. The governor is not in a position where he can put education in a neat little compartment and consider only the "professional" aspects of its needs. He must consider it as part of an overall state program which is politically oriented. Any state governor will experience tremendous pressure to do this or that for education, for highways, for the aged, for other state institutions, and so on. What he recommends for education will often be a mixture of politics and practical necessity. A governor knows, perhaps better than any other state official, the political glitter or dynamite lurking in educational plans and proposals. Any recommendation on education which comes from the governor's office in any state is apt to be a bundle of compromises hopefully designed to please everyone, prayerfully designed to alienate as few as possible. Although some may protest that this casts the schools in the role of political football, others may recognize that on the state level, education and politics are inseparable.

THE LEGISLATURE

In terms of the actual educational program in the state and the degree of involvement of the state government in school matters, the state legislature is most important, for it determines the amount of state money which will be available for schools and it also provides a great deal of direction on a multitude of school problems. As in the case of the governor, the legislature may or may not operate independently from any formal organization for education which may exist on the state level. In every case, however, where money is appropriated, or where the legislature is called upon to implement some program through legislation, the legislature can be counted upon to exercise a certain amount of independent judgment. In practice this means that even the most carefully laid plans of the governor, other agencies of government, or interested groups or individuals, can expect some modification in the hands of the legislature. More often than not these modifications are politically motivated. For example, a very comprehensive program calling for a rather drastic increase in state taxes may fall short of its goal in a legislature which is not inclined to pass new revenue measures.

The legislature cannot consider education as a special problem, but must view the needs of schools within the larger context of the needs of state government. Education bills, like every other measure before the legislature, get the regular treatment of the normal process of the legislature. Such bills are introduced (frequently at the behest of interested groups or interested state agencies), assigned to a committee, and wait their turn for hearings and open debate on the floor. In most states some concession is made to the importance of the schools in that there are standing committees in each house on education.

The extent of legislative control and influence over the state's public and private schools is great. State legislatures have complete control over the size and composition of school districts and their organization. In this respect the legislatures in some states may determine the composition of the school boards, including the size of the board and the qualifications of its members, as well as the terms of office of school board members and their manner of election. Directly or indirectly the state legislature may determine the administrative structure of the school district. The legislature can set the qualifications for district superintendents and can provide certification programs for the position. In some cases the legislature may provide teacher-administrator ratios, and it may spell out the functions of the school district in such detail that the organization of the administrative structure must be made with an eye toward legislative requirements. For example, the legislature may establish a guidance program in schools of a certain size. In order to implement the program, the administrative office of guidance director may become a necessity. Similarly, the legislature may provide for certain supervisory functions which require the attention of an assistant superintendent and a staff of curriculum supervisors.

Beyond this, the legislature may enact laws providing for the minimum number of school days and other matters pertaining to pupils in the schools of the state. There are laws in some states which determine the size of classes, the total number of students teachers may teach, the health needs of students, the manner and form of attendance records, and the transportation of students. The state legislature can determine the qualifications for teachers on specific levels and in certain subjects; it can determine the legal liability of teachers and other school officers and employees; and it can provide a whole scale of legal provisions directly concerning teachers, such as tenure, sick leave, teachers' oaths, pensions, and retirement plans.

With regard to school finance the legislature is in a very significant position, for it determines the amount of state aid; it frequently establishes the legal framework for bond issues and bond elections, or implements constitutional provisions which do so; it can fix minimum salary schedules for teachers; and it may fix local taxing limits for school purposes, or implement constitutional provisions on such limitations. These are only a few examples of the way the legislature of any state may be involved in the educational policy and processes of the state.

Perhaps more important than the actual functions of the legislature with regard to education is the way the legislature goes about making the decisions which involve the schools. Legislative decisions on school matters are made from at least three different frames of reference. All of these involve political values in some way. The first basis for legislative action in school matters is the implementation of constitutional provisions or court decisions which have interpreted the state constitution. In some cases the constitution may be rather explicit in its direction to the legislature; in others the provision in the constitution may provide the legislature with a great deal of discretion in implementing its provisions. For example, the constitution may establish a specific mill levy for educational purposes, and the legislature may have no choice but to implement the constitutional provision or work for a constitutional amendment. In another state the constitution may merely declare that the legislature is charged with the establishment of property tax mill levies which will insure an "adequate" system of education, thus giving the legislature a great deal of flexibility in establishing tax rates for the purpose of school support. A federal court may declare a state law or constitutional provision which establishes separate schools for Blacks and whites a violation of the national Constitution, and direct the schools within the states to proceed to integrate schools "with all deliberate speed" as the Supreme Court did in *Brown v. Board of Education of Topeka*. Even with such a specific direction, the legislature may still procrastinate in implementing the decision, or it may even attempt to overcome the effects of the decision in one way or another. Even where the mandate from the Constitution or the courts may be perfectly clear, what the state legislature does about educational problems, or any other state problem for that matter, depends on the political values and the environment in which the legislature operates. In total, any state legislature may be more interested in the desires of the voters on the issues, education included, than they are in any model program or improvement desired by any single group of professional educators, state boards of education, the governor, or others. In this context, a constitutional or court mandate to the legislature may be modified, hampered, or expedited by political conditions and values.

A second basis for legislative action in states which provide for it is through initiative (twenty states) or referendum (twenty-two states). The initiative is a means of popular legislation. In states where it exists, a certain percentage of legally registered voters (from 3 per cent to 15 per cent) can sign a petition to have an issue placed on the ballot in a special or general election. Generally speaking, such initiated measures on school problems originate with school people; that is, organizations of school administrators, the classroom teachers' organization, or some other such school group. In some states, initiated measures require a majority vote of all those voting in the election, while in others merely a majority of those voting on the issue itself is sufficient to pass it. In some states the initiative, once approved in a legal manner, can become law without legislative action; in others, legislative action is necessary to implement it. School people have used this method where it is available with varying degrees of frequency and success. Generally speaking, initiated measures are difficult to pass and have not proved very promising as a major method for the solution of educational problems. In states where the procedure exists, however, it has had the effect of sometimes causing school people to realize that their fate and the adequacy of the school program as they see it is a political problem of the first order. Campaigns for or against initiated school matters proceed in a manner which differs little from campaigns for political office and other political programs. In order to succeed, school people have generally found it necessary to use the time-worn techniques of political persuasion in initiative battles.

The referendum is much more dependent upon legislative action than the initiative. Generally, the referendum is a measure which is referred to the vote of the people by the legislature itself. School measures are occasionally handled in this manner. Where the provision for referendum exists, a legislature faced with a serious problem of inadequate finance for schools might prefer that a measure which would require a rise in taxes be referred to the people. This can become a means of relieving the legislature of the political responsibility for making a decision which might be unpopular with the voters. Most states which have the referendum require petitions signed by from 5 to 10 per cent of the legal voters in the last gubernatorial election before the measure can be placed on the ballot.

A third basis for legislative action in educational matters is the most common; that is, the legislature acting on its own initiative. This may be somewhat misleading, since it is possible that the legislature may not possess its own initiative in any practical sense. In any event, the normal process of legislation involves the push and pull and compromise aspect of party and pressure politics. In the case of normal legislation, the legislature will almost always ask for advice or guidance from any number of sources. On school matters it is not uncommon for bills affecting the schools to originate with the school people or some organization representing school people. Once a friendly legislator can be prevailed upon to introduce the measure, the forces for and against it begin to marshal their troops. In a typical state legislature, the bill may be referred to the committee on education in either house, where it is debated, investigated, hearings are held, and it is ultimately tabled, killed, or reported to the floor for action. In this committee process, the committee may call upon the governor, the state administrative officers who have some responsibility in education, teacher groups, school administrators, businessmen, representatives of taxpayers' associations, and others who are interested, pro or con. The result is never what the advocates of the bill hoped for, nor is it ever what its opponents hoped for. It is essentially a compromise between the conflicting and opposing forces in the state. Anyone who harbors notions that school matters are nonpartisan or nonpolitical is expressing a naiveté about the political process that borders on ignorance.

STATE ADMINISTRATIVE STRUCTURE

It is difficult to generalize about the administrative structure of education in the United States. In the first place, there are many types of administrative structures on the state level. In the second place, there is great variety in the power which is exercised on the state administrative level. In some states the constitution or the laws of the state have established an administrative structure with great discretionary powers, while in others the organization and functions are spelled out in such detail that there are very few. Some generalizations can be safely made, however. Every state has some kind of chief school officer, who may be either elected or appointed. If he is appointed, it is usually by the governor or by an elected board of education. His term of office frequently coincides with that of the governor and other top level state administrative posts. The qualifications for office of state superintendent vary from almost nonexistent ones to very rigid educational and experience qualifications. The duties of this office are generally fixed by either constitutional or statutory provision. Normally the chief state school administrator has rather standard administrative duties. They include planning on a state-wide basis, supervision of the state's school system, and policing the qualifications of teachers in the public schools. This policing duty may range from perfunctory supervisory duties in some states to that of official certification officer in others. The chief state school officer also has duties as the coordinator of educational programs and policies in the state; in some states he provides opportunities for inservice training or for research in education, and in some he has extensive budgeting responsibilities.

Whether this office is appointive or elective, the chief state school officer is intimately involved in the political process. However selected, he is part of the administrative staff of the executive department and shares in the responsibilities and duties of whatever party happens to be in power. Even where party responsibility does not exist, he is appointed by a board or a governor selected through the political process. Like any administrative officer on any level of government, he is sure to be beset with all kinds of political pressures from all kinds of sources, above and below. Since the chief state school officer serves a single-purpose clientele, he is frequently in close touch with the school people. This relationship can be formal or informal. However, the administrative structure for education is set up in the state, the chief state school officer must work closely with teachers' organizations, professional organizations of school administrators, and school-oriented groups such as the PTA. Whether he is appointed or elected, the smooth functioning of his office depends on good relations with his clientele. In order that he may perform his functions properly, all states have provided the state school officer with a staff which makes up some sort of a state department of education. These staffs are generally organized according to function; that is, there may be a director in charge of administration of certification laws, one in charge of administration of the school lunch program, another in charge of curriculum matters, another in charge of reorganization, and so on.

Finally, on the state level, every state has some kind of state board of education. Like the chief school officer, this board may be elected or appointed. In the states as a whole, thirty-two state boards are appointed by the governor, and ten are elected by popular vote. In the other states a variety of methods are used to select the state board members. In one state they are elected by the state legislature, in another they are appointed by the chief state school officer, and in a third, they are elected by conventions of local school boards. Three states have a mixture of elected and ex-officio appointed boards.[13] The state board or its equivalent may have widely varying powers from one state to the next. In some states the board has a great deal of discretionary power and wields a great deal of policy-making authority; in others the board is little more than a figurehead with most of the real policy-making authority resting with the state legislature. State boards may have quasi-legislative authority in education. For example, if a state legislature has delegated to the state board the power to determine certification requirements for teachers, it has delegated what amounts to a legislative power. State boards also have administrative powers in that they are generally charged with the responsibility of seeing to it that the policy of the legislature with regard to education is carried out.

From the local voter in the local school district to the state level, the schools are intimately involved in the political process and political values. Not to recognize this is to overlook one of the most important facts of the political process and the educational scene. The welfare of pupils, teachers, and patrons is tied closely to political values, structure, and process. Attempts to overlook this fact have created some difficult problems for school people. The most difficult is a general lack of understanding on the part of the public and school people about how educational problems are met and solved. No longer is education a strictly local problem which concerns only the voters or patrons in a small and narrowly defined geographic area. The problems associated with the schools have become a state and national problem. Education ranks as the major problem of state

---

[13] Van Miller, *The Public Administration of American School Systems* (New York: Macmillan, 1965), p. 126.

government. In view of its importance as a major function of state government, the citizen-voter, and particularly the educator, must understand how problems get solved in education. On the state level this problem-solving process in education is actually a political one, and its solution is no different than that for any other problem facing state government. The citizen-voter and the educator must recognize the interrelationship between educational problems and the political process if intelligent solutions to school problems are to be found.

REFERENCES

American Association of School Administrators. *School District Organization.* Washington, D.C.: NEA, 1958.

Bailey, Stephen K., Richard T. Frost, Paul E. Marsh, and Robert C. Wood. *Schoolmen and Politics.* Syracuse, N.Y.: Syracuse Univ. Press, 1963.

Beach, Fred F., and Robert F. Will. *The State and Education.* Washington, D.C.: U. S. Dept. of Health, Education, and Welfare, Office of Education, 1960.

Bollens, John C. *Special District Governments in the United States.* Berkeley, Calif.: Univ. of California Press, 1957.

Chase, Francis S., and Edgar L. Morphet. *The Forty-Eight State School Systems.* Chicago: The Council of State Governments, 1949.

Cubberley, Ellwood P. *Public Education in the United States.* Rev. ed. Boston: Houghton Mifflin, 1934.

Ellul, Jacques. *The Political Illusion.* New York: Alfred A. Knopf, 1967.

Ferguson, John H., and Dean E. McHenry. *The American System of Government.* 7th ed. New York: McGraw-Hill, 1963. Part IV.

Goldhammer, Keith. *The School Board.* New York: The Center for Applied Research in Education, Inc., 1964.

Gross, Neal. *Who Runs Our Schools?* New York: John Wiley & Sons, 1958.

Hansen, Kenneth H. *Public Education in American Society.* Englewood Cliffs, N.J.: Prentice-Hall, 1963.

Hartford, Ellis Ford. *Education in These United States.* New York: Macmillan, 1964.

Lind, Loren. "The Politics of Subterfuge." *This Magazine is About Schools.* 5, I:178–185 (Winter 1971).

Martin, Roscoe C. *Government and the Suburban School.* Syracuse, N.Y.: Syracuse Univ. Press, 1962.

Masotti, Louis M. *Education and Politics in Suburbia: The New Trier Experience.* Cleveland: Press of Case Western Reserve Univ., 1967.

Masters, Nicholas A., Robert H. Salisbury, and Thomas H. Eliot. *State Politics and the Public Schools.* New York: Alfred A. Knopf, 1964.

Meranto, Philip J. *School Politics in the Metropolis.* Columbus, Ohio: Charles E. Merrill, 1970.

Miller, Van. *The Public Administration of American School Systems.* New York:Macmillan, 1965.

National Education Association. *Research Report, 1963-R12, Estimates of School Statistics, 1963–1964.* Washington, D.C.: Research Division, 1963.

————. *Research Report, 1969-R15, Estimates of School Statistics, 1969–1970.* Washington, D.C.: Research Division, 1969.

Salisbury, Robert H. "Schools and Politics in the Big City." *Harvard Educational Review.* 408–425 (Summer 1967).

Thurston, Lee M., and William H. Roe. *State School Administration.* New York: Harper & Row, 1957.

Weinberg, Meyer. *Race and Place: A Legal History of the Neighborhood School.* Washington, D.C.: U.S. Office of Education, U. S. Government Printing Office, 1967.

10

The National Government, Education, and Values

With each passing year, the national government becomes more deeply involved in educational matters, a situation that is viewed with mixed feelings in our society. There is an ambivalence about the role which the national government should play in education. Some cheer every new educational effort it makes, while others view such efforts with despair.

Whether one favors increasing activity in educational matters by the national government, or only limited action, depends upon the social, political, and economic values one holds. Many arguments over increasing national involvement in education have revolved around the question of states' rights, or the extension of "big" government at the expense of the state in our system. Other problems which have created heated controversy in recent years have included the Supreme Court's interpretations of the First and Fourteenth Amendments as these have involved freedom of religion and the meaning of equality. What follows in this chapter is a brief discussion of the basis for the states' rights argument, a discussion of the principle of federalism applied to education, and a discussion of federal aid and values.

THE PRINCIPLE OF FEDERALISM AND THE SCHOOLS

A major school problem in recent years has been closely related to a general political problem long a controversial issue in our society; that is, the growth of government, especially the growth of the national government. This, in turn, has created problems in the area of federal aid to education. To understand these problems, one should understand the meaning of federalism.

Education in the United States provides a good case study of federalism in operation. In the heat of the argument over the question of federal aid to education, the schools' relationship to the principle of federalism as a governmental system is frequently overlooked. The following discussion will attempt to define federalism and indicate how public education fits into the scheme of federalism in the United States.

Federalism Defined

As a political concept, federalism may be defined as a system in which there are two levels of government with certain more or less clearly defined areas of authority and responsibility established by constitution, law, or custom. The levels of government in the United States are, of course, national and state. The division of authority and responsibility in the United States is more or less clearly laid down in the Constitution. The model of federalism in the United States takes shape generally from Articles I, IV, and VI of the Constitution and the Tenth Amendment. Section Eight of the first article enumerates the powers of Congress; Section Nine presents specific limitations on Congress. The first two sections of Article IV describe the relationship between the states, and provide that "Full Faith and Credit shall be given in each State of the public Acts, Records, and judicial proceedings of every other State." In addition, Article IV declares that "The Citizens of each State Shall Be entitled to all Privileges and Immunities of Citizens in the several States." Article VI declares that the Constitution of the United States is the "supreme Law of the Land," while the Tenth Amendment states that the powers not delegated to the national government by the Constitution "are reserved to the States respectively, or to the people." In total, these constitutional provisions establish an operational definition of federalism in that they attempt to define the general areas of authority and responsibility of the state and national levels of government; enable the system to function smoothly by establishing a system of state equality in the public acts of the states; and provide for a kind of national citizenship which enables freedom of movement and action for citizens throughout the system. Beyond this, they provide a means for adjustment of differences between states, between a single state and the national government, or between national and state law.

In practice these provisions are subject to widely differing interpretations. Public education has not been spared from such conflicting interpretations of the Constitution in recent years. The debate over federal aid to education has involved many aspects of the Constitution. To some, the constitutional provisions cited spell a clear division of powers between the national government and the states, and any power exercised by the national government which is not expressly provided in the Constitution is viewed with alarm and as an encroachment on the part of the national government into areas of power which are reserved to the states under the Constitution. The major point of this argument is that since education is not mentioned in the Constitution, the national government should therefore exercise no authority in this area. On the other hand, there are those who believe that absence of the mention of education in the Constitution does not arbitrarily exclude the exercise of national power in this area. The advocates of federal aid point to other sections of the Constitution which they claim give a clear legal mandate to the national government to exercise power in the area of education. Most frequently used in this argument is the phrase in the Preamble to the Constitution, which states that the government of the United States was formed by the people to "promote the general Welfare." In addition, those who advocate the propriety of national action on educational matters point to the so-called "elastic" clause of Article I, Section Eight, which states that Congress shall have the power "To make all Laws which shall be necessary and proper for carrying into Execution the foregoing Power, and all other powers vested by this Constitution in the Government of the United States. . . ." Some see in this clause—in its responsibility for providing for general welfare, its stated power over taxation, commerce, and other stated powers—a clear constitutional duty for Congress to act in the educational field. More recently, a new phrase has come into vogue, which describes federalism as "creative-federalism." This term implies joint cooperative efforts by the states and the national government and attempts to minimize arguments over the locus of powers. "Creative-federalism" advocates seem more concerned with attacks on problems which are at once local and national in character than they are with the classical definition of federalism.

In practice, when applied to a specific issue such as education, the definition of the proper constitutional role of the national government and the states is not clear-cut. Perhaps some clarification can be provided in a review of what has actually happened in the historical development of education in the federal system.

A Brief History of Education and Federalism

Any history of education in the United States is replete with examples of involvement of the national government in education in spite of the fact that education is not specifically mentioned in the Constitution. There seemed to be little doubt on the part of the framers of the Constitution that the national government could act in the area of education without fear of contradicting the Constitution. Washington, Madison, and others had become interested in the creation of a national university as one of the new government's first orders of business. They even proposed that the Constitution contain a provision for a national university. The records of the Constitutional Convention at Philadelphia in 1787 indicate that some of the delegates felt national power under the Constitution was ample without specific reference to a national university. Indeed, Washington and the four presidents who followed him each recommended the establishment of a national university.

There is nothing in the discussion on the proposals to establish such a university to indicate that the Founding Fathers or the early leaders of the new nation were opposed to the creation of a national university on the grounds that the Constitution did not permit national action in this area.

Even before the Constitution was adopted, the Articles of Confederation government accepted a role in the promotion of public education. The Land Ordinance of 1785 provided that the sixteenth section in every township be set aside for the support of education. Two years later, in a more comprehensive manner, Congress enacted another ordinance which provided that the Northwest Territory be divided into not less than three or more than five states. With regard to education, the third article of the Ordinance of 1787 stated that "religion, morality, and knowledge being necessary to good government and the happiness of mankind, schools and the means of education shall be forever encouraged." The provisions of the Ordinance of 1785 were applied, and every sixteenth section was set aside for the support of education. In the case of Ohio, which was admitted under the terms of the Northwest Ordinance, two additional townships "near the center" and "of good land" were set aside by Congress for the development of a literary institution in that state. The four other states which were formed out of the Northwest Territory followed the pattern established in the admission of Ohio, with a total of three sections in each state set aside for educational purposes. In 1826 the land which was acquired as a result of the Louisiana Purchase "was brought by act of Congress under the same general principle."[1] The original Atlantic seaboard states were concerned about the educational provisions of the Ordinance of 1787 since they, too, were attempting to establish funds for the development of common schools. Some of the older states without land felt cheated since they were not able to share in the provisions of the Ordinance of 1787. This was a particularly sticky problem since several states held western lands before the Articles of Confederation government was established and had ceded these lands to the national government as one of the conditions for entering the Confederation. Virginia ceded its western claims in 1784, New York in 1782, and other states in the early 1780's. By the time Ohio was admitted in 1803, all of the states had relinquished claims to western lands. However, many of these states, particularly New York and Connecticut, contained hundreds of thousands of acres of undeveloped and unclaimed land which they were able to sell over the years. Connecticut and New York, moreover, had set aside lands even before 1800 for purposes of education, and both states were able to create permanent school funds from public land sales within their boundaries.

Even so, the states with limited public lands were not completely satisfied.

---

[1] Edward H. Reisner, *Nationalism and Education Since 1789* (New York: Macmillan, 1922), p. 342.

Partly to mollify these dissatisfactions, Congress established a policy which gave to states 5 per cent of the proceeds from the sale of public lands within their boundaries, provided the states would agree not to tax federal property. In addition, the national government gave certain salt and waste lands to the states which they could then improve and sell and use the proceeds as they saw fit. The states with limited public lands were finally placated by the provisions of the Surplus Revenue Deposit Act of 1836, which provided for a distribution of a United States Treasury surplus of twenty-eight million dollars. This surplus had accrued from the sale of public lands and the high tariffs of the 1820's and early 1830's. Several states used their share of this money to establish a common school fund.

Congress again concerned itself with a program of national education after the Civil War. Some kind of program had to be established to provide for the newly freed Blacks. The immediate needs of food, clothing, and shelter were provided in an act passed in March 1865, which established the Bureau of Refugees and the so-called Freedman's Bureau. Not only were the freed slaves given some of the bare essentials of life under the provisions of this legislation, but in some places the bureau provided a kind of rudimentary education in reading and writing for all ages.

The confusion and disorganization attending the period after the Civil War encouraged another approach to education. In 1870 Representative George F. Hoar, a Massachusetts Republican, introduced a bill in Congress to provide for a national system of education. Representative Hoar was concerned about the sort of schooling that southern states were apt to provide for the newly freed Blacks, and he must have seen the political possibilities in a nationally controlled educational system. Representative Hoar's bill never got out of committee.

In 1867 Congress created the Department of Education in the national government for "the purposes of collecting such statistics and facts as shall show the condition and progress of education in the several States and Territories and of diffusing such information respecting the organization and management of schools and school systems, and methods of teaching as shall aid the people of the United States in the establishment and mainte- nance of efficient school systems, and otherwise promote the cause of education throughout the country." Heading the Department of Education was the commissioner of education, with very little authority and very little responsibility. His major function, as defined in the act creating the depart- ment, seemed to be that of general collector and disseminator of educational information, as well as advisor to those who wished to seek his advice. In spite of these meager beginnings, the creation of a department of education was a big step forward in the involvement of the national government in education.

During this same period the national government became involved in education through the Morrill Act of 1862. Under the provisions of the Morrill

Act, each state was granted thirty thousand acres of public land (or its equivalent in money) for each of its congressmen. The proceeds from the sale of this land were to be used to establish colleges of agriculture and mechanical arts. An interesting feature of the Morrill Act was that the national government, through its own initiative, was encouraging a new kind of college in the United States. Until this time the major programs in higher education had been classical in nature. The Hatch Experiment Station Act in 1887 extended the idea of the Morrill Act in providing some $15,000 annually to each state to establish agricultural experiment stations at the land-grant colleges. The Second Morrill Act of 1890 provided annual federal appropriations of $15,000 with increments of one thousand dollars per year until the annual sum reached $25,000 for land-grant colleges.[2] By 1906 the annual appropriation was raised to $20,000 for each state.

Supplementing and continuing the program of agricultural and mechanical education subsidized by the national government, the Smith-Lever Act of 1914 provided that the national government would match contributions of states which wanted to provide a program of agricultural extension. This program provided for direct education of farmers through the office of the county agent. A few years later, the Smith-Hughes Act made funds available on a matching basis for industrial, commercial, and domestic science subjects for the secondary schools.

Following the Smith-Hughes Act of 1917, the teaching of agricultural and vocational subjects was further encouraged by Congress in the George-Reed Act in 1929, the George-Ellzey Act in 1934, and the George-Deen Act in 1936. In addition to these efforts in vocational and agricultural education, the Great Depression saw many other educational efforts by Congress. Some of the most notable of these were the National Youth Association (NYA), the vocational rehabilitation program of the Social Security Act of 1935, the Civilian Conservation Corps (CCC), and the school lunch program. Although the NYA was not a direct educational program of the national government, the funds provided to students of high school and college age to assist them in their education were a real contribution to individuals. Under the NYA program, students were given an opportunity to work in the school and assist teachers in all sorts of ways. The stipend for these jobs was an hourly rate which averaged about fifteen dollars per month. There can be little doubt that this amount, although small, allowed many to continue in school who would otherwise have had to drop out. The CCC was a direct national educational program of sorts. At its height, the CCC had more than a quarter of a million youths at work in national forests, on national highways and roads, and with flood control projects and other such programs. The CCC also undertook a limited amount of formal education.

---

[2] R. Freeman Butts and Lawrence A. Cremin, *A History of Education in American Culture* (New York: Holt, Rinehart & Winston, 1953), p. 427.

The national government became directly involved in vocational education under the provisions of the Social Security Act. Under the provisions of the act, millions of dollars have been spent by the social security system for direct costs of training the handicapped. In addition to these programs, the Public Works Administration and the Works Project Administration of the 1930's assisted the states and local communities in building schools, providing for adult education, citizenship education, and certain kinds of vocational education.

The greatest single financial contribution by the national government for education to date has been the Servicemen's Readjustment Act of 1944, popularly known as the G. I. Bill of Rights. The original G. I. Bill provided varying amounts of education for more than eight million World War II veterans at a total cost of nearly $15 billion. This program was renewed after the Korean War, and has once more been activated for veterans of the Viet Nam conflict.

The trend toward increasing national participation in the educational scene continues. National activity in education includes everything from the distribution of surplus property to grants to foreign countries. During the 1969–1970 school year, Congress appropriated nearly $3.2 billion for U.S. Office of Education programs. This is a rapidly growing figure, as witnessed by the fact that the 1965–1966 appropriation was approximately two billion dollars.[3] Indeed, the national government has become so involved in educational finance that any total cited becomes quickly dated.

The national government is deeply involved in a tremendous variety of educational activities. By far the most significant on the present scene are the various titles of the general Elementary and Secondary Education Act approved by Congress in the spring of 1965. Under its provisions, the national contribution to education totaled $1.3 billion for the first year. The Elementary and Secondary Education Act opened the door for a very extensive program of federal aid. Since 1965, federal support of education has continued to be significant. Of a total appropriation of more than $3.6 billion for the U.S. Office of Education for 1969, elementary and secondary educational activities received more than $1.4 billion. The contribution for higher education grew from a total of slightly over $500 million in 1965, to nearly $700 million in 1969. Added to these broad general programs, the national government is involved in a myriad of others—some old, some fairly new—which vitally contribute to the support of education on the local, regional, and national levels. The following list should give some general idea of the kinds of educational programs in which the national government is financially involved.

---

[3] National Education Association, *Estimates of School Statistics, 1965–1966* (Washington, D.C.: Research Division, 1965), (R-17).

A Partial List of Programs for Which Federal Funds
Were Appropriated in 1970[4]

Elementary and Secondary Education

 School assistance in federally affected areas (National Defense Education Act, Titles III, V, and X)

 The Education Act of 1965 (includes programs of aid for poverty areas, provides funds for textbooks, libraries, research and development, educational centers, teacher training, etc.)

 Indian education

 Education for dependents of military personnel overseas

 Vocational education

 School assistance in special areas

 Teaching and teacher training grants, Educational Exchange Program

 Dependent and neglected children in institutions

 Supplementary educational centers and services

 Library resources

 Dropout prevention programs

 Bilingual education programs

Higher Education

 National Science Foundation

 Basic research and research facilities in United States educational institutions

 Training grants

 Fellowships

 Veterans' education

 Traineeships

Adult Education

 Veterans' education

 Vocational and technical training

 Indian education

 Adult basic education

 Manpower development and training

 Work Incentive Program

 Cooperative Extensions Program

 The Migrant Worker Program

Loan Programs

 Private school loans

 Student loan programs

 College housing loans

School Services

 School lunch program

 Job placement for high school seniors

---

[4] Based on various bulletins and reports of the United States Office of Education.

A Partial List of Programs for Which Federal Funds
Were Appropriated in 1970 *(cont.)*

School Services (cont.)

Bus transportation, military dependents

Library Services Act grants

Aid to school dropouts

Deprived Children

Neighborhood Youth Corps

Community action programs

Upward Bound

Head Start

Follow Through

Vista

Job Corps

The Teacher Corps

International Education

AID cooperative projects

Grants for observation and advisory services

Educational Exchange Program

Peace Corps program

Clearly the efforts of the administration and Congress during the years from 1964 to 1968 launched the national government into many new programs and efforts in the educational arena. Indeed, the national government had become so involved in educational programs and educational finance by the time the Nixon administration took office that any radical change in programs or funding seemed unlikely. Although this was generally true, there have been some subtle but perhaps significant changes during the Nixon administration. Possibly the greatest difference between the Nixon and Johnson administrations has been that the focus of leadership is different. Much of the leadership for new programs and funding came from the administration during Johnson's term in office, while President Nixon has seemed more content to leave the initiative with Congress. However, major concerns with economy during the Nixon years have had their effect on educational programs. Most of the major programs of the Elementary and Secondary Education Act and the Higher Education Act have been cut back in the interest of economy. In other areas, the Nixon administration has indicated an interest in studying the complex involvement of the national government in educational programs with a view toward economy and reorganization of educational activities. The major titles of the Elementary and Secondary Education Act have been studied with a view toward reorganization and a more effective distribution of existing funds. Student loan programs have been studied along with the Job Corps and the Head Start program. There have been significant increases in vocational education programs and a new federal biligual education program was launched in 1969.[5] Generally, the first years of the Nixon administration experienced no dramatic new national programs in education, nor were there any serious retreats from major existing programs. The recommendations for new programs have been modest when compared to the efforts of his predecessor. In a special message to Congress on March 3, 1970, President Nixon announced that he was setting up a Commission on School Finance to "analyze the fiscal plight of public and non-public schools," and was requesting $25 million for the establishment of experimental schools, that he was requesting $200 million for a "Right to Read" program which would attack reading problems in the schools, and that he was going to ask Congress for $52 million for pre-school programs.[6] The general role of the national government in education remained fairly intact during the early years of the Nixon administration. Perhaps its attitude toward nationally funded programs for education can best be summed up by what the president said in early March 1970: "I have called for fundamental studies that should lead to far-reaching reform before going ahead with major new expenditures of 'more of the same.'"[7] In this context President Nixon has proposed the creation of a "National Institute of Education," composed of outstanding scholars whose role would be to establish priorities for education, develop criteria for evaluation of new programs, and offer advice to state and local agencies.

FEDERAL AID AND VALUES

The preceding discussion of the involvement of the national government in education should serve to demonstrate that the national government is deeply committed to public education in spite of the fact that education is not mentioned in the United States Constitution. Those who oppose national involvement in education or federal aid to education point, as means of support for their position, to the Constitution and to the tradition of development of education in the United States. Similarly, those who favor federal aid point to a long history of national educational programs of every description as evidence that there is no constitutional obstacle to limit the

---

[5] *Federal Aid: New Directions for Education in 1969–1970, Education U.S.A.* (Washington, D.C.: National School Public Relations Association, 1970), pp. 1–31.
[6] Editorial Research Reports (Washington, D.C.: Congressional Quarterly, Inc., April 15, 1970), p. 282.
[7] Editorial Research Reports, p. 284.

national government in this area of activity, nor is there any tradition of non-interference in education by the national government. This may be one of those strange debates in which both sides are correct. In reality, there has been an ambivalent development of national involvement in education in the United States. This ambivalence has expressed itself by action on the part of the national government in areas in which states have been unwilling or unable to act, while at the same time observing the principle of state authority in educational matters.

It cannot be denied that federal aid to education is a fact of our times. Nor can it be denied that federal aid to education has a long and honorable tradition dating to the debates over the question of the establishment of a national university in the Constitutional Convention of 1787. Similarly, there can be no doubt that education has traditionally developed in the United States with the individual states holding the major responsibility, involved in the greatest expenditure by far, and exercising virtually total control over their individual state systems of education. This ambivalent, or perhaps coordinate, development of education in the United States is confusing for many who argue the merits or lack of them in federal aid to education. Perhaps the recent debate over federal aid should not properly be viewed as a constitutional argument or a debate over the propriety of federal aid in terms of tradition. The recent debate merely uses such authority as the Constitution and tradition to support a case for either side. The real issue in federal aid may very well be the changing nature of the federal system as it has come to be viewed by conservative and liberal forces in the twentieth century. Certainly, as far as national-state relations with respect to the schools are concerned, "creative-federalism" is a more apt term than "federalism."

Viewed in this light, control of education by the national government is not the real issue. The real issue is the expansion of power of the national government, not only in education but a general expansion of power and activity. Those who oppose this trend in government may see education as the last stronghold of the state's legitimate power, or they may see federal aid in education as just another indication of an all-powerful national government attempting to encroach upon the powers of the states. Of course, such a view may be held for a variety of reasons. The expansion of national power may be viewed as a negation of a whole theory of government. In an earlier era a high value was placed on individualism and a laissez-faire government. Any expansion of governmental power may be seen as destructive of individual rights. Those who express this latter view have a tendency to see the state and local government as close to the people and responsive to their desires, and the national government as far removed and sometimes hostile. Lastly, some view involvement of the national government in any new program as a serious threat to the American system as they understand it.

Those who favor an active national government may see education as a key to progress for the nation. An individual holding this view may believe the state is failing in its responsibility to provide an adequate education for the youth of the nation, or he may view efforts on the part of the state as too slow and ineffective in meeting the needs of the society. Those who hold this latter view have no real fear of an all-powerful national government, and see no real conflict between the states and the national government. Advocates of federal aid see federalism as a growing and cooperative process rather than as a fixed system. Such persons would deny that states have absolute authority in certain areas such as education, and that the national government is one of strictly defined and subsequently limited powers. This argument denies that it necessarily follows that increasing power by the national government decreases the freedom of the individual. In the case of education, those who favor federal aid may do so because they honestly feel that the aid and direction which can be provided by the national government provide greater individual freedom in that they can make available greater educational opportunities to individuals denied them under a system which is almost totally controlled by the states. A temporary compromise was reached with the passage of the 1965 Elementary and Secondary Education Act. This, like many important measures, was a compromise between contending forces, between those who desperately needed funds but who abhorred federal control, and those who did not view federal control as an unconditional evil. The present huge federal aid program leaves most of the control of education in the hands of the states. As needs and demands grow, the debate over who should control education will continue.

The argument, of course, is a long way from being settled. The machinery exists for its gradual resolution, however. It exists in the basic nature of the federal system of government. Specific issues will be resolved in the future just as they have been in the past—by the expression of the representatives of the majority. The national government is deeply involved in education because programs have been voted by Congress. Each has been seriously debated in Congress and the advantages and disadvantages have been subjected to the bright light of public opinion. This process will continue. In education, as in other areas in which the national government has become concerned, the government has moved because there have been needs and demands for increased services. Where other agencies of government on the state and local level proved unable financially, or unwilling politically, Congress attempted to meet the need. This has been the story of the development of a national system of highways, a national program in agriculture, the social security program, and so on. It has also been true in education, and doubtless will continue to be so in future years.

It is becoming increasingly apparent that the future will see vast increases in national spending for education. The national government is already a significant part of the financial picture in education, and it is not unrealistic to presume that within a very few years it may be providing as much as one quarter of the total funds for education. Most of the serious opposition to large federal aid programs has been overcome, and few educators today show any openly. The new programs have somehow been made palatable, even to former opponents, by repeated assurance that federal aid will not be followed by federal control.

The following is not to be considered as an argument against federal aid, for it has been an evolutionary development that is natural and probably necessary. Federal aid in its present scope and in its future potential, however, holds certain political implications which have yet to be faced by educators and the public. In their zeal to avoid the charge of "federal control," politicians and educators who have been preparing the general outline of federal aid in large amounts for elementary and secondary education seem deliberately to have avoided certain large questions which must ultimately face them. Some of these are the old political questions which have surrounded public education in the United States throughout our history. There may never be any final answer, but we must continue to ask them. Some, however, are new questions which grow out of the environment in which we find ourselves. The most important of these include the following:

1. Who should be educated and at whose expense?
2. How much and what kind of education should be provided at public expense?
3. To what extent should political action attempt to implement programs which lead to equalization of income through education?
4. How should the race for international supremacy condition our educational goals and objectives?
5. Who should make the decisions for education?
6. Is increased centralized planning necessary in education? If so, does it have a price tag?

There remains a good deal of healthy disagreement on the questions of who should be educated and at whose expense in our society. The general consensus at the present writing seems to be that everyone should be educated at public expense. Presently, there is little responsible argument against this general goal. The argument comes more over where the money will come from than over the general goal of education for every individual to the limit of his capability, even though it is tragically apparent that rhetoric exceeds performance. The money is coming in increasing amounts from the federal government, and this trend will undoubtedly continue in the future. The old fear—federal aid means federal control—has been somewhat subdued in recent years due partly to repeated assurances on the part of congressional leaders that there are "no strings attached." Perhaps more important, opposition has seemed to dwindle because of the prospect of huge sums, and the educational fraternity is currently displaying a certain reluctance to look a gift horse in the mouth. In spite of such assurances of little or no control, the control is there. Although the specific appropriation may be very general and may allow state governments, school districts, and other agencies complete discretion in the manner in which the federal money is to be spent, every appropriation by Congress is made as a political gesture. Every appropriation tends to answer the second question posed in this section: How much and what kind of education?

Every educational appropriation by Congress has to be justified on some political basis which is national in character. This can range from a national concern for poverty to the question of national survival in a nuclear age. At first, the quantity becomes some political leader's educated guess. This may be in the form of a recommendation that Congress appropriate a billion dollars a year to combat poverty. A bureaucracy has already grown around the anti-poverty educational program. Needs are more closely scrutinized by those in the field, and the educated guesses have tended to become statements of real need based on volumes of facts and figures. These are compiled by the field workers and channeled up through the new bureaucratic structure into committees on appropriation in Congress. Similarly, in the beginning, the matter of what kind of education becomes an educated guess. The statistics of unemployment are summarized and analyzed; current demands in the economic system are matched with supply. Generalized conclusions are reached which have led to the kind of educational programs which meet some current pressing need in terms of labor supply. The political appeal of preparing unemployed youth for jobs which are going begging is irresistible. Its political promise becomes even greater when it assures quick results. As in the case of quantity, what began as somebody's educated guess, when enacted into law, enables the creation of a bureaucratic structure to formalize the process. Studies can now be made under the general provisions of the law. Needs are carefully and accurately assessed and recommendations made for more money for extension of the program. The central issue here, however, is not with the amount of money, but with the kind of education. Once a program is outlined and initiated, it tends to continue in operation as long as the need exists—sometimes even beyond this time. Larger questions about the kind of education are seldom asked once a program is underway. The speed with which a kind of "defensive bureaucracy" develops is both amusing and frightening. For example, educators have preached pre-school training for years, and some states assumed this responsibility. Few, however, got really excited or emotional about pre-school programs. On the other hand, give the pre-school program a title like Head Start, involve thousands of people in the program, tie it in with a general political platform, and an instant bureaucracy develops which can oppose any cut in the program with the passion and zeal of a missionary.

One is tempted to wonder where all this energy came from. One might raise the question: Why wasn't some of this energy exerted earlier in state legislative chambers?

A third major political question which must be kept before the public is: To what extent should political action attempt to implement programs which lead to equalization of income through education? Equalization of income has come to be identified with the greatest good for the greatest number in our society. However, we have generally tended to view with suspicion those who would "rob from the rich and give to the poor." In a society which professes to believe strongly in individualism and emphasizes individual liberty and freedom in the economic as well as the political realm, the idea of the redistribution of wealth has always been, and continues to appear, an alien, if not radical, idea. Although the federal income tax does effect some redistribution in practice, many Americans have held to the old liberal classical economic ideal of individualism. In spite of arguments by an articulate minority to the contrary, the income tax has not resulted in socialism as an economic system. It has not proved disastrous to private initiative, nor has it substantially altered the existence of economic classes in our society. The approach which the United States has taken in its attempts to make the society economically more democratic, that is, to minimize great differences in wealth and class, has been an educational approach.

Most students of our society would agree that the existence of rigid economic class structures presents a serious obstacle to the realization of the democratic ideal. A most important part of the American dream has been the idea that any individual who puts forth the necessary effort can "reach the top." This has been true in enough cases in our past to give the dream some genuine validity. Certainly this aspect of the American dream has great political appeal. In today's technological society, the political aspects of the dream have undergone a rather subtle change. Individual opportunity to move up the ladder of economic success has been replaced to some extent with the concept of collective opportunity. This is stated in political platforms and promises and political action in the form of legislation, which enhances all kinds of expression for whole groups. The advocates of equality have been successful in writing laws which formalize equality for minority groups in our society. More recently, the philosophy has expanded to include a whole economic class—the poor. The argument advocates moving the whole society upward on the economic scale, with special attention given to the very lowest economic group. This is an equalitarianism which is quite different from the older and more alien idea of taking from the rich and giving to the poor. Indeed, it doesn't have the same effect. Classes remain, but there are few tears shed over their existence. They are tacitly accepted as the way things are. The rich can become richer, but not at the expense of the poor. Rather, the argument now runs: Everyone becomes richer, especially the poor. The most obvious means for attainment of this goal, of course, is education. Education is the surest way, in a technological society, for the individual, for whole groups or classes, to move forward. Of course this does little to effect a basic change in economic class structure. What it does instead, is to enhance a most basic American accomplishment; that is, it enables our society to continue to have the richest poor in the history of civilization. Thus political expressions of equalitarianism have tended to compromise the utopian ideal of a classless society with the reality of classes, and have found in education a practical means for a greater equalitarianism. Moreover, it can be argued that such equalitarianism is not achieved at the expense of individualism. That this has not been a planned effort or one with a long theoretical background is remarkable in itself. It is essentially pragmatic, and there is some hope that it will be successful. Theory in this area will not determine future action. Future action will be determined on the basis of the success or failure of investment in education to provide a kind of equalitarianism which does not destroy the traditional ideal of individualism.

A fourth question—How should the race for international supremacy condition our educational goals and objectives?—has serious political implications. It involves an extension of American nationalism, or at least a dedication to its preservation. The race for supremacy is fed partly by fear, partly by pride. From the beginning of the cold war, political leaders have insisted on a strong national defense in the face of very real threats from our enemies. At times during the past twenty-five years, the fear of possible attack has resulted in almost total mobilization of the society. During the last twenty-five years, even in periods of relative calm, huge sums have been spent on national defense. Moreover, national defense has come to have a very comprehensive definition since the end of World War II. The threat of total war, or the fear of it, real or imagined, requires a kind of total preparation unknown in any previous period in our history. It has been under this threat, and the resultant fear, that the purposes of education in American society have been somewhat redefined. The old idea of education as a means of providing for intelligent and enlightened citizens has become instead a mobilization of the resources of education for purposes of national defense. The National Defense Education Act is a good case in point. Because of the fear of total war, the national government has been able to promote and finance large educational programs which might never have been considered during more stable times. Each succeeding year witnesses new programs in education financed wholly or in part by the national government, and based on the premise that the new programs are necessary for our national defense.[8]

National pride has also been an important factor in expanding the role of

---

[8] A different point of view is presented in Seymour Melman, *The Depleted Society* (New York: Holt, Rinehart & Winston, 1965).

the federal government in education. Perhaps the best single illustration of this phenomenon is the space race. There can be little doubt that the early Soviet lead in the space race was a serious blow to American pride. Perhaps the success of Sputnik I in 1957 had more effect in getting Congress to consider greater expenditures in education than all the previous carefully considered and intelligently made arguments combined. Since 1957, great sums have been spent for improving and expanding the teaching of scientific subjects in the public schools and colleges. Catching up and ultimately winning the space race became a national preoccupation which threatened the position of baseball as the number one spectator sport. National pride, as well as some fear, is involved in the space race. It is the sort of contest that Americans seem to thrive upon. Few in our society question the importance of the space race and even fewer perhaps question that education will somehow play a vital role in the outcome.

Such overriding considerations as the question of national defense and those raised by the space race seem to have automatically decided for us who should make the decisions for education. Events have made many decisions for us. The size, scope, and technology of war and the space race have overcome the old arguments of whether the national government or the states should make educational decisions. A good argument might be made for the position that most of the really important decisions, most of the innovations in education in the past twenty-five years, have been implemented by the national government, not by the leaders among the individual states. National defense is, of course, a national concern, and the educational programs which have been initiated and financed by the national government have been the most notable developments in education in the past twenty-five years.

Finally, the questions of decision-making and planning have great political implications. The really big decisions affecting education are no longer made on the local level. The implications of national policy for education may seriously modify the role of education in our society. The tradition of educational decision-making has been one of individualism and localism in the past; that is, the individual decided in his own case how much and what kind of education he should have. To this was added the concerns of the state. States early determined what minimum education should be, and in a general way, the kind of education which was necessary for effective citizenship and an orderly society. As industrialization and urbanization of the society proceeded, the role of the state government became increasingly important. Increasingly, the state was deciding who should be educated, at whose expense, and the kind of education that should be provided. A trend that began in a large way in the 1930's and has accelerated in the last thirty-five years is becoming more apparent—the individual is coming to have less to say about his own education and the society is assuming a greater burden of decision-making. Technology, the economic condition of the society, and the imperatives of the hot and cold wars, appear to be making many educational decisions for us. Educational planning in the face of these conditions is becoming more common. Schooling has become essential in order for the individual to find a useful place in the society. Evidence of the recognition of these forces is seen in the various guidance and counseling programs in the schools. The existing comprehensive testing programs are justified on the grounds that they help students find their place in a complex technological society. In the face of this increasing complexity, the individual is becoming increasingly more helpless, increasingly more dependent upon guidance, direction, and planning from some outside source. The "other-directed" individual, at least in an economic sense, may not only be increasing in number in our society, but the condition of the society may be such that greater planning is necessary. Already, urban schools are deeply involved in much "directive" counseling on the basis of a formal testing program.[9] With increasing frequency, students are evaluating education in terms of what it does for them economically. Education which leads to immediate employment in a good secure job is a good education, in the view of many students.

This condition raises a genuinely serious question which goes right to the heart of our political values: To what extent will the increased planning affect the traditional value of individualism? How to match people with jobs, human resources with needs, and individual aptitudes with needs of the society become problems for planners in a technological society. How these things can be accomplished without great sacrifices of individual freedom and occupational free choice in our society will be one of the most serious and continuing political-educational problems in our future.

REFERENCES

Allen, Hollis P. *The Federal Government and Education.* New York: McGraw-Hill, 1950.
Butts, R. Freeman, and Lawrence A. Cremin. *A History of Education in American Culture.* New York: Holt, Rinehart & Winston, 1953.
Congressional Quarterly Services. *Federal Role in Education.* Washington, D.C.: Congressional Quarterly Inc., 1965.
Fellman, David (ed.). *The Supreme Court and Education.* New York: Bureau of Publications, Teachers College, Columbia Univ., 1960.
Garber, Lee O. "Four Church-State Controversies: How They Affect Education." *The Nation's Schools.* 69:66–68 (June 1962).
Gross, M. L. *The Brain Watchers.* New York: Random House, 1962.

---

[9] For a well-reasoned criticism of specific counseling based on test results, see M. L. Gross, *The Brain Watchers* (New York: Random House, 1962); B. Hoffman, *The Tyranny of Testing* (New York: Crowell-Collier, 1962); and the February 1965 issue of the *American Psychologist,* which is devoted to an assessment of the school testing program.

Hanna, Paul R. (ed.). *Education: An Instrument of National Goals.* New York: McGraw-Hill, 1962.

Hoffman, B. *The Tyranny of Testing.* New York: Crowell-Collier, 1962.

Hovde, H. O. "Brief Survey of Federal Aid to Education." *National Association of Secondary School Principals Bulletin.* 45, I:96–101 (Feb. 1961).

Melby, Ernest O. *Freedom and Public Education.* New York: Frederick Praeger, 1953.

Melman, Seymour. *The Depleted Society.* New York: Holt, Rinehart & Winston, 1965.

Meranto, Philip. *The Politics of Federal Aid to Education in 1965: A Study in Political Motivation.* Syracuse, N.Y.: Syracuse Univ. Press, 1967.

Munger, Frank J., and Richard F. Fenno, Jr. *National Politics and Federal Aid to Education.* Syracuse, N.Y.: Syracuse Univ. Press, 1962.

National Education Association. *Research Report, 1965–R17, Estimates of School Statistics, 1965–1966.* Washington, D.C.: Research Division, 1965.

Reisner, Edward H. *Nationalism and Education Since 1789.* New York: Macmillan, 1922.

Roszak, Theodore (ed.). *The Dissenting Academy.* New York: Random House, 1967

PART FOUR
Special Problems Involving Values and Schooling

Chapters 11 to 14 are addressed to the general question: Can the schools change values? Perhaps it is not so much a question of whether the schools can change values as it is a tacit recognition of the fact that values change and that there are certain conditions and forces which are directly related to the schools and which directly involve the schools in the process of change. These are the forces in the society which the schools cannot ignore. The content selected to illustrate the particular role of the school in this process of change, or perhaps to illustrate the need for the school as an agent of change, includes forces operating within the environment which are more or less impersonal, yet demand change on a broad social scale. The increased militancy of the teacher and his growing political consciousness are among the forces just now awakening which are sure to have some effect on the role the schools are to play in the future. Similarly, the great push for realization of idealized political values such as equality, freedom, and justice for minorities has already greatly affected the goals of education as well as the organization of the schools. Nearly every aspect of American life has been influenced in some way by the force of technology. An impersonal force in a changing environment into which students will move as they complete their formal schooling, technological development has a great effect on political values as they are expressed in terms which affect educational goals, programs, teachers, school organization, and most of all—students. No attempt is made in this section to deal with all of the forces which exert pressure for change in the schools; but teachers, technology, and human values should be considered illustrations which demonstrate that the schools can be a vital part of the process of change at least as they reflect change in the society.

11

The Changing Role of the Teacher

The history of teachers' activities in the political arena has been a dreary one in many ways. It has been characterized by ineffective organization for political purposes and an absence of any firm and continuing goals, a difficulty in agreement on priority needs in education and the frustration of serious and prolonged failures. Even the casual observer of the educational scene today may be struck with public displays of teacher dissatisfaction in communities across the land. Yesterday's image of the little old lady teacher with hornrims has been replaced with one of a sign-carrying militant in many school districts. In recent years, teachers have struck in several major cities and have staged walkouts and "professional holidays" in several states. In some instances, the strikes have been long and bitter, as in the case of New York City in the early sixties and Los Angeles in 1970. In the spring of 1968, about half the teachers in the state of Florida submitted their resignations, and the ensuing battle between teachers, the legislature, and the governor of Florida gained national notoriety. In the spring of 1970, Kentucky's twenty-five thousand teachers struck for a week, and even in the face of court injunctions prohibiting such action, succeeded in gaining some concessions from the Kentucky legislature. During the sixties, several states and dozens of school districts were the object of sanctions imposed by the National Education Association at the request of state and local affiliates.

The frustration and attendant militancy on the part of teachers may be due in part to the inability of the schoolteacher in our society to work effectively in the political process. There are many reasons for this, and it will be the task of this chapter to look into some of them in detail, examining what the teacher wants, describing how the teacher has worked for what he wants, and analyzing the successes and failures of the political efforts of the teacher.

There is some evidence that teachers are making new demands, that they are moving to new definitions of their role, and that they are willing to adopt new techniques to achieve the things they desire. Finally, some special problems created by the educational "establishment" will be discussed.

IS TEACHING A PROFESSION?

Within the limited context of his work, what the teacher considers valuable for himself as well as the schools seems to involve two very general areas. The first has to do with his professional status or dignity; the second involves adequate financial recognition.

Webster's New World Dictionary defines a profession as:

> A vocation or occupation requiring advanced training in some liberal art or science, and usually involving mental rather than manual work, as teaching, engineering, writing, etc.; especially medicine, law, or theology. . . .

Almost twenty-five years ago, the National Education Association suggested that a profession should embrace the following criteria:

1. Involves activities essentially intellectual
2. Commands a body of specialized knowledge
3. Requires extended professional preparation
4. Demands continuous inservice growth
5. Affords a life career and permanent membership
6. Sets up its own standards
7. Exalts service above personal gain
8. Has a strong, closely knit professional organization[1]

Although there are many such lists, we are no closer to a clear definition of the so-called "professional" teacher today than we were twenty-five years ago. There is some indication that the younger, more militant teacher of the seventies may be less concerned with the abstractions of "professionalism" as defined by some educational authority or national group than he is with such bread and butter issues as salary, fringe benefits, and working conditions. Indeed, in many of today's classrooms, the so-called "professional criteria" of an earlier generation of teachers seems strangely archaic. Even so, there continues to be a serious division of opinion on the matter of professionalism. This division is a split between the traditional-minded teacher who has certain ideas about professionalism and vocal emergent groups which are challenging these ideas. It is not uncommon, for example,

---

[1] National Education Association. "The Yardstick of a Profession," *Institutes on Professional and Public Relations, 1938–1947* (Washington, D.C.: Division of Field Services, 1948), p. 8.

for the tradition-oriented teacher to refer to his colleagues who are strong advocates of bread and butter issues such as salary and working conditions as "non-professional" in their attitude. On the other hand, some teachers may feel that inadequate salaries, lack of community respect for their position, and their general status in the community indicate that they are not regarded as professional people. Teachers frequently compare their lot with that of the more clearly identifiable professions of law and medicine, and some conclude that they fall short of these professions in many ways. In searching for conditions which separate or distinguish them from the professions of law and medicine, many teachers settle on the differences in financial reward for their services and the general attitude of the public toward them.

Whether or not teaching is truly a professional calling, there may be general agreement among teachers concerning what constitutes professional dignity. Professional dignity involves a whole scale of values and problems in education. A most important aspect of professional dignity from the classroom teacher's point of view is the esteem in which his position is viewed in the community. The esteem in which any professional is held in our society is closely tied to the size and source of income. However, there is more involved in the respectability of a profession than cold cash. From the teacher's viewpoint, professional dignity involves the recognition of his academic preparation and the privilege to speak as an expert in his area of preparation. Recognition of academic preparation is necessary on the part of peers, the school administration, students, and the general public. In theory at least, degree of expertise should contribute to one's standing in the eyes of his peers. The kind of respect which grows out of professional competence is perhaps most easily gained with one's peers or with the teacher's administrative superiors in the school situation. Moreover, the teacher who has gained respect through his professional competence is sure to know he has it. This is true since respect can be made evident in many ways. For example, when a school principal or superintendent receives a request for someone on his faculty to speak before some outside group and the administrative officer refers the request to a member of his faculty on the basis of his professional competence in the subject matter, such a request can be a gratifying expression of confidence in the teacher as a professional. Similarly, the teacher whose advice on some subject in his area of teaching is sought out by his colleagues or by some administrative authority has the respect of those seeking the advice. Unfortunately, such respect is not always in evidence in the public schools.

Similarly, students show their respect for the competence of the teacher in many ways. Students may respect teachers who are properly assigned and know the subject they are teaching. Teachers who are poorly prepared can expect little respect from students. Students indicate respect for professional competence of the teacher in a number of ways. When they are challenged by a teacher, they have ways of showing it. In the questions they ask and their general attitude toward the teacher in and out of class, students directly indicate their respect or lack of it.

This has become a particularly acute problem for many teachers in recent years in school districts throughout the nation. This is especially the case in secondary schools which tend to reflect the larger society with all its divisions and problems. Fueled by the national problems of race, ghettos, poverty, and war, student frustrations have increased on the secondary school level as they have on the college level. Secondary school students in hundreds of school districts have been demanding a greater voice in determination of school policy, curriculum decisions, and other matters. With increasing efforts to provide integrated education, racial problems in schools have become so commonplace that they are hardly newsworthy. Regarding problems associated with race, teachers have often been directly involved. Students have accused teachers of prejudice and have demanded their dismissal. Secondary schools have been plagued with sit-ins, student strikes, and riots, not infrequently initiated by teacher actions involving students. Unquestionably, disorders in the public high schools have been most common in schools which have been recently integrated. A study made by the Syracuse University Research Corporation in 1970 found that urban integrated schools were the most likely to experience student disruption. The Syracuse research group found that "85 per cent of the nearly 700 secondary schools involved in the study experienced some kind of disruption in the period 1967–1969."[2] In considering causes for school unrest, the Syracuse study reported that major reasons for student dissatisfaction were rigid school rules, curricula which students considered irrelevant, and teachers who failed to understand their students' needs and interests. Although these have been long-standing problems in the public schools, they have become more acute in schools which have been integrated in recent years. This is true because many such schools continue to cling to a white, middle-class-oriented curriculum and predominantly white faculties, in the face of increasing numbers of students who are neither white nor middle-class.

With each passing year there seem to be fewer school districts where teachers can expect the unquestioned obedience of their students. Increasingly, students are demanding competent, fair-minded, and democratic teachers. Increasingly, students are becoming more articulate about what they call "student rights." Perhaps the greatest tragedy lurking in this situation is that there is very little present evidence to indicate that secondary schools beset with these troubles are making any serious efforts to correct them. Although there are some schools with a longer experience in integration, faculties who really care about students, institutes and inservice work in human relations, and revised curriculum, the most common reaction to

---

[2] *Newsweek,* 19 Oct. 1970, p. 80.

student violence appears to be to increase the number of guards. Moreover, in too many instances the greatest outcry for "protection" seems to come not from students, administrators, or even from parents, but from the teachers themselves. This is a direct admission of failure, for it is extremely difficult for students to respect the professional competence of teachers who play the role of prison guards.

Parents and lay groups also indicate respect, or lack of it, for teachers in a number of ways. The teacher may be asked his opinion on community problems, asked to speak to a variety of local groups, or consulted on any number of problems facing parents. These demands, although they may be burdensome, are all expressions of faith in the teacher's professional competence. A total lack of respect for the professional competence of teachers is expressed in other ways. When teachers are not consulted on matters in which they consider themselves competent and to which they feel they could make a genuine contribution, they may feel slighted. Indeed, they may interpret such neglect of their counsel as a direct or implied insult to their competence. Finally, in communities where a large number of parents are willing to picket the school administration or the local school, demanding the dismissal of prejudiced teachers, there is obviously a total lack of respect for the professional competence of teachers.

Lack of respect is indicated when the teacher is not consulted by school administrators on matters which vitally concern him. An unfortunate, but not unheard of, expression of such lack of professional respect on the part of the school principal is the situation in which a teacher is assigned courses to teach outside his major area of training. The attitude that the well-prepared teacher can teach anything might be great reasoning for those who are faced with making up class schedules, but it does very little to elevate the dignity of teaching. Perhaps nothing destroys the professional image more quickly than the obvious incompetence of the practitioner.

Total lack of respect for the professional competence of the teacher is approached when communities establish formal or informal bans on teacher participation in community activities. In communities where the teachers are effectively barred from political activity and are generally less active as citizens than the population generally, there may be some justification for questioning the respect the community has for the professional competence of the teacher. This kind of lack of respect occurs most frequently in middle-class suburbia. Frequently in the inner-city schools, the problem is reversed. That is, the teacher is often a suburban commuter to his place of employment. A stranger to the ghetto, he arrives at his post at the last possible moment in the morning and sometimes beats the children out of the building in the evening. Such a teacher makes no effort to participate in the affairs of the community in which his school is located. Indeed, he deliberately avoids them. Such an attitude does not go unnoticed by his students or their parents. Teachers who perform their duties in this manner could not be called professional no matter how the term is defined, and it is doubtful that the residents of the community they serve think of them as professionals.

The teacher may sometimes be puzzled about how the matter of professional competence becomes established in the community. In nearly any community in any given year, it would not be surprising to find a local physician or lawyer speaking out on educational problems about which he knows very little, while the school people remain silent because they are not asked to speak. There are times when this process seems to be carried to extremes. So the most successful and highly respected local physician becomes an expert on education, on politics, on tax policies, on local government, and so on, while the local social studies teacher remains silent, for if he speaks out he may do so at the risk of his job. Part of this attitude may be due to the fact that the teacher may be considered a public employee, while the physician is considered a private citizen and is speaking as such. However, some of it is related to the matter of the dignity and respect which surrounds the medical profession and the lack of such respect for teaching. In such circumstances, the teacher cannot help but wonder about the criteria which a community may use in judging professional competence. Clearly, the medical doctor may be somewhat out of his area of professional competence when he is expressing his private views on political issues. It may be that his opinion is respected not because of his specialized knowledge on political issues, but because of his success in his own area of competence. Success in one of the established professions has apparently given the successful practitioner a certain amount of license in our society.

Viewed realistically, the teacher's desire to become a truly active citizen-participant may be a dream that will be difficult to realize. The problems raised by active teacher participation in the burning political issues of the day are many. Foremost among these problems is the fact that the teacher is, after all, a public servant who gains his livelihood from the public treasury. This fact places some subtle restrictions on the teacher as a participating citizen. Once he signs a contract with a public agency, the school board, he has placed certain limitations on his ability to speak and act freely in politics. His role in the society is not unlike that of other government employees, state and national, who are employed under the conditions and restrictions of the civil service system. In most states, and in all cases in the federal civil service, the government employee has certain legal restrictions on his political activity. The basic philosophy underlying such restrictions is that the employee of the government has a direct and personal vested interest in politics which properly should be controlled and restricted. This philosophy is beginning to affect teachers directly. A few states already make certain provisions limiting political activities of teachers. Some state legislatures have passed laws which see the political candidacy of teachers as a conflict of interest. Some states have constitutional provisions which have been interpreted to deny teachers the privilege of serving in the state legislature or state office at the same time they have contracted for a teaching position.

Traditionally, teachers have appeared reluctant to become involved in politics. Perhaps one of the reasons for this is that teachers, as a group, tend to be politically conservative. If conservatism is defined as a reluctance to take risks and an inclination to support the established order, a majority of American teachers think of themselves as conservative. In a 1960 poll by the National Education Association, which asked teachers if they thought they should work actively as members of political parties, only half the teachers believed that they should. In 1964, the NEA asked teachers how they classified themselves in terms of political philosophy. The combined total of those who thought of themselves as conservatives or tending to be conservative was 61.1 per cent.[3]

This conservatism, often expressed in the reluctance of teachers to become involved in politics, is curious in view of the fact that any direct improvement in the economic conditions of teaching depends almost completely on the political process. Such inconsistent attitudes on the part of teachers are one of the findings of Harmon Zeigler's study of Oregon teachers in the mid-sixties.[4] Among other things, the study attempted to determine reasons for the relative political inactivity of teachers in Oregon. Although Zeigler's generalized conclusions apply to the Oregon population he sampled, they present some interesting bases for speculation about the political life of teachers in general. Among other things, Zeigler found a significant number of teachers in his Oregon sample who were cynical about the political system, and alienated from it. He defined political alienation as "the sense of being left out of the political process."[5] His study indicated that downward-mobile males (those whose economic status was lower than that of their fathers) and upward-mobile females were extremely alienated from the political system. The classifications established in the study placed about 33 per cent of the Oregon teachers in the downward-mobile category, about 15 per cent in the upward-mobile category, and the remainder were classified as "stationary."[6] Zeigler found that the greatest inhibiting factor felt by teachers regarding their political activities came not from the community or outside pressure groups, but from within the school system itself. Teachers, particularly those who considered themselves conservative, expressed real fear of sanctions which might be imposed by the administrative hierarchy.

It should be obvious to any casual observer of the school scene that the last

---

[3] National Education Association, *What Teachers Think: A Summary of Teacher Opinion Poll Findings, 1960–1965* (Washington, D.C.: NEA, 1965), p. 51.
[4] Harmon Zeigler, *The Political Life of American Teachers* (Englewood Cliffs, N.J.: Prentice-Hall, 1967).
[5] Zeigler, p. 42.
[6] Zeigler, pp. 34–35.

few years of the sixties witnessed tremendously increased political activity by teachers. Indeed, in some states and localities, walkouts, demonstrations, and strikes have been blatantly political in the sense that they have been executed at a time when the legislature was considering important school matters. It is possible that the increasing militance of teachers' organizations, their willingness to indulge in open confrontations, has given teachers the necessary anonymity and security to become active. Obviously, it is quite a different thing to join with a large organization in political activity, even overt political activity such as carrying a picket sign, than it is to stand on a political soapbox as a single individual. If a major reason that teachers have tended to be politically timid is fear of administrative sanctions, as Zeigler's study suggests, certainly a strong classroom teachers' organization would contribute in a major way to the elimination of that fear. As teachers become better organized, it is possible that they will also become a more potent political force. Perhaps the most significant contribution such organization can make to the individual teacher is increased awareness of his political role in the system. With success, his alienation most certainly would diminish, and perhaps most important, his image as a professional might be enhanced.

Another important aspect of professionalism from the teacher's point of view is the matter of competence in knowledge and skills. But what is competence in teaching? Perhaps dignity and respect come to the physician and lawyer because it is a relatively simple matter to evaluate their work. The physician's failures may die or lie ill, while his successes recover. The lawyer's failures may go to jail or "pay up," while his successes are outside and solvent. In a word, the products of these professions are measurable in a very realistic way. Not so with teachers. The fact that "everybody" knows Miss Jones is a good teacher may mean that nobody knows. What constitutes good teaching, in spite of considerable research on the subject, remains one of the most knotty problems in education. Even in cases where Johnny seems to be learning his lessons well under the guidance of a particular teacher, who knows to what extent that teacher is responsible for Johnny's success? There are so many variables in teaching. What sort of background for this particular study did Johnny have? Is the teacher merely capitalizing on spadework done by Johnny's previous teacher or teachers? Is there some personal relationship between Johnny and his teacher which enhances the learning situation? These and other questions continue to obscure a clear definition of good teaching.

One thing all teachers can agree upon, however, is that their chances of doing a good job of teaching in the eyes of their students, peers, administrators, and patrons is handicapped or enhanced by the conditions under which they are expected to work. Most important among the conditions which many teachers believe make some difference in their effectiveness are such factors as class size and total number of students, the physical environment, the availability of the necessary tools, and a clear understanding of major areas of responsibility.

Research on class size as related to teacher effectiveness is presently inconclusive. In the minds of most teachers, however, there is little question that they can be more effective with a smaller number of students. This does not mean that there is a magic size of maximum efficiency, say twenty-five or thirty students to a room, although this continues to be a popular class size in the minds of teachers, parents, and administrators. Professional-minded teachers are concerned about meeting individual needs in their classrooms, and it is logically reasonable if not empirically true that a teacher has a better chance of attending to individual differences and needs in a small class than a large one. This would appear to be especially true in the lower grades and in the skill subjects where students are first learning to read, write, spell, and make some sense out of the mysteries of arithmetic. Experienced teachers know that it is absolute folly to attempt to meet the learning as well as the emotional needs of young children in the lower elementary grades where they are jammed together with forty or more to a room. In such a situation (which sadly exists in too many American schools) one can only marvel at how the teacher is able to maintain his mental stability from one day to the next.

Teachers also know that an attractive and pleasant physical environment is important to learning. Students who are uncomfortable have a difficult time concentrating on the business at hand. Physical discomfort brought on by extremes in temperature, drab rooms, and generally inadequate facilities are not conducive to good learning. However, these things by themselves do not make learning impossible. The poor teacher might still be poor with one child in a million-dollar classroom equipped with all manner of technological aids and contrivances, but the good teacher should be made a better one in a favorable physical environment. Prospective teachers should know, however, that there still remains a chance that their first job may find them in rooms which present a threat to life and limb. Although great improvements in physical facilities have been made in the past twenty-five years, there are still schools in which teachers and children may face the daily threat of falling chunks of plaster or worse.

The tools of the trade have traditionally borne a close relationship to the image of professionalism. In comedy skits, the "quack" practitioner is frequently characterized as one who uses rather unconventional tools. Mechanics' pliers for the dentist and wood saws for the surgeon have long been popular comedy props for the depiction of the quack. Similarly, not many people are ready to trust a lawyer whose office consists of the jump seat of an old automobile which he uses literally to "pick up" clients from the scene of an accident. Most people, if they can afford the fee, prefer the mahogany-paneled office, well equipped with good furnishings, the best magazines, and crisply efficient office help. The teacher, too, may gain some personal satisfaction, if not professional status, from a well-equipped classroom.

Tied closely to the image of professionalism is the matter of a clear definition of proper areas of responsibility for the practitioner. The teacher who is called upon to do all sorts of menial tasks may not only suffer physically from such ordeals, but also sacrifice professional dignity. Such housekeeping functions as clerical work and extra-class responsibility including policing the grounds, taking tickets at football games, and so on, may fit well into the plans of certain school administrators, but these activities do little to elevate the status of teaching as a profession. For a teacher to have professional status, the tasks he undertakes must be of a professional nature. He must be employed in the area of his competence and not become a "hired man" around the school. A good rule of thumb to follow in this respect is the same one which is followed in many large business organizations, that is, the rule of comparative advantage. No self-respecting professional businessman would be caught doing work which can be done by someone of lesser talent. The classical example in economics of the theory of comparative advantage is that of the executive and his typist. Even though the executive may be able to type more proficiently than his typist, he delegates the typing to the typist since he can more advantageously employ himself in other tasks. The rule of thumb provided by the professions and by most businessmen is that the time of the professional should be spent in those activities which he is most qualified to do. Unfortunately, this simple guideline of economic efficiency has not yet been widely applied to teaching. As a result of doing many menial and clerical duties, the teacher's professional status may be lowered—not only because even the dullest student recognizes the low level of such activities, but because it takes valuable time from greater responsibilities. Moreover, a most deplorable condition may exist in some schools where the teacher's worth is evaluated not in terms of professional competence, but in terms of how well he performs these housekeeping functions. Each year many a promotion is earned by teachers who are willing to do any number of "dirty jobs" which need to be done, which have absolutely no relationship to the professional competence of the teacher.

Rare is the community which does not call frequently on its teachers to spend precious hours with the Boy Scouts, various fund drives, the annual daisy bazaar, or what have you. Although some of this activity is an important facet of active citizenship, there are limits. The school administrator or the community which makes unreasonable demands on the teacher's time outside his area of competence thinks little or cares little about the teacher's need to spend more time preparing for his major function—that of guiding the learning of his charges. It is, in a way, a recognition that there is nothing really professional about teaching.

Still another aspect of professionalism in teaching is the opportunity (or lack of it) provided for the teacher to improve the skills of his profession. The true professional knows what is going on in his profession. He is dedicated to his work to the extent that he finds keeping abreast of his field a genuine responsibility. Many teachers are unable to do this. For those teachers who feel a genuine dedication to their profession and who are unable to keep up with it, the frustration and disappointment can become overpowering enough to cause them to leave teaching. Coupled with the opportunity to improve skills, which is implied in professionalism, is the opportunity to do research for the purpose of expanding and improving the profession. Little opportunity is provided in teaching for this sort of activity.

The foregoing discussion may suggest that teaching generally falls short of many of the criteria of professionalism. Individual teachers and individual schools may have achieved a professional status, but in many other cases there remains a long road ahead. All of the foregoing problems are related in one way or another to the problem of finance. But more than this, perhaps, such problems are related to the inability or unwillingness on the part of teachers to work for their own professional improvement. Fortunately, this situation is rapidly changing. Teachers are better organized and they are demanding results from their leadership. The real emergent power group in education may well be the rank and file classroom teacher. Interested first in his own welfare, he can do much in an incidental way to change the image of the teacher, to generally improve conditions, and perhaps ultimately cause some basic changes in curriculum, school organization, and other aspects of the school which are steeped in an old tradition dependent for its continuance upon a subservient, uncomplaining, and ineffectively organized teacher.

DIFFERENTIATED STAFFING AND PROFESSIONALISM

One solution which has been offered to help solve some of the professional problems of teachers is differentiated staffing. Although definitions vary greatly, differentiated staffing refers to the organization of teaching personnel in ways which will make the best use of their special competencies and talents. Advocates of differentiated staffing have claimed that it can solve the problems of teachers in ways ranging from reducing teaching load to providing significant increases in salary for outstanding teachers. Critics often see it as a scheme to quietly introduce the concept of merit pay without the necessity of increasing total salary costs. Whatever its strengths or weaknesses, differentiated staffing appears to be an idea which has caught the imagination of school boards and taxpayers throughout the nation.

Although the notion of merit pay for outstanding teachers and the use of "sub-professionals" or "teacher aides" has a long history, the idea of differentiated staffing has gained recent publicity through its adoption in Temple City, California, in 1967 and in three Florida counties in 1968.[7] The Temple City model provides four distinct teaching levels, each with different responsibilities and salaries. The lowest level in terms of salary and responsibility is the "associate teacher," whose major responsibility is classroom teaching. Next in line, the "staff teacher" holds responsibility for small group instruction and individual help for students, as well as some responsibility for curriculum development and supervision. At the third level, the Temple City plan provides for a "senior teacher," who serves as a consultant to the associate teachers, works with inservice training, and generally attempts to improve instruction. At the top of the hierarchy, the "master teacher" is responsible for district-wide research and curriculum development.

The Florida model is much more comprehensive, in that it provides for eight levels. At the bottom of the model are three non-tenured positions, "teacher aide," "educational technician," and "assistant teacher." The highest level of preparation required for these positions is an associate degree (two years of college) for the assistant teacher. In the Florida model, the major teaching responsibilities fall on a tenured "associate teacher" and "staff teacher." The three top positions in the model are that of "senior teacher," "teaching curriculum specialist," and "teaching research specialist."

Although there are other models which vary in the degree of differentiation and complexity, most plans for differentiated staffing have features in common. A major feature of all plans is the provision for differentiated salary. Thus, in the Florida model, the lowest rank, that of teacher aide, has a salary range of $3,500 to $4,500, while the top position, that of teaching research specialist, provides a salary range from $17,500 to $19,000 (1969). Another common feature of all plans is that the system is hierarchical in nature, in that duties and responsibilities on each level are clearly defined and progressively more comprehensive. All the plans for differentiated staffing provide succeedingly higher levels of preparation. Thus, the plans provide employment as teacher aides for those with little or no college training, but require a doctorate for the highest level positions. Those employees whose educational attainments are less than those necessary for full teacher certification are often called "para-professionals" or "sub-professionals."

Given a large number of students and teaching positions with which to work out such schemes, it should be obvious that taxpayers might easily be convinced that differentiated staffing could provide more "teachers" for their children without an increase in cost. On the other hand, experienced certified teachers can be sold on the system because it may relieve them of some of their nonprofessional duties, while at the same time promising to signifi-

---

[7] "Differentiated Staffing," *The Nation's Schools* (June 1970), pp. 43–46.

cantly increase their salaries. With such obvious advantages, it is not surprising that twenty-two state legislatures have already established guidelines or policy statements which enable local school districts to utilize teacher aides, while at least eight others were considering such action in 1970.[8] In view of the long struggle on the part of teachers' organizations for more stringent certification laws in every state, the speed with which legislators have acted to permit non-certified personnel to work with children in classrooms is amazing. No doubt the Elementary and Secondary Education Act of 1965, which provided financial support for teacher aides, paraprofessionals, and auxiliary personnel, has had something to do with the speed with which schemes of differentiated staffing have been adopted. The popularity of simple and complex schemes of differentiated staffing might also say something about the relative strength of teachers' organizations. A similar scheme called "medic," which has been devised to relieve the medical doctor of some of the more routine cases, has met with serious criticism and resistance from the organized nursing profession. Doctors have not been critical because they are in a position to control entrance into the system. The skilled trades have succeeded in a continuing policy of extremely long apprenticeship programs as a deliberate method of limiting the supply of skilled workers. Teachers, on the other hand, even though they have been plagued with the problem of oversupply in recent years, have not strongly resisted efforts to provide sub-professional assistance, even though its implementation is beyond their control. This is not meant as an unconditional criticism of differentiated staffing. Obviously, teachers have long been called upon to perform menial and clerical tasks which required little formal training. Nor is there any question that most teachers have desperately needed assistance. For the most part, however, teachers have labored for reduced work loads in the form of smaller classes and the induction of more fully certified teachers into their ranks, and have simultaneously pressured school boards and legislatures for better salaries. For teachers who have struggled so long for a more meaningful voice in matters which vitally affect them, there are serious dangers lurking in differentiated staffing. It is conceivable that the introduction of large numbers of sub-professionals into teaching could seriously weaken existing teachers' organizations. When "marginal" employees are introduced into the system, it is possible that they might be grateful for any employment. As non-tenured sub-professionals they may feel reluctant to join teachers in their efforts to improve the profession. It is also possible that an indiscriminate use of sub-professionals could reduce the need for fully certified teachers, which could have the effect of creating teacher surpluses. This, in turn, might seriously hamper the

---

[8] Laurel N. and Daniel Tanner, "The Teacher Aide: A National Study in Confusion," *Educational Leadership* (May 1969), pp. 765–769.

bargaining position of teachers. Another problem which teachers have yet to face is that of who makes the decisions in differentiated staffing schemes. As things now stand, it is obviously not the classroom teacher, even though these decisions vitally affect his conditions of employment. For example, most differentiated staffing schemes seem to place responsibility for the selection of the top positions in the hands of administration. Where this is true, the vital questions concerning what to teach, how to teach, and the organization of instruction are answered from the top down. In this system, the voice of the classroom teacher on most vital issues can easily be muted. In a real sense, the backbone of the system, the certified classroom teacher, is caught in the middle of the system—directed from the hierarchy above, and not necessarily supported in his professional demands from those below him. Moreover, the system can operate in a way which severely limits the number of prestigious and high-salary positions, effectively blocking the great majority of certified teachers from positions of real influence and power.

Obviously, these problems and others which may develop in schemes of differentiated staffing are based on the assumption that school boards and school administrators which serve them do not always act in the best interests of the professional teacher. What may be great for school administrations and large taxpayers may not always work well for teachers and students. At any rate, it would not be greatly surprising to discover that teachers may resist wholesale implementation of differentiated staffing, for they have long argued that their years of preparation have meant something in terms of the competencies they offer the local school district. Perhaps their arguments have been based on an erroneous assumption. Perhaps it is true that much of what is done by the certified teacher can be done by people with less formal training and experience. If, indeed, the public discovers that nearly anyone can teach, then arguments over issues of professionalism in education are largely academic.

TEACHERS' ORGANIZATIONS AND PROFESSIONALISM

If the teacher is dependent upon the political process for success in his search for professional identity, it might be profitable to examine how he works for what he values. Generally, the teacher has worked through his organizations—the National Education Association, and more recently the American Federation of Teachers. He has been an active lobbyist in Congress and before the state legislatures; he has made use of groups outside of teaching to push his causes; he has resorted to direct pressure of various kinds; and he has utilized the techniques of propaganda in order to gain public support for his goals. These are all techniques employed by the classroom teacher as his power emerges through recognized teachers' organizations.

Professional Organizations

There are two major teachers' organizations in the United States. These are the National Education Association, which has a membership of approximately one million, and the American Federation of Teachers, which claims approximately 250,000 members. Since there is a total of about 2.2 million, one can conclude that the public elementary and secondary teachers are not as well organized as they might be. However, membership is growing in both groups, and for the last decade there has been a thriving competition for membership between the NEA and the AFT.

The National Education Association was first organized in 1857 as the National Teachers Association. Thirteen years later, in 1870, it combined with the National Association of School Superintendents and the American Normal School Association, and its name was changed to the National Education Association. In 1884 the organization held a national convention in Madison, Wisconsin, which was attended by representatives from throughout the country. Eight years later, in 1892, the NEA appointed its first important committee to investigate conditions and practices in the public schools. From that time until the present, it has been an established organization. The NEA was chartered by Congress in 1906 and established its headquarters in Washington, D.C. in 1920.[9] At present the work of the NEA is directed by a president elected by the delegates to the representative assembly. It employs a salaried executive secretary and more than one thousand other employees. The organization of the NEA consists of fourteen divisions, thirty-three departments, and twenty-six commissions and committees, which deal with everything from professional ethics to school surveys.

There are clear indications that the new breed of teachers want to be professional. They are elated when asked to consult with others as recognized experts in their various fields. They are demanding, through their organizations, a greater voice in policy which concerns them. They desire to be active citizens. They continuously plead for working conditions which are professional in quality, and they are much concerned as individuals and as a group with the opportunity to improve their skill and do research in their areas of specialization.

Professional status for teachers generally is possible, and indeed exists, in some communities and for some teachers, but professional status for most teachers is going to cost a great deal more money than is presently being

---

[9] Raymond E. Callahan, *An Introduction to Education in American Society* (New York: Alfred A. Knopf, 1956), pp. 418–419.

expended on education. The teacher, as he is represented by his professional organizations, realizes this today more than he has at any other period in history. The teacher realizes his function is a public one, dependent upon public funds. He knows that the road to success lies generally in political activity, and his successes will depend to a great extent on his success in the political arena.

The National Education Association is governed by a representative assembly consisting of some eight thousand delegates. Each local association is entitled to one delegate for each one hundred of its NEA members; state associations are allotted one delegate for each one hundred members up to a total of five hundred members, and thereafter one delegate for each additional five hundred members. The assembly meets annually and acts as a legislative body in establishing the general policies of the association. The administrative policy is carried out by a board of directors composed of at least one NEA director from each state who is nominated by state associations and elected by the representative assembly. The board of directors also has several ex-officio members. An executive committee of eleven members serves as the interim policy-making body between sessions of the representative assembly. The day-to-day operation of the association is conducted by an executive secretary and more than one thousand employees.

The major functions of the National Education Association include publication of several journals and hundreds of books, reports, research studies pamphlets, and yearbooks. Its Research Division provides data on many aspects of education in the United States. There are committees and commissions in the National Education Association which deal with special problems of teachers, ranging from academic freedom to professional improvement. In recent years, the National Education Association has been particularly active in its efforts to influence national educational legislation and the improvement of salaries and working conditions of teachers on the state and local levels. The NEA has worked for federal aid for education, improvement of teacher retirement and social security benefits for teachers, reorganization of school districts, integration of public schools, opposition to merit ratings, and other matters of a teacher welfare nature. This is a new program for the NEA, which reflects the new militancy of the teacher. This program contrasts sharply with earlier goals of the NEA, which were concerned, for the most part, with working for what was loosely referred to as "professional" standards, which meant, in an earlier era, such things as the improvement of teacher certification laws.

The American Federation of Teachers is affiliated with the AFL-CIO. Although there were some scattered cities which had teachers' unions before 1916, the first national convention and affiliation of the American Federation of Teachers with the AFL took place in Chicago in 1916. During 1918 and 1919, the AFT enjoyed a brief period of success when it claimed eleven thousand members, more than the NEA of that period. From 1919 to 1929, the labor movement in the United States generally declined in strength and the AFT suffered from some anti-labor sentiment during the period. From 1929 to 1939, the American Federation of Teachers grew more rapidly, from a membership of six thousand to approximately thirty thousand. After World War II, the AFT experienced rather rapid growth from about twenty thousand members in 1947 to its present membership of approximately 250,000. The federation is organized under a paid president and sixteen non-salaried vice-presidents who are its regional representatives. Together these officials make up the executive council of the union.

The AFT is based on the idea of craft unionism, and claims to be the only true teachers' organization. This claim is based on the argument that full-time administrators are not in key positions in the union. The AFT views the educational organization as comparable to a business organization. They often compare the school board to the governing board of a corporation and see the office of superintendent as "management." The union sees a basic conflict of interest between teachers on the one hand and the administration and school board on the other.

General policy for the AFT is considered at its annual convention. Delegates to the convention are elected by affiliated locals, and each local union is entitled to one delegate for the first twenty-five or fewer members and one delegate for each twenty-five additional members up to five hundred, an additional delegate for each fifty members beyond five hundred up to one thousand. For locals with more than one thousand members, one delegate is allotted for each one hundred members in excess of one thousand.

Typical goals of the AFT in recent years have included collective bargaining for teachers, the extension of social security for teachers, desegregated schools, and a strong favorable position on federal aid to education. In terms of teacher welfare, the union has advocated a single salary schedule, opposed merit pay, and supported tenure laws and minimum salaries.

The decade of the sixties was characterized by much competition between the two major teachers' organizations. Although there had been a long rivalry between the NEA and the AFT, the bitter battle between the two organizations in New York City in 1960 was certainly a landmark. The battle began with a one-day strike sponsored by the United Federation of Teachers, a local union affiliated with the AFT. The union was attempting to force the board of education to bargain collectively with teachers in New York City. It was also attempting to gain recognition as the sole bargaining agent for forty thousand New York City teachers. The board agreed to allow an election so that teachers might decide which organization was to represent them in their discussions with the board. Both the NEA and AFT conducted feverish campaigns to gain the support of a majority of teachers. In the election the AFT affiliate gained a clear majority of the votes cast.

Following the significant victory in New York City, the AFT was encouraged in its efforts to organize teachers in other major cities. In order to combat this threat, the National Education Association established the Urban Services Project (currently, Urban Services Division), designed to make the organization more effective and popular with urban teachers. There followed a series of battles in dozens of major cities in the United States, between the NEA and AFT, for the loyalty of urban teachers. Although the NEA was successful in many cities, the AFT made serious inroads and won elections in Detroit, Cleveland, Philadelphia, Boston, Chicago, Rochester, Baltimore, and Washington, D.C., along with many other smaller cities. The immediate local result of this competition was an attempt on the part of both organizations to prove to their prospective membership that their organization was more willing to go to any lengths to improve salaries and working conditions. Consequently, both organizations became much more militant than they had ever been. Neither appeared reluctant to call for walkouts, sanctions, or strikes. In the face of such militancy, school boards tended to make concessions, and both organizations gained membership among urban teachers. Most significantly, the battles of the sixties seemed to bring the organizations closer together in terms of general goals and the means they were willing to use in reaching them. By the end of the sixties, the real differences between local militant classroom teachers' associations (whether or not they were affiliated with the NEA) and the local teachers' union, seemed minor. Indeed, the goals and tactics had become so similar in some localities that mergers of the two groups were accomplished. Since 1968, the delegate conventions and leadership of both organizations have been seriously considering a merger of the two groups. Even though the idea has been voted down by the NEA Association Classroom Teachers Division, the possibility for merger in the 1970's seems real enough. The issues which have divided the groups no longer loom as large. The two major issues which have historically divided the AFT and NEA were the fact that the NEA permitted administrators to become members and the AFT did not, and the fact that the AFT has been affiliated with the AFL-CIO.[10] Both organizations have been moving away from these positions on the local level. The classroom teachers' associations on the local level have not only moved to exclude administrators, but in some instances have virtually declared their independence from the NEA. Simultaneously, large union locals, which have always had a great deal of local autonomy, have tended to move away from affiliation with AFL-CIO. Thus in spite of the bitterness of the conflict between the two organizations in the past, most observers concede that a complete merger of the AFT and NEA is a real possibility. The next decade may determine the direction which will be taken by the classroom teachers of America.

---

[10] Myron Lieberman, "Implications of the Coming NEA-AFT Merger," *Phi Delta Kappan* (November 1968), pp. 139–140.

Clearly, whatever direction is taken by the teachers, the rivalry between the two groups may have outlived its usefulness. The competition did serve to awaken leadership in both groups concerning the strongly felt needs of teachers. Beyond a certain point, however, such rivalry tends to become so divisive that both parties stand to lose. Obviously, organization is important to teachers because it gets results. Just as obvious is the need for what amounts to an effective "closed shop" if teachers are to negotiate with boards from a position of strength. Nor is this an unrealistic goal. It is perfectly natural that teachers' organizations should work toward monopoly representation at least within a given school district. The history of group action in our society has been a history of attempts on the part of organizations to achieve monopoly. Moreover, those which have been successful are the ones which have approached monopoly control.

Any group of workers, semiprofessional or professional, needs a nearly unanimous agreement on the organization which will represent it. This is true whether the representation is made before the owners or management of private industry or before the public and its agencies. Division of teachers into competing groups only tends to weaken their position. Near monopolization of membership is the only realistic approach to teacher organization. Monopolization is necessary for the obvious strength which comes from unity. Teachers need unity because of the vast size of the educational enterprise, coupled with the great complexity of issues and problems facing education. For those who fear the power of monopoly, there are precedents in our society for internal and external control designed to protect minorities and provide majorities with a free choice.

There is reason to believe that teachers will continue to work towards a united front. The "rules of the game" are pushing them rapidly in this direction. Already the rules of collective bargaining or collective negotiations are a common part of the educational scene. Collective agreements between teachers and boards of education can only stimulate efforts on the part of teachers to work together. This is true because the basic rule of collective bargaining is that teachers must agree, via popular election, upon the organization that will speak for them. Collective bargaining or collective negotiations thus bring some order out of the confusion of demands made by conflicting groups.

Lobbying

A major method used by teachers in attempting to gain their goals is lobbying. Both the NEA and the AFT engage in lobbying activities before the national legislature. In these activities teachers' organizations have a sort of built-in advantage which should operate in their favor. As with any other lobbying group interested in the welfare of its constituents, the teachers' organizations tend to identify their own interests with the public good. For years Americans have heard various pleas from special interest groups claiming that what was good for them was good for the country. Subsequently, Congress and the general public have been bombarded from time to time with propaganda designed to demonstrate beyond the question of a doubt that what is good for the farmer, the businessman, the worker, or whatever, is good for the country. In their lobbying efforts, teacher representatives have used these time-worn tactics. However, to argue that what is good for the children is good for America has great appeal. It is a believable plea. A major problem has been that there have been times when the teachers themselves have not been entirely in agreement upon what is good for the children. The changing position on federal aid to education on the part of the National Education Association is a good case in point.

There can be little doubt, however, that the lobbying activities of teachers' groups enjoyed some success. The creation of a separate United States Office of Education in 1939 was made partly as a response to pressure to do so from teachers' groups. Similarly, making the United States Office of Education part of the Department of Health, Education, and Welfare in 1953 constituted a genuine recognition on the part of the executive department of the increasing importance and stature of education in our society. Part of the credit for the recent Elementary and Secondary School Act is claimed by the teachers' groups which had been advocating federal aid.

Lobbying techniques used by educational groups are not very different from those of any other pressure group. The teachers' organizations, like other lobbyists, write bills or urge individual members of Congress to do so. Congressional committee hearings on educational bills are well attended by representatives of teachers' groups. Both the NEA and the AFT have been known to urge their membership to "write their congressmen" on behalf of legislation pending before Congress. Beyond these more obvious efforts to influence legislation, teachers' groups have worked to develop close relationships with the agencies of government, such as the United States Office of Education, which make recommendations to Congress for action on educational plans and programs. The same sort of clientele relationship has developed between the United States Office of Education and teachers as those which have long existed between the Department of Agriculture and farmers or between the Department of Labor and labor unions.

Lobbying by educational groups has been much more obvious and active on the state level than on the national level. This is true, of course, since the state legislature provides the bulk of the money and outlines many details of the educational program. On the state level, the school interests have utilized every means known to lobbyists in an attempt to convince the legislature of the legitimacy of their cause. In many states teachers' organizations may quietly (sometimes openly) work for the election of a governor and legislators who will be "friendly." Governors have been prevailed upon by every device known to politics to outline programs for the legislature which will favorably reflect teachers' demands. Friendly legislators, who are sometimes teachers themselves, are prevailed upon to introduce bills in behalf of the teachers. In some states in the recent past, teachers have been known to descend en masse upon the state legislature while it was considering an important educational bill.

The Use of Front Groups

Teachers have been somewhat handicapped in their ability to use the influence of groups outside their own membership in the advocacy of their cause before the legislature. Cooperation among various pressure groups pleading cases before the state legislature and before the national Congress is a common practice in the American political system. Farm groups have been known to cooperate with labor groups, business groups with patriotic groups, and so on. However, teachers seem to have experienced some trouble in this respect. Generally, it has not been difficult for teachers to gain support from the Parent-Teacher Association and organized labor on the state level. Rarely does the Parent-Teacher Association openly oppose the legislative program of the teachers' organizations. PTA's have a history of working closely with classroom teachers, are generally aware of the most serious educational problems, and normally make a sincere effort to lend their weight to support teachers' requests before legislative bodies. The labor unions have also been friendly toward teachers in most states. This is particularly true where teachers are members of the American Federation of Teachers. It has not been uncommon for organized labor to lobby actively before the legislature for increased aid to education. Rarely does organized labor actively oppose educational programs which have been proposed by recognized teachers' groups. There have been a few exceptions to this policy in recent years when there is a strong division of the teachers between the American Federation of Teachers and the National Education Association. Where the views of these groups are in conflict before the legislature, obviously the AFL-CIO and other labor unions side with the teachers' union. Generally, however, organized labor has lobbied openly for increased federal aid for education, extending minimum compulsory school age, increased appropriations for the common schools, and other programs and policies which have been in the interests of teachers and their organizations.

Beyond the labor union and the PTA, teachers have been hard pressed to gain real support for their goals. In many instances groups which profess to be interested in "good" education on the local scene either remain silent before the legislature or quietly do what they can to oppose teachers' demands. In many instances of opposition by such groups, the motivation appears to be primarily economic. Even state school board associations have been known to oppose teachers in their demands for financial support for schools. Very often the school board associations express concern about the cost of teachers' demands, and may be more concerned about increased taxation than they are in teachers' demands. A similar conflict of interests may be found in certain business groups such as the Chamber of Commerce, certain farm groups, patriotic groups of various complexion, and others which appear to be willing enough to provide good schools, but express reluctance, sometimes in a loud and clear voice, when the legislature is considering increased appropriations for the schools. In a very real sense the teacher stands almost alone as he attempts to convince the legislature of the need for increased appropriations for education.

Direct Pressure

Laboring under such handicaps, teachers have become more militant in their demands in recent years. Following the example of other groups, teachers are more frequently resorting to direct pressure on the local and state level in an attempt to publicize their cause and in an attempt to pressure the legislature into action. Although for many years the pressure has existed in the form of a high rate of teacher turnover in states which have consistently low salary schedules or poor working conditions or both, the supply of teachers has somehow managed to meet the demand. More recently, teachers have been acting in unison and have engaged in various activities in order to call attention to their problems. Although the NEA and the AFT both officially frown upon strikes as a sanction, the membership in both of these groups has resorted to strikes on many occasions during the last decade. The strikes which have occurred are wild-cat strikes; that is, they do not have legal status in either the NEA or AFT constitutions, and have been short-lived. In a move to keep pace with its membership, or perhaps to provide leadership for its membership, the NEA has recently added the term "sanction" to school terminology. "Sanction," in the jargon of economists, has generally referred to some overt action on the part of the worker or the employer to force attention to demands. In the language of organized labor, the ultimate sanction which unions can employ is the strike. Since the NEA has a no-strike policy, its sanction must stop short of the strike. When the NEA imposes a sanction, it is, in effect, employing a form of boycott, a time-worn and effective device that has been used by organized labor. When the NEA imposes a sanction on a school district (or perhaps an entire state as in the cases of Utah, Oklahoma, and Florida) it is merely informing its membership that that school district or state is an undesirable place to work and teachers who agree to work there are not living up to the ethical standards of the profession. The sanction thus is a form of blacklisting by the NEA. It is also a kind of strike without a strike. That is, the NEA sanction, if totally effective, sets up a picket line which will not be crossed by the dedicated membership.

A final direct pressure worth noting is the so-called "professional holiday." This tactic has not been incorporated as an official policy of either the NEA or the AFT, but local classroom teachers' organizations have used it in some localities. The professional holiday might best be described as a one-day protest walkout. It differs from a strike in that generally there are not specific contract issues at stake. As it has been used, it is normally only a one-day affair, and no picket lines are established. In practice it has been used to call public attention to the plight of teachers.

There can be little question that strikes, and the threat of strikes, professional holidays, and sanctions, have proved effective weapons for teachers. It is more than simple coincidence that most of the large urban school systems which experienced teacher strikes during the sixties also happen to be near the top nationally in teacher salaries. Moreover, in specific cases boards have been forced to bow to some of the demands of striking teachers in order to reopen the schools. In several states and dozens of local school districts during the 1969–1970 school year, for example, militant action in one form or another resulted in favorable settlements for teachers. NEA sanctions in Idaho, Florida, and Kentucky no doubt had some effect on increased legislative appropriations in those states. Local district teachers in New Jersey and New York benefited from strikes and threatened strikes during the 1969–1970 school year. During that year walkouts and threatened walkouts in widely scattered localities from Pennsylvania to California resulted in increased salary schedules for teachers. In several school districts in Pennsylvania; Denver; Los Angeles; and Wichita, Kansas, strikes and threatened strikes resulted in better contracts for teachers. Perhaps even more significant than salary and fringe benefit gains is the fact that in recent years teachers in hundreds of school districts across the country have won the right to negotiate collectively with their boards.

Propaganda

Finally, a common tactic used by teachers in working for their political goals is the use of propaganda. Teachers have utilized, with varying degrees of success, direct and indirect techniques of propaganda. The direct propaganda effort is generally well planned and well executed by the national teachers' organizations and their state and local affiliates. Both the NEA and the AFT have made serious efforts in recent years to alert the public to the needs of teachers and to the needs of education generally. The educational fraternity has a built-in advantage when it comes to the promotion of education. Education is something in which most people deeply believe. Although there may be differences of opinion on how much education, or how the program for education should be organized, there is very general agreement on the great value of education to the society. In the language of the expert on propaganda, education is an "ingratiating term." As such, everyone is for it, just as they are for motherhood, flag, and country. The educational pressure groups have used this fact to advantage in that they frequently phrase their arguments in terms which advocate an improved educational system in the interests of the society and for the good of the children. In their struggle for more adequate support for education, the educational groups tend to identify their own good with the general good, or their purposes with the children of the society. Such groups then proceed to use the facilities of mass media with material which associates the goals of the educational groups with the general idea of improved education. This, of course, is a time-worn and generally successful technique of propaganda, and the educational pressure groups would be doing a real disservice to their membership if they neglected its use.

Perhaps there are many more local illustrations of the use of direct propaganda than there are national or state examples. Most frequently one may find rather well planned and executed propaganda campaigns conducted on the local level to push over a bond issue or to expand the program of the local school, to consolidate school districts, or some other program or problem. Bond issue campaigns are often characterized by educational programs of varying duration in which the voters of the community are treated to the needs of the school in terms which make it almost inhuman to resist. This should in no way be construed as a criticism of such tactics, since it would be incorrect to assume that all direct propaganda for any cause is an unconditional evil. Propaganda, for whatever purpose, can only be evaluated in terms of the cause it serves. Obviously, it is impossible to be totally objective about ends or causes. The purpose of this analysis is merely to point out that school people tend to be realistic when they recognize that they are operating in an environment which may require the methods of propaganda.

Indirect methods of propaganda are also employed by school people. "Indirect methods of propaganda" as used here means that which is generally unplanned, not part of any specific goal or educational program. The most obvious example of such propaganda is the classroom teacher who works on his students whenever the oportunity arises, attempting to convince future citizens of the needs of the educational system. In its most crude form, this can be illustrated by the classroom teacher who harangues students about his long hours and low pay. (In certain chronic cases the point is made as if the students themselves are responsible.) One scarcely need comment on the problems created by this kind of propaganda. School people have also resorted to rumors of various sorts in order to get a point across. It is not uncommon, for example, for the word to get around that certain aspects of a program might have to be curtailed if a bond issue fails. Open houses during Education Week can and have been used to point up the needs of a school system to the patrons.

SUCCESSES AND FAILURES

There can be little question that the lot of the teacher and of education generally has improved over the last generation. To what extent the efforts of teachers in politics can be credited with this improvement is hard to determine. In terms of absolute gain, the educational enterprise has had some tremendous growth in the last generation. Teachers' salaries have improved. The national average teacher's salary for elementary and secondary schools was $1,441 in 1940 (a fairly prosperous year), while thirty years later the average had risen to $8,901. During the decade of teacher militancy, average salaries rose from $5,174 in 1960 to $8,901 in 1970. However, these were years of serious inflation, and the gain in terms of real income was from $5,174 in 1960 to $6,866 in 1970. Thus, in spite of strenuous efforts on the part of teachers to improve salaries during the period, there has been no dramatic breakthrough.

Even though teachers are better off now than they were a generation ago, when compared to gains in the general economy and to other occupational groups, teachers have not done so well. The nation is much more prosperous today than it was thirty years ago. The gross national product in 1940 was a little over one billion dollars a year, while in 1970, it approached one trillion dollars. In terms of percentage of the total of the gross national product, education just about kept pace during the thirty years from 1940 to 1970. However, this increase took place in the face of a burgeoning increase in school population. In 1940, there were twenty-eight million students enrolled in public and private elementary and secondary schools, while in 1970, there were about sixty million. In order to keep even, the share of the gross national product for education would have had to double. Moreover, when compared to other occupations requiring equal training time, teaching lags far behind. The average beginning salary for all fields requiring a bachelor's degree as a minimum entering requirement in 1971 was $9,361 for males and $8,256 for females. For teachers, the average beginning salary with a bachelor's degree in 1971 was $6,850.[11] It is interesting to note that those employed in most of these fields are not organized as teachers are. They hold professional positions in engineering, accounting, sales, chemistry, mathematics, and others.

In other respects teachers have made some gains. Although it is difficult to generalize, since the system of local support for education allows such wide variations in school programs, working conditions have improved over the past two or three decades. The movement for consolidation has improved assignment possibilities, and it may be that today teachers are assigned in areas of their competence more than was the case three decades ago. It is

---

[11] National Education Association, *Financial Status of the Public Schools* (Washington, D.C.: Committee on Educational Finance, 1971), p. 17.

also true that even though building needs have not kept pace with demands, the situation at present may be better than at any time in history. There exist today many teaching aids which were unheard of thirty years ago. Faculty lounges are a rather common feature of new school buildings, another convenience uncommon in the schools of yesterday. In total, however, working conditions still remain a major problem for teachers. Class size remains a problem. In addition, the improvement in education has actually increased the burden the teacher has to bear. The modern school performs many more functions than its predecessor of a generation ago. The guidance and counseling movement, new innovations such as team teaching, special classes for the gifted and underprivileged, new programs in vocational education, the explosion of materials for teaching, and so on, have placed new responsibilities on the school without providing enough additional help to implement the new programs properly. In all too many cases, the burden of new ideas and programs has fallen on the existing staff which already had more than it could do effectively. The following example should illustrate the problem. No self-respecting school wants to be without a testing, counseling, and guidance program. In order to implement such a program, a large staff may be necessary. Because of lack of funds, a school district may undertake a comprehensive guidance and counseling program by employing a guidance director and parceling out the bulk of the work of the implementation of the program to the existing staff, which is already overworked.

Such a situation may be peculiar to education. It may not exist in any other large organized group in our society. Automation—the improvement of processes in industry, agriculture, and other areas of our society—has generally resulted in a better life for its participants. In education, sometimes the innovations—increased knowledge about learning and improved facilities—have resulted in a greater burden. The difference may be in leadership. Educational leadership has been somewhat altruistic (or ignorant) in its approach to innovation and expansion to meet pressing needs. New programs, new equipment, and new ideas have been quickly adopted without giving serious consideration to necessary staffing for implementation of the innovation. To cite one specific example, there can be little question that the introduction of audiovisual aids has been a great boon to teaching. Even where the school system has a special director of audiovisual aids who is willing to assist the teacher in his employment of them, the final responsibility for their use rests with the teacher. There can be no question that the use of such aids can improve teaching. However, to utilize them properly requires extra preparation. The proper use of films, tapes, the overhead projector, and other such devices is time-consuming. No self-respecting professor in any college of education would suggest these aids as short cuts to effective teaching. The net result of these innovations is an increased work load for the teacher in school systems which do not adequately provide the additional staff to implement the innovations properly.

However, as any experienced teacher can testify, there have been some real gains. Perhaps the propaganda efforts of the educational pressure groups have had some success. Surely the public is more school-conscious than it was a generation ago. Whether this is due to the more obvious needs of the technological society or to the efforts of teachers' pressure groups is problematical. The lot of the teacher has improved in certain respects. He does, in many cases, have a better place to work. The physical surroundings have improved dramatically in the last generation. The teacher does have more specialized help, and even though this may mean more work in some cases, it may diminish his work load in others. In addition, state legislatures have provided sick leave, retirement benefits, group insurance, and other fringe benefits. Where tenure laws exist, the teacher may be more secure in his position than he was a generation ago. Perhaps the greatest failure of teachers in politics has been that the teachers and their representatives have failed in their efforts to gain financial support in large enough quantities to keep pace with the growing needs of education in the society.

In summary, there can be little question that the teacher is changing his image. His image is no longer the old "school marm," a dedicated old maid who was satisfied with the nonpecuniary rewards of teaching. The new image is that of an emergent group of young teachers, male and female, who openly demand an adequate salary and an adequate standard of living. The new image reflects a kind of new-found self-confidence on the part of the teacher—confidence in the sense that he is prepared to do the job that the community expects of him and confidence in the sense that he has found the means to improve his own welfare through organizations dedicated to some real bread and butter issues facing teachers. A great part of this new confidence may be due to the realization on the part of teachers that they may have the political muscle needed to achieve some genuine progress in the things they value. Teachers may be on the threshold of the realization that what they believe about their own welfare and about the needs of the schools may really make a difference.

WHO MAKES THE BIG DECISIONS IN EDUCATION?

It is possible to overstate the present power of teachers acting as a group, since the successes and failures of teachers have been rather dependent upon the organization in education, as this organization permits the development of effective leadership and as this leadership reflects the desires of the rank and file in the classroom. The big decisions in education, on teacher welfare, as well as on other matters in which teachers have a vital and direct interest, depend to a great extent on the leadership that has developed within the organization of education. Very generally this organization may be classified as formal and informal. The formal organization is that which is provided by law, while the informal organization is that which may have a quasi-legal standing, but is outside the formal legal framework for education.

The formal government agencies would include the United States Office of Education, the state departments of education, and various other state and local agencies and officials which are constitutionally or legally created agencies or officials. These agencies and officials were described in the preceding section. There can be no doubt that they exercise a great deal of power to influence important decisions in education. The power of the formal structure is clearly established by state constitutions or by national or state legislative enactments. At their present stage of development, state educational agencies have widely varying power. In some states they have almost dictatorial powers with respect to curriculum, textbook selection, school finance, and other matters, whereas in other states, control from the state administrative agencies is very loose. The formal structure of state administration for education is rapidly changing, however. The amount of power and leadership the formal organization is able to muster is rapidly increasing. Early in 1965 President Johnson recommended that Congress provide funds which would strengthen state departments of education. This recommendation was implemented by Congress in the Elementary and Secondary Education Act of 1965.

The funds provided under this act since its creation have provided an opportunity for some effective leadership from state departments of education. New programs have been initiated in elementary and secondary education in nearly every state since 1965. State departments of education have been able to add staff in nearly every area and to create new offices and divisions. In the process, state departments have become more powerful in the decision-making role, and the United States Office of Education has transformed itself from a relatively insignificant federal office to one of real power and potential for leadership in education. As funds for education increase on the national level, the possibilities for the exercise of greater leadership through legally established formal agencies of government will be enhanced.

Some critics of education charge that there is an "educational establishment" in the United States. The term is used here to denote that group of individuals representing large school systems, governmental agencies, and various organizations and associations that exercise influence on the big decisions in education, but have no formal legal status. There can be little doubt that such an establishment exists. The National Education Association, with its many divisions and departments, might be considered as part of this educational establishment. The NEA is frequently included in any definition of the educational establishment because of its particularly influential position with the legally established agencies of government. The NEA is frequently called upon to furnish expert advice to the United States Office of

Education, and has provided a rather fertile training ground for personnel who move from the NEA operation in Washington to the United States Office of Education. Some critics maintain that the NEA and the United States Office of Education have something which approaches an interlocking directorate. However, this does not imply that this is an unconditioned evil. The United States Office is not unlike any other agency of government, in that such agencies tend to work as closely as possible with their clientele. Certainly the relationship between the NEA and the United States Office of Education is no closer than that which exists between the Federal Power Commission and the oil and gas industry or that which exists between the Department of Agriculture and various farm groups. As greater funds become available for the formal legal agencies, one can only speculate concerning the effect this will have on the establishment. It is doubtful that there will be much change in view of the fact that membership in the so-called establishment includes many of the officials in the national and state formal bureaucracies.

Many of the groups which are affiliated with the NEA may exercise some influence on national and state legislatures, and particularly upon the state and national agencies which are responsible for various aspects of the educational system. For example, the national leadership of the National Council for the Social Studies might be sorely disappointed if they were not consulted by governmental agencies which deal with matters which vitally affect their interests. Similarly, the Association of Secondary School Principals, the Association for Supervision and Curriculum Development, the Association for Student Teaching, and other groups affiliated with the NEA make every effort to keep abreast of national and state developments and are always ready to work with the legally established agencies of government in order to promote their interests. There are many examples which indicate that these professional groups have in some cases initiated new programs which have been enacted into law and administered by legally constituted authority. There have been other cases in which such groups have opposed innovation and have stood solidly and sometimes effectively for the status quo.

Another group of extralegal agencies which should be noted are the various accrediting associations. There are four major accrediting associations in the United States—the Middle States Association, the Southern Association, the North Central Association, and the Northwest Association—which play a significant role in American education. These groups have absolutely no legal status. Membership in the regional association is very important to the vast majority of schools and colleges, however. These groups set up criteria for membership and establish examining committees to determine the extent to which member schools in the association are living up to the standards fixed by the association. The National Council for Accreditation of Teacher Education was established with the help of the NEA, and its major function is the evaluation of teacher education programs in colleges of education throughout the country. It has been charged that these groups are subject to domination by professors in colleges of education. Because this interlocking relationship between formal and informal groups and individuals exists, one hears the accusation that there exists in the United States an educational "establishment. Those who take this position point out that there is a close working relationship among the leaders of the various accrediting associations, the NEA, and the official state and national agencies of government. It is true that the same names in education do appear with uncanny regularity, and that a few hundred of these leaders appear to have a great deal of influence nationally. On the state level, informal control is sometimes even more obvious. In many states veteran teachers can list the names in the informal educational power group without hesitation.

In spite of this, the establishment appears loosely organized. Perhaps it might be more correct to say that there is not a single monolithic educational establishment in the United States, but a series of them—sometimes at odds with each other. It would be extremely difficult to determine, at any given time, the goals and philosophy of all the professional education groups. This is partly due to the autonomy of many of the groups and partly due to the loose character of their organization and leadership. The "official" policy of the NEA itself is difficult to determine. Although the policy-making process of the NEA may be less than completely democratic, neither is it completely totalitarian. Its policy has been changing and shifting through the years. There appears to be very little evidence that the professional groups which are affiliated with the NEA are following any "party line," as is sometimes implied in the criticism of the educational establishment. Although there is a "ruling clique" in some of the professional groups, power is held ever so tentatively, and the groups themselves are rather loosely organized. Most of the professional groups affiliated with the NEA conduct most or all of their business in a single annual national convention and through a system of standing committees. These committees are very often made up of members who are widely scattered geographically and who meet no more than once or twice a year. Obviously, such loose organization encourages the type of individual who enjoys power. This situation does enable a few individuals in each organization who are willing to devote time and energy to conferences and committee meetings to dominate the organization if they are so inclined. Although there has been some of this in educational circles, it is no more a problem in education than it is in other representative organizations in our society.

The fact remains, however, that there is, in nearly every state, a rather small and loosely organized group of educators, usually comprised of a few leading superintendents in the state, a few professors of education from the colleges and universities, and the top hierarchy of the state education agencies which may call most of the shots in education. Very often these are the same people who serve on NCATE teams, are active in the regional accrediting associations, and have very real power in determining what the educational program of a given state will be. To ignore this informal power structure would be to disclaim one of the facts of life in education. Moreover, in some states this informal power structure constitutes serious problems for education; that is, it may tend to resist change, keep a tight rein on the power structure, be dedicated to a tried and true routine, and will at times attack critics with the viciousness of a mother defending her young. Where such a situation exists, real progress in education is difficult to come by.

As the expenditure for education increases and as greater emphasis is placed on organization for education, the problems of leadership in educational decision-making will increase. There may be no reasonable or practical way of avoiding the formal and informal power structures which presently exist in education. However, there are ways of assuring that the leadership in education is responsible and responsive both to the needs of the teachers they serve and to the public generally. Most important, perhaps, is the need for better public knowledge of the educational structure and the educational function. As it now stands, the variety of professional organizations in education not only is a mystery to the public, but to some extent, remains a mystery to large numbers of teachers in the public schools and colleges. Such ignorance is inexcusable in the days of mass media. Certainly, every effort should be made to bring about a situation in which the professional groups are as responsive as possible to their membership. Methods must be discovered which will enable teachers to work more actively in their own professional groups to keep leadership responsible. Ways must be explored which will involve the public more directly in the educational system which vitally affects their interests, not only on the local level but on the state and national levels, where many of the big educational decisions are made.

Disagreements on what the schools ought to do—what is most valuable in education—disagreements between teachers, the formal and informal leadership, and the public, will continue to plague the schools until means are found to provide free and open public discussion over differences in values among these groups. No individual or group has really anything to lose in such discussions of what is most important for the teacher, the schools, and the children.

REFERENCES

Bailey, Stephen K., Richard T. Frost, Paul E. Marsh, and Robert C. Wood. *Schoolmen and Politics.* Syracuse, N.Y.: Syracuse Univ. Press, 1962.
Barzun, Jacques. *The Teacher in America.* Boston: Little, Brown, 1945.

Callahan, Raymond E. *An Introduction to Education in American Society*. New York: Alfred A. Knopf, 1956.

Commission on Educational Reconstruction. *Organizing the Teaching Profession*. Glencoe, Ill.: The Free Press, 1955.

Graham, Grace. *The Public School in the American Community*. New York: Harper & Row, 1963.

Hook, Sidney. *Education for Modern Man*. New York: Alfred A. Knopf, 1963.

Keppel, Francis. *The Necessary Revolution in American Education*. New York: Harper & Row, 1966.

Kimbrough, Ralph B. *Political Power and Educational Decision-Making*. Chicago: Rand McNally, 1964.

Lieberman, Myron. *Education As a Profession*. Englewood Cliffs, N.J.: Prentice-Hall, 1956.

————. "Implications of the Coming NEA-AFT Merger." *Phi Delta Kappan*. 139–140 (Nov. 1968).

Lindsey, Margaret (ed.). *Teacher Education: Future Directions*. Washington, D.C.: Association of Teacher Education, 1970.

Masters, Nicholas A., Robert H. Salisburg, and Thomas H. Eliot. *State Politics and the Public Schools*. New York: Alfred A. Knopf, 1964.

National Education Association. *Financial Status of the Public Schools*. Washington, D.C.: Committee on Educational Finance, 1970.

————. *The Status of the American Public School Teachers*. Washington, D.C.: NEA Research Bulletin XXV, Feb. 1957, No. 1.

————. *What Teachers Think: A Summary of Teacher Opinion Poll Findings, 1960–1965*. Washington, D.C.: NEA, 1965.

————. "The Yardstick of a Profession." *Institutes on Professional and Public Relations, 1938–1947*. Washington, D.C.: Division of Field Services, 1948.

The Nation's Schools. "Differentiated Staffing." 85:43–49 (June 1970).

Phi Delta Kappan. "The Educational Establishment." 46:190–194 (Dec. 1964).

Riccio, Anthony, and Frederick R. Cyphert (eds.). *Teaching in America*. Columbus, Ohio: Charles E. Merrill, 1962.

Roberts, Joan I. *Scene of the Battle: Group Behavior in Urban Classrooms*. Garden City, N.Y.: Doubleday, 1970.

Rosenberry, Morris, Edward Suchman, and Rose Goldsen. *Occupations and Values*. New York: Free Press of Glencoe, 1957.

Silberman, Charles E. *Crisis in the Classroom*. New York: Random House, 1970.

Stinett, T. M. *Professional Problems of Teachers*. 3rd ed. New York: Macmillan, 1968.

————. *The Teacher and Professional Organizations*. Washington, D.C.: NEA, 1956.

Tanner, Laurel N. and Daniel. "The Teacher Aide: A National Study in Confusion." *Educational Leadership*. 765–769 (May 1969).

Wesley, Edgar B. *NEA: The First Hundred Years*. New York: Harper Brothers, 1957.

Wynn, Richard. "Teachers are Entitled to Job Satisfaction." *The Nation's Schools*. 55:43–45 (May 1955).

Ziegler, Harmon. *The Political Life of American Teachers*. Englewood Cliffs, N. J.: Prentice-Hall, 1967.

12

Human Relations, Political Values, and Education

In many ways, the United States is a society in crisis. For nearly a decade, scarcely a day has passed that has not witnessed some serious problem related to race, youth, war, poverty, or pollution. Certain radical groups such as the Weathermen vow that they will destroy the system through violence, while the establishment insists that law and order must prevail at all costs. By the end of the sixties militant Blacks were demanding a section of the United States as a separate nation, while police were launching commando-type raids on Black Panther headquarters. Organized and self-appointed radicals were building bombs and using them on public buildings. Citizens were arming themselves, fearing the possibility of mass disorder. The last decade has witnessed the bombing of police stations and snipers' attacks on police officers patrolling their beats. In most major American cities it was no longer safe, by 1970, for the unprotected citizen to walk the streets.

Many of these problems and others like them grew directly out of an almost total failure of the society to deal with its immense problems in human relations. At present these problems loom so large that they involve all of the established agencies and institutions of government, law enforcement agencies, political parties, the political process, and leaders. The problems are due to years of economic and social neglect of large segments of our population. Thus, with each passing year, the young; the black, brown, and red minorities; and the poor seem to become more seriously alienated from the system. The present alienation and attendant unrest seem to date from the Civil Rights movement of the mid-sixties, which was characterized by peaceful marches and passive resistance in scattered locations, mostly in the South, in protest to unequal treatment and open discriminaton against Blacks. Gains were made through peaceful protest, but the accomplishments seemed small and painfully slow to the more radical leadership in the movement. In major cities, millions of poor and Black citizens became progressively more frustrated and alienated from the system as their demands were met with promises from political leaders and very little action. In city after city, after the summer of 1965, requests turned to demands and the advocates of violence and destruction were able to initiate actions which led to rioting, looting, and burning. Even cities which had prided themselves on good race relations were rudely shocked into reality in the late sixties. Following the example of Black activists, student radicals successfully closed universities, engaged in the destruction of university property, and generally demonstrated their impatience with the system. The established order, the elected political leaders, at first seemed hesitant to react to the disorder and violence. It was not long, however, before the established forces reacted. Force was met with force, as police moved in to establish order. Although the general attitude of the forces for law and order was not quite so harsh on the college and university campuses, and serious personal injury was somehow miraculously avoided for a time, the campus confrontations reached a climax with the death of four students on the Kent State University campus.

Thus, for the most pessimistic, the society appeared on the verge of literally falling apart on several occasions in the late sixties. This was particularly true for those who were close but impartial observers of any of the large disruptions in the cities or campuses. A more optimistic view might be that at any given time only a miniscule part of the population was involved in acts of violence and disruption, and that for the overwhelming majority of the population, it was business as usual. Whatever position one takes, the violence and troubles which have beset this country in the sixties do indicate some measure of failure on the part of the society to move in positive directions on its most basic political, social, and economic problems. The decade of the seventies did begin with a serious sense of frustration and division in the society.

It will be the purpose of this chapter to attempt to determine what, if anything, the schools can contribute to ameliorating some of the frustration and healing some of the divisions. It should be obvious that some agency or agent of the system must assume responsibility for the task of rebuilding. Not that the physical destruction has been so great that a major effort is needed. There can be little doubt that property can be protected and that large-scale destruction of the physical landscape can be avoided. What needs rebuilding are attitudes and hopes—the attitudes of those apathetic citizens who see no real problem, and whose solutions are the simple use of force and repression; and the hopes of those who have been without hope that the system knows of their existence. This is clearly an educational task to be seriously undertaken.

Moreover, the rebuilding process must be successful, because a highly

developed technological society is too easily sabotaged, too easily destroyed, even by a pitifully small minority. No society can long endure
destructive attacks against its physical appurtenances, and any society is
even more susceptible to wholesale rejections of its system of values and
institutions. The most genuine threat to our existence is not the threat to our
material possessions, for they are easily replaced, but the threat to our basic
beliefs, values, and institutions. Extremists on both the right and the left
stand in constant opposition to the democratic political process, political
parties, the courts, the system of representation, a fundamental belief in the
law, and most significantly, the process of rational decision-making. If these
institutions are destroyed, however lacking or sorry they may be, it is unlikely
that they will be reconstituted by those who were successful in their
destruction.

Obviously, the school plays a key role in the twin processes of preservation
of democratic institutions and their utilization in a program of meaningful
reform. Tragically, it may be that of all social institutions, the school has
failed most miserably in its tasks. At the very least, school leaders and
teachers must share some of the responsibility for the problems of society,
any society. The schools seem to have failed most tragically in not developing
thinking citizens dedicated to the principles of rational discussion and
democratic change. Certainly teachers must assume some responsibility for
failure if they are concerned only with the indoctrination of established
"truths." The major question facing teachers now and for the next generation
may be: Can the schools as a social institution, and teachers as individuals
do anything to consciously improve the human conditions of the society? In
this task, a genuine concern and a high priority for human relations may be
the first order of business. Nor does this mean that we can continue in the
future with old habits and patterns.

If one were to ask them, most elementary school teachers would insist that
a major objective of their teaching is to improve human relationships. For
many teachers, especially on the elementary level, improving human relations is translated in operational terms to mean such things as "learning to
appreciate differences" or "helping the students understand children who
are different from themselves" or "promoting cooperation in the schoolroom." Obviously, even in operational terms, the concept of human relations
is a broad one.

Perhaps it would be helpful to look at the record of the schools in their
human relations role in an attempt to discover any successes which can be
built upon, and any failures which might be avoided. The record is both good
and bad. With regard to the "Americanization" of large numbers of immigrants, the record, although spotty, has been generally good. Insofar as
the schools have contributed to the present unrest in colleges and universities—unrest which stops short of violence, merely questions the existing
order, examines instances of injustice, advocates greater freedom and

equality, and demands more relevant education—the record has been good. With regard to the schools' contribution to the poor, the Black, and other minorities, the record has been dismal.

What follows in this chapter is a brief discussion of the general dimensions of some of the more pressing problems in human relations facing our society—problems with which the schools are vitally concerned. Major assumptions in this chapter are that the schools cannot ignore problems in human relations, and that the school can have some impact on their improvement. The discussion which follows assumes that many intergroup problems and conflicts are based on strongly held values and beliefs, and that the schools can accomplish something which contributes to possible changes in these values. This does not mean that the schools should teach a particular set of values. However, since the school is a social institution, children from different backgrounds and different views and values are thrown together and have to live with each other in that environment. Thus, the manner in which the schools go about the business of teaching the children can have some effect on values, however small, which in turn affect problems in human relations. Although it is true that the schools can promote the status quo in human relations, they can also move in the direction of progress, or they can be essentially retrogressive in their effects on problems in human relations. In a very real way, teachers can consciously work to improve human relations, or they can encourage tensions and open conflict between groups. However, it is assumed that our society has reached a state in its development where it is impossible for teachers to do nothing. Some action must be taken. Action is being forced upon the schools in the form of the militancy of minorities, the urban and interdependent nature of the society, and the international image we feel we must portray. These are all political aspects of the human relations problem which is a dimension that is causing the greatest amount of anxiety on the present scene, yet may promise the greatest amount of hope in the long run. Whatever its promise, there can be little doubt that political expressions in this area vitally affect the schools.

MAJOR PROBLEMS IN HUMAN RELATIONS

Since it is such a broad concept, it may be impossible to provide a clear definition of human relations. It is possible that the term "human relations" can mean anything one wants it to mean. As it is used in this chapter, human relations may be defined as the interaction of individuals which reflects values or the process of valuing. In this definition, interaction implies that a meaningful definition of human relations involves action or behavior of one sort or another. This action or behavior is based on deeply held beliefs or feelings of individuals toward other individuals or groups, and these beliefs or feelings are not necessarily based on factual knowledge, but on values which are the result of total life experience. Finally, the process of valuing is the manner or technique by which conclusions are reached, decisions are made, or roles are defined, wherever human interaction takes place.

Within the meaning of this definition, the schools have a significant role to play. The schools can have *some* effect on total life experience for good or ill; they can have a *great* effect on the process or technique of valuing. Of course, life experience and the process of valuing can have great effect on the behavior of human beings as they interact. This definition of human relations is not an abstraction. It is assumed that a meaningful definition of human relations is a real problem—a daily problem facing the schools. To illustrate the complexity of the problem, this chapter will deal briefly with the problems of race, nationality, and population mobility as examples of major problems in human relations.

Race

Our inability as a nation to improve greatly the relations between Blacks and whites has been one of our most notable social failures. Anyone who reads the newspapers is aware of the tremendous scope of this problem. In recent years, Blacks have resorted to something which approaches armed rebellion against what they consider to be white-dominated communities, in order to publicize their grievances. Wherever they are heard, the complaints are almost always the same. Black leaders object to second-class citizenship, and list such grievances as lack of adequate representation in the councils of government, poor housing, unemployment, and unequal school opportunities as major and continuing problems. These grievances know no real geographic boundaries within our nation. Moreover, the Black is not the only minority group which faces these problems. Others, including Chicanos, Puerto Ricans, and Indians, have similar problems in certain sections of the country. In a way, the militant Black is speaking for these minorities as well as for himself.

The problems between Blacks and whites have persisted since the abolition of slavery, in spite of the fact that we have had more than a century to do something about them. Some of the responsibility for racial problems rests with the schools, since it is at least possible that in more than a century the schools might have succeeded in the improvement of interracial understanding if this had been a considered part of their responsibility. Apparently it has not been. Perhaps the reasons for the schools' inability to deal with the problem might be better understood if one could understand the general nature and scope of the problem.

A basic difficulty has been the inability of many individuals in the society to define the problem clearly. The fact that it is difficult, if not impossible, to define race except in terms of skin pigmentation in our society bothers few Americans who admit to being prejudiced, and perhaps even fewer who claim that they are not but act as if they are. Clyde Kluckhohn stated that a biological definition of race "is used to designate a group of organisms that physically resemble one another by virtue of their descent from common ancestors."[1] In order to remain "pure" in a biological sense, it would be necessary for the organism to remain in complete physical isolation. For this reason, Kluckhohn describes race as a "myth" and he asserts that racial classifications are misleading or meaningless in view of current knowledge about human inheritance. The only certain thing about race, in Kluckhohn's words, is that "in the modern world many peoples react suspiciously, defensively, or hostilely toward individuals who differ in obvious physical characteristics such as skin color, hair form, and nose shape."[2]

Beginning with the definition, there are many popular myths about race. Some who claim prejudice against the Black point to his general inferiority and attempt to prove their case by citing "evidence" in support of theories which claim that Blacks are biologically inferior to and less intelligent than whites. The implication, always, is that equality is a "natural" impossibility. This kind of thinking persists in spite of evidence to the contrary. Mendelian genetics long ago demonstrated the fallacy of the biological inferiority argument. With regard to intelligence, many studies have indicated that there are no significant differences between races.[3] An early study on intelligence by Benedict and Weltfish, which has been much quoted, provides information on this point and lists the results in a simple chart.

Median Scores on A.E.F. Intelligence Tests[4]

Southern Whites	
Mississippi	41.25
Kentucky	41.50
Arkansas	41.55
Northern Negroes	
New York	45.02
Illinois	47.35
Ohio	49.50

---

[1] Clyde Kluckhohn, *Mirror for Man* (New York: Fawcett, 1965), p. 93.
[2] Kluckhohn, p. 94.
[3] A notable exception is the study by Arthur R. Jensen reported in the *Harvard Educational Review* (Winter 1969).
[4] Ruth Benedict and Gene Weltfish, *The Races of Mankind* (Washington, D.C.: Public Affairs Press, 1946), no. 85, p. 18.

More recent studies tend to support these findings. Researchers who have studied the problem of race and IQ are careful to point out that any intelligence test has a cultural bias in that those who live in a rich cultural environment have a better chance for a high score. In the Benedict and Weltfish study, the major conclusion reached about differences in intelligence between Blacks and whites tested was that "the differences did not arise because people were from the North or South, or because they were black or white, but because of differences in income, education, cultural advantages, and other opportunities."[5]

In addition to a belief that a particular race may be intellectually inferior, the deeply prejudiced person may charge that members of a minority race are lazy or lack ambition, or that they are shiftless and immoral, and prefer to live in squalor; and may resort to other such labels which tend to identify the racial minority as inferior. The fact that none of these labels can be scientifically supported seems to make very little difference to the person using them. Indeed, even in the face of a considerable amount of evidence which can effectively challenge such notions about race, individuals may continue to cling to their prejudices.

Yet this seems to defy reason. If prejudice is based simply on ignorance of facts, it would seem reasonable to assume that the solution to such prejudice would be merely to provide the prejudiced person with the true facts and he would change his attitude. Unfortunately, it is not such a simple problem. In reporting several experimental studies on attitudes, Berrien and Bash[6] concluded that it is difficult to alter attitudes simply with intellectual arguments or a mass of facts. Comparisons have been made of college students before and after a regular college course in race relations which dished out a healthy portion of facts, and these appeared to cause no significant change in attitudes. In other studies with college students, there seemed to be little relationship between the student's knowledge of the history and problems of the Black and his attitude toward them.

The matter of what causes negative attitudes toward ethnic out-groups continues to be an unsolved problem. Some studies lean toward an explanation of such attitudes as a basic personality problem, while others favor an explanation of such attitudes as an outgrowth of prejudice. An early classic study on personality as a cause of attitudes is *The Authoritarian Personality.*[7] The general thesis of this study is that persons who hold negative attitudes toward minority racial, religious, or ethnic groups tend to be different personalities than those who are nonprejudiced. According to the findings of

[5] Benedict and Weltfish, p. 19.

[6] F. K. Berrien and Wendell H. Bash, *Human Relations: Comments and Cases* (New York: Harper & Row, 1957), pp. 147–149.

[7] T. W. Adorno, Else Frenkel-Brunswik, Daniel J. Levinson, and R. Nevitt Sanford, *The Authoritarian Personality* (New York: Harper & Row, 1950).

Adorno and others, the authoritarian personality is not only prejudiced, but may be mentally ill. Such a personality displays superstition; shows tendencies to make rigid moral judgments, to express an unhealthy disrespect for the weak, and to classify everything into categories of black and white or good and evil; and may exhibit serious hostility and distrust toward strangers. Such persons often view the environment as threatening. Many studies which followed the Adorno study tended to support its conclusions.[8]

However, at least one study suggests that attitudes are more than a matter of personality. A recent Cornell study on prejudice suggested that all behavior is a reflection of personality in some way. That is, everything a person does is some reflection of his personality. However, the authors of the Cornell study suggested that "many attitudes and behaviors are so widely shared in standardized forms that the mere presence of an item in a particular person tells us very little about the distinctive modes of personality functioning in that person."[9] In other words, prejudice might very well be some kind of standardized form which, in some persons, may be somewhat independent of personality type. That is, it is possible to hold strong prejudices which seriously affect attitude and behavior without being generally authoritarian. For the schools, the implications of these kinds of studies are that it is extremely difficult to attack prejudice by teaching facts in the classroom.

This raises a very significant question of why the myths persist in the face of facts which deny them. This question, of course, goes right to the heart of the problem of prejudice. Sociologists, anthropologists, psychologists, and others have offered explanations for prejudice and many would agree with Kluckhohn's explanation that "race prejudice is, fundamentally, merely one form of scapegoatism."[10] He pointed out that when the security of individuals or the group is threatened, they tend to seek scapegoats. Thus, much prejudice is based on fear. Kluckhohn rejected economic conditions as a basic cause of prejudice. He took the position that economic conditions perhaps encourage prejudice, and race problems may begin as economic problems, but become social and cultural in nature as soon as the minority attains awareness of the values of the dominant group and develops articulate leaders.[11] Some would agree that economic conditions are mere stimulants to prejudice, and that basic causes are more easily explained by

---

[8] Richard Christie and Peggy Cook, "A Guide to the Published Literature Relating to Authoritarian Personality 1956," *Journal of Psychology* (April 1958), vol. 45, pp. 171–199.

[9] Robin M. Williams, Jr., *Strangers Next Door* (Englewood Cliffs, N.J.: Prentice-Hall, 1964), p.111.

[10] Kluckhohn, p. 120.

[11] Kluckhohn, p. 121.

psychology than by economics. Some authorities on the subject explain prejudice as a means of deflecting aggressions created by personal frustrations. The following explanation is provided by Peter I. Rose:

One goes through life seeking gratification for felt needs, and, while many such needs have their origin in the organic structure of the individual, there are others which are culturally determined. These are learned early in life and are canalized and directed toward certain goals. When goal-directed behavior is blocked, hostile impulses are frequently created in the individual, who, unable to determine the real source of his frustration and in an attempt to overcome it, manifests "free-floating aggression." Such undirected aggression finds a "legitimate" point on which to focus that becomes a substitute for the actual frustrating agent. Usually the target is weak and unable to strike back. This process is well known: The boss berates his employee, who takes it out on his wife, who then in turn berates the children. And so it goes.[12]

This explanation goes a long way toward helping one understand how prejudice grows and is nurtured. It explains to some extent the deepest kind of prejudice, which appears to have economic motivation in certain geographic areas where poor whites and Blacks are competing for the same jobs. It explains why racial hostility is a psychological necessity for some who are so low on the social scale that they need someone lower—a scapegoat upon whom they can pin all of their personal frustrations, all of the ills of the society.

Whatever its causes, the problems which prejudice creates for the schools are many. It prevents groups from working together effectively, it blocks effective learning of content which is necessary for intelligent and enlightened citizenship, it is an expensive social disease even in a dormant stage, and frightening when it is active. Moreover, the problem is a huge one. Non-white students in the public schools constitute a little more than one-tenth of the school population. An overwhelming majority of these are from families in the very lowest income groups, who have not been able to give their children the kinds of opportunities which provide the background necessary for success in school. Many of these children are hungry, poorly housed, poorly clothed, and alienated from a system which has provided them with so little. For many, the schools are an unfriendly place and the teachers and school administrators are viewed as enemies. In many inner-city schools where the population is nearly 100 per cent Black and poor, the school more nearly resembles a prison than a place of learning. Armed

---

[12] Peter I. Rose, *They and We, Racial and Ethnic Relations in the United States,* Studies in Sociology No. 22 (New York: Random House, 1964), p. 88.

guards roam the halls, violence between students is an almost daily occurrence, physical attacks on teachers are common, and real learning is almost impossible in the classroom.

The school cannot avoid its share of the responsibility for such conditions. The schools have not only reflected the prejudice and racism which exists in society; all too often they have promoted it. They continue to promote racism through a policy of homogeneous grouping and track systems which separate whites and non-whites within the walls of a school. School boards and administrators continue to resist attempts to redraw school attendance boundaries which would provide a greater mix of poor Black students and middle-class whites. School officials sometimes appear more interested in real estate development than in children, as evidenced by the policy in recent years of building new schools in open spaces in suburban areas while neglecting inner-city schools. Teachers contribute to racism by insisting on homogeneous grouping, neglecting slow learners, and openly displaying their own prejudice in the classroom and the teachers' lounge.

National Origin

In some parts of the country, nationality has constituted a problem in human relations. Much of what has been said in the preceding section about prejudice can be applied historically to foreigners who immigrated to America in large groups beginning in the 1830's and continuing until the outbreak of World War I. Many of these groups suffered the same type of hostility in the past which is presently being experienced by Blacks. Of course some groups still experience the problem. This is particularly true of the large waves of our most recent immigrants—the Mexicans and the Puerto Ricans.

With regard to immigrants generally, one has to admit that in spite of the problems in human relations which grew out of mass immigration waves throughout our history, our national record has been a good one. For more than a century Emma Lazarus' words which appear at the foot of the Statue of Liberty were literally true:

> "Keep, ancient lands, your storied pomp," cries she,
> With silent lips. "Give me your tired, your poor,
> Your huddled masses yearning to breathe free,
> The wretched refuse of your teeming shore.
> Send these, the homeless tempest-tossed, to me!
> I lift my lamp beside the golden door."

And millions of them came—the Germans and Irish in large waves from 1840 to 1880, followed by millions of Italians and southern and eastern European Slavs in the years from 1880 to 1914. It is impossible to overestimate the impact of these large numbers of immigrants on certain communities in the United States. In total, from 1820 to 1960 some thirty-four million Europeans immigrated to our shores. During a single nine-year period between 1900 and 1912, more than two million Italians and almost three million Slavs left their homelands to come to America.[13] More than half of these settled in a few of the larger cities in the East. These new immigrants changed the character of cities where they massed in large numbers. In some cities, such as Buffalo, New York, Chicago, Pittsburgh, and Boston, it was possible to walk for blocks within the city as recently as the 1920's and hear not a word of English spoken.

That these numbers of immigrants created serious problems in human relations is a matter of record. Many of the immigrants were "different," and being different, they aroused hostility and prejudice among the "native" population. They were different in many respects. A vast majority of them from the non-English-speaking countries could not speak the language. Most were almost totally without funds. Most were from a rural environment in Europe which was little changed from the feudal way of life of the Middle Ages. For many, the move to America was not only a move in space but a move in time. For those who settled in the large cities in the early twentieth century, it was like moving to the new environment from the twelfth century. Many were Roman Catholics who moved into predominantly Protestant communities. All of them brought customs and folkways from the old country.

Perhaps the first and most serious problem for the new immigrant from whatever country was that of learning the language. This was necessary in many cases in order to secure employment. The author's father, who immigrated from Yugoslavia in 1909, described this problem:

I arrived in the United States with only one change of clothing and eighty cents American money. I was more lucky than some. My sister was already living in Gary and her husband had a good job in the mill there so I was able to live with my sister and her husband and children. They all helped me with my English. My first problem was to find a job so I had to learn how to ask for work. For the first few days, along with tips on how to act, I was taught a single sentence which I repeated over and over. That sentence was: "You got work for me?" After a few days I had it learned well enough and I had practiced it before the family and they judged that I was ready to look for work. They also needed the money I could provide because they were not so well off. Well, I got on new work clothes which my brother-in-law bought for me and I went to the mill. I marched up to the cage but I was scared and some nervous.

---

[13] Bureau of the Census, *Statistical Abstract of the United States* (Washington, D.C.: U.S. Government Printing Office, 1960).

The boss said: "Well, what do you want, bohunk?" I was so nervous he had to ask me again and I said: "You vurk for me?" He really laughed and said: "No, I don't think so." He then said some other things I don't remember or didn't understand and I got out of there. It took me about three months before I could find work.

Of course there were many other problems in addition to language. The new immigrant generally knew nothing about living in the city, about how he was expected to act; he knew nothing of the customs or politics of his newly adopted country. How many must have longed for a return to the simple life of the European peasant! Many of the immigrants were almost totally "ignorant" in almost any way in which their native neighbors wanted to use the term.

Considering the size of the problem, how did the immigrant manage not only to survive, but to become a fully accepted part of the society? The theories which explain this phenomenon have come to be known as assimilation, amalgamation, and cultural pluralism.[14] Assimilation has been the story for many. Generally defined, it means that many immigrants were able to adopt virtually all of the customs and values of the white, native-born, Protestant, middle-class Americans. In many cases, even his name was changed when the new American became a citizen. Where foreigners were able to assimilate, the transition and almost full acceptance into the community were perhaps most simple. Of course, it goes without saying that this process was much easier for the native residents than for the foreign-born.

Many immigrants were able to become effectively amalgamated into American society. Some Americans with a predominant northern European heritage were able to make the adjustment by preserving the "best" of the traditions of Europe while accepting most of the values of the new society into which they came. This was a two-way street. The established citizens gave a little in the process; that is, some of the European traditions and values were blended with the mixture that was American and the result was a fairly well-integrated whole.

In many cases, the solution provided was that of cultural pluralism; that is, the foreign-born tended to keep their customs and values and live in ethnic colonies scattered in cities and rural areas across the country. To this day one can find these patterns throughout the United States. The idea of cultural pluralism came to be generally accepted in the United States and even justified in terms of the richness that such variety provided for American life.

The European immigrant was able to overcome major problems of adjustment because he was able to find work, and through the income it provided, he became more "American" in character. He was also able to organize in

---

[14] Rose, pp. 50–57.

various ways for political action. He was able to elect his own kind to office and become a genuine political power in many localities. In some instances, ethnic groups became a significant political force in state and even national politics. In a word, the immigrant was able to work politically for his own benefit and acceptance in the society. In addition, the European immigrant has been able to break out of the ghetto. It is possible that economic affluence provided this opportunity, although it took more than a generation in most cases. In general the immigrant was able to find his place as a fully participating citizen if he wished to make the effort. More than this, he had some real effect on shaping the traditions which constitute the mainstream of American society. Finally, the schools did contribute somewhat to the "Americanization" of the immigrant. In many cases they taught his children the language and worked some modification on old country values.

Whatever the approach taken by immigrant groups or individuals, the result has been good; there proved to be room for them here, and although the immigrant faced prejudice and hatred which sometimes flared into open violence, gradually these problems diminished until today nationality, by itself, seems to be a minor problem in human relations. The open prejudice has largely evaporated, except toward the newest immigrants, the Mexicans and Puerto Ricans, who suffer many of the same indignities as the earlier immigrants. The Jews also seem to experience some of the same problems regardless of their date of entry.

For the Mexicans and Puerto Ricans, the problems are more complicated than for earlier immigrants. This is true for many reasons. Most important, many are dark skinned, a problem that the European immigrant can't possibly imagine. Also important is the fact that the newer immigrant is unskilled in a much more advanced technology than that which faced the earlier unskilled European. It is important to realize that the Black, the Puerto Rican, and, in many areas of the country, the Mexican, cannot copy the pattern of success followed by the European immigrant. They can advance through work, they can work through the political system for recognition, the school can help them, but there is always that final and obvious limitation which bars them from complete acceptance.

Population Mobility

Beginning early in the nineteenth century and continuing to the present, increasing urbanization has been the pattern of population development in the United States. In the years since the beginning of World War II, however, a new kind of population has been creating problems in human relations for every community agency, including the schools, namely, the tremendously accelerated population movement from the rural areas of the country into the large cities. The pattern of migration has not changed greatly, for there has always been rural-to-urban movement, but now there are such great numbers of people and different kinds of people involved. Of course, many of the recent migrants to cities have been Blacks from the rural areas of the South. Some of the problems related to the Black minority were discussed in the preceding section. In addition to southern rural Blacks, however, hundreds of thousands of rural poor whites have been on the move. The schools have been directly affected by many of the problems created by this movement.

No large American city with a million or more inhabitants has been able to escape the invasion of rural poor whites. This influx had become such a problem in Chicago by the late 1950's that local citizens tagged the newcomers with the derogatory term "hillbilly." This is a tag that has stuck and has become a popular stereotype for rural poor white newcomers in a score or more of America's largest cities. In the late 1950's Norma Lee Browning of the *Chicago Tribune* described Chicago's problem in this fashion:

> Chicagoans long accustomed to living in a melting pot of mixed nationalities and creeds have become suddenly aware of a "new breed" of transients moving in whose rural customs and culture-patterns are as incomprehensible to us as dial telephones are to them.
>
> They're American-born white skinned natives, with no racial, religious, or language characteristics (except southern accents) to set them apart as an ethnic group. Yet as a group with specific, recognizable culture patterns that are completely alien to urban life, they pose one of the most serious social problems in Chicago's projected plans for industrial expansion . . . the so-called poor white migrant with low educational background who shirks responsibility in his new surroundings is causing trouble. This type is commonly called "hillbilly."[15]

Miss Browning reported that the living pattern of the so-called "hillbillies" was similar wherever one found them. These she described as "disgraceful"; including such conditions as community toilets and kitchens, "mixed-up" families with all kinds of relatives living together, frequent moving without bothering to pay the rent, "primitive" concepts of sanitation, "resistance to public health measures, immunization and education." Miss Browning quoted one school official as saying that the "hillbillies" were harder to reach than the minority groups. He called them the "most withdrawn, clannish, non-conformist rugged individualists of any of Chicago's new resident groups." The story can be repeated a hundred times in many cities across the country.

The scope of this problem nationally is difficult to determine, since the census data is not broken down in a manner which enables one to determine the precise number of poor white citizens who migrate to the cities. However,

---

[15] Norma Lee Browning, "New Breed of Migrants City Problem," *Chicago Daily Tribune,* 4 March 1957.

one can make certain generalizations about total numbers of migrants to cities which may give the reader some general notion of the scope of the problem. During the decade between 1950 and 1960, the urban population of the United States increased by 29 per cent, while the rural population declined by 1 per cent.[16] Out-migration from the rural areas came largely from the South and the Midwest, where agriculture has been declining for the last twenty-five years. Many have left the southern hill regions for greener pastures. The mountainous portion of the southern states has been an area of serious economic hardship and chronic unemployment for more than fifteen years. In the words of Donald J. Bogue:

> Under the combined impact of the pull of large metropolitan centers in all directions outside, this area has suffered a very severe out-migration. Despite the fact that its birth rates are very high, between 1950 and 1960 it grew at a rate of only 5.1 per cent, the slowest growth rate for any of the economic regions.[17]

This region of the country contributed vast numbers of poor white citizens to the cities which surround it. Other areas of the nation have had similar pockets of poverty which contributed to poor white migration to cities near and far. One can only guess at the total number on the move in the past twenty-five years, but there can be little question that the numbers have been significant for many cities throughout the country.

In every city where they have migrated in substantial numbers, the rural poor whites have created tremendous problems for the schools. Aside from increased burdens on school facilities, the teaching staff, and the like, in some cities these new residents have created major problems in human relations. A most serious problem was suggested in the material cited from the *Chicago Tribune*. These people are "different." They are unfamiliar with the ways of the city, and in some places are looked down upon by the lowest strata of the city's classes. In some cities they have become the new scapegoat—the breeders of trouble—the hopelessly stupid, immoral, and generally uncouth group. The new scapegoat is often blamed for many of the city's ills, including high taxes for welfare, a high crime rate, the existence of ghettos, poverty, and so on. For the deeply prejudiced, there never need be any reason to substantiate these charges, nor are they interested in facts. For the schools, the problems in human relations, already serious enough, are further complicated by the new arrivals. In some cities the newcomers have moved into the ghetto and they live in close proximity to large numbers of Blacks. Of course they must send their children to schools with extensive

---

[16] Donald J. Bogue, "Population Growth in the United States," *The Population Dilemma,* ed. Philip M. Hauser (Englewood Cliffs, N.J.: Prentice-Hall, 1963), p. 87.
[17] Bogue, p. 88.

racial mixtures. The result is the mixing of children from social groups which are very possibly the most antagonistic toward each other of any groups in our society. The result for the schools can be disastrous.

The preceding examples of major problems in human relations which plague our society and which the schools are forced to face are certainly among the most serious, but they do not by any means constitute a complete list. Other serious problems in human relations may be related to questions of religious differences, youth-adult conflicts, and many others. The foregoing discussion merely cites examples of the tremendous scope and complexity of the problem of human relations which faces the society and provides a great challenge for the schools.

CAN THE SCHOOLS CHANGE VALUES?

It should be rather obvious from the foregoing that in many of the hard-core problems in human relations there will be little improvement until there is some change in values. Most of what happens to strongly held values is more apt to come from the general environment than from the schools. However, the forces in our society which are presently working for improvement in the most difficult problems of human relations are going to affect the schools. Indeed, the school is already one of the key social agencies that must deal with these forces.

What are these forces which are working for change in values? Arnold Rose has suggested some of the most important forces which were working for social change with reference to Blacks. Some of these apply to other groups as well. He lists the following as being responsible for "the rapid change in race relations since 1940":[18]

1. Technological advance
2. The high level of mobility of the American people
3. Economic prosperity
4. The organization and political education of minority groups
5. American awareness of world opinion
6. Consistent support for civil rights on the part of the Supreme Court
7. Propaganda and educational efforts for more equal implementation of civil rights.

Interestingly, the schools are not listed. Rose points out that industry and technology have had several effects on Blacks, moving them in large

---

[18] Arnold M. Rose, "The American Negro Problem in the Context of Social Change," *The Annals of the American Academy of Political and Social Science* (Jan. 1965), vol. 357, pp. 1–18.

numbers to the city, where they have been able to earn more and, in most cases, live better. They have also gained political expression in the cities and their children are probably better educated. They have been able in many cases to include themselves in the mainstream of the growing and increasingly more prosperous economy. The most serious exceptions to this are the unskilled Blacks who become technologically unemployed. However, Rose points out that these can be trained and that, as they are trained, the gap between Black workers and others in the society will narrow.

Perhaps the most hopeful movement for change is the increasing political awareness of Blacks. The Black through his own efforts, and in many cases without the support of sympathetic whites, has been able to call attention to his problems through protest and pressure. These methods are not at all new to the American scene, as they have been used by farmers, laborers, and other groups working for reform throughout our history with varying degrees of success. Therefore, it is natural to expect a large racial minority to use such methods.

The law has been used to improve the lot of Blacks. The last generation has seen the elimination of the "white primary"; the decline of the "separate but equal" doctrine in public schools and public facilities; the end of legal support for segregated parks, playgrounds, and libraries; the end of discrimination in federal jobs through the Fair Employment Practices Act; and a host of other legal improvements in their position via the Civil Rights Act of 1964. This act promises some genuine voting equality for the first time in many areas; it makes integrated public facilities a reality in many cases; it bars racial discrimination in any program involving federal aid; it prohibits discrimination by employers or unions; and it enables Blacks to bring suit in federal courts to protect these rights.

In a word, Blacks have gained more in the last few years than they have in the century since abolition. In spite of the fact that they still have a long way to go, and their persistent demands are for better housing, an end to discrimination in housing, improved educational opportunities, and full employment equality, there can be no question that their position has substantially improved. Nor can there be any question that Black groups have discovered organization for political power as an effective weapon in working for their own full legal equality as citizens. Moreover, most Americans will readily admit that Blacks are justified in this cause and though they may not actively support them in their drive for full legal equality, most are not openly against them. There are pockets of resistance, and there will continue to be. Prejudice dies hard, but the means for making some dent in it are at hand. The first reaction to Black militancy might be an increase in hostility from whites who claimed to be "on the fence" on the issue of racial prejudice. In the long run, however, there is every reason to hope that gains by Blacks will be gains for the population generally. That is, as Blacks gain full legal equality and are able to improve their economic position and educational level, and as they gain a greater share of the "good" things of life which our society has to offer, the things these accomplishments will do for the Black population should tend to lessen prejudice and racial conflict. This optimism is based on the condition that the society will continue to prosper economically and that a fair and equitable share of the "good" things for Blacks will not mean less for everybody else; that is, as the economy grows, everyone becomes more prosperous, including (perhaps especially) poor Black citizens. Optimism is also based on the condition that the present Black movement does not result in Blacks thinking of themselves solely as Blacks—that they do not completely reject the white citizen as an unyielding enemy. Although there is some evidence that this has already happened, hopefully it involves only a small minority of Blacks. Most continue to cling to the hope of equality and are more than willing to work through the system for equal rights and a greater measure of social justice. The real challenge of the future is not a Black challenge but a white one. If whites persist in denying the full rights of citizenship to Blacks through formal and informal means, the only result can be a growing and frightening apartheid. Each new rejection and denial on the part of the white majority brings new recruits to the Black separatist movement, and fuels the fires of militancy. On the other hand, if a majority of whites accept full and equal citizenship of Blacks, there is great reason for optimism.

There is, therefore, some reason for guarded optimism. At least the possibility of improvement exists. Forces at work in the community—the same forces which improved conditions for other minorities in our society—have improved the lot of the Black minority. Indeed, all non-white minorities will continue to profit from a growing technology, increasing mobility, economic propserity, and most of all, their own political action. Moreover, the law, as it attempts to implement basic rights and correct basic injustices, promises real hope for minorities.

The optimism expressed here for a rational solution to our major human relations problem can be expressed in the face of, in spite of, the problem of color. This is where the schools can provide some genuine leadership. Every study that has been made of the problem of prejudice supports the finding of the Cornell studies which simply state: "Out of hundreds of tabulations, there emerges the major finding that *in all the surveys in all communities and for all groups, majorities and minorities, the greater the frequency of interaction, the lower the prevalence of ethnic prejudice."*[19]

The schools already play a vital role in the process of interaction between groups, and will continue to play a greater role. Even where there is a reluctance on the part of the community to have the schools play this role,

---

[19] Williams, p. 168.

they really have no choice. The law which forces desegregation, and the progressive communities which promote integration, can provide real leadership in the improvement of human relations. There is simply no realistic, rational, or human alternative. It is not so much a question of whether or not schools can change values which affect human relations, it is more an imperative—the schools *must* do something. They are forced to face the problem legally, and under present national policy, they are threatened with economic sanctions if they do not, since federal aid can be withheld if schools do not observe the provisions of national law and court decisions dealing with the problem of equality.

The question is, *will* they? In all probability the schools will continue to reflect the social environment in which they find themselves. Crusading superintendents will continue to lose their jobs when they attempt to move schools ahead of the community on matters involving race relations. But the social environment is rapidly changing. Perhaps the greatest hope for the schools as an agent of change in the broad general area of human relations rests with the children and the young teachers of America. In the discussion of values in the first chapter, we cited Spindler's hypothesis to the effect that some students and younger teachers tended to be on the "emergent" end of an emergent-traditional value continuum. Where the values of the younger generation are in the process of change, the school can facilitate the process by providing experiences for interaction. This is being done. Perhaps even strongly held prejudices of a specific teacher, where such exist, will prove incapable of seriously modifying the general movement in the direction of improved relationships among children. Of course, the teacher who deliberately works to improve human relationships will be faced with increasing chances for success in our society. The great emphasis which has been placed by the national government on improving this aspect of our society and the funds which are presently being provided to work with the culturally and economically deprived can speed the process of improved human relations.

If they would, there is much that teachers could do to improve the society. Teachers more than any other group should be trained to recognize and deal with prejudice when they see it in their classrooms. School officials and teachers, both as individuals and through their professional groups, could cry out against injustices and keep the public aware of the problems. School systems could stop, as quickly as possible, all practices which are prejudicial and discriminatory in nature, including homogeneous grouping, track systems, and other artificial segregation policies. Teachers could make their classrooms exciting places for learning rather than dismal detention wards. Teachers could get more involved in political action on the local, state, and national level, and plead for public support for better facilities. They could inform the public about the number of children they see each day who are hungry, educationally retarded, poorly housed, and poorly clothed, rather than leaving this task to outside critics. In a word, teachers could become responsible citizens concerned more for the welfare of children and the future of society than for their own narrow interests. They could work in their professional groups to make these groups more responsive to tne really desperate problems of children. Teachers, acting in concert, could serve as a national conscience on the really serious problems in human relations which face this society.

We end this chapter with qualified optimism. The long-range solution to improved human relations rests with the society. The forces for improvement have always existed and continue to express themselves with increasing frequency. Conditions are improving and will continue to improve. The challenge to the schools may very well be that of a careful study of the forces that breed prejudice and the promotion of their understanding in the young. More than this, as a major social institution the school is cast in the midst of social change, and can be a real force in the speed and direction of this change.

REFERENCES

Adorno, T. W., Else Frenkel-Brunswick, Daniel J. Levinson, and R. Nevitt Sanford. *The Authoritarian Personality.* New York: Harper & Row, 1950.

American Assembly, The. *The Population Dilemma.* Englewood Cliffs, N.J.: Prentice-Hall, 1963.

American Association of School Administrators. *School Racial Policy.* Washington, D.C.: The Association, 1966.

Benedict, Ruth, and Gene Weltfish. *The Races of Mankind.* Washington, D.C.: Public Affairs Press, 1946.

Berrien, F. K., and Wendell H. Bash. *Human Relations: Comments and Cases.* New York: Harper & Row, 1957.

Browning, Norma Lee. *"New Breed of Migrants City Problem."* Chicago Daily Tribune. 4 March 1957.

Christie, Richard, and Peggy Cook. "A Guide to the Published Literature Relating to Authoritarian Personality 1956." *Journal of Psychology.* 45:171–199 (April 1958).

Fuller, Buckminster. *Utopia or Oblivion: The Prospects for Humanity.* New York: Bantam Books, 1969.

Grimes, Alan P. *Equality in America.* New York: Oxford Univ. Press, 1964.

Handlin, Oscar. *The Newcomers: Negroes and Puerto Ricans in a Changing Metropolis.* Cambridge, Mass.: Harvard Univ. Press, 1959.

Kluckhohn, Clyde. *Mirror for Man.* New York: Fawcett, 1965.

Koestler, Arthur. *The Ghost in the Machine.* New York: Macmillan, 1968.

Lane, Howard, and Mary Beauchamp. *Human Relations in Teaching.* Englewood Cliffs, N.J.: Prentice-Hall, 1965.

Miller, Herman P. *Rich Man Poor Man.* New York: Thomas Y. Crowell, 1964.

Morgan, James N., Norma Meyers, and Barbara Baldwin. *Income and Welfare in the United States.* New York: McGraw-Hill, 1962.

Mueller-Dedham, Albert. *Human Relations and Power.* New York: Philosophical Library, 1957.

Petersen, William. *Population.* New York: Macmillan, 1961.

Rose, Arnold M. "The American Negro Problem in the Context of Social Change." *The Annals of the American Academy of Political and Social Science.* 357:1–18 (Jan. 1965).

Rose, Peter I. *They and We, Racial and Ethnic Relations in the United States.* Studies in Sociology No. 22. New York: Random House, 1964.

Taeuber, Conrad and Irene B. *The Changing Population of the United States.* New York: John Wiley & Sons, 1958.

Taeuber, Karl E. and Alma F. "White Migration and Socio-Economic Differences Between Cities and Suburbs." *American Sociological Review.* 29, II: 718–730 (Oct. 1964).

Williams, Robin M., Jr. *Strangers Next Door.* Englewood Cliffs, N.J.: Prentice-Hall, 1964.

13

Technology, the Schools, and Values

Technology may be one of the major forces to influence values and education in any society. It is possible that in the highly developed industrial nations of the world, technology may constitute an impersonal force which tends to create its own values. This could happen in a society which is developing so rapidly that it seems as if the machine is in control and man is merely an awed or subservient observer. In the words of Robert L. Heilbroner:

> In an age when it is possible to write seriously about a Death-of-the-World machine, it is hardly necessary to waste words on the power of technology to affect society. The shoe is now on the other foot: the brooding question is no longer what technology will make of man, but what man can still accomplish in the face of his technology. And it is not merely the apocalyptic potential of nuclear warfare which thus tilts the scales. At least in the Western world, where the typical landscape is industrial, where human life is sustained by the ceaseless operation of an enormous technical apparatus, where mechanical contrivances have penetrated into the smallest interstices of private life, it is not mere rhetoric to ask if Things are not already in the saddle, riding Man.[1]

If, indeed, things are "in the saddle, riding Man," there may be little that the schools can do but recognize the fact and resign themselves to the role of chief camp follower of technology, wherever it leads. This is essentially a pessimistic view in which the schools would play a vital, albeit somewhat passive, role. It is pessimistic in the sense that it declares that man no longer

---

[1] Robert L. Heilbroner, "The Impact of Technology: The Historic Debate," *Automation and Technological Change*, The American Assembly, Columbia University (Englewood Cliffs, N.J.: Prentice-Hall, 1962), p. 7.

has any effective control over his destiny, that the machine-gods that he has created could destroy him physically in the horror of massive war or that they could destroy his independent spirit by predetermining his vocation, his interests, his way of life. In either case, he may be effectively dead. Fortunately, the history of technology presents a brighter alternative. That alternative is the prospect of a utopian material existence whose broad outlines are determined by man, not for him. Whatever position one chooses to take, that of a utopian existence or a nightmarish hell, or anything in between, there can be little doubt that schooling enters the picture.

This chapter will be concerned with the broad general question of the effect of technological development on the values held by our citizens and the role of the schools in a rapidly developing technological society. It will also provide a brief definition of technology; a discussion of technology, change, and values; and a discussion of the role of the schools in a technological society.

A DEFINITION OF TECHNOLOGY

Most definitions of technology attempt to make some distinction between science and technology, but suggest a close relationship between the two. Most definitions suggest that technology grows out of science or scientific discovery. Such a definition is provided by Walter Buckingham,[2] in which he defines science as "knowledge, systematized and formulated to discover general truths." Technology is defined as "science applied to the industrial arts." But technology is more than applied science. Such a definition does not make clear the effect of the application of science on social institutions. It is the relationship between science and social institutions which is most significant as far as the schools are concerned. Obviously, the application of science to the production and modification of material objects in an indus trial society has brought tremendous changes, not only in the material aspects of our culture, but in its institutional and social aspects. The level of technological development has a great effect on the way man lives. It is a genuine force in determining the kind of work he does, the manner in which he provides shelter, the kind and variety of food he eats, his means of transportation, and so on. More than this, the level of technology in a society influences the social institutions in the society. The law tends to reflect the level of technological development; family relationships are influenced by it; primary and secondary social groups are influenced and sometimes determined by it; and the political and economic systems and social class are all touched by it. Most significantly, for our purposes, the school comes under

---

[2] Walter Buckingham, "Gains and Costs of Technological Change," *Adjusting to Technological Change,* ed. Gerald Somers, *et al.* (New York: Harper & Row, 1963), p. 2.

the influence of technological development. How the school is organized, what it must teach, the qualifications of its teachers, and the nature of its students are all influenced by the level of technology. This is the social face of technology. In a sense, the social face of technology is what man does with science and invention and its application; that is, the social uses which are made of technology.

Traditionally, Americans have been a little reluctant to confront this aspect of technological development, and perhaps only a few are really concerned about it. Many may view technological advance as a self-evident good. As Max Lerner points out:

> The Big Technology has been for Americans what the Cross was for the Emperor Constantine: *In hoc signo vinces.* It set the pace for an impressively swift and thorough conquest of a new environment and of world leadership. The American has been a machine-intoxicated man. The love affair . . . between the Americans and their Big Technology has been fateful, for it has joined the impersonal power of the machine to the dynamism of the American character.[3]

The problem with this "love affair" is that man can get emotional about technological accomplishments and fail to consider rationally the social implications of technological advance. Robert K. Merton[4] sounds this warning when he points out that the good of technological advance must be judged only in terms of the conditions of the society; that is, if technology is "good" it is due to its good effects on the human condition. The "things" of society, its material goods and objects, have no meaning outside a human one.

The problem of attempting to decide what is "good" about technology is a difficult one, because it is intimately tied in with the values man holds. Perhaps, as Paul Goodman suggests,[5] technology has already been "oversold." Certainly the technicians, the scientists, and the engineers must bear some brunt of the responsibility for air fouled by their inventions, garbage created by conveniently packaged products, huge roadways which bulldoze neighborhoods and destroy the landscape, and the inhuman application of technology to warfare. Computers and other mechanical devices can hopelessly complicate and impersonalize bureaucracies in business, government, and education. Already the little plastic credit card has become a major means of survival for many. As Goodman points out, it is possible to diminish the quality of life with technological improvements. "There are ingenious devices for unimportant functions, stressful mazes for essential functions,

---

[3] Max Lerner, *America as a Civilization* (New York: Simon and Schuster, 1957), p. 227.
[4] Robert K. Merton, *Social Theory and Social Structure* (New York: Free Press of Glencoe, 1957), p. 562.
[5] Paul Goodman, "Can Technology Be Humane?" *New York Review of Books,* 20 Nov. 1969.

and drastic dislocation when anything goes wrong, which happens with increasing frequency. To add to the complexity, the mass of people tend to become incompetent and dependent on repairmen. . . . "[6]

A BRIEF HISTORY

The pace of technological development has been so rapid that few have had time to reflect on its history. For practical purposes of solving problems brought about by the rapidly accelerating body of scientific knowledge and its application, many are more interested in where they are than how they got there; that is, many students of society are more interested in the kinds of human problems which are wrought by scientific and technological advance than they are in how these problems came about, just as they are more interested in human problems created by machines than they are in the way the machine operates. However, a brief history of technological development can more clearly outline the problems which surround it.

The history of man's view of technological development reveals that many of the problems created by technology in an earlier century remain with us. Although the history of technology can be traced to the ancient Greeks and beyond, modern problems of technology might begin with the growth of the nation-state and the development of national economic systems. The modern debate over technology—whether it is an unrestrained good or an unconditioned evil—was outlined in Adam Smith's *Wealth of Nations.* Smith's view of technology was optimistic, because he believed that technology permitted a greater division of labor which, in his view, was a major contributor to the wealth of nations. Technology permitted a greater division of labor, since the introduction of machines enabled goods to be produced more cheaply. This, in turn, increased demand for goods and for labor to produce them.[7] As a result, the wealth of the nation would grow, the market would expand, and general prosperity would follow.

Not everyone shared Smith's view. In specific instances in which machines had the immediate effect of replacing workers and causing serious local unemployment, workers did not take kindly to the introduction of technology. Such was the case of the Luddites in England, who wrecked and burned the machines which were designed to liberate them from their toil. Marx predicted this kind of reaction to the machine. He could see nothing but disaster resulting from technological development under a capitalist system. He felt that the displacement of workers, which would inevitably result from the introduction of machines, would cause serious under-consumption

---

[6] Goodman, p. 29.
[7] Heilbroner, p. 9.

which, in turn, would lead to the eventual collapse of the system. Even though history demonstrates that the gloomy predictions of Marx were in error, critics continued to find faults with technology. Social reformers of every hue continued to lament the ill effects of technology long after Marx. The protest took many forms. Labor groups in the developing industrial nations continued to view the machine with alarm and blamed many of the economic ills of the society on its introduction. Early in the industrial development of the United States, reformers protested against the deadening routine that enslaved the industrial worker, a protest that continues to be heard in more sophisticated forms.

In spite of these dissident voices, however, America has generally viewed technological development with optimism.[8] Utopian novelists of the late nineteenth century expressed the hope that the machine would create an abundance that would serve to liberate mankind. In *Looking Backward, 2000–1887,* Edward Bellamy in 1888 welcomed even the routine that accompanied the introduction of the machine. He envisioned a utopia of a highly disciplined army of industrial workers which he compared to the organization of a modern military system. Even the despair sounded by the so-called "technocrats" during the days of the Great Depression failed to dampen general enthusiasm for technological progress, because economic progress and growth continued to contradict the gloomy forebodings of the critics.

More recently, a new kind of spectre has been raised to stir the conscience of a nation of people bent on technological progress. This is the spectre of the completely automated citizen. In *1984*, George Orwell draws a particularly gruesome picture of the ultimate end of a technological society. Similar warnings are sounded in John Hersey's *The Child Buyer,* and Aldous Huxley's *Brave New World.* These are different from the older criticisms of technology. The pictures drawn by Orwell and Huxley are not those which depict human suffering in the form of unemployment caused by technological displacement. These critics admit that material utopia is possible, but raise the question of price. In a word, they are suggesting that material utopia may be achieved only at the expense of intellectual and spiritual freedom.

Thus, the argument continues. For nearly two hundred years Western man has viewed technology as a mixed blessing at best. There have always been critics who see technology as an unconditional evil. Still the general optimism persists. This is true partly because technology does provide a better life and most importantly, perhaps, because it is always extremely difficult for the current generation, at any period in time, to see any alternative to rapid technological development. It is possible that most

---

[8] Oscar Handlin, "Science and Technology in Popular Culture," *Daedalus, Journal of the American Academy of Arts and Sciences* (Winter 1965), p. 160.

Americans realize that it is a force that cannot be stopped—we cannot get off and walk, so we must ride along with it and perhaps do what can be done to point it in the right direction.

TECHNOLOGY AND CHANGE

There can be little doubt that technology is an important vehicle for change in any society. The most obvious changes which are encouraged by the application of science to man's way of doing are the physical changes in the landscape. Certainly technological development has played an important part in changing the American landscape from a rural agricultural landscape to a nation of factories and cities. This process of urbanization has proceeded from the application of water and steam power to the textile industry of the Northeast to the highly sophisticated application of space science to the race for the conquest of space. With each passing decade the physical characteristics of change become more obvious. Dramatic changes in the landscape have become so common in recent years that great and complex technological installations which seem to grow up almost overnight in some isolated pasture get hardly a nod from the passer-by. Explosive technological development has become a way of life, accepted and hardly noticed.

This is the physical face of technology, and it is a constantly changing one. Technology brings more than physical change, however. The great material and environmental changes which are wrought by the application of science can also result in changes in ways of believing, feeling, and thinking; in short, changes in values.

The underlying cause of these changes has always been subject to serious academic argument. For some, all change begins in the mind of man. This is a comfortable belief in the age of big technology, for it assumes that man can quite consciously control his ideas, and thus the technology which his ideas create. Some, however, would agree with Engels' materialistic conception of history that "the ultimate causes of all social change and political revolutions, are to be sought, not in the minds of men . . . but in changes in the mode of production and exchange. . . . " This impersonal and materialistic view of the role of technology can lead to some rather frightening conclusions. It can become an argument for *laissez-innover* or a kind of freedom for technologists which existed in the old laissez-faire concept of capitalism. The principle of *laissez-innover* assumes that technological innovations will automatically operate for the benefit of mankind rather than for the private gain of the inventor. A major problem with this philosophy is that the inventor is no longer a single individual acting in a competitive market place, but the research and development establishments of large corporations. At least one critic[9] suggested that the normal tendency of uncontrolled technology would be to increase the concentration of decision-making power in the hands of the largest scientific bureaucracies. Thus, the good or ill of any specific technological application is not evaluated in human terms, but in terms of its economic returns.

It really matters little what position one takes; the fact is, big technology is upon us and it does influence values. Attempting to determine whether technology, in all of its dimensions, has its origin in the mind of man or if it can become a kind of self-generating and somewhat uncontrollable force is like the old "chicken and egg" argument. Such an argument poses unanswerable questions. For example, who can know with certainty whether the railroad was responsible for mass migration into the American West or whether the mass migration encouraged the building of rail lines westward? It was probably a little of both in addition to a number of other variables. These might include: the increasing commercialization of agriculture, the lure of natural riches, and the dreams and ideals of man. So it is with other technological developments. Do men build power installations which result from the technological application of atomic science as a deliberately planned effort to provide for the known power needs of an area, or is this technological development an inevitable outgrowth of the "accidental" discovery of atomic power?

Perhaps this is not the real issue. Many Americans care little about academic arguments which deal with the philosophical questions surrounding technology. They merely accept big technology as a fact of their existence, and tend to judge it in terms of what it does for them in a material sense. The real issue may be the manner in which technology changes the culture and, subsequently, the values held in any given culture. Technology does cause great change in a society, which inevitably affects ways of doing as well as ways of thinking. A few illustrations should demonstrate the point.

One of the most obvious changes wrought by technology in any society is the pattern of work and subsequent attitudes about work. Lerner points out that the old generalizations about work no longer apply in the "New Society." "The greatest change has come about in the gospel of work."[10] This was the belief in the basic necessity of work and the human dignity which could be found in "useful" occupations. Through much of our history, work has been valued for its own sake. It was a virtue which was closely associated with morality and religion. The advent of machine technology spelled doom for this concept, but it was a long time dying and the death was painful. This is illustrated in the heartbreaking ballad of John Henry who gave his life in

---

[9] Suzanne Keller, *Beyond the Ruling Class* (New York: Random House, 1963).
[10] Lerner, p. 238.

competition with "the monstrous strength of the steam crane."[11] The world of work has not really been the same since. For what "dignity" could be found in the miserable textile mills, the grimy coal pits, and the monstrous steel mills of an industrialized society? As technology expanded and as jobs became more dehumanized, man came to realize that his job was just a living and had little else to recommend it. As the process of dehumanization of work continues at an accelerating pace, it becomes increasingly difficult to convince children whose parents may hold such jobs that there is an intrinsic dignity in work. More often such children are apt to feel that the value of work is more in the things it will buy than in the work itself.

Besides affecting the worker's attitude toward his job, technology has had a great deal to do with the kind of employment that is available. Certainly it has had a tremendous effect on extending the possibilities for different kinds of work. The fact that technology has created countless numbers of new jobs and many entirely new occupations is already an old story. Accompanying this cornucopia of occupational variety has come an increasing emphasis on specialization. With each new technological advance in any given area, the necessity for specialization is increased. At levels above the routine ma-chine-tending positions created by technology, there has grown a tremendous variety of new jobs. This presents its own peculiar problems. A most serious one is the narrow specialization required of many of the important new jobs. The mere accumulation of knowledge made possible by techno-logical development has made it increasingly difficult for one to master a small segment of a single specialty. Although the effect that such specialization is having on innovation and research is not clearly known, many writers have expressed concern in recent years over the problems it creates. Reference was made earlier to the changing character of invention and innovation. It is becoming increasingly difficult for a single individual working with limited resources to invent anything significant. With increasing frequency, invention is proceeding out of some team effort which has great financial support. Moreover, as technology develops, feedback and interre-lated processes may reduce the demand for independent invention. Processes of invention and production tend to become increasingly interrelated and interdependent. Progressively the system could demand fewer innovators, less inventiveness, and a reduced need for such skills, while at the same time markedly increasing the need for high-level technicians. For example, hundreds of thousands of high-level technicians could spend decades on the single problem of applying what is known about the power of the atom to practical uses. The successful technician has already become the new "hero," replacing the inventor-hero of an earlier generation. But heroes are few by definition. In a highly specialized work force, the mass of workers

---

[11] Lerner, p. 239.

perform miniscule and unchallenging tasks for which they are greatly overtrained. Automation and cybernetics divide work into extremely simple units which require only a small fraction of the workers' skills. When workers are aware that their intelligence and skills are not fully utilized, the possibility for frustration and alienation from the job is greatly enhanced.

Another example of change brought about by technology is that of consumption. Of course, one of the most obvious advantages of technology is the tremendous increase in production which can result from its application. For the mass of consumers, technology has resulted in a tremendous expansion of material goods which can be enjoyed. Within this century the basic needs of man—his shelter, his food, and his clothing—not to mention the means by which he moves about, his forms of relaxation and entertainment, and so on, have been revolutionized by technology. Not only does he have completely new products from which to select, but the variety which exists has vastly increased his possibilities for selection. Moreover, the changes have been rapid. They have come in this generation. A favorite preoccupation of middle-aged Americans seems to be that of remembering how things have changed from "the old days." The kind of life that is possible in this generation would have been pure fantasy for the last.

There can be little doubt that the abundance encouraged by technology has some effect on values. This point has been made many times in recent years in such works as John Kenneth Galbraith's *The Affluent Society,* David Potter's *People of Plenty,* and Vance Packard's *The Status Seekers.* Scholars, teachers, journalists, and preachers have been warning us in recent years that we are too much concerned with the material things in life and that we have been neglecting the human and spiritual aspects of our existence. Critics of this consumers' never-never land are quick to point out that Americans spend more on cosmetics, tobacco, and liquor than on public education. However, the case is easily overstated. In the words of Max Lerner:

> It remains true, however, that there are more good things available to a higher proportion of Americans than in any other society. This is not a matter of piglike, sensuous reveling in material things. The long-established image of America as a golden sty is a stereo-type with more envy and ignorance than truth. The vast array of available commodities has become an American way of living, but it does not follow that Americans are more likely than others to confuse living standards with life values, or mistake good things for the good life. Many Americans—like many other human beings—do live by things as well as among them. But many others know that, like the machine, the shopwindow crowded with glittering items carries no ethic with it. It does not become an end in itself except for the impoverished of spirit, who are to be found in any civilization. What is true in America is that

they find it easier to disguise their impoverished spirit behind the gaudy raiments of a consumer's plenty.[12]

One of the most noticeable changes in the landscape, which has been encouraged by industrial and technological development, is the urbanization of the society. This, too, has its derivative effects and causes some modifications in values. On the contemporary scene, the machine continues to draw men from the countryside and concentrate them in large numbers in and near the cities. Sometimes it works the other way; the concentration of population in the form of skilled labor has attracted the machine in some areas in recent years. Either way, the result is the same. The urbanization encouraged by technology has changed traditional values.

In many instances technology does more than encourage urban migration—it forces the issue. The decision to move to the city is always an individual one, but with the advent of technology it is not always a free choice. The tenant farmer may move to the city because he lacks any real alternative. His usefulness on the farm may have been effectively ended by the introduction of technology in agriculture. In the city his way of life and, perhaps, his values, become subject to change.

The old value of individualism, that of the Jeffersonian ideal of the small self-sufficient landholder, is certain to face some modification in a giant industrial metropolis. Similarly, the classic economic ideal of free enterprise is seriously modified when the cost of establishing a successful business is above the means of most. Horatio Alger stories are no longer popular. They have been replaced with success stories whose plots contain new values. These are the values of the security of an interesting and long-tenure career, with the major hope being the ability to move up through the organization. The new stereotype of success is not the poor, but honest boy who makes good through hard work and fortuitous good circumstance, but the highly trained, fun-loving, well-turned-out, junior executive type characterized by the advertising industry. This is the man who reads the right books, wears the proper brand of clothing, keeps his breath sweet-smelling with the proper mouthwash, smokes the right cigarette, drinks only the best booze, and in general, makes it clear that he is on his way up. This is the "organization man" of William H. Whyte, Jr. Even this theme can be overplayed, for it is possible that many continue to believe that the shortest route to success is through hard work and honest effort. The fact that in some circles such a belief may be considered a meaningless platitude demonstrates the extent to which the "real" world of technology has had its effect on values.

As a final illustration, industrialization and technology have had the effect of disrupting the old family pattern in the United States. The particular kind of

---

[12] Lerner, pp. 251–252.

life required of a technological society has made old patterns of family relationships obsolete. The working wife is a common feature of the technological age. In addition, the house in the city or its surrounding area no longer has room for grandparents. Even if it did, the mobility required of a highly industrialized society makes the extended family unrealistic. More likely, grandparents are in a rest home if they are not able to care for themselves, or in some distant place which is still nostalgically called home by the younger generation. Even the old concept of "home," which implies the permanency of at least a generation of residency, may die effectively with the present generation, taking with it a whole bundle of values associated with the semipermanent "homestead" as a way of life.

TECHNOLOGY AND EDUCATION

The possibilities of discussion of the effect of technological development on the manner of life and on values are many. But what does this have to do with the schools? Clearly, changes induced by technology pose some challenging problems for the schools. Some of the effects of technology on the schools have been direct. Of course, the schools have been part of advancing technology in that they have generally reflected technological advances and have employed its devices. These reflections have been in the form of new buildings, gadgets and equipment of all kinds, books, and new materials for teaching. The modern, well-equipped classroom can be a technological marvel. The lectern can be wired for sound with a built-in overhead projector which almost eliminates the need for the chalkboard. The lectern has become an electronic console where the push of a button can bring down maps, bulletin board displays, or whatever. A second push, and the whole assembly slips silently back into its slot. Another button controls the film projector, which can thread itself and be started and stopped at will. Sensitive microphones are placed around the room in case the students are moved to comment on the proceedings. All the while the whole lesson is being recorded on video tape so that it can be shown to other classes in the future. Finally, hidden cameras are recording the class from all angles so that researchers and prospective teachers can study what is going on in a given teaching situation. Of course, if anybody misses anything, the whole business is programmed for teaching machines. Perhaps the only step left in the complete automation of the classroom is to build a robot teacher—a phenomenon that is closely approached by placing a television set in the classroom. In some experimental elementary schools a great quantity of routine learning has become programmed and automated.

The expansion of technology into the classroom has been nothing short of revolutionary in the last decade. The quantity and variety of hardware boggles the mind of the experienced teacher and calls seductively to fresh college graduates. In many schools teachers now can choose from one or more of the following media aids to instruction:[13]

programmed texts
audio and video recording equipment
telephone lectures
telelecture
sound slides and filmstrips
teaching machines
computer-assisted instruction
student response systems
television
teaching kits

simulated activities
single-concept films
learning carrels
learning laboratories
information storage and retrieval
automated test scoring
systematic educational programs
computerized requisitioning
computerized resource listings

Perhaps the ultimate in technologically assisted education was described in George Leonard's "Kennedy School" of the year 2001.[14] The heart of Kennedy School is the "Basic Dome" which houses forty "learning consoles" and a large number of "learning displays." The learning display, "about ten feet square, is reflected from the hologram-conversion screen that runs all the way around the inner surface of the dome. The image appears to stand out from the screen in sometimes startling colors and dimensions. The screen is slightly elevated . . . so that everyone . . . can view all of the learning displays."[15] At Kennedy, all of the child's learning is arranged by computer. "As the child takes his place at the learning console he puts on his combination earphones and brain wave sensors so that Ongoing Brain Wave Analysis can become an element in the dialogue. . . . Once the computer picks up the child's ongoing brain waves, it immediately begins reiterating . . . his last learning session. . . ."[16] If the child is satisfied that he understands his last lesson, he punches a button and the computer immediately begins searching for material that will match his level of learning, and a new lesson is underway. Leonard's Kennedy School may appear to border on fantasy, but its creator claims that the technology already exists which would enable such a school to be built.

In addition to obvious gadgets which are directly engaged in schooling, technology has had many indirect effects on the schools. In a very real sense, the school reorganization movement has been an outgrowth of technology. Although it would be impossible to pick up every thread of this development, a few illustrations should serve to demonstrate the point. The automobile, in

[13] This is an incomplete random list from several sources. Particularly useful sources on media are the journals *Audiovisual Instruction* and *Educational Media*.
[14] George B. Leonard, *Education and Ecstasy* (New York: Dell, 1968).
[15] Leonard, p. 148.
[16] Leonard, p. 148.

making us more mobile as a population, also had the derivative effect of creating a demand for bigger and better roads. As mass production in automobile assembly helped bring the price within the means of most Americans, the whole process was accelerated. Communities on wheels with convenient and rapid transportation from place to place soon began to question the need for isolated schools. Paralleling this development, of course, were a myriad of other technological developments making new demands on the labor supply. One of the results of all this was the school reorganization movement. The technology of transportation had made isolated rural schools obsolete. In addition, the economics of technology was demanding a kind of schooling that the small rural school could not provide. Technology demanded a dramatically broadened curriculum including all manner of new and exotic training on the high school level which could not be housed, staffed, or equipped in the old small rural school.

The derivative effects of this process were numerous. To mention one, teacher training has been greatly affected by it. The teacher, like millions of others in our society, has been forced to become more specialized. Reorganization of schools has enabled greater specialization and has created its own demands for highly specialized preparation. The very character of schooling has been changed by the labor demands of big technology. Not only have new subjects and whole new courses of study been added, but the old standbys have been modified by it. It is now possible for some students to take such courses as "English for Secretaries," or "Civics for Industrial Arts Majors," or "Economics for Homemakers" in secondary schools and colleges in nearly any state. Such titles have bowed to the reality of a highly specialized technological environment. Even the old classical courses have been affected. Many English literature teachers must spend hours wrestling with such questions as: "How can I make *Pilgrim's Progress* relevant to today's society?" or "What are the values of *Beowulf* in twentieth-century America?" Indeed, such weighty questions often consume the time of the teacher and his students for the first week or so of any such course. Moreover, no self-respecting English literature instructor would fail to accept the challenge to speak on some such topic as: "*Romeo and Juliet* as it relates to present-day problems of the teenager in a technological society." In all fairness, however, one must admit that there remain a few teachers who are satisfied with the classics merely because they are good reading. Even so, such justification for many youths, as well as adults, has to be couched in terms which "fit" the technological age. Thus, the teacher and student who merely like to read good literature may be forced to explain apologetically that this is important in a society where so much leisure time is created by technology.

Technology has created an environment which contains the potential for revolutionary change in the role of the schools. The great and serious immediate implications of technology for the schools are that it can free human resources for social rather then economic production, and it can narrowly specialize the functions of the school. Finally, technology has revolutionary implications for educational planning.

Technology does free human resources in that a highly developed nation does not find it necessary to devote all of its physical energy to providing for minimum physical needs. This surplus of human resources could be diverted to noneconomic production whose major purpose might be the general improvement of the society. This is a tough problem in an essentially capitalist society, since the market place is such an important factor in determining the allocation of resources, including human ones. Unfortunately, there is no real market place in human relations. This does not mean that Americans have pursued their economic interests in the market place at the expense of their humanity; quite the contrary has been true. Every generation has produced its philanthropists, its unpaid social workers, its citizens dedicated to the service of their fellow man. But this has been almost incidental to the main purpose—that of building the economic strength of the individual, the family, and the nation. It has been a largely unplanned and somewhat haphazard effort. Moreover, those who have been inclined, for one reason or another, to be strong advocates of social production have been reminded that this inclination has a Marxian flavor about it. There is, of course, a reasonable answer to this challenge. Certainly Marx was not the first to think in broad humanitarian terms, nor can his contemporary followers claim exclusive rights. There is much evidence on the present scene that citizens are interested in social production. In most interesting ways, the young are expressing very active interests in their fellow man. There is evidence of this in the popularity of the Peace Corps and Vista programs, not to mention the great number of church groups and fraternal organizations which have enabled countless numbers of young people to work in the interests of humanity with little or no pay. There is, moreover, some evidence that the youth of our society is having some serious pangs of conscience about a grossly materialistic outlook on life. There are many illustrations in the secondary schools, colleges, and universities across the country where young people are expressing renewed interest in spiritual, moral, or humanitarian values as opposed to materialist ones.

Assuming that technology does free man for such considerations, many problems remain. Social development makes great demands on a population. It is not the kind of process which can be limited to a few who may dabble in it for a limited period of time. Social development, if it is to be productive, needs great numbers of men and women who are schooled in the broad areas of the humanities, not a small handful of starry-eyed, youthful enthusiasts who can become quickly disillusioned when utopia is not achieved during spring semester. Social production may be the most difficult work there is in any society. The real hope for socially useful pursuits is that technology can free man for these pursuits and the schools can prepare him to pursue them intelligently. But the success of social production will be determined not so much by the efforts of the few, as by the education of the many. This clearly implies that a broad general education for everybody is of vital importance.

The schools, however, can move in the other direction; that is, technology can be read as a mandate for greater specialization. Unfortunately, there is accumulating evidence that this is precisely what is happening in our schools. The knowledge industry has become big business. Some of America's largest corporations, including IBM, Xerox, Raytheon, and General Electric, have recently acquired textbook companies and have become enthusiastic producers of educational hardware. Many companies would be quick to agree with the definition of the instructional process offered by Raytheon: "printed matter plus apparatus, plus electronic equipment, equals learning."[17] One can't help but wonder where the teacher fits in. The real problem facing the schools in this development is a deep philosophical one. It is very likely that the major motivation of large corporations is not philanthropy, but profit. Although it is difficult to find fault with the profit motive, it does create certain problems when applied to schooling. A major problem is really one of unfair competition. Part of the unfair competition danger is the old fear of monopoly with all of its resultant evils. Thus, the very large corporations have an advantage over smaller concerns interested in educational hardware.

When applied to educational hardware, however, the evils of monopoly go far beyond basic economic problems. Schools are concerned with teaching and examining cultural values. If large corporations gain monopoly power over the devices and gadgets which teach the young, they have achieved powerful tools for influence. Teachers have always had this power, but it has not been concentrated. Anything approaching monopoly power over educational technology is a frightening prospect.

More than this, there is evidence that teachers, school administrators, and the general public tend to view the introduction of technology into education as an absolute good. This may be true because technology gets measurable results. Not that the very human teacher does not, but the teacher is in no position to compete with the claims of corporate enterprise. In the interest of creating a market for its goods, industry is willing to prove that its product is a good one. Thus, the educational hardware industry stands ready to spend huge sums to test and evaluate its educational hardware, computers, machines, and teaching kits so that the public and even the teachers are satisfied that they are getting their money's worth. Few stand ready to

---

[17] Efrem Sigel, "The Education Industry," *School Management* (Oct. 1968), p. 92.

question the fact that certain educational tasks can be more economically performed by machines than by man. Even fewer question the validity of the tasks themselves. Those who stand ready to question the educational tasks undertaken by industry and the effectiveness of technological devices are faced with pitifully small resources with which to research and evaluate their position.

The results of such unfair competition are already beginning to be felt. Certain traditional tasks of teachers are, in fact, being performed by machines. Teacher training is being affected in that increasing emphasis is being placed on the teacher to become an operator of machines and hardware. In such programs the learning process tends to be reduced to what amounts to an engineering system. It is possible that the centuries-old designation "teacher" may in some future year become "learning engineer." Already there is much concern for developing "systems" in education. In the words of one educational writer:

> In the teacher-based system . . . we have the problem of creating the sort of teacher who can organize, structure, implement, experiment with, and, in a word, engineer learning situations that are effective and operationally efficient in human terms. . . . Teachers will use technology, or they will run the risk of being replaced by it.[18]

Such specialization can be dangerous, since it can further dehumanize the technological process. Specialization can produce men whom Alfred Whitehead, in *The Aims of Education,* characterized as men with "minds in a groove." Such "grooves" can effectively prevent them from considering problems other than their own, and the results, in the words of Whitehead, are: " . . . the directive force of reason is weakened. The leading intellects lack balance. They see this set of circumstances or that set; but not both sets together." The program of the schools can, of course, encourage this lack of balance. It already is, in some places, by providing a completely technical curriculum for certain students. In other places the schools have attempted a compromise that results in a two-track system. This consists of a purely technical education for some and a general education for others. If the social needs of man are to be identified and dealt with, such a system may be dangerous. A more realistic approach might include a study of man along with the development of special skills. Anything less makes Orwell's *1984* much too realistic a possibility. Even at the risk of appearing hopelessly out of step with the times, the schools cannot, nor should they, be concerned mainly with the immediate employment needs of business and industry in the society. Schooling has to be more than this. In a technological society which

---

[18] James J. Thompson, *Instructional Communication* (New York: American Book, 1969), p. 41.

professes to be democratic, it may be true that the schools must be all things to all men. Perhaps there is no other real choice.

Of course, the impracticality of being all things to all men looms large in any given time. Even though our schools may embrace such a single comprehensive goal, getting there presents some problems. Out of all the vast possible areas in which schooling can assist its citizens in developing occupational and social skills, at any given time the mere size of the job will require some selection of those which are most important. This means planning. The implications for planning raise other significant questions. Who is to do the planning? What criterion will be used for the direction the school program should take? These and other questions of a similar nature are not easily answered. However, if the schools are viewed as social institutions which must be out ahead of technological developments, rather than institutions which merely follow where the developments lead, planning is necessary. How this is to be accomplished may be too tough a question to answer at this stage in our development. The alternative to such planning, of course, is that the schools continue to do what they have been doing in a general way—attempt to keep up, attempt to meet the most pressing needs and demands of a technological society, and hope for the best. Given the complexity and pace of technological development, perhaps this is really all the schools can be expected to do. It is always difficult, even if desirable, to plan for the unknown needs and demands of a society. Nor does the lack of highly organized planning for the future necessarily mean that no planning is possible. A minimum of such planning is essential for the public schools merely to anticipate real physical needs such as space, buildings, number of classrooms, equipment, and so on. In the normal process of meeting current pressing needs, there is always time to reflect on possible future needs. Thus, planning proceeds even though it may appear haphazard and uncollected. Perhaps this is the way it should be. It does provide a delightful flexibility and may lessen the possibility of tragic error that could lurk in more formal planning.

What this says, in effect, is that the schools in our society are in an ambivalent position relative to the force of technology. Certainly the force is recognized, but it is also played down; the schools have acknowledged the force in countless ways and have attempted to deal with it on its own terms, but they have not been dominated by it. The old ways continue to exist even when attempts to justify them in contemporary terms may seem pathetically ridiculous. Yet, school people and the public generally continue to find values in the old ways, in the old curricula and the classical content. Perhaps this is as it should be. For who can oppose this kind of ambivalence, this kind of a pluralism, in a public school system which represents an ambivalent and pluralistic society?

What then are the effects of technology on the American school system?

Obviously, there is no precise answer to this question. Just as obvious is the fact that short of more directive planning, the schools may be more characteristically reflecting technological development than influencing its direction. Moreover, it seems doubtful that most Americans, if given the choice, would choose to have greater planning than presently exists. Nor does this have to mean that the schools are the prostitutes of technology. They mirror its force, but are not captivated by its image. Instead, they explore and explain it, criticize and praise it, resist and encourage it. Above all, the schools cannot ignore technology, nor do they try. In this sense technology is a force for change in the schools as in other aspects of the society. As the schools reflect and respond to the changes wrought by technology, they help each new generation transcend the old. It is in this manner that the schools change society. They do not consciously reconstruct it, but they help the young understand the changes that technology brings.

REFERENCES

Allen, F. R., H. Hart, D. C. Miller, W. F. Ozburn, and M. F. Nimkoff. *Technology and Social Change*. New York: Appleton-Century-Crofts, 1957.

American Assembly, The. Columbia University. *Automation and Technological Change*. Englewood Cliffs, N.J.: Prentice-Hall, 1962.

Braibanti, Ralph, and Joseph J. Spengler (eds.). *Tradition, Values and Socio-Economic Development*. London: Cambridge Univ. Press, 1961.

Dupre, J. Stefan, and Sanford A. Lakoff. *Science and the Nation*. Englewood Cliffs, N.J.: Prentice-Hall, 1962.

Evans, Luther H., and George E. Arnstein (eds.). *Automation and the Challenge to Education*. Washington, D.C.: NEA, 1962.

Ferkins, Victor C. *Technological Man: The Myth and the Reality*. New York: Mentor, 1969.

Fuller, Buckminster. *Education on Automation*. Carbondale, Ill.: Southern Illinois Univ Press, 1962.

Galbraith, John Kenneth, and Molinder S. Randhawai. *The New Industrial State*. Boston: Houghton Mifflin, 1967.

George, F. H. *Computers, Science and Society*. New York: Prometheus Books, 1970.

Ginsberg, Eli. *Technology and Social Change*. New York: Columbia Univ. Press, 1964.

Goodman, Paul. "Can Technology be Humane?" *New York Review of Books*. 27–34 (20 Nov. 1969).

Graham, Grace. *The Public School in the American Community*. New York: Harper & Row, 1963. Chapter 5.

Handlin, Oscar. "Science and Technology in Popular Culture." *Daedalus, Journal of the American Academy of Arts and Sciences*. 156–171 (Winter 1965).

Hoselitz, Bert F., and Wilbert E. Moore (eds.). *Industrialization and Society*. New York: UNESCO, 1960.

Keller, Suzanne. *Beyond the Ruling Class*. New York: Random House, 1963.

Kreps, Juanita M. *Automation and Employment*. New York: Holt, Rinehart & Winston, 1964.

Leonard, George B. *Education and Ecstasy.* New York: Dell, 1968.

Lerner, Max. *America as a Civilization.* New York: Simon and Schuster, 1957. Chapter 4.

Merton, Robert K. *Social Theory and Social Structure.* New York: Free Press of Glencoe, 1957.

Moore, Wilbert E. *The Impact of Industry.* Englewood Cliffs, N.J.: Prentice-Hall, 1965.

Mumford, Lewis. *The Myth of the Machine: The Pentagon of Power.* New York: Harcourt Brace Jovanovich, 1970.

Sigel, Efrem. "The Education Industry." *School Management.* 89–126 (Oct. 1968).

Somers, Gerald G., Edward L. Cushman, and Nat Weinberg (eds.). *Adjusting to Technological Change.* New York: Harper & Row, 1963.

Thompson, James J. *Instructional Communication.* New York: American Book, 1969.

White, Leslie A. "Energy and the Evolution of Culture." Reprinted from *The Science of Culture.* Indianapolis, Ind.: Bobbs-Merrill, 1964. Reprint Series in the Social Sciences.

14

Can the Schools Change Society?

American schools have changed the society and they will continue to do so. This change is not difficult to measure, for we can determine in a very general way that there are fewer illiterates in our society than at any time in history, that the millions of immigrants who landed on our shores have been somehow blended into the broad pattern of life that is American, and that schooling has been a major vehicle for progress—intellectual, social, political, and economic. However, the role of the schools in determination of the quality and direction of change has been less obvious and more difficult to measure. It is possible to praise the schools for their accomplishments or damn them for their deficiencies. No honest man can be totally consistent in his approach, since the schools perform many functions that cannot possibly be all "good" or "bad" by any standard against which they are judged.

Any past or present judgment of the schools is always made according to some value criterion. A totally objective view may not be possible in a pluralistic society which must encompass and tolerate a wide range of attitudes, beliefs, and values. Thus, judgments about the quality of the school program, its teachers and its administrators, its plans and its hopes are always made from some value orientation. Similarly, judgments about the direction the schools are taking or ought to take are always made within the context of some value orientation. It is therefore impossible to assess accurately the qualitative accomplishments of the schools in any objective fashion or to present a strong case for the direction which the schools should take and expect unanimous agreement. If this situation seems hopelessly confusing, we should consider the alternatives. It is doubtful that most Americans, if given the choice, would accept any alternative to this kind of confusion. There isn't any question but that the schools can be used in a deliberately planned way, to achieve certain and specific goals—that they can and have been used in some societies to produce a homogeneously uniform citizen. Most Americans would view this use of the schools with horror, for it raises questions which we cannot answer. If the schools are to work consciously toward the reconstruction of the society, whose plan will they follow? Whose values will be taught? What kind of a society should the schools produce? Of course, we shall continue to ask these questions, search for answers, and work for agreement on common goals and aspirations; but the very difficulty of finding these answers must force us to the conclusion that the schools may not be able to change the society in any planned and deliberate manner.

SERIOUS OBSTACLES TO CHANGE

One must admit, however, that the society changes and the schools change with it. The central question which might be raised in America may be: Are the schools adequate for present needs? In some respects they are clearly inadequate. One could point to the lag between curriculum development and the needs of the environment, inadequacies in teachers and their training, communities which fail to recognize the need for change, and the search for easy solutions to difficult school problems.

The present school scene is characterized by concern from many sources about the adequacy of the curriculum. There have been many criticisms within the last fifteen years that the existing school curriculum is not meeting the needs of children who must function in the latter part of the twentieth century. This concern is not a new one, for it has been characteristic in our society for each generation to examine what the schools are doing in the light of real or fancied needs of the environment. Probing questions were asked by the so-called progressive reformers of the 1930's and 1940's regarding the school curriculum; many progressives rejected the traditional study of disciplines and advocated a curriculum based on problems facing youth and society. Wholesale elimination of traditional disciplines was not advocated, but it was proposed that the content be rearranged in a manner which promised relevancy in a rapidly changing social order. Although the impact of the progressive reformers was a serious one, they were not completely successful in their attempts to revise the curriculum.

The present generation is experiencing a new flurry of interest in the curriculum, and it has many new features that distinguish it from that of the generation of progressive reformers which preceded it. This generation of reformers is most notable, perhaps, in its inability to find agreement. Not only does honest disagreement exist, but it seems to be welcomed by those vitally concerned with curriculum reform. Some hold to the old progressive view that content in the public schools should be based on real life and the needs of youth, and such reformers are concerned with what they view as a serious gap between what the school does and what the environment demands.

Others in this generation of curriculum reformers advocate a curriculum for the public schools which is organized on the basis of systematized fields of study in which the major ideas and principles from recognized and organized fields of knowledge get central recognition. Still others are engaged in a search for central principles or a central theme such as "culture" which will provide a general key for organization of content. Some are eclectic in their approach, and are attempting to incorporate many ideas and principles in reform proposals. All, however, are in general agreement that the existing curriculum is not doing the job—that there is a wide gap between what the school is teaching and what ought to be taught. Always the justification for any proposal is made in the light of the gap between what the school teaches and what the reformer sees as necessary for intelligent life and informed participation in a rapidly changing society.

Recurring cycles of interest in the school curriculum are understandable in a society in which change is such an obvious fact of life. Each generation is forced to look at its schools, because each generation is faced with a new set of problems, a new environment, which the upcoming generation of school children must face. In a dynamic society which is characterized by revolutionary developments in science and technology, by rapidly changing patterns of economic and social life, by an increasingly complicated and complex existence—where change is the rule rather than the exception—it is not only necessary, but vital, that those responsible for the schooling of the young ask questions of their schools. A central question will always be: What knowledge is most useful for our future citizens? With each passing year this question becomes more difficult because of the increasing possibilities from which to select. The very bulk of possible contents makes some kind of selection necessary, while the demands of the environment make the proper selection vital.

Nearly everyone agrees that the curricula in many public schools are dated in general and specific ways, but few agree on how the problem should be solved. Nor is this the extent of the problem, for even if agreement were reached on what the schools should teach, the new curriculum, once adopted, would almost immediately become dated. This is because the environment does not stand still. Those who work in the schools should recognize the very real difficulties involved in curriculum planning and revision. It is no easy task at best, nor is it ever a finished one. It is a task which will always be before us, one for which there will never be a completely satisfactory solution. This difficulty is partly due to the fact that the knowledge with which the curriculum deals is constantly changing and expanding, and partly due to the time lag, unavoidable in a democratic society, between the needs of the environment and the implementation of changes in the school curriculum. If real progress is to be made, the task of curriculum reform should have high priority. Although it would appear that there has been a great deal of activity in curriculum reform in recent years, the vast majority of schools continue to operate as if they were living in the nineteenth century. Efforts on the part of the national government, which has spent millions in curriculum development on the elementary and secondary level, have not yet had a great impact on the overwhelming majority of schools. This continues to be true even though regional laboratories have been established in an attempt to implement new ideas developed through national curriculum projects. The few states that have attempted to provide leadership for the radical change needed have met with extremely limited success. The most significant and sweeping changes have taken place in local school districts and in single schools. Non-graded elementary schools, flexible scheduling, the use of available technology, inquiry-oriented study, the adoption of new materials and techniques, and so on, have been introduced in only a handful of schools. Perhaps even worse, thousands of school districts continue to operate as they have in the past, with little concern for reform.

Another noteworthy inadequacy of the present school system has to do with teachers. The best curriculum in the hands of a poorly trained teacher can fail in its purposes. The greatest geniuses available can be set to work on curriculum revision and the results of their efforts can gain wide popular acceptance, but if those who are to implement the curriculum are something less than brilliant, or if they resist constructive innovation in the curriculum, the efforts of genius are wasted. This has been and continues to be a serious problem in American schools. It is serious because the public schools continue to find it difficult to attract and hold the best that society has to offer to staff its classrooms. Public school teaching in America has never been a calling which attracted the very best talent available. Although the reasons for this are legion, the results are quite clear. Genuinely creative teachers are rare. Innovation in the way of new curricula, new methods, and new ideas too often die from lack of nurture in the hands of those who neither understand nor care.

Many are in teaching only as a temporary expedient until something better turns up. Others who might provide vigorous and exciting experiences for children have their strength dissipated by the necessity of finding extra work to supplement meager income. The societal cost of this condition is immense. Nor does the responsibility for it rest with the teachers—it rests with the society which may find it easier to accept the fact that some of its teachers are not adequate to their task than to face what needs to be done to correct this problem.

Teachers, of course, can be very little better than the preparation they receive in the colleges and universities responsible for their training. In recent years teacher education programs have come in for their share of criticism, which has been eagerly devoured by a public looking desperately for an easy explanation—a convenient scapegoat upon which to pile all of the invective for ineffective and poorly prepared teachers. Admitting that teacher education programs have weaknesses, that they may be slow to change in the face of great needs for change, it is also true that if teacher training is poor, it may be merely a symptom rather than a major cause for poorly prepared teachers. In a very direct way, teacher training is only as good as the society wants it to be. More than this, it is only as good as the product which feeds it, the students who elect this course of study. Like many elementary and secondary teachers, professors of education know, in specific terms, what could be done to improve teaching. Every legislative year, in nearly every state legislature in the Union, proposals are made which are designed to improve teacher training. Although some of these may be in the nature of idle dreams, many are based on sound research or at least on reasoned and careful consideration. Each year, proposals reach state legislatures in the several states which would increase the quantity and quality of the prospective teacher's preparation in content, methodology, and psychology; extend and improve the student teaching experience; and provide greater resources for experimentation and research in learning, techniques of teaching, and the organization of the curriculum. Most of these proposals are never funded, not because they lack merit or have not been carefully studied, but very often because the legislature represents a public which is reluctant to accept their cost. In teacher training, as in the teachers it employs, the public gets about what it is willing to pay for.

Even if the public were willing to bear the cost, reform in teacher education is difficult to achieve. The great bulk of undergraduate teacher training is controlled by college professors who are oriented toward and have genuine vested interests in their own particular discipline. Much of what passes for general education for prospective teachers in undergraduate training programs consists of separate courses in the various academic disciplines, which may or may not have any clear relationship to what prospective teachers need to make them competent. Thus, the overhaul of general training programs for prospective teachers is particularly difficult because those who are in charge of any revision are always those who have the vested interests in their own discipline and in the courses which are offered within that discipline. As often as not, teacher education committees, charged with the responsibility for developing teacher education curricula, are staffed with a majority of professorial members who have seldom, if ever, stuck their heads inside an elementary or secondary school classroom. Such professionals may clearly understand what is needed to produce historians, physicists, biologists, or mathematicians, but they often lack understanding of what is needed to produce classroom teachers in those disciplines. Similarly, colleges of education are staffed with those who may be more concerned with making their particular specialty a required part of every prospective teacher's preparation than they are with meeting the real needs of the classroom. Thus, meetings of learned professionals who are faced with revision of teacher education curricula frequently deteriorate into dissertations by individual faculty members who attempt to justify what they are presently doing. The result is built-in resistance to change, with each new generation of professionals defending and supporting their own training of a generation earlier, and imposing it upon succeeding generations of prospective teachers.

Because of the particular conservatism of the colleges and universities regarding curriculum revision, the task of innovation has rested primarily with the public schools. Much of the initiative for retraining and implementation of new ideas in teaching has come from the public schools themselves through inservice programs. Unfortunately, few public schools provide great opportunities for inservice training or adequate time for planning or research. Where inservice training is neglected, it is difficult for teachers to keep up in their field, innovation is discouraged, and the quality of teaching can decline. Although some school systems make provision in one way or another for inservice training, these opportunities may be limited or poorly planned. Similarly, planned programs of research on school problems, although increasing in number, have been extremely limited in the past. Although huge efforts to provide a kind of inservice training have been made by various programs of the national government under the umbrella of the National Science Foundation and the National Defense Education Act, these efforts have affected only a relatively small percentage of the total number of teachers, and even these sometimes fall short of their goals. In some cases the summer institutes have been little more than refresher courses in various disciplines, which have offered old approaches to old courses and have accomplished little in the way of meeting real public school classroom needs. Moreover, many of the best public school teachers have found the institutes a door of opportunity which led directly out of the public school classroom into college teaching.

Time for planning and research is all too often lacking in the public schools. Even though there are many great ideas lying around ready to be implemented by interested public school teachers, it may be that they do not have time to implement them. Burdened with the pressure of doing what has to be done—teaching the existing courses, grading papers, attending meetings, participating in extra-class activities of various kinds—the teacher may have little time to improve what he is doing, much less consider a complete overhaul. Effective and significant change takes planning and study, neither of which is possible in very large amounts for the average public school teacher. Yet, if needed changes are to come to the classroom in curriculum or methodology, they must be implemented by the classroom teacher who understands them and is enthusiastic about them.

If the schools are to meet the demands of a rapidly changing environment, and teachers have little time to consider these demands, perhaps the responsibility for innovation rests with various administrative personnel—special supervisors, the principal, and the school superintendent. Although it may be true that most innovations in the schools are instigated by administrative personnel, it may be futile to seek needed change from this source. Administrators cannot know everything; they can be really expert in only a narrowly limited sense. Supervisory personnel are not always noted for their depth of knowledge of the content of the curriculum, educational psychol ogy, or methodology, and perhaps it would be impossible to train anyone adequately in all these areas. Certainly the general curriculum supervisor who is responsible for several content areas cannot be knowledgeable in all. At best, his professional training may be limited to certain broad principles dealing with the general subject of curriculum. Some training may be so general in nature that it offers little help in dealing with genuine substantive problems of a specific content or discipline. The principal of the school may be more broadly trained and his surface knowledge of what is actually going on in the classrooms of his school may be so insignificant that his suggestions appear naive to the experienced teacher.

The superintendent may be even less competent to deal with specific curriculum problems which attempt to meet the need for change. Add to all of these problems policy-makers in the form of school board members, who can be almost totally ignorant of educational processes as they relate to general and individual needs and who might be inclined to take a conservative view toward innovation, and one is in a situation where change is difficult. Where these conditions exist, the school may not only be inadequate as an institution capable of meeting the present needs of the environment, but there may be little hope that it ever will be.

This kind of organization for formal education in American communities, where it exists, may reflect prevailing community attitudes which fail to recognize the need for change. Where the prevailing community attitude toward the schools is that of silent advocacy of the status quo, it may be reflected in the kind of teachers hired in the system, the treatment they get and what is expected of them, the kind of administrative structure which exists, and the prevailing physical atmosphere. School buildings may be neglected, or, when new ones are built, they may be built along traditional lines with a major concern for cost rather than needs of a modern program; materials may be inadequate; innovative teachers and administrators may be looked upon with contempt and suspicion; and curriculum may remain unchanged year after dreary year.

The foregoing discussion presents only a few of the more obvious ways in which some schools may not be adequately prepared to meet the demands of a rapidly changing environment. There are many other problems which could be discussed. However, this does not mean that the situation is hopeless, for there are many ways in which some school systems are attempting to meet the needs of contemporary society.

INNOVATIVE FORCES

Some examples of the more obvious forces which are tending to push schools into a more active role are increasing public awareness of the potential of the schools as a major weapon to combat poverty, awareness of the need for new approaches to school problems, the militancy of the teacher, the drive for equality on the part of minorities, and the force of technology.

During the last decade, as in no period in our history, the schools have become part of a broad political and economic program which promises reform and change in education. Schooling has been tied to the age-old dream of political equality in a way that makes it seem practical. Politicians and political platforms of the last decade on both the state and national levels of government have held forth the promise that the schools may provide the shortest route to the elimination of the worst of our social and economic problems. This has very great implications for the schools in that the promise is believable and large numbers of voters appear willing to support it. The promise offers great hope while providing a solution that is practical. It puts our best talent to work devising new ways in which the schools may better attack serious economic and social problems such as poverty, ghettos, inequality, and so on. More than this, Congress has been willing to vote funds to implement new educational programs designed to attack specific problems.

In addition, there is an increasing awareness that solutions to school problems demand new appraches. New alliances have been formed between educators, disciplinary scholars, psychologists, methodologists, and classroom teachers which provide real promise for breaking the traditional curriculum pattern in the schools. The so-called modern science and math curricula have evolved out of such cooperative efforts. Similar efforts are currently underway in the social sciences, English, and other curricula in the public schools. Cooperative efforts at curriculum revision and experimentation which are currently underway are more numerous and varied than at any period in our history. Never before have so many public and private resources been expended on study and revision of the school curriculum. Never in our history have so many people, representing such a wide spectrum of interests and abilities, been involved in a serious consideration of the public school and its offerings. Whereas the curriculum efforts of the progressive reformers of an earlier generation were limited in scope and often privately financed, and they provided little in the way of controlled experimentation, the efforts of the last decade have been broad in scope, often financed by the public, and have offered a wide range of experimentation in locations scattered across the country. Experimental schools and programs in traditional schools, which have been rare exceptions in our past, are growing in number.

Another force pushing for change is the new militancy of the teacher, which has taken many forms in recent years. Strikes and walkouts by teachers have grown in intensity and frequency. Although the effectiveness of various forms of militancy is difficult to measure, they have at least attracted public attention to very real problems in education and have resulted in improved conditions in some states and localities. Whatever the result, teachers are demonstrating that there is some hope in protest, that there is some strength in militant organization, and that the teacher can use the time-worn devices of pressure. It is possible that such militancy will increase in future years, for this is the kind of protest which claims a just cause; teachers have identified their cause with the good of the children and the good of the society. Change has already occurred in the face of such militancy, and even limited success will bring more demands and more change. This is not to argue the fact that such change is prima facie "good" or that militant techniques are "good." It is merely to point out that teachers are becoming aware that they can be a major instrument in the process of change, and that as a solidly united group they can exercise some real influence on teacher welfare and other aspects of the school program.

The drive for equality on the part of minority groups, especially Blacks, has already worked some changes in schooling as well as in the society generally. No one can deny that Blacks have been instrumental in getting new definitions of the Fourteenth Amendment through the Supreme Court and in providing some initiative for extensive civil rights legislation. For many years the drive for equal treatment under the law has centered its attention on the schools. This has been a generally successful drive in that it has gained the support of the law and the courts. Although equal educational opportunity is a long way from realization, giant strides have been made and there is no evidence that those who have been denied equal educational opportunity will stop short of success. Already the movement has seriously questioned local community values which deny equal educational opportunity. Already the movement has shaken local beliefs, attitudes, and prejudices to their roots. It has not been an easy battle, for a frontal assault on deeply held values never is; but it has generated change. It has set change in motion in communities where change was not thought possible. The pressure brought by Blacks and their friends has opened school doors that were closed, it has seriously challenged the existing social structure within the school in some areas, it has questioned the homogeneity of school boundary lines, and most significantly, perhaps, it has forced many a citizen to examine his own values and his own conscience. Whether or not the schools will be able to meet the challenge imposed upon them by the efforts of such pressure remains to be seen. Here, indeed, is a case in which a social movement is forcing the issue. It is forcing the schools to deal with problems which for years they may have elected to ignore.

Finally, the force of technology has pushed the school to the forefront as a central societal institution which must deal with the problems of technology and attempt to help the society understand its meaning. Of course, the force of technology has already hit the schools in a direct way. It has made revolutionary changes possible in school buildings, in the organization of curricula, and in materials and methods of teaching. In addition, it has encouraged the same kind of concern for specialization in teaching as it has in other occupations.

In a wider sense, technology is changing the society in a revolutionary and dramatic manner. Each year it creates entire new industries; it speeds the process of obsolescence in goods, services, and jobs; and it creates serious problems of adjustment for individuals. Although it may not be possible for the schools to keep ahead of technological development, they must at least be able to accept and explain it. The schools must be able to interpret and analyze technological development with a view toward facilitating the material and human progress that can be realized from the application of science to man's needs. It is imperative that the schools consciously undertake this task, since no other institution in our society is geared for the challenge. Such a challenge means that the schools are forced to accept the interpretation of social change as a major role. In the case of the need for understanding the change wrought by technology, the question which school people must ask is not: Can the schools change society? but What is the human meaning of change?

THE FUTURE OF EDUCATION

It may be a truism that the changing environment of the future will force changes on the schools almost in spite of anything we do or do not do in the way of building school systems to train citizens for a new society. The demand for new skills and new knowledge is a fact of our times—a demand which the schools cannot realistically ignore. How well the schools can do what society expects of them depends largely on the support which society is willing to furnish them. There is a reason to hope that society will increase its support of its schools. Not only is there greater public and political awareness of the importance of schools and schooling, but the increased affluence of the society has enabled consideration of large increases in expenditures for schools without neglecting other public and private demands.

Whatever the results of increasing public support, the public is looking toward the schools with new hope. Many in our society are looking toward the schools to help find long-range solutions to some of our more serious problems. The reasons for this increased interest in the schools are numerous and varied, but of all those that can be imagined, the ones which could be classified as economic in nature would certainly top the list. More of our citizens are coming to realize that one cannot function to the limit of one's ability in a technological society without formal preparation, which can come only through schooling. Citizens, industrialists, governmental agents, and public and private groups of all descriptions are turning to the schools to provide the kind of manpower needed in this age. The great majority of our citizens are more aware of the economic necessity of education today than they have been at any time in history. With each passing year, the old dream of equal economic opportunity is coming to be more closely tied to the idea of equal educational opportunity. The economic advantages of education into and beyond the secondary school level are becoming abundantly clear to most citizens.

Government, as it represents the society, has become directly interested in education for political reasons which may have roots in the economics of education. Concern for national economic well-being is at once political and economic. The desire for full employment and full utilization of national material and human resources may be a political desire, but it is at heart an economic problem. Human resources which are not properly trained to do the necessary tasks in a technological society are wasted resources. Such waste has become a political issue which has national as well as international implications. The problem of wasted human resources is most frequently described in terms of the numbers of our citizens on welfare or those who are unemployed or underemployed. Almost without exception, schooling in one form or another is believed to provide the most promising solution for these political and economic problems.

In spite of the huge problem of wasted human resources, there can be little doubt that the American educational system has been a resounding success in providing the skills and abilities needed in the economic system. If there is a general condemnation that can be leveled against American public education in this century, it is that in spite of its Herculean efforts to provide mass education, it may have done so at the expense of the genuine needs of individual children. In our overwhelming desire to provide something for everybody, we have overlooked some very basic human problems. The schools continue to neglect the poor and the minorities, and they continue to fall considerably short of any humanitarian ideal.

The poor, and many Blacks, Indians, Chicanos, and other minorities, are being neglected by the system. Compared to the white middle-class majority, the poor child or the minority child has a much greater chance of attending school in a dilapidated or deteriorating building. The children of the poor and the minorities have a greater chance of getting inadequate facilities and inexperienced or poorly qualified teachers. The poor and the minorities have a weak voice in the educational decision-making process in most communities. An overwhelming number of children from these groups are behind in reading and other basic skills at whatever grade level they are found in the public schools. Children of the poor and minorities are most apt to drop out of school before they graduate from high school. An insignificant number of them find their way into colleges and universities. Large numbers of them find their way into tracked programs in vocational training for dead-end jobs and severely limited careers. Many are alienated from the school system, as well as the society, at an early age.

This kind of neglect would be serious enough if it involved only a handful of children. Unfortunately, it involves millions, perhaps as many as one-quarter of the total school population. This is America's greatest educational problem, and will undoubtedly continue to challenge us for years to come. The solutions will have to be large and revolutionary. Hundreds, perhaps thousands, of schools in urban as well as rural areas have no legitimate educational defense, no real possibility for ever becoming places where learning can occur. These are the urban schools, where discipline is maintained only by brute force, and the small rural schools in abject poverty. Not only do these schools fail to provide anything approaching equal educational opportunity, it is doubtful that they provide any positive educational opportunity at all. The sooner they are eliminated, by whatever means, the better. The school people, working in concert with the public through the political process, must find solutions to the gigantic problems of educational neglect if we are to have a future. No society can afford neglect of this magnitude, particularly a society in which inequities are so public and obvious. Ways must be found which directly attack the problems of neglect. A start was made in the mid-sixties with the Elementary and Secondary Education Act and the various anti-poverty measures. Great and intensive efforts by local, state, and national governments need to be made to build on the success of these programs. Teachers, working through their professional organizations and the political process, need to speak out against injustices and inequities in the system. It would seem that the major responsibility for informing the public, where neglect is such that learning is difficult or impossible for large numbers of children, rests with the teachers. Where social neglect is such that the children are being deprived of a meaningful education, it is not only the teacher's right as a citizen to make these deficiencies known, but his responsibility as a professional. Moreover, if the society is to survive, teachers must demand that the organizations which represent them work tirelessly toward genuine educational equality. Certainly, the society has the means to do more than provide a few model schools for ghetto children and satisfactorily train the children of the middle classes. More than anything else, basic improvement in the educational system may involve basic changes in public values and the priorities which grow out of them. This could very well be the most challenging educational task of the future.

The most basic challenge to public education in recent years has been the charge that the schools tend to dehumanize and alienate children. Much of the so-called "free school movement" of the 1960's grew out of such criticism. Dissatisfied with what they called closed or authoritarian schools, individuals and groups established alternative schools, commonly called "free schools" in hundreds of communities during the sixties. The movement seemed to reach a peak in 1970 when more than 600 such schools were listed by the *Free School Clearing House*. In the early seventies, the movement began to subside as some of the early experiments failed and as the public schools co-opted part of the movement by establishing their own alternative schools. However, the free school movement has become so large that it is unlikely that it will soon fade from the landscape.[1] It is interesting to note that much of the enthusiasm for free schools has come, not from the minorities and the poor, but from middle-class critics of public education.

Perhaps the greatest failure of the American educational system in this century is its inability to demonstrate any genuine humanitarian purpose. In this sense, it not only fails the poor and the minorities in the society, but all children. Although the scope of this failure is immense, it is most acute, perhaps, in the sense that the schools have generally failed to develop thinking citizens. Although the schools cannot assume the whole guilt for problems of hate, prejudice, rape of our environment, drugs, alienation, indifference, and injustice, they share some of the burden. If there is to be any general improvement in the quality of life, regardless of how it might be defined, it would seem that the school would bear a major share of the burden of improvement. Yet, the schools do little in any conscious way to improve the quality of life. Too often, the local school is too caught up in its own carefully defined bureaucratic functions to be concerned with the

---

[1] Volumes have been written on the free school movement of the 1960's. The best material may be found in various free school clearinghouses such as: *Education Switchboard* (1380 Howard Street, San Francisco), *Free School Clearinghouse* (1609 19th Street, Washington, D. C.), and *New Schools Network* (3039 Deakin Street, Berkeley, California). Also useful are periodicals such as: *Big Rock Candy Mountain* (Partola Institute, 115 Merrill Street, Menlo Park, California), *Outside the Net* (P. O. Box 184, Lansing, Michigan), and *Whole Earth Catalog* (558 Santa Cruz Avenue, Menlo Park, California). By far the most thorough and scholarly effort on the recent free school movement is *The Free School Movement,* by Jerry C. Long (Unpublished Ph.D. dissertation, Oklahoma State University, May 1972).

general condition of the society. More often than not, these functions are stated in operational and functional terms which involve, for the most part, imparting specific knowledge and teaching specific skills. The success of the school is then measured in terms of its production of knowledge and skills. In this process, humanitarian goals tend to get neglected or ignored. Thus, schools which can train future scientists, mathematicians, engineers, historians, or skilled workers tend to be the best schools because they are turning out a serviceable product. Success of individuals in this system is measured more by the contribution which can be made to the productive process than anything else. Rewards are also based on the individual's value to the productive process. The resultant neglect of problems in human relationships is evident. Helping children learn about their own humanity and their relationship to others, teaching them to think rationally and reflect on their system of values, is not a central purpose of the typical American school. Until it becomes at least a major purpose of schooling, we will continue to excel in gross national product and fail in solving human problems.

Index

A B C D E F G   7 6 5 4 3 2